DEMOCRACY AND LIBERTY

William Edward Hartpole Lecky

DEMOCRACY AND LIBERTY

by WILLIAM EDWARD HARTPOLE LECKY

Volume II.

*Liberty*Classics

INDIANAPOLIS

ACE -2315

LibertyClassics is a publishing imprint of Liberty Fund, Inc., a foundation established to encourage study of the ideal of a society of free and responsible individuals.

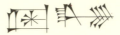

The cuneiform inscription that serves as the design motif for our endpapers is the earliest known written appearance of the word "freedom" (ama-gi), or liberty. It is taken from a clay document written about 2300 B.C. in the Sumerian city-state of Lagash.

Photograph by Louis Mercier.

Democracy and Liberty was first published in March 1896 by Longmans, Green and Company in London. During that year it was printed three more times. This Liberty Classics edition of 1981 is based on the second edition of 1896.

Library of Congress Cataloging in Publication Data

Lecky, William Edward Hartpole, 1838–1903.
  Democracy and liberty.
    Originally published: London; New York: Longmans, Green, 1896.
    Includes bibliographical references and index.
    1. Democracy. 2. Liberty. I. Title.
  JC423.L4 1981   321.8   80-82371
  ISBN 0-913966-80 (set)   AACR2
  ISBN 0-913966-82-7 (v. 1)
  ISBN 0-913966-83-5 (v. 2)
  ISBN 0-913966-81-9 (pbk. set)
  ISBN 0-913966-84-3 (pbk.: v. 1)
  ISBN 0-913966-85-1 (pbk.: v. 2)
  10 9 8 7 6 5 4 3 2 1

CONTENTS OF THE SECOND VOLUME

CHAPTER 6 (*continued*)

CHAPTER 7

Sunday Legislation

Marriage Laws

Various Forms of Imperfect Marriages and Marriage Disabilities

CHAPTER 8
SOCIALISM

Socialism in Germany

CHAPTER 9
LABOR QUESTIONS

CHAPTER 10
WOMAN QUESTIONS

DEMOCRACY AND LIBERTY

CHAPTER 6

(continued)

There is one other subject connected with religious liberty that is likely to occupy a large share in the attention of the democracies of the future. It is the position and the aggressive policy of the Catholic Church. Of all the judgments of the great thinkers of the eighteenth century, none have been more signally falsified than those which they formed of the future of the Catholic Church. With scarcely an exception, they believed that its sacerdotal, superstitious, intolerant, and ultramontane elements were silently fading away; that it was taking more and more the character of a purely moralising influence; and that all danger of antagonism between it and the civil power had passed for ever. The delusion lasted for several years after the French Revolution, and it may be very clearly traced in the speeches and writings of the chief advocates of Catholic Emancipation. Many of them lived to acknowledge their mistake. There is a characteristically cynical saying attributed to Lord Melbourne, that on that question 'all the d———d fools in England predicted one set of things, and all the sensible men in England another set, and that the d———d fools proved perfectly right, and the sensible men perfectly wrong.'

I have been told on excellent authority, that Macaulay once

expressed in more decorous language a very similar view. 'I do not mean to take the white sheet,' he is reported to have said, 'for I acted honestly and conscientiously, but I now see that all we did for the Catholics has turned out badly.' The belief that Protestant and Catholic would become almost indistinguishable in the field of politics, and that the association of disaffection with Catholicism was purely casual and ephemeral, has proved ludicrously false, and in Ireland, as on the Continent, the question of priestly influence in politics is one of the most pressing of our time.

Looking back with the cheap wisdom which is supplied by the event, it is not difficult to trace the causes of this disappointment. In the comparatively narrow sphere of the United Kingdom, much is to be attributed to a strangely unbroken series of legislative blunders. Strong arguments have been urged in support of the opinion that some legislation resembling the Irish Penal Code against the Catholics was inevitable after the great social and political convulsions of the Revolution; but two parts of these laws had an evil influence of the most profound and enduring kind. The laws forbidding Catholics to purchase or inherit land, or to acquire lasting and profitable land-tenures, had the effect of producing in Ireland the most dangerous of class divisions; while the laws preventing or restricting Catholic education reduced the Catholic population to a far lower level of civilisation than their Protestant countrymen. When, at last, the hour of emancipation struck, the difficult task was most unskilfully accomplished. By the Irish Act of 1793 the vast ignorant Catholic democracy were granted votes for which they were utterly unfit, while the intelligent and loyal Catholic gentry were still excluded from Parliament, and thus prevented from exercising over their poorer co-religionists the guiding and restraining influence which was pre-eminently wanting.

The education of the priests was equally mismanaged. There was a moment when it would have been quite possible to connect a seminary for the special education of priests with Dublin University, and thus to secure for the teachers of the

Irish people a high level of secular education, and close and friendly connection with their Protestant contemporaries. If this course had been adopted, and if it had been combined with a State payment of the priests, the whole complexion of later Irish history might have been changed. But the opportunity was neglected. The priests were left wholly dependent on the dues of their people, and they were educated, apart from all the great secular influences of their time, in a separate seminary, which soon became a hotbed of disloyalty and of obscurantism. Then followed the shameful frustration of Catholic hopes at the time of Lord Fitzwilliam, and of the Union, which left a deep stain upon the good faith of the Government, and added immensely to Catholic disloyalty. Nothing, in the light of history, can be more clear than that it was of vital importance that the Legislative Union should have been accompanied by the three great measures of Catholic Emancipation, the commutation of tithes, and the payment of the priests; but all these measures were suffered to fail. The Catholics remained outside Parliament till a great agitation had brought the country to the verge of civil war. The tithe system, which, more than any other single influence, tended to disorganise and demoralise Irish country life, was suffered to continue unchanged for thirty-eight years after the Union, and State payment of the priests, which nearly all the best judges had pronounced essential to the tranquillity of Ireland, was never accomplished.

It was a strange story, and it seems all the more strange if we compare it with the corresponding measures about the English Catholics. The concession of the suffrage to the vast ignorant majority of Irish Catholics was a measure of great danger, and it was accomplished in 1793; but the English Catholics, who could be no possible danger to the State, were excluded from the franchise till 1829. The Irish Catholics were admitted, before the close of the eighteenth century, to the magistracy, to degrees in Trinity College, to membership of lay corporations, and to every rank in the army except that of general of the staff. In England, for many years after this concession, they could neither be magistrates, nor members of corporations, nor enter the universities, nor legally hold any rank in the army. In Canada, on the other hand, all offices were open to them.[1]

The ill-fate that hung over British legislation about the Catholics still continued. The permanent insanity of George III. in 1812 removed what at the time of the Union had been deemed the one insuperable obstacle to their emancipation, and the Catholics were then perfectly ready to accept a State endowment for the priesthood, and, at the same time, to concede to the Government a right of veto on the appointment of their bishops. But the ascendency of the Tory party and the ability of Peel succeeded in again deferring the settlement of the question, and, in consequence of the postponement, a new agitation arose under O'Connell, which enormously increased its difficulties. O'Connell induced the Irish priesthood to repudiate the 'securities' which they had previously accepted, and which Grattan and most of the other leading advocates of Catholic Emancipation had considered essential to its safe enactment. He gave the agitation an entirely democratic character, dissociating it from the property of the country, and placing the priesthood at its head. The creation of the Catholic Association in 1823 marked the triumph of his influence, and the election of 1826 showed clearly the instrumentality by which it was worked.

The Chief Secretary, Goulburn, described this election in some striking letters to Peel. 'Never,' he wrote, 'were Roman Catholic and Protestant so decidedly opposed. Never did the former act with so general a concert, or place themselves so completely under the command of the priesthood; and never did the priests assume to themselves such authority, and exercise their power so openly in a manner the most extraordinary and alarming.' 'The priests exercise on all matters a dominion perfectly uncontrolled and uncontrollable. In many parts of the country their sermons are purely political, and the

---

[1] May's *Const. Hist.* ii. 366.

altars in the several chapels are the rostra from which they declaim on the subject of Roman Catholic grievances, exhort to the collection of rent,[2] or denounce their Protestant neighbours in a mode perfectly intelligible and effective, but not within the grasp of the law. In several towns no Roman Catholic will now deal with a Protestant shopkeeper in consequence of the priest's interdiction, and this species of interference, stirring up enmity on one hand and feelings of resentment on the other, is mainly conducive to outrage and disorder. . . . It is impossible to detail to you in a letter the various modes in which the Roman Catholic priesthood now interfere in every transaction of every description; how they rule the mob, the gentry, and the magistracy; how they impede the administration of justice.[3]

The evil culminated in 1829. The necessary measure of Catholic emancipation was conceded, but it was conceded not by the triumph of its advocates, but by the intimidation of its enemies. It was carried by a ministry which was placed in power for the special purpose of resisting it, and avowedly in consequence of a great priestly and democratic agitation, and through fear of civil war. Except the disfranchisement of forty-shilling freeholders, no measure was taken to regulate and moderate the change. An oath, it is true, was imposed on Catholic members, binding them in very solemn terms to use no privilege the Act gave them 'to disturb or weaken the Protestant religion or Protestant government of the United Kingdom.' But this oath was soon treated, with the full approbation of the priests, as a dead-letter.[4] No step was taken

---

[2] *I.e.* the Catholic rent paid to O'Connell and his Association for carrying on the agitation.

[3] Sir Robert Peel's *Private Correspondence*, pp. 416, 418–19.

[4] Sir R. Peel, in his speech on the Irish Church Establishment, April 2, 1835, expressed very clearly the intention of the authors of the Act. 'In 1829, the civil disabilities of the Roman Catholics were removed by the Legislature, and the measure by which that object was effected partook also of the nature of a compact, as distinguished from an ordinary law. . . . By that Act the Protestants of Ireland were led to believe that all

for the endowment, or the discipline, or the better education
of the priesthood, or for the prevention of exercises of ecclesiastical authority that are subversive of civil rights; while the
exclusion of a few eminent Catholics from promotion to which
they were most justly entitled contributed immensely to ex-
asperate the leaders and perpetuate the agitation.

The Whig party had long believed that, if Catholic Emancipation were conceded, the Irish priests would become a great
restraining and moralising influence on the side of the law.
Many of them, both before and after Emancipation, have been
so, but it cannot be said that in general this hope was realised.
In 1847, Lord Minto was instructed by the British Government
to bring their conduct before the authorities at the Vatican,
and Lord Palmerston, who was then Minister for Foreign Affairs, wrote him a letter containing the following instructive
passage: 'You may confidently assure the Papal authorities
that at the present in Ireland misconduct is the rule and good
conduct the exception in the Catholic priests; that they, in a
multitude of cases, are the open, and fearless, and shameless
instigators to disorder, to violence, and murder, and that every
day and every week the better-conducted, who are by constitution of human nature the most quiet and timid, are being
scared by their fellow-priests, as well as by their flocks, from
a perseverance in any efforts to give good counsel and to restrain violence and crime. Major Mahon, who was shot the
other day, was denounced by his priest at the altar the Sunday
before he was murdered. He might have been murdered all
the same if the priest had not denounced him, but that denun-
ciation, of course, made all the people of the neighbourhood

---

intention to subvert the present Church establishment, as settled by law
within these realms, was most solemnly disclaimed and utterly abandoned. They were assured, on the obligation of an oath, that no privilege
which the Act confers would be exercised to disturb or weaken the Protestant religion or the Protestant government within these realms. . . . .
They little thought that, within five years from the passing of that Act,
the power which it conferred would be exercised to subvert the Church
establishment, so far as regards the property of the Church.'

think the deed a holy one instead of a diabolical one. . . . I really believe there never has been in modern times, in any country professing to be civilised and Christian, nor anywhere out of the central regions of Africa, such a state of crime as now exists in Ireland. There is evidently a deliberate and extensive conspiracy among the priests and the peasantry to kill off or drive away all the proprietors of land, to prevent and deter any of their agents from collecting rent, and thus practically to transfer the land of the country from the landowner to the tenant.'[5]

The accompanying memorandum of Lord Clarendon, who was then Lord Lieutenant, states the facts in more moderate terms, and throws some light upon their cause.

'With respect to the priests,' he writes, 'I must again report that, as a body, there is not in the world a more zealous, faithful, hardworking clergy, and most of the older priests are friendly to order, to education, and to the general improvement of the people. There are, however, some unfortunate exceptions, but it is among the younger clergy, the curates and coadjutors, that the real mischief-makers are to be found. . . . There are at this moment numerous cases in which, if evidence could be procured, a prosecution could be sustained against priests as accessories to atrocious crimes by the inciting language they have held to people over whose minds they exercise an absolute control. . . . From different parts of the country, and from persons upon whose veracity I can confide, I hear either that a landlord has been denounced by name from the altar in a manner which is equivalent to his death-warrant, or that persons giving evidence against criminals are held up as public enemies and traitors, or that people are advised to assemble in mobs and enforce their demands upon individuals. It was only yesterday that I heard of a priest (in the diocese of Dr. McHale) addressing a man in the chapel, and telling him that he would not curse him, because the last man he had cursed died directly, but that before the blossom

---

[5] Ashley's *Life of Palmerston*, ii. 49–50.

fell from the potato he would be a corpse. This man's offence
was having given evidence in a court of justice against a party
that had broken into his house and robbed him. I have sworn
depositions now lying on my table in proof of acts of this
kind, but the deponents dare not come forward and openly
give their evidence, for they say—and I know it to be true—
that their lives would not be worth twenty-four hours' purchase. Indeed, to prevent any misunderstanding upon this
subject, the priest usually defies any person to give information of what he has been saying, and warns them of the
consequences.

'The result of all this is . . . that the clergy, to maintain their
position, must still pander to the passions of their flock. In
places—and there are many—where a priest friendly to order
and anxious for the real welfare of his people has given good
advice, and intimated that among those present in the chapel
there were some who had been guilty of such-and-such
crimes, the individuals alluded to will come forward and bid
him hold his tongue, and threaten him with vengeance if he
proceeds. I could multiply facts and details *ad infinitum*, for
every day some fresh case comes to my knowledge. . . . Wherever the priests so misconduct themselves, there the people
are always found to be the most turbulent and wretched. The
indignation, and, I may add, shame, of the respectable Roman
classes are extreme. . . . I feel sure that a Papal prohibition to
take part in political agitations and to make use of the places
of worship for secular purposes, would be received as a great
boon by the well-disposed priests (*i.e.* the majority of the
clergy), who, when they become agitators, yield to intimidation, and are compelled to act against their judgment. If they
could appeal to the sanction of the Pope's authority for confining themselves to their spiritual duties, they would not fear
to have their chapels deserted, and thus find themselves destitute of the means of subsistence.

'To the best of my belief, the bishops are not in the habit of
punishing such misdeeds as those I have alluded to. They may

do so; but I have neither official nor private knowledge of the fact, and, if they do, their interference is not very successful.'[6]

These extracts will sufficiently explain the nature and causes of a priestly despotism in Ireland which probably, on the whole, exceeds that in any other European country. It is of a somewhat peculiar character, for the political element largely mixes with the religious one. The priests are at once intimidated and intimidators, and their power is often used in ways wholly unsanctioned by the doctrines of their Church. In all those large fields of morals in which they are supported by a healthy moral feeling among their congregations their conduct has usually been exemplary. In those cases in which the moral sense of the community has been gravely perverted, a great proportion of them have either shared, or yielded to the perversion, and they have often lent all their influence to support it.

The events of the last few years have abundantly shown that the evils indicated by Lord Clarendon have not disappeared. The nature, methods and objects of the great recent agrarian conspiracy have been established beyond all reasonable controversy by an exhaustive judicial inquiry before three eminent English judges, and the sworn evidence they have accumulated and the judgments they have given are open to the world. They have pronounced, among other things, that the movement was 'a conspiracy by a system of coercion and intimidation to promote an agrarian agitation against the payment of agricultural rents, for the purpose of impoverishing and expelling from the country the Irish landlords, who were styled "the English garrison;"' that the leaders of this conspiracy were active inciters to an intimidation which produced crime and outrage, and that they 'persisted in it with knowl-

---

[6] Ashley's *Life of Lord Palmerston*, ii. 50–53. Lord Palmerston considered that in this letter Lord Clarendon understated the case. He writes to Lord Minto, 'You may safely go further than Clarendon has chosen to do.'

edge of its effect.'[7] In every stage of this conspiracy the Catholic priest has been a leading actor. Nearly always he has been the chairman of the local Land League, has collected its subscriptions, inspired its policy, countenanced, at least by his silence, the outrages it produced, supported it from the pulpit and from the altar. It is a memorable and most characteristic fact, that during the 'no rent conspiracy,' when the sheriff's officers appeared to enforce the law, the chapel bells were continually rung to summon rioters to resist, or to enable the defaulting farmers to baffle their creditors by driving away their cattle.[8] The fraudulent conspiracy known as the Plan of Campaign, and the 'elaborate and all-pervading tyranny'[9] known under the name of boycotting, have been both formally condemned by the highest authority in the Catholic Church; but Catholic priests have been among their warmest supporters and their most industrious instigators, and the men who, in defiance of the censure of their Church, most steadily practised, preached, and eulogised them have been, and are, favoured guests in Catholic episcopal dwellings.

Nor is this all that can be truly said. Under the teaching of the Catholic clergy the moral sense of great masses of the Irish people has been so perverted that the most atrocious murders, if they have any agrarian end, carry with them no blame, and their perpetrators are sedulously sheltered from justice. It is impossible to disguise the significance of the fact that nearly all those murderers who have been brought to justice have been Catholics; that nearly all of them have gone to the gallows fortified by the rites of their Church, and professing the most complete and absolute submission to its commands; and yet, that scarcely in a single instance have they made the only reparation in their power, by publicly acknowledging their guilt and the justice of their sentence. I do not suppose that any English minister would venture to propose that a

---

[7] *Report of the Special Commission*, 1888, pp. 119–20.
[8] See Clifford Lloyd's *Ireland under the Land League*, pp. 150–151, 154, 161.
[9] *Report of the Special Commission*, 1888, p. 53.

murderer who sent his victim into another world 'unhousel'd, disappointed, unanel'd,' with all his sins upon his head, and with no possiblity of obtaining spiritual consolation or assistance, should himself only be allowed to receive such consolation up to the moment of his conviction. But it may be doubted whether any other single measure would do so much to strengthen criminal law in Ireland.

After the well-known murders that were committed in the Phoenix Park in 1882, protests of more or less sincerity expressing horror at those murders were put forward by popular leaders. But no one who knows Ireland will deny that, when the perpetrators were detected and brought to justice upon the clearest evidence, the strong popular sentiment was in their favour. Those who were present have described the crowds outside the prison-gates at the time of the execution, kneeling on the bare ground, and praying with the most passionate devotion for men whom they evidently regarded as martyrs. One member of the band, it is true, was excepted, and became the object of ferocious hatred; but he was hated, not because he was a murderer, but because he saved his life by giving evidence against his fellow-culprits. It is well known that James Carey was afterwards most deliberately murdered, and that his murderer, having been tried by an English judge and jury, was duly hanged. It is not so well known that in the principal Catholic cemetery of Dublin an imposing monument was soon after erected—as far as I know, without a single ecclesiastical protest—to the murderer of Carey, with an epitaph holding up that murderer, in language in which religion and perverted patriotism are grotesquely mixed, to the admiration and imitation of his countrymen.[10] There is, probably, no other Christian country in which such a thing could have

---

[10] The reader may be interested to read the whole of the epitaph, which I have copied in Glasnevin Cemetery. At the top is a dove in the midst of vines, and around it the incription, 'Thy Will be done.' Then follows: 'In Memory of Patrick O'Donnell, who heroically gave up his life for Ireland in London, England, on December 17, 1883.'

happened. There is certainly no Catholic Government that would have permitted it.

The enormous accession of political power which recent legislation has given to the Catholic priesthood in Ireland is very evident. Its whole tendency has been to diminish and destroy the influence of the propertied classes. The ballot, which was supposed to secure freedom of vote, has had no restraining influence upon a priesthood who claim an empire over the thoughts and secret actions of men; and it is stated on good authority that in cases where the secret sentiments of the voters were suspected they have been continually induced to pass themselves off as illiterate, in order that they may vote openly in the presence of their priest. This much at least is certain, that in a country where an excellent system of national education has been established since 1834, and where the average children are certainly far quicker than in England in acquiring instruction, more than one elector out of every five at the election of 1892 professed himself to be an illiterate.[11] The suffrage has been so lowered as to place an overwhelming proportion of power in the hands of the classes who are completely under priestly influence, and that influence has been strained to the utmost. Some recent election trials have brought vividly before the world the manner in which it is exercised; which was, indeed, well known to all who are acquainted with Irish life. We have seen a bishop, in his pastorals, dictating the political conduct of the voters with exactly the same kind and weight of authority as if he were prescribing a fast or promulgating a

---

'Not tears, but prayers, for the dead who died for Ireland.

'This monument was erected by the grateful admirers of his heroism in the United States of America, through the *Irish World*, and forwarded by a Ladies' Committee of New York—Mrs. F. Byrne, Mrs. Maggie Halevey, and Ellen A. Ford. R.I.P.'

[11] See a most curious parliamentary return moved for by Mr. Webster (Feb. 20, 1893). Out of 395,024 votes polled in this election, 84,919 were set down as illiterates. In Great Britain the proportion of illiterates among the electors is about 1 in 100.

theological doctrine. We have seen the whole body of the priesthood turned into electioneering agents, and employing for political purposes all the engines and powers of their profession. The chapel under this system becomes an electioneering meeting. Priests vested in their sacerdotal robes prescribe the votes of their congregations from the altar, from the pulpit, and, as there is good reason to believe, in the confessional, and every kind of spiritual threat is employed steadily, persistently, and effectually to coerce the voters.[12] Few things in politics are more grotesque than a system of legislation which, in the name of Liberal principles, has been endeavouring in every possible way to break down the influence of property, loyalty, and intelligence at elections, and has ended in constituting over a great part of Ireland a monopoly of power in the hands of the priesthood which is quite as absolute as the monopoly that existed in the darkest days of

---

[12] See especially the South Meath Election petition, tried before Mr. Justice O'Brien and Mr. Justice Andrews, November 16, 1892. A report of the trial has been published, and is very deserving of a careful study. I will only quote the following extract from the charge of Judge O'Brien (a fervent Catholic): 'Some other matters have been introduced into the case which are, of course, of an extremely delicate and painful character—all the incidents connected with the confessional. Whether it was right or wrong to give that evidence, whatever view may be taken of it on any side or in any respect, the evidence was of an unusual and an unprecedented kind. The statement was that several clergymen, the names of whom are mentioned, had canvassed voters in the confessional; and there is no person at all—there is no Catholic—who cannot understand the tremendous importance of evidence of that kind. In all the instances but one undoubtedly the communication was after the confession was over; but there was one incident—a tremendous and unexampled incident—in which this interference with the franchise—entirely innocent, I believe, and from the purest reasons and motives, according to the evidence—was allowed to intrude into the mysterious sanctity of the Divine commission itself, and in which the absolution of the penitent was postponed at least, owing to the construction possibly made to depend upon the vote he gave. . . . I certainly do unhesitatingly come to the conclusion that, if the Rev. Mr. Fox did undoubtedly speak in confession to this man concerning his vote, he certainly did so in the strongest sense of his own duty.'

Tory ascendency, and which is certainly immeasurably more prejudicial to the interests of the Empire.

The influences affecting Catholic affairs in Ireland stand somewhat apart from those that have acted upon Continental Catholicism, but a few words may be sufficient to describe the causes that falsified the predictions of the best European judges of the eighteenth century. Something was due to the violent reaction in the direction of religion which followed the horrors of the French Revolution, and, at a later period, of the Commune; and also to the extremely subversive doctrines relating to the foundations of religion, morals, and property, which have of late years been widely disseminated. Probably still more is due to the rapid, and for the most part silent, spread of scepticism and indifferentism among the laity in nearly all Catholic countries. It has detached from all religious practices and controversies numbers who, in another age, would have proved the chief moderating and restraining influence in the Church, and it has thrown the direction of that great organisation more and more into the hands of priests and fanatics. At the same time, the very violence of the conflict between the Church and its opponents has accentuated on each side the points of difference, and the great confiscations of ecclesiastical property have tended powerfully in the same direction. In a Church which is established and endowed, in which secular tribunals have a great place, and which has large termporal and secular interests, there will always be much that diverts or moderates the fervour of the sectarian spirit. But when the priest is nothing but a priest, and when his power and dignity rest exclusively on his sacerdotal character, he will naturally exalt it to the highest point, and the interests of the Church will become the passion of his life. In Protestant Churches, there is a marked difference between the moderation that is displayed and the latitude of opinion that is permitted in established Churches, and the narrower and more intolerant dogmatism that usually prevails in free Churches; but in all branches of Protestantism the marriage of the clergy, and the family interests and affections it entails, have greatly mitigated the purely theological spirit. In Catholicism, with a celibate clergy, with a doctrinal system intended to exalt to the highest degree sacerdotal dignity, and with a Church organisation that is eminently fit to attract to itself the kind of enthusiasm and devotion which is elsewhere attracted to the country, this sacerdotal spirit is incomparably more intense, and the men who converted the priesthood into a mere salaried body, and divested them of all temporal dignity, have unconsciously laboured to strengthen it. It was noticed during the last General Council that, of all the bishops, those who were most conspicuous for their independence and their moderation were the Bishops of Hungary and Croatia; and the manifest explanation was, that they were among the few bishops who were neither disestablished nor disendowed, and that the sentiments of the great nobleman blended in them with the sentiments of the priest. The Italian priests are, probably, at least as superstitious in their theological belief as their colleagues in France, but their fanaticism is much less, and they arouse far less hostility among their people. One great reason of this appears to be, that a small plot of land is attached to each parish in Italy; that the Italian priest, for the most part cultivating it himself, acquires the tastes, habits, interests, and sympathies of a small farmer, while the French priest is a priest, and nothing more, and all his interests are those of his Church.[13]

A change which has taken place in many countries in the internal arrangements and discipline of the Church has also tended greatly to give the priesthood a more restless, aggressive, and intensely sacerdotal character. Formerly the position of the parish priest was usually a very independent and secure one, much like that of an Anglican rector. It has been of late the policy of the Church to make it more precarious, and to make the priest much more dependent on the goodwill of his bishop.

The increase of Catholic enthusiasm over large portions of

---

[13] See Laveleye, *Le Gouvernement dans la Démocratie*, i. 121–24.

the Continent in the latter half of the present century has been very remarkable. Few pages in the history of the nineteenth century will be hereafter regarded as more curious than the revival, in a scientific and highly industrial age, on a vast scale, of the mediæval pilgrimages, with all their old accompaniments of visions and miracles. It is true that, like most successful movements of this century, it has been due not to one but to many impulses, and that these are by no means exclusively religious. Politics have borne a large part; and the period when the pilgrimages assumed their greatest prominence was in the few years that followed the war of 1870, when the French Catholic party were labouring desperately to kindle a strong Legitimist as well as religious fanaticism, for the double purpose of placing the Comte de Chambord on the throne of France, and of restoring the temporal power of the Pope. Apparition after apparition of the Virgin Mary was announced, accompanied by prophecies foreshadowing these events, and the great pilgrimages that were organised were almost wholly in the hands of the Legitimist party.[14] Speeches, hymns, banners, and emblems continually pointing to the speedy restoration of the Monarchy of the White Flag, gave them the character of great political demonstrations.

Other motives may be traced which are not very unlike those that have contributed considerably to the success of the great Primrose League in England. The pilgrimages were under very aristocratic guidance, and large classes who were struggling on the verge of good society found that by throwing themselves into the movement their social ambition was largely helped. The desire for change and for new and strong emotions, which is so characteristic of our time, bore a large

---

[14] Much information on this subject will be found in the very interesting work of the Abbé Michaud, *L'Eglise Catholique Romaine en France*. See especially pp. 54–92. The illustrious Bishop Dupanloup clearly saw the danger of this multiplication of pretended prophecies; see his *Lettre sur les Prophéties Contemporaines* (1874).

part. The love of pleasure was gratified by a gigantic excursion, and the love of show by the pomp of a great religious ceremony; the organisation of a pilgrimage introduced a new interest and animation into dull country life; the banner, which was only authorised when a given number of pilgrims had been enlisted, and the enrolment of the largest contributors in 'the book of gold' deposited at Lourdes, created a keen emulation.[15] Great local and material interests grew up in connection with the pilgrimages. Miraculous waters were widely sold, and much charlatanism, of which the priests were probably very innocent, was connected with them.[16] Cures were accomplished, as is always the case under the influence of a strong enthusiasm; and, as is also always the case, they were multiplied and magnified a hundredfold. The pilgrimages acquired the popularity of a new and greatly advertised remedy, and the mere assemblage of vast, enthusiastic multitudes kindled by the force of contagious sympathy an ever-growing flame.

---

[15] There is an excellent account of the way in which pilgrimages are got up in Hamerton's *Round my House*, pp. 265–72; see, too, Michaud, 332–36; Burnouf, *Le Catholicisme Contemporaine*, pp. 242–45.

[16] M. Michaud quotes the prospectus of a liqueur called L'Immortelle which was on sale: 'Cette délicieuse liqueur composée avec de l'eau de la fontaine miraculeuse de Lourdes, et avec des plantes et des fruits recueillis dans les splendides vallées de Cauterets, &c., possède, avec le parfum le plus suave, les qualités qui en font une liqueur hygiénique par excellence. Prise avant le repas elle dispose à l'appétit; mais au lieu d'abrutir et de tuer, comme le fait l'absinthe, elle ouvre l'esprit et donne la vie. Prise après le repas elle parfume la bouche, active la digestion, et fait éprouver un bien-être que ne saurait procurer le meilleur cognac ou la plus délicieuse chartreuse,' &c. (Michaud, pp. 335–36).

Paul Bert, in one of his speeches (January 21, 1879) on the education question, mentions, as a fact which he had verified, that some Catholic students were accustomed, when presenting themselves for their examination for the 'baccalauréat,' to put drops of Lourdes water into their ink-bottles, in order that they might win at the examination (*Morale des Jésuites*, p. 591). M. Zola's great novel on the subject of Lourdes has appeared since these pages were written, and I need only refer to it.

New and comparatively obscure forms of devotion rose rapidly into popularity. The devotion of the Sacré Cœur which grew out of the visions of Marie Alacoque at Paray-le-Monial at the close of the seventeenth century, and which was especially favoured by the Jesuits; the devotions connected with St. Joseph, to which Pius IX. gave a great impulse; the innumerable works of charity and piety associated with the Society of St. Vincent de Paul, have been the most remarkable. A vast network of confraternities, 'cercles,' Catholic Committees, and other organisations has grown up over France for the purpose of acting on different classes of society, directing, stimulating, and organising religious fervour and propagandism. 'Christian Corporations' and 'Catholic workmen's clubs' especially multiplied. In 1878 there were said to have been more than four hundred of these clubs in France, with nearly 100,000 persons enrolled in them, and a law which was enacted in 1884, giving fuller powers to syndicates or trades unions, greatly assisted them by giving them a new right of holding property.[17]

It is impossible in a work like the present to give any adequate account of the vast mass of zeal which has been poured into these various channels, but a careful study will amply repay those who take a serious interest in the religious history of the nineteenth century. Millions of copies of tracts and catechisms for young children and for the poor were scattered abroad, and many of them were pervaded by a superstition as gross and by an intolerance as intense as any that existed in the Middle Ages. Education especially has been the field in which the Catholic priests have shown themselves most active, and there was a period when, in nearly every grade, French education was mainly dominated by their influence.

All this was accompanied by a strong movement towards religious centralisation. Under Pius IX. the power of the

---

[17] Hurlbert's *France*, pp. 380–83, 388–89. Pressensé, *La Liberté Religieuse*, pp. 71–72. See, too, Michaud, *L'Eglise Romaine en France*, pp. 254–69; Burnouf, *Le Catholicisme Contemporaine*.

Jesuits enormously increased in the Church, and the whole tendency of the 'Univers' and of its remarkable editor, Louis Veuillot, was to supersede the influence of the bishops by the more direct action of the Jesuits and of the Pope. The Gallican theory of Catholicism, which gave the French Church a large measure of independence, was definitely overthrown, amid the almost complete indifference of the great body of the laity, who had once been its most ardent supporters; the type of Catholicism identified with the great names of Lamennais, Lacordaire, Montalembert, and de Falloux, which was strongly anti-Gallican, but at the same time on its political side sincerely liberal, was equally crushed. The definition, in 1854, of the doctrine of the Immaculate Conception by Pius IX., without the convocation of a General Council, prepared the way for the declaration by the General Council of 1870 that the Pope was infallible in faith and morals; and although some obscurity was still suffered to rest upon the conditions under which this infallibility was called into action, it was left to the Pope himself to define the frontier of his own inspiration. All over Catholic Europe the triumph of the Ultramontane theory was recognised as a great step to complete centralisation, converting the Church from a limited into an absolute monarchy. If the power of the bishops over the parish priests was increased, their own power in the government of the Church was materially diminished. The saying attributed to the old Duke de Sermoneta was as true as it was witty: 'They entered the Council shepherds—they came out of it sheep.' By committing itself to the infallibility of the long line of Popes the Church cut itself off from the historical spirit and learning of the age, and has exposed itself to such crushing and unanswerable refutations as the treatise of Janus and the Letters of Gratry. But if Catholicism has dissociated itself more and more from the intellect of Europe, and become more and more incredible to the small class of earnest, truth-seeking scholars, it has greatly increased its power of acting on vast ignorant democracies. A cause which is embodied in a single man is, with such democracies, far more popular than a cause which rests upon any abstract principles or on any governing class, and the Church acquired a greatly increased discipline and concentration, and a much greater power of carrying out a policy independently of all local and national influences.

It had already abundantly shown that its old spirit of intolerance was not abandoned. This was clearly manifested in the Encyclical Letter of Gregory XVI., which was issued in 1832, condemning the prevailing doctrine that men of upright and honest lives might obtain salvation in any faith, tracing to this noxious source the 'absurd and erroneous opinion, or rather form of madness, which was spread abroad to the ruin of religious and civil society,' that 'liberty of conscience must be assured and guaranteed to every one,' and condemning in terms of equal violence unrestricted liberty of publication. In the Concordat with Spain in 1851, and in the Concordat with the Republic of the Equator in 1862, it was expressly stipulated that 'no other forms of worship than the Catholic one should be tolerated' in the land. 'That each man is free to embrace and profess the religion which by the light of his reason he believes to be true;' 'that the Church may not employ force;' 'that Church and State should be separated;' 'that national Churches may be established which are not under the authority of the Roman Pontiff;' 'that it is no longer expedient that the Catholic religion should be considered as the only religion of the State, to the exclusion of all other forms of worship;' 'that in countries called Catholic the public exercise of their own religions may be laudably granted to immigrants;' 'that the Roman Pontiff ought to come to terms with progress, liberalism, and modern civilisation,' are among the propositions enumerated in the famous Syllabus of 1864 as authoritatively condemned by the Church. The meaning and scope of such condemnations are clearly shown by the formal ecclesiastical condemnation of the laws or institutions which, in Belgium, Austria, Spain, Tuscany, Bavaria, and some States in South America, have in the present century established freedom of religious worship and accorded civil rights to

members of different creeds.[18] As late as 1884, Pope Leo XIII.
delivered an allocution to the assembled Cardinals, in which
he denounced, as one of the worst crimes of the Italian Government, that Protestant doctrines were openly taught and
Protestant churches established in Rome itself with complete
liberty and impunity and under the protection of the laws.[19]
As late as 1893 the leading ecclesiastical authorities in Spain
protested against the opening of a Protestant church in
Madrid as an insult to their faith.[20]

At the same time, when Governments based on other principles have been established, the Church has usually accepted
them, has authorised Catholics to swear allegiance to them,
and has used all her spiritual influence to direct and mould
them to her ends. Veuillot, in a striking sentence, expressed
with great candour the policy of his party. 'When you are the
masters,' he said to the Liberals and Protestants, 'we claim
perfect liberty for ouselves, as your principles require it; when
we are the masters we refuse it to you, as it is contrary to our
principles.[21]

The use of distinctly spiritual influence in politics has been
one of the gravest difficulties in Catholic countries. The following, for example, is part of an address issued in 1872 by
the Cardinal Archbishop of Chambery to his clergy. 'Monsieur
le Curé, next Sunday, the 7th inst., the election of a deputy
will go on in each commune. . . . Reduce on this day the
parish service to a low Mass celebrated early in the morning.

---

[18] The texts of some of these condemnations will be found in Janus; in
the introduction of Laveleye to Minghetti's treatise on Church and State
(French translation); in Laurent, *De l'Eglise et l'État*, p. 111; and in Mr.
Gladstone's pamphlet on Vaticanism. See, too, an excellent chapter in
Laveleye's *Le Gouvernement dans la Démocratie*, i. 146–56.

[19] The text of this important allocution will be found in the pamphlet of
Laveleye, *La Crise récente en Belgique* (1885), p. 29.

[20] See a curious notice of this episode in the *Dublin Review*, April, 1893,
pp. 463–64.

[21] Laveleye, i. 187–88.

Recommend all your electors to go and vote, and to elect a good Catholic. Tell them that it is for them an obligation of conscience under penalty of grave sin. Take care that there is no abstention in your parish.[22] In Belgium and in French Canada, as well as in Ireland, priests have been among the most active electioneering agents, and their success has always depended mainly upon their spiritual authority. In Italy, the Pope gives the order which causes great multitudes of electors to abstain from elections. In France, when divorce was established, the ecclesiastical authorities did not content themselves with the legitimate course of informing their flocks that good Catholics must not avail themselves of the privilege granted by the law. They proceeded, 'with the express approbation of the Pope,' to issue a declaration directly attacking the administration of public justice, by pronouncing that no Catholic judge could legitimately grant a divorce, and no Catholic advocate plead for one.[23] In Germany, the Catholic party have not only won a great victory, but have also formed a distinct and powerful party, and German politics largely depend upon its bargains with the Government. When a ministry had introduced some measure for the increase of the army or navy, on the ground that it is essential to the security of the country, it has more than once happened that the vote of the Catholic party could turn the scale, and that their vote depended avowedly on the concessions on purely Catholic questions that the Government were prepared to make. In Germany, a priesthood far more educated and intelligent than in most countries have thrown themselves heartily into politics, and have done so with brilliant success. The remarkable triumph of the Catholic party at the election of 1890 appears to have been generally attributed by friend and foe to their skilful conduct, and it placed no less than twenty-three priests in the Reichstag, while twenty-seven others sat in the sub-

---

[22] Michaud, p. 52.

[23] May 27, 1886. See *Revue de Droit International*, xxi. 615.

ordinate German parliaments.[24] Leo XIII. has been much praised in England for the direction he gave to the French Catholics to rally round the Republic. The measure may have been a wise one; but it is surely a startling thing when Frenchmen who have been long attached to the Royalist or Imperialist cause consider themselves bound by their religious duty to abandon the politics of their lives at the order of an Italian priest.

The Catholic Church is essentially a State within a State, with its frontiers, its policy, and its leaders entirely distinct from those of the nation, and it can command an enthusiasm and a devotion at least as powerful and as widespread as the enthusiasm of patriotism. It claims to be a higher authority than the State: to exercise a Divine, and therefore a supreme, authority over belief, morals, and education, and to possess the right of defining the limits of its own authority. It also demands obedience even where it does not claim infallibility; and it claims a controlling influence over a vast and indefinite province which lies beyond the limits of authoritatively formulated doctrine. The Council of the Vatican laid down that all Catholics, whatever may be their position, 'are subject to the duty of hierarchical subordination and of a true obedience, not only in the things that concern faith and morals, but also in those which belong to the discipline and the government of the Church spread throughout the universe.' On the strength of this decree, and on the strength of various Papal encyclicals, or instructions relating to political or social matters, attempts have been made to draw the whole fields of politics, political economy, and social questions within the empire of the Church, on the ground that particular courses adopted on all these questions may promote or impede its interests. In the words of Cardinal Lavigerie, 'In the order of facts which practically interest religion and the Church' the counsels or precepts of the Vicar of Christ have an absolute

---

[24] See Kannengieser, *Catholiques Allemands*, p. 76.

right to the submission of Catholics. To dispute this, and to draw distinctions between less authoritative and more authoritative Papal commands, is, according to the Cardinal, 'a grave error, condemned by the Council of the Vatican with the other errors of ancient Gallicanism.[25]

The Church has in every parish one or more priests entirely devoted to its service; it exercises an enormous influence over the whole female population, over the education of the young, over the periods of weakness, sickness, enfeebled faculties, and approaching death. It meddles persistently in domestic life, dictating the conditions of marriage, prescribing to the parent the places of secular education to which he may or may not send his children, interfering between the husband and the wife, and between the parent and the child. It orders all men, under pain of eternal perdition, to attend its ministrations, to obey its precepts, to reveal in the confessional the inmost secrets of their hearts. It professes also to possess spiritual powers which furnish it with extraordinary means of levying taxation. Its teaching about purgatory and Masses, acting, as it does, with peculiar force in the moments of bitter bereavement and in the terrors of approaching death, will always, in a believing Catholic country, secure it an ample independent revenue; and it has in every Church a tribune where its priest can harangue his congregation without the possibility of discussion or reply. Being itself independent of all Governments, and using all Governments for its own purposes, it has much to hope, as well as something to fear, from the transfer of the chief political power in the world to the most ignorant classes, and the modern tendency of most Parliaments to break up into small groups is exceedingly favourable to its influence. No other body possesses in so high a degree the power of cohesion, or can carry out more effectually the policy which has been successfully pursued by the Irish members in the Imperial Parliament. Its leaders are well aware of

---

[25] See on this subject *La Papauté, le Socialisme et la Démocratie* par A. Leroy-Beaulieu, pp. 61–71.

the enormously disproportioned power that can be exercised in a divided and balanced Parliament by a small group of earnest men who are prepared to subordinate to their special objects all national and party interests. It has also a rare power of waiting for opportunities, often suspending its claims, never formally abandoning them.

Such an organisation cannot be treated by legislators as if it were simply a form of secular opinion, and many good judges look with extreme alarm upon the dangerous power it may acquire in the democracies of the future. In the writings of Laveleye this fear continually appears in the darkest colours; but it must be remembered that Laveleye was a Belgian, and that Belgium is one of the countries where the religious conflict has assumed its acutest form. It is impossible, however, to be blind to the consensus of opinion on this subject which has grown up among the statesmen of most Catholic countries; and the tendency of historical research in Protestant countries is in the same direction. One of the facts which have been most painfully borne upon the minds of the more careful thinkers and students of the present generation is, how much stronger than our fathers imagined were the reasons which led former legislators to impose restrictive legislation on Catholicism. Measures of the Reformation period which, as lately as the days of Hallam, were regarded by the most enlightened historians as simple persecution, are now seen to have been in a large degree measures of necessary self-defence, or inevitable incidents in a civil war. As a matter of strict right, a Church which is in its own nature, in principle, and in practice persecuting wherever it has the power, cannot, like other religions, claim toleration; but all enlightened Protestant and free-thinking opinion would accord it to Catholic belief and worship in the amplest manner. But when the Catholic priests claim to be invested by Divine authority with the prerogatives of teaching, commanding, excommunicating, and forgiving sins, and when, by virtue of their spiritual authority, they attempt to dictate the politics of their congregations, the case cannot be lightly dismissed with mere commonplaces about religious toleration. Two things, at least, may be confidently stated. The one is, that when a large proportion of the electors in a nation submit to such dictation, that nation is very unfit for representative institutions. The other is, that a priesthood which acts on such principles must hold a position essentially different from a Protestant clergy.

In my own opinion, the danger of priestly ascendency is very serious in particular countries and provinces, but is not serious in the world at large. No one who takes a wide and impartial survey of the broad current of human affairs can fail to see that it is not running in the direction of priestly power. It is surely a significant fact that the whole aggregate political force of Catholicism in the world has not been sufficient to maintain the small temporal dominion of the Pope, although Popes who were pronounced to be infallible had declared with the utmost emphasis and authority that the maintenance of this dominion was of vital importance to the Catholic Church. In countries where almost the whole population had been baptised into the Catholic faith, the once terrible weapon of excommunication has proved absolutely idle. Who can fail to be struck with the contrast between the modern Popes, who have been vainly appealing to all Catholic kings and peoples to restore Rome to their dominion, and the ancient Popes, at whose command, during nearly two centuries,[26] the flower of martial Christendom poured into the Holy Land, and the chief sovereigns of Europe consented to subordinate all temporal objects to the recovery of Jerusalem from the infidel? If there ever was an occasion in modern times when priestly influence seemed likely to triumph in France, it was during the deep depression which followed the disasters of 1870, when a Legitimist Parliament was elected, and assembled at Bordeaux. All the moral conditions of a great ecclesiastical revival seemed there, and strong political interests seemed turning in the same direction. It was widely believed in Ger-

---

[26] The First Crusade took place in 1096. The loss of Ptolemais, the last Christian possession in the East, was in 1291.

many, and was openly predicted by Bismarck, that France would place herself after her defeat at the head of the Catholic interest of Europe, and endeavour to paralyse German unity by acting through priestly influence on German Catholics.[27] But all such predictions proved absolutely false. The result of the struggle was the total defeat of the Clerical party and the establishment of a fiercely anti-Clerical republic.

Nearly the whole Catholic world in the present century has based its constitutions and its religious legislation on principles that have been condemned by the Church. Full religious liberty, to which she is bitterly opposed, has been almost everywhere established. Civil marriage, which she hates, has passed into the legislation of most Catholic countries. National education, over which she claims an absolute directing power, has in most countries been wrested wholly or in a large measure from her hands. In an age in which, under the influence of democracy, the government of the world is passing more and more into uninstructed hands, no great importance may be attached to the fact that, in the literature of nominally Catholic countries, really Catholic literature holds only an infinitesimal place. It is, however, a more important fact that the press, which represents political force much more faithfully than literature, has long been mainly anti-Catholic, or at least completely indifferent to Catholic teaching. In no other department, indeed, have the Catholic party failed more conspicuously in establishing their influence.

Nor does the popular sentiment in democratic countries show any real signs of returning to the Church. There is, indeed, something in the meddling, monastic, inquisitorial, and pedagogic spirit of priestly government that seems to produce an altogether peculiar irritation in masculine natures. The Roman Government, during the days of the Papal ascendency, was a backward and ignorant Government, honeycombed with abuses, but it was neither extravagant, nor

---

[27] See a striking passage of a speech of Bismarck quoted by Pressensé (*La Liberté Religieuse*, p. 155).

cruel, nor grossly oppressive; it secured for those who lived under it an assured peace and a unique dignity in the world, and it was presided over by a most amiable and well-meaning, though somewhat vain and foolish, old man. There have assuredly been many worse Governments, but few appear to have excited more animosity among its subjects.

The most unjustifiable and contemptible of all recent revolutions is, probably, that which in 1889 destroyed the monarchy in Brazil, deposing after a long, prosperous, and eminently beneficent reign one of the most enlightened and accomplished sovereigns of our age. He was, however, a kind of modern Prospero, caring more for scientific studies than for the government of men, and under his culpably indulgent rule traitors were suffered for at least twenty years to preach treason and form conspiracies with impunity. They succeeded at last, and power fell for a time into the hands of a small group of pretentious, philosophical pedants of a sect which modestly claims for itself the government of the world.[28] Their State papers are a curious study, and have, I suppose, seldom been surpassed in grandiloquent absurdity. As might be expected, these men did not long hold power. Their chief in a short time 'quitted'—in the words of their National Congress—'the objective life for immortality,'[29] and the direction of affairs passed into the strong hands of a series of ambitious soldiers, under whom a once prosperous country has been steadily traversing the well-known path to anarchy and bankruptcy. The significance of the story, however, lies in the fact that the one real

---

[28] 'Au nom du passé et de l'avenir, les serviteurs théoriques et les serviteurs pratiques de l'Humanité viennent prendre dignement la direction générale des affaires terrestres, pour construire enfin la vraie providence morale, intellectuelle et matérielle; en excluant irrévocablement de la suprématie politique tous les divers esclaves de Dieu, catholiques, protestants ou déistes, comme étant à la fois arriérés et perturbateurs' (Aug. Comte, *Catéchisme Positiviste*, Preface).

[29] See *L'Idée Républicaine au Brésil*, par Oscar d'Araujo, p. 126. This silly book, written for the purpose of glorifying the revolution, contains much evidence of the treachery by which it was effected.

public motive that seems to have entered into this revolution was the fear that in the near future priestly influence might acquire a dominating influence in the Government. The Brazilian Constitution of 1891 disclosed clearly the intense hatred of clerical influence that had silently grown up among a people who by race, religion, and circumstances might have been supposed to be one of the most Catholic in the world. Not only was complete religious liberty guaranteed; not only was every civil post, from the highest to the lowest, thrown open to men of all religions; not only was every vestige of privilege withdrawn from the Catholic clergy—it was further provided that civil marriage alone should be recognised by the Republic; that all teaching in public establishments should be exclusively secular; that all cemeteries should be secularised, and placed under the administration of the municipal authorities; that no Church or form of worship should receive any subvention or special privilege from the Government.[30]

In France, some good judges believe that it is quite possible that a strong and despotic monarchy may again exist, but nearly all admit that this can only be on the condition that it is entirely free from sacerdotal influence; and many think that over large tracts of France, if the State endowment were withdrawn, it would be impossible to maintain the Catholic worship. The hatred with which priests and priestly interference are regarded by great masses of the population seems hardly comprehensible to a Protestant mind; and it will have been observed how frequently the anti-Catholic measures, which English opinion has regarded as most oppressive, have been speedily followed by Government successes at elections. In nearly all Catholic countries some measure of the same spirit may be traced. Even in Ireland it is beginning to grow up, and it is probable that the manner in which the priests in that country have been seeking to maintain their power, by tampering with the first principles of honesty and morality, will be soon found to have undermined, in a great part of the

---

[30] Dareste, *Les Constitutions Modernes*, ii. 648–50.

population, the moral foundations on which all religious beliefs and Churches must ultimately rest.

This at least is certain, that the triumph of Ultramontanism
in the General Council of 1870 gave the signal for a new and
formidable schism between the Catholic Church and lay opinion, and became the starting-point for much new restrictive
legislation on ecclesiastical matters. In Austria, Count Beust
at once declared the Concordat of 1855 null and void; and a
law of 1874, to which I have already referred, gave the Government a right of veto over all ecclesiastical appointments
that are not made by the sovereign, and also a superinten-
dency over all ecclesiastical proceedings, and provided carefully against abuses of ecclesiastical authority. In Switzerland,
where the sword had been drawn and lives had been lost in
a religious war as recently as 1847, the decrees of the Vatican
and the aggressive policy of Bishop Mermillod at once produced a renewed, though happily a bloodless, conflict. Immediately after the declaration of Infallibility a law was voted
in Geneva obliging all Catholic congregations to receive a
fresh authorisation from the Council of State, and making
their continued existence dependent on its pleasure. The
Pope took a step very similar to the English Papal aggression
by creating a new bishopric of Geneva, and appointing the
Abbé Mermillod as bishop, and soon after as vicar-apostolic.
But in Switzerland he was met by a very different kind of
resistance from the abortive Ecclesiastical Titles Act, which
some English writers are accustomed to represent as so intolerant. The Government refused to recognise the new bishopric, or to allow the new bishop to exercise his ecclesiastical
functions, and, as he declined to obey, he was banished from
the country, and an article was introduced into the revised
Federal Constitution of 1874 providing that no bishopric may
be established on Swiss territory without the approbation of
the Government. By the same Constitution no convents or
religious orders could be founded, and those which had been
suppressed could not be restored. Neither the Jesuits nor any
affiliated societies were permitted to exist in any part of Swit-

zerland; all participation of their members either in Church or school is prohibited, and the Federal Government reserves to itself the right of extending similar treatment to all other orders that might introduce danger and disorder into the State. The public schools are gratuitous, open to the members of all creeds, without prejudice to their freedom of conscience and belief. The right of marriage is placed under the protection of the Confederation, and no 'confessional motive' is allowed to impede it, and the right of disposing of the places of burial is retained in the hands of the civil powers. Liberty of conscience and belief is pronounced inviolable; but it is essentially a liberty of individuals, and it is pushed to such a point that it deprives Churches of all restraining and disciplinary powers over their members. 'No one can be constrained to take part in a religious association, to follow a religious teaching, to accomplish a religious act, or to incur any punishments of any kind on account of his religious opinion.'[31]

It was, however, in the cantonal legislation that the severity of the conflict was most shown. Several of the cantons, and among them the important cantons of Berne, Geneva, and Neuchatel, following in the steps of the Civil Constitution of the clergy which had been created by the French National Assembly in 1789, took the bold step of requiring the election of the parish priests by the people, and of vesting full powers of directing the manner of religious services, the uses to which the churches might be applied, and the instruction of the young, in a parish council consisting chiefly of laymen, and chosen by the general vote of the parishioners. Such a measure, basing the whole ecclesiastical system on popular election and on lay control, was directly opposed to the theory of the Roman Church, and one of its results was that, while it was emphatically condemned by the Pope, the Old Catholics, who consented to adopt it, acquired a great place in Swiss Catholicism. Some measures of extreme and unjustifiable

---

[31] Dareste, i. 496–97.

severity were taken. A bishop of Bâle was accused, and finally exiled from his diocese, for having excommunicated two priests who had preached the doctrines of Old Catholicism, and a large number of priests who adhered to him were deprived of their positions. The Canton of Berne even attempted to expel from their parishes all priests who were not elected. The Federal Council and Chamber ultimately declared this measure inconsistent with the Constitution, and pronounced that the Infallibilists had a full right of constituting themselves an independent community; but in a considerable part of Switzerland all public subsidies were withdrawn from those who refused to accept the elective system. The new centralisation at Rome was thus met by a decentralisation so complete that in each parish the parishioners might determine by election the type of doctrine and the character of worship. The avowed object was that each Catholic should have the right of rejecting the doctrine of infallibility, and in order to make the democratic ascendency more complete the priests were required to submit to periodical re-election. The same system was extended, in the Canton of Berne, to the Protestant Churches, which could only retain their subsidies from the State by relinquishing all power of enforcing unity; and this system was sanctioned on appeal by a majority of the electors. [32]

In Prussia, and, in a less degree, in all Germany, still more strenuous measures were taken. Bismarck wrote to Count Arnim that the effect of the decision of the Council of the Vatican was to reduce the bishops to mere 'functionaries of a foreign sovereign, and of a sovereign who, by virtue of his claimed infallibility, is the most absolute monarch on the globe'; he dilated in public on the dangerous power the Pope had now acquired of meddling with and controlling the internal affairs of Germany; and he issued a circular despatch to the German ambassadors, directing them to call the atten-

---

[32] Pressensé, *La Liberté Religieuse depuis 1870*, pp. 250–333; *Revue de Droit International*, xv. 70–72, 77–84; Adams and Cunningham,*The Swiss Confederation*, pp. 177–88, 274–75.

tion of the Governments to which they were accredited to the changed position of the Pope, and to the expediency of coming to some agreement about the conditions on which alone the election of ensuing Popes should be recognised.

Legislation of the most drastic kind was at once adopted. In 1872, a German law was carried making every ecclesiastic who, in the exercise of his religious functions, treats public affairs before an assembly in such a way as to imperil public peace liable to two years' imprisonment; and another German law banished the Society of Jesus and all orders that were in relation with it from German soil, and enabled the Government by a simple measure of police to expel from the Empire any German who belonged to them. In the same year a Prussian law placed all schools, whether they were free or public, under strict Government inspection and control. In the following year the famous Falk laws were passed, which transformed the whole condition of Catholics in Prussia. The separate, isolated, and exclusively clerical system of education, which contributes more than any other cause to the worst characteristics of the priesthood, was put an end to by a law which compelled the ecclesiastical students to receive their education in a national university; or in an authorised seminary. Such seminaries were only authorised in towns where there was no university; they were required to fulfil the same conditions as State establishments; and every step of the education of those intended for the priesthood was submitted to strict Government inspection and control. By other laws the conditions of entry into the priesthood were regulated by the Government; all acts of ecclesiastical discipline and all episcopal condemnations were made subject to the High Court of Justice, which has a right of adjudicating upon them on appeal; and it was expressly enacted that no judgments emanating from an ecclesiastical authority of foreign nationality should have force upon German soil. At the same time, great facilities were given by the Government for the construction of a Church on the basis of Old Catholic doctrine.

Such measures inevitably involved a fierce war between the State and the Catholic Church, and the lay authority encountered an intense and courageous resistance. Three articles in the Prussian Constitution guaranteed to the Evangelical Church and to the Roman Catholic Church the right of governing themselves freely, disposing of their goods, and providing for ecclesiastical nominations, and also gave a legal sanction to the relations between religious societies and their superiors. A law of 1873 modified and restricted these liberties, and in 1875 the three articles were altogether abolished. A long succession of other measures were taken, breaking down the whole system of Catholic government. Civil marriage was established, and the control of burials was taken from the Church; ecclesiastics who refused to obey the new laws were made liable to imprisonment, banishment, fines, and deposition. In 1873 the Cardinal Archbishop of Posen and the Archbishop of Cologne were thrown into prison, and ultimately banished. In 1874 a law was passed providing for the appointment of administrators over the vacant dioceses and parishes. The chapters might elect the substitutes for the bishops, subject to the approval of the Government; but if they refused to do so the civil power appointed them, and in some cases the places of the banished priests might be filled, as in Switzerland, by election. In all parts of the German Empire, ecclesiastics who had been deprived of their functions by a regular judgment might be deprived of their nationality and banished from the country.

The old Pope threw himself into the conflict quite as vehemently as the Prussian statesman. Cardinal Hohenlohe had been selected without any previous consultation to represent the German Empire at the Vatican, but the Pope refused to accept him. Shortly after the first ecclesiastical law had been carried the Pope received a deputation from German Catholics, and in reply to their address he complained bitterly of the persecution which the Church was undergoing in Prussia, and, alluding to the vision in Daniel, he predicted that the little stone might soon fall from the mountain which would shatter the feet of the Colossus. In the beginning of 1875 he issued a fierce Encyclical pronouncing the new legislation invalid, as being contrary to the Divine institution of the Church, and excommunicated all persons who accepted from the temporal power the investiture of which the bishops had been deprived. On the other side language was used about the supreme authority of the State over all religious bodies which seemed an echo of the language of Hobbes in the seventeenth and of Rousseau in the eighteenth century. Except in the case of clergy who were attached to public institutions, the State subsidies were withdrawn from dioceses in which the bishop or his administrator refused to accept the new laws. The Old Catholics were permitted to hold their services in the Catholic parish churches, or to have a proportionate share of the Church lands and revenues. All conventual establishments were abolished; all Catholic religious orders were banished from the Prussian soil.

It was stated on good authority in the beginning of 1875 that no less than five bishops had been imprisoned and six others fined, and that about 1,400 priests had been either fined or imprisoned. Nearly the whole Prussian episcopacy were acting in defiance of the laws, either refusing to submit the programmes of their clerical seminaries to Government inspection and approval, or expelling or excommunicating Old Catholics, or appointing priests to spiritual charges without reference to the civil authorities.

The Cardinal Archbishop of Posen was under arrest for more than two years, and a Bishop of Trèves died in prison.[33] In several dioceses all ecclesiastical subsidies from the State were suspended for periods ranging from five to ten years.[34] The resistance encountered among the German Catholics showed clearly the power of their faith, and was probably not anticipated by the framers of these laws; and it also soon became evident that the Old Catholic movement, though sup-

---

[33] Kannengieser, *Catholiques Allemands*, pp. 30–31.
[34] Ibid. p. 218.

ported by a few great scholars and very excellent men, was
never likely to furnish a dominant or even an important element in German Catholicism. It experienced the fate of most
half measures. Serious and independent inquirers, who based
their faith upon evidence, nearly always went much further,
while those who were indisposed to such inquiries soon acquiesced in a new doctrine, and remained attached to the body
which represented in visible and unbroken continuity the old
framework or organisation of the Church. In 1881 it was stated
in the Prussian Parliament that, owing to the laws making it
penal for any priest whose appointment had not been sanctioned by the Government to perform the offices of religion,
601 Roman Catholic parishes were left without curates, and
584 with only half their requisite number.[35] Politically, the first
and most serious effect of the laws was to consolidate into a
single party in the Reichstag the Catholic members from all
parts of the Empire. Under the consummate leadership of Dr.
Windthorst they steadily increased, and in 1878 they num-
bered 103. In spite of the great preponderance of Protestantism
in the German Empire, the Catholic party was now the most
powerful single party in its much-divided Parliament.[35]

The persecution—for it had come to amount to nothing
less—soon ceased. The death of Pius IX., and the accession
in 1878 of a much more intelligent Pope, brought a spirit of
moderation to the Vatican; and the fact that the French Government had engaged in a violent ecclesiastical contest was
probably not without some influence at Berlin. The kaleido-
scope of German politics took a new pattern. The great and
imperious statesman who presided over it was always accustomed to concentrate his undivided efforts on an immediate
and pressing object, and in order to attain it he has never
hesitated to enter into new combinations, discard old allies,
and connect himself with old enemies. Socialism, not Ultramontanism, now seemed to him the pressing danger, and he

---

[35] *Annual Register,* 1881, p. 250.
[36] Kannengieser, p. 38.

also desired to carry out a policy of economical protection which was very displeasing to his former allies. For the success of his new policy Catholic assistance was required. He probably perceived that his crusade against the Church had been based upon a profound miscalculation of moral forces, and he retraced his steps with a promptitude and completeness that would have ruined the reputation of a weaker man. 'The moment,' he once said, 'the interest of the country requires me to put myself in contradiction with myself, I shall do it.' Almost immediately after the accession of the new Pope overtures were made to the Vatican; the diplomatic relations which had been broken off in 1874 were restored. Dr. Falk, who was most directly concerned in the ecclesiastical laws, was put aside, and the great statesman, who had so lately dilated on the danger of the Pope meddling with the internal affairs of Germany, began a negotiation with the Pope for the purpose of inducing him to put pressure upon the Catholic members in order to induce them to vote for the anti-Socialist laws and for a law in favour of a Government monopoly of tobacco. Bismarck now declared that the anti-Catholic laws had been measures of war, which had become unnecessary since a new spirit of conciliation prevailed in the Vatican; that parts of them were shown by experience to be wholly useless; and that, if they were now abolished, they could always, in case of danger, be re-enacted. A law was carried through the Prussian Parliament giving the Government a discretionary power of applying or not applying the chief portions of them, and this measure was only a prelude to their almost complete repeal.

The Pope was much inclined to do as the Prussian statesman desired, but he would not as yet openly disown the Catholic party in the Reichstag, and he found that party by no means prepared to take its German politics implicitly from Rome. A long period of skilful bargaining ensued, conducted between the Prussian Government and the Vatican behind the back of the Catholic party in Germany. One of the most curious incidents in the negotiations was the selection by Bis-

marck of the Pope as the arbitrator in a dispute which had
risen between Germany and Spain about the Caroline Isles.
To the great indignation of the German Ultramontanes, the
Pope consented to allow the Prussian ecclesiastics to notify
their appointments to the Government before they were carried out, and he afterwards acquiesced in the governors of
the provinces retaining a very limited veto on the appointment of parish priests. A proposal to restore the three abrogated articles of the Prussian Constitution was defeated in
1884,[37] but nearly all that was important in the Falk laws
speedily disappeared. The banished prelates were restored.
The payment of the priests in the dioceses where it had been
suspended was resumed. The bishops regained almost complete liberty of ecclesiastical discipline, and full power of exercising their spiritual functions outside their own sees. The
measures that had been taken for controlling and directing
the education of priests, which formed, perhaps, the most
really valuable portion of the new laws, were unconditionally
surrendered, and, with the important exception of the Jesuits,
the religious congregations that had been banished or dissolved were restored to their former position. A sum of
twenty millions of marks was in the coffers of the State, representing the ecclesiastical revenues which, during the years
of conflict, had been unpaid. After a long controversy this
sum was restored to the Church, and distributed among the
dioceses from which it had been withheld.[38]

The repeal of the Falk laws was the price paid by Prince
Bismarck for a new act of Papal interference in his favour. The
question of the military Septennate was pending, and the
Pope undertook to persuade the Catholic party to vote for it.
Greatly to their credit, the leaders of the party, though declaring their complete submission to the Papacy on all questions of religion, declined to take their orders from Rome in
a matter of purely secular German politics. They were taunted

---

[37] Dareste, *Les Constitutions Modernes*, i. 184.
[38] Kannengieser, pp. 220–55.

by Bismarck with their disobedience, but they persevered, and their votes contributed to throw out the Bill. A dissolution and general election followed, and two letters were then published, written from Rome by Cardinal Jacobini to the Nuncio in Munich, urging the Catholic party to support the Government, and predicting that by doing so they would obtain a revision of the Falk laws. The triumph of the Government at the election of 1887 was probably largely due to this Papal interference, and the author of the Culturkampf was thus enabled to carry out his policy. The subsequent measure abolishing the anti-Catholic laws was the subject of direct negotiation with Rome; and when the Catholic leaders raised some difficulties about its terms, a letter was written by the Pope himself to the Archbishop of Cologne, directing them to vote for it.[39]

It was a strange and unexpected transformation-scene. The Catholic party found themselves censured and disavowed by the Pope, and Bismarck attained the immediate object of his policy; but the victory was dearly purchased. It was purchased by a complete and humiliating abandonment of the policy which had been so recently and so deliberately adopted. A precedent full of danger had been established, and the interference of the Papacy with purely German affairs had been not only permitted but invited. Above all, a separate Catholic party had been created in the Reichstag, which remains to the present day a distinct, dangerous, and distracting element in German politics. One of its principal objects has been to increase clerical influence over education, and there was a moment in 1891 when the Government favoured its policy; but on this subject public opinion in Germany proved so strong that the proposed measure was withdrawn.

In Germany, the war against the Catholic Church was waged by men who were for the most part firm believers in Christianity, or at least in Theism. It was a conflict between a

---

[39] See an interesting article on this subject, by Valbert, in the *Revue des Deux Mondes*, March 1, 1887. See, too, the *Annual Register*, 1887, and Kannengieser, *Catholiques Allemands*.

despotic and highly centralised Church and a State which was
more and more aspiring to be the supreme moulder and reg-
ulator of national life. In France, the conflict took a somewhat
different form, and broke out at a somewhat later period. The
few years that immediately followed the declaration of infallibility, the Franco-German War, and the horrors of the Commune, were in France years of reaction, during which clerical
influence seemed to spread. The real battle was waged, as it
is always likely to be waged in our day, on the question of
education.

In the Consulate and in the early days of the Empire the
First Napoleon had founded on the ruins of the educational
institutions that were shattered by the Revolution a great system of secondary education. Although religious teaching was
given in the lyceums and other institutions which he created,
these establishments were essentially lay, military, and highly
centralised bodies under the direct control of the Government,
and their supreme object was to cultivate civic and military
virtues—to foster the ideals and the habits of a nation of soldiers. The Imperial University, which he founded in 1808, had
a similarly secular character, and it was given a complete authority over the public teaching of the Empire.[40] It was not in
any degree an anti-Christian body. It professed to take as the
basis of its teaching 'the principles of the Catholic religion;'
but it was essentially a lay body, and very free from direct
ecclesiastical influence. The clergy had their 'great seminaries,' or special schools of theology, under the exclusive direction of the bishops; but it was decided by a decree of 1809 that
no one could enter them who had not received a degree from
the Imperial University; and when the clergy began to found
'small seminaries,' which were represented as preparatory
schools for the larger seminaries, but which also admitted lay
pupils, the Government decided 'that all such schools must
be governed by the University; that they could only be organised by it, and ruled by its authority, and that no teaching

---

[40] Simon, *Dieu, Patrie et Liberté*, pp. 120, 124–25.

could be given in them except by members of the University.[41] Very little, however, was as yet done for primary education, and the few schools that were founded for the education of the poor were chiefly placed under the care of religious teaching bodies, which had begun to re-establish themselves in France. They were authorised to teach by the Grand Master of the University.

With the Restoration ecclesiastical influence in French teaching rose rapidly. A strong clerical element was planted in the government of the University, and gave rise to much intestine struggle and some repressive measures. A few very able men, among whom Royer-Collard and Cuvier were the most conspicuous, at this time devoted themselves to education. But the character of education was in a great measure transformed. It was noticed as a characteristic fact, that the classes, which under Napoleon had been summoned by the beat of the drum, were now summoned by bells, and the military aspect of education was replaced by a clerical aspect. The 'small seminaries' became recognised ecclesiastical schools under purely ecclesiastical direction; they appear to have been for a time free from University inspection and control, and they were allowed to receive pupils intended for all professions. Between 1821 and 1828 a large number of religious associations were authorised to establish elementary schools, and 'a letter of obedience' from the Superior-General of the order to which he belonged was accepted as a sufficient certificate of the ability of the teacher. At the same time the Government of the Restoration was far from desiring to surrender the education of France into the hands of priests, and especially of Jesuits. An ordinance of 1828 placed the secondary ecclesiastical schools, in a great measure, under the rule of the University, and their professors were obliged to affirm in writing that they did not belong to any religious association not legally established in France.[42]

---

[41] *Ibid.*; Cousin, *Huit Mois au Ministère de l'Instruction publique; Mémoires de Guizot*, iii. 67–68.
[42] See two articles by Duruy, *Revue des Deux Mondes*, May 15, June 1, 1879.

The Government created by the Revolution of 1830, for the first time, undertook on a large scale public elementary education in France. The charter guaranteed its liberty, and the great measure of Guizot in 1833 carried it into effect. The French statesman declined to adopt the system of compulsory education which had been decreed by the Convention in 1793, and which was actually in force in Prussia and in the greater portion of the German States. At the same time, he wished that primary education should not be a monopoly, and that secular schools and religious schools should have full liberty to develop and compete. With the object of providing efficient teachers for the former the normal schools, which had been founded in 1810, were greatly extended, while the free schools fell chiefly into the hands of religious associations encouraged and assisted by the Government. In the Chamber of Deputies there was a strong feeling against the influence of priests in schools, and in favour of the complete independence of teachers; but Guizot himself was a vehement advocate of religious education, and he succeeded in carrying out, if not all, at least a great part of his design. 'Popular education,' he afterwards wrote, 'ought to be given and received in a religious atmosphere, in order that religious impressions and habits may penetrate from every side. Religion is not a study or an exercise, to which a particular place or hour can be assigned. It is a faith, a law, which should be felt everywhere and at all times, and on no other condition can it fully exercise its salutary influence.'[43]

Such a passage marks clearly the great change which has passed over the prevailing ideas in France, and indeed in most countries. In founding municipal schools, Guizot insisted that the curé, or pastor, should always be a member of the superintending committee, and that the exclusive appointment of the teachers should be with the Minister of Public Instruction. In the Chamber of Deputies both of these provisions were at first rejected, but by the persuasion and influence of Guizot they were finally inserted. In a circular

---

[43] *Mémoires*, iii. 69.

which was drawn up by Rémusat, and addressed by Guizot to 39,300 elementary teachers in France, they were reminded that elementary education has never really flourished 'where the religious sentiment has not been combined in those who propagate it with the taste for enlightenment and instruction.'[44] The law of 1833 expressly stated that 'the wish of the parents should be always consulted and followed in what concerns religious teaching,' and by multiplying schools of different denominations, forbidding proselytism, and exempting children in mixed schools from teaching of which their parents disapproved, this plan appears to have been usually carried out.[45]

This law had an enormous effect in developing primary education in France. The enfranchisement of education which it began was completed by the very important law of 1850, under the Republic, which broke down the monopoly of the University over secondary education. This body had long been the object of bitter attacks of the Clerical party, on account of the essentially lay character which, in spite of all efforts to tamper with it, it still retained, and the cry of monopoly which was raised against it won many democratic votes. Democracy, indeed, has in general very little sympathy with corporations which represent a high, austere standard of knowledge and research. From this time secondary education as well as primary education became open, all persons of twenty-five having a right to open schools, even though they are not members of the university, provided they fulfil certain specified tests of competence and character; and the members of religious communities were not excluded. A Supreme Council of Education was established, in which the University was represented, but which also included four bishops or archbishops and other important functionaries.

It is not necessary to follow the subsequent modifications

---

[44] See the text of this circular in Barnard's *System of Instruction in different Countries*, ii. 278–80.

[45] See Arnold's *Schools and Universities on the Continent*, pp. 87–88; Simon, pp. 340–45; Cousin, *Rapport sur l'Instruction primaire* (Fragments littéraires), pp. 96–145.

that were introduced into the law. It is sufficient to say that the Jesuits, and a number of other religious associations which were closely allied with the Jesuits, flung themselves with great zeal into the field of education that was opened to them, and, although their success in the higher forms of education was not conspicuous, a great part of popular education passed gradually into their hands. In 1874, it was estimated that about a third of all the children, and an immense majority of the girls who were educated in the primary schools, were educated by teachers belonging to religious congregations.[46] These bodies had great advantages. Many men, and most women, desired an essentially religious education for their children. The pressure of Church influence was steadily exerted in favour of the Church schools, and great voluntary organisations, indifferent to gain, and animated by a strong religious zeal, had manifest economical advantages. In several indirect ways the Government and the municipalities appear at this time to have favoured them, and in the schools for girls the teachers belonging to religious orders were not obliged to give the proofs of efficiency required from lay teachers.[47] The Christian Brothers, who were a recognised order, but who were in close alliance with the Jesuits, were the most successful in primary education. They appear to have had at one time no less than 2,328 public schools in their hands.[48] In secondary education the Jesuits and some affiliated orders had an overwhelming preponderance. Some of these organisations, and especially the Jesuits, had no legal existence in France, and had been completely excluded from all education, before 1850.[49] It was contended, however, that the liberty of teaching which was proclaimed by the Constitution of 1848, and regulated in its exercise by the law of 1850, virtually abolished these restrictions. In 1874 there were fourteen Jesuit col-

---

[46] Michaud, *L'Église Romaine en France*, pp. 302–303.

[47] Ibid. pp. 290–303.

[48] See an article of Albert Duruy, 'L'Instruction Publique et la Démocratie' (*Revue des Deux Mondes*, 1 Mai 1886).

[49] See *Discours de P. Bert*, 21 Juin 1879; *La Morale des Jésuites*, p. 577.

leges in France, containing about 5,000 pupils, and fifteen others directed by the order of the Marists.[50] A law of 1875 gave the Catholic bodies the right of constituting themselves into distinct faculties and granting degrees, thus breaking down the last vestige of the University monopoly.

This was one of the last acts of the very Catholic Assembly which sat immediately after the disasters of the war. Very soon, however, a new spirit began to prevail in French politics. It had already in 1874 found a powerful organ in M. Challemel-Lacour, who, in a speech of great force and eloquence, contended that France was taking a false line in education; that a teaching which was wholly based on the doctrines of the Syllabus, and imbued with all the superstitions of Ultramontanism, was radically and essentially opposed, not only to the teachings of modern science, but also to the principles on which republican government must rest; that it was a patriotic interest of the most vital kind to prevent the youth of France from being educated in anti-revolutionary principles by a reactionary priesthood; and that if this were not done, the next generation of Frenchmen would be completely alienated from both civil and religious liberty. 'The moral unity of France' was represented as the chief end of French education; and it was especially deplored that the French youth, having been separated into two sections in the primary and in the secondary schools, were no longer likely to be brought together in the classes of the same University.[51]

Candid men will, I think, admit that there was a large measure of truth in these representations. Foreigners are too apt to judge modern French Catholicism by its best intellectual products. They judge it by the noble sermons of Lacordaire; by the writings of Montalembert, or Ozanam, or Dupanloup; by the exquisite tenderness and grace that breathe through the religious sentiment of the 'Récit d'une Sœur.' Many things in these writings must wither before the touch of an impartial

---

[50] Michaud, p. 305.
[51] Simon, *Dieu, Patrie et Liberté*, pp. 176–87.

and scientific criticism. Much of this religious sentiment seems to me more akin to the hothouse than to the mountain, to the hectic of consumption than to the flush of health; but no religious nature can fail to feel its beauty and purity. These writings, however, do not represent the strongest influence in French Catholicism. The newspaper which long reflected most faithfully the opinions of the French clergy was the 'Univers,' and Louis Veuillot probably exercised in his generation more influence than any other single man in the French Church. I do not know where, in modern times, the religious sentiment has assumed a more repulsive form. He watched with the aspect of a caged tiger all the developments of religious and intellectual liberty around him, pursued with untiring and scurrilous ferocity every Catholic who showed any sympathy for tolerance or any appreciation of goodness outside his own body, and exercised for a long period a kind of reign of terror in the Church. With the great secular world he had little or no direct contact, but the spirit of Veuillot passed largely into the education of the young. The collection of extracts from Catholic educational works which was afterwards brought by Paul Bert before the public showed very decisively how profoundly superstitious and intolerant was much of the prevailing teaching in France; and Catholic nations have very generally agreed about the tendencies of Jesuit education. The success of Germany in the late war had opened French eyes to the supreme importance of national education, and it was felt that it was only by a great effort of internal regeneration that France could regain her position among the nations of the world. The great outburst of pilgrimages and miracles in the first years after the war was attributed by most Frenchmen quite as much to deliberate imposture as to ignorant credulity; and the manifest efforts of the priesthood to turn the force of superstition in the direction of monarchy, as well as their attempt to overthrow the Liberal republic in the May of 1877, kindled a firm and not unnatural indignation. The elections of that year brought strong Republicans to power, and it is by no means surprising that a war against the Church should have begun, which speedily passed beyond all the bounds of reason and moderation.

The first measure, however, was probably neither unwise nor unjust. The Supreme Council of Education was remodelled so as to consist entirely of members of the great teaching bodies; the episcopal element was eliminated from it, and the free schools were only represented in a very small degree. The exclusive right of conferring degrees was restored to the University, and no independent institution was permitted any longer to assume that title. But another step followed, which at once threw France into a paroxysm of agitation. It was the famous Clause 7, which forbade not only the Jesuits, but also all other congregations which were unauthorised by law, from taking any part in teaching either in public or private schools, though they were not prevented from being tutors in private houses.[52]

This article was in perfect accordance with the law as it had existed before 1850. It was an echo of the ordinance of 1828, and it was far from suppressing religious teaching, as a large number of religious corporations were authorised by law and fully permitted to teach, provided they fulfilled the same conditions of efficiency as lay teachers. The Jesuits, however, and several minor congregations devoted to teaching, were unrecognised, and under the system of liberty which had existed since 1850 they had set up a multitude of popular schools. There were said to have been at this time no less than 141 nonauthorised congregations in France, 125 of them of women, and 16 of men; 640 establishments were in their hands; 62,000 pupils were educated by them, and 9,000 of them were taught gratuitously. The measure for their suppression was profoundly unpopular. The majority of the 'conseils généraux' were opposed to it, and about 1,700,000 signatures were appended to petitions against it. It passed through the Chamber

---

[52] Simon, *Dieu, Patrie et Liberté*, p. 219.

of Deputies, but the Senate, recognising the strong adverse tendency of opinion, threw it out by 148 votes to 120.[53] M. Ferry, however, was determined not to be baffled. He availed himself of a legal power which had long been obsolete, and in March 1880 decrees were issued breaking up and dissolving all religious congregations unauthorised by law.

The measure was undoubtedly legal, but it was at the same time violent, despotic, and unconstitutional. The congregations that were assailed had long existed in France publicly and unmolested, and they had thrown themselves into the work of education and invested large resources in educational purposes with the full knowledge of every successive Government. A minister who has asked and been refused the sanction of Parliament for a particular policy, and who then proceeds to carry out that policy by other means without parliamentary sanction, may be acting in a way that is strictly legal, but he is straining the principles of constitutional government. In modern English politics we have had a somewhat similar case, when a minister submitted the question of the abolition of purchase in the army to the decision of Parliament, and, having been defeated in the House of Lords, proceeded notwithstanding to carry the measure into effect by the exercise of a power of the Crown which had been reserved under a statute of George III. The French measure was not only violent, but in a great degree useless, for it was not difficult for the members of most of the congregations to continue their teaching by transforming themselves, under ecclesiastical authority, into congregations that were duly authorised by law. If the decrees had been directed solely against the Jesuits, they would probably not have been very widely unpopular, and some of the best judges in the Radical party desired at least to limit them to this order. M. de Freycinet, who had succeeded M. Waddington in the French ministry, made a conciliatory speech, plainly pointing to such limitation; and the Prefect of Police,

---

[53] See the articles of Albert Duruy *Revue des Deux Mondes*, 1 Juin 1879; Jan. 1880; 15 Juin 1882; 1 Mai 1886.

on whom the task of carrying the decrees into effect would chiefly devolve, made strong representations in the same sense. M. de Freycinet, however, was unable to carry his colleagues with him, and was obliged to retire from the ministry, and M. Ferry obtained full power to carry the decrees into effect.

The cry of persecution was at once raised. The congregations put out a manifesto declaring that they were only intended for prayer, education, and charity, and that they were not in alliance with any political party. In October the measure of suppression began. There were numerous arrests. Doors were broken open; convents were barricaded and fortified. There were constant threats of armed resistance, and the Host was exposed, and women prayed day and night in the chapels of the menaced buildings. At Lyons some blood was shed. At Tarascon the somewhat absurd spectacle was exhibited of the public force laying siege to a convent during several days. In Paris there were grave fears that there might be formidable disturbances, and it was resolved to proceed with extreme secrecy and at a very early hour of a dark winter morning. 'Since the Coup d'État of December 2,' wrote the Prefect of Police, 'such precautions have never been taken.' The secret was well kept, and on November 5 the blow was struck. At five in the morning a combined force of police and soldiers simultaneously surrounded eleven convents in Paris. By 9 A.M. all was over. About sixty persons in the convents were arrested for resisting the seizure.[54]

The result of all this was that many hundreds of men were driven out of their homes and scattered abroad, proclaiming themselves martyrs and awakening over a wide area strong sympathies and bitter resentments; and, in the end, the mea-

---

[54] See a curious account of these measures by M. Andrieux, who was charged with the task of carrying them out (*Souvenirs d'un Préfet de Police*, i. 210–233, 288–301). See also Duparc et Cochin, *Expulsion des Congrégations Religieuses*. A vivid picture of the feelings aroused among pious Catholics will be found in the Letters of Mrs. Craven, in her *Life* by Mrs. Bishop.

sure was so much relaxed in its practical application that the Jesuits alone appear to have been effectually expelled from French education. The other congregations, who formed four-fifths of the male unauthorised orders,[55] continued, under the shelter of a precarious toleration and by some mutual compromises, to carry on the work of education much as before; and the female unauthorised congregations were not molested. But the chasm between the Catholic and freethinking sections of the French people was greatly deepened.[56]

The suppression of the unauthorised orders, and especially of the Jesuits, affected chiefly secondary education, for religious education in primary schools was, for the most part, in the hands of authorised congregations.[57] A law of 1882 provided that the heads of all private establishments of secondary education must have graduated at the University, and received a certificate of competence from a commission in which the University element preponderated.[58] Two laws which were enacted in the preceding year obliged all who were engaged in primary education in public and private schools, with a few specified exceptions, to provide themselves with regular certificates of competence, and at the same time made primary education in the public schools absolutely gratuitous.[59]

The next important measure to be noticed is the law of March 1882, making primary education obligatory for all children between six and thirteen, excluding all religious teaching from the public schools, and abolishing the provisions of the law of 1850 which gave ministers of religion rights of direction and inspection. This law has sometimes been misrepresented. It did not attempt to suppress all religious education. Primary

---

[55] Simon, p. 227.

[56] Compare Beaussire, 'Questions de l'Enseignement sous la Troisième République,' in the *Revue des Deux Mondes,* June 15, 1882; Simon, pp. 228–34.

[57] Simon, pp. 311–12, 323.

[58] Ibid. p. 320.

[59] June 16, 1881.

instruction might be still given, either in public schools or in free schools, or in the family by the father, or by any one he might appoint; but every child educated in the family was liable to an annual examination, beginning at the second year of obligatory instruction, and relating to the subjects taught in public schools, and if the result of the examination was unsatisfactory the parent was compelled to send the child to some public or private school. In the family, of course, religious teaching was entirely unrestrained. In the private schools it was 'facultative;' but in the public schools it was absolutely prohibited. The majority in a commune, though they were compelled to endow their school, had no power of relaxing the rule, and they were expressly prohibited from granting any subvention to private schools.[60] The public schools were alone endowed. All religious emblems in them were forbidden; and the rule against religious teaching was in some cases so strictly enforced that the mere mention of the name of God was forbidden. The Senate endeavoured to mitigate the measure by an amendment providing that, on the demand of the parents, ministers of different creeds might give religious instruction in the schoolroom on Sundays and also once a week after school hours; but this amendment was rejected by the Chamber of Deputies, and it was finally decided that no religious teaching of any kind could be given in the Government schools. On one day of the week, however, in addition to Sunday, the law provided that there should be a holiday in the schools, in order that parents might provide, 'if they desired it,' religious instruction for the children outside the scholastic buildings.

Considered in itself, the system of purely secular State education is not in any way irrational or irreligious. It simply means that the State, which is an essentially lay body, undertakes during a few hours of the day the instruction of the young in certain secular subjects which men of all creeds and

---

[60] Pichard, *Nouveau Code de l'Instruction primaire*, pp. 2–4. This work gives the text of all the laws and official circulars relating to primary education.

parties believe to be highly important to their temporal interest. It is the task of the parents to provide during other hours for such religious education as they desire, and one day in seven is reserved, and a great profession is endowed for the express purpose of religious teaching. The contention that all secular teaching should be conducted in a religious spirit or atmosphere holds a very much larger place in theoretical discussions than in the reality of things. Everybody who has been at an English public school knows how naturally and how strictly religion is allocated to particular times. The many hours of school life that are spent in learning Greek or Latin, or mathematics or geography, or English composition or modern languages, or other secular subjects, are hours with which religion has not, and cannot have, any more to say than it has with the ordinary work of the shopman at his counter or the clerk in his office. Very few parents would think it necessary to inquire into the religious opinions of the tutor who gives their children daily lessons in drawing, or music, or foreign languages. Every one, too, who has any practical experience knows that branches of education like physical science, or history, or even moral philosophy, which have, or may have, some real connection with religious teaching, may be largely and profitably taught without raising any question of controverted divinity.

If this is true of the education of the upper classes, it is at least equally true of the education of the poor. The great mistake in their education has in general been, that it has been too largely and too ambitiously literary. Primary education should open to the poor the keys of knowledge, by enabling the scholar to read, not merely with effort, but with ease and with pleasure. It should teach him to write well and to count well; but for the rest it should be much more technical and industrial than literary, and should be much more concerned with the knowledge and observation of facts than with any form of speculative reasoning or opinions. There is much evidence to support the conclusion that the kinds of popular education which have proved morally, as well as intellectually, the most beneficial have been those in which a very moderate amount of purely mental instruction has been combined with physical, industrial, or military training. The English half-time system of education, which was introduced at the recommendation of the Commission which sat in 1833 to inquire into the condition of factory children, appears to have been extraordinarily efficacious in diminishing juvenile crime, as well as in developing capacity, and the same system has been successfully adopted in the army and navy schools, in district poor-law schools, in industrial and reformatory schools, and in the great schools established by the Children's Aid Society of New York. Some of the most competent judges in England have arrived at the conclusion that an education conducted on such lines is the most powerful of all instruments for raising the condition of the most neglected and demoralised classes of society.[61]

For a long time the State took no direct part in education. If it now equips boys for the practical battle of life, it has done a good work, even though it leaves the care of those religious questions on which men are profoundly divided to the home, the Church, and the Sunday-school.

It is the custom of many writers, and especially of Catholic writers, to inveigh against purely secular education as if it were morally worthless, or even morally pernicious. I believe this to be a grave error. Religion is probably the most powerful, but it is by no means the only, influence by which character can be formed. Military discipline, the point of honour, the creation of habits, contribute powerfully to this end. It is quite true that a merely intellectual education does not fundamentally change character; but, by giving men a clearer view of their true interests, it contributes largely to the proper regulation of life; by opening a wide range of new and healthy interests it diverts them from much vice; by increasing their capacity for fighting the battle of life, it takes away many

---

[61] There is a remarkable paper on this subject, called *The Elementary Education and the Half-time System*, by Sir Edwin Chadwick (1887). See, too, Dr. Richardson's *Health of Nations*, i. 161–305.

temptations, though it undoubtedly creates and strengthens some; and it seldom fails to implant in the character serious elements of discipline and self-control. It especially cultivates the civic and industrial virtues with which the Legislature is chiefly concerned.

When the public opinion of a country favours such a course, a Government is certainly not to be blamed if it confines itself in its public schools to a good secular education which brings children of all denominations together, leaving full liberty to religious teachers to teach their different views to the members of their congregations, either in the schools after class-hours, or in other places. An educational system ought, however, to be an elastic thing, meeting, as far as possible, the wishes of many parents, the requirements of different classes and forms of opinion; and in countries where an unsectarian or purely secular system of public education prevails, it will usually, I believe, be found a wise policy to give some help also to purely denominational institutions, provided that no child is obliged to attend a religious teaching to which its parents object, and that sufficient proofs are furnished of educational efficiency.

In Protestant countries it has also been proved by experience that it is perfectly possible to unite with secular education a certain amount of unsectarian and undogmatic religious teaching. When the School Boards were first established under the Act of 1870, and all religious catechisms and formularies were excluded from the Board schools, Lord Russell strongly advocated the simple reading of the Bible, accompanied by undogmatic explanations. I can well remember the scorn with which this suggestion was received in some theological circles, and the triumphant arguments by which it was shown that an undogmatic religious teaching was an impossible thing, and that the teaching of any one who attempted it must be hopelessly indefinite and misleading. The best answer to these arguments is, that the great majority of the School Boards of England adopted the suggestion of Lord Russell, and made Bible-reading, either without note or comment, or accompanied by simple explanations of an undogmatic character, a leading feature of their teaching; and although some agitation against it has recently arisen, that agitation has been almost wholly extraneous, and appears to have received no support from the parents of the children. Substantially, the religious teaching in the Board schools meets the wants of the overwhelming majority of the parents who make use of them. It is carried on under careful supervision; the teachers are under a strong obligation of honour not to give any controversial bias to their lessons, and with ordinary tact and goodwill they have no difficulty in carrying out their instructions.

Such teaching, no doubt, is not all that theologians would desire, and a large field remains for the priest, the clergyman, and the Sunday-school teacher, but, as far as it goes, it is undoubtedly a great moralising and elevating influence. It is difficult to exaggerate the moral advantage of an early and complete familiarity with the Biblical writings. In after-years the pupils may form widely different judgments of them. Some may hold, with the strictest type of Evangelicals, that every word had been written by Divine dictation, and, disregarding all questions of date or context, or conflicting statements or tendencies, they may be always ready to quote some detached fragment of the Sacred Book as decisive in controversy. Others may look on the Bible as a collection of documents of many different ages and degrees of merit and authority; as the literature of a nation, frequently recast and re-edited, reflecting the conceptions of the universe and the moral ideas and aspirations of many successive stages of development; conveying much valuable historical information, but with a large mixture and environment of myth. But in the one case, as in the other, a familiarity with the Sacred text seldom fails to do something to purify, elevate, and regulate the character, to exalt the imagination, to colour the whole texture of a life.

Even on its purely intellectual side its value is very great. It is related of one of the semi-pagan cardinals of the Renaissance that he dissuaded a friend from reading the Greek Testament lest its bad Greek should spoil his style. But it may be truly said that the pure, simple, and lofty language of the English Bible has done more than any other single influence to refine the taste of the great masses of the English people. It is the most powerful antidote to vulgarity of thought and feeling. If, as is not impossible, the result of educational and theological disputes is to banish all direct religious teaching from Government schools, it is much to be hoped that the simple reading of the Bible without note or comment may at least remain.

The system of education which was adopted by most of the English School Boards was not original. It was, in its main features, a copy of a far older system which has been one of the most successful in the world. There is probably no other single institution to which America owes so much as to the common schools which were established in New England more than two hundred years ago, and which have gradually extended to nearly all parts of the United States. These great free schools are entirely unsectarian and essentially secular, but they are usually opened and closed by a simple prayer, and portions of the Bible are usually read in them without note or comment. Any teacher who taught in them anything hostile to religion, or to any particular creed, would be at once dismissed. They have done more than any other single influence to unify the nation, by bringing together children of different classes and of all religious denominations, and nearly all the greatest and best men that America has produced have concurred in the opinion that, while they have incalculably raised the intellectual level, they have at the same time had moral effects of the most beneficial kind.[62] A great system of voluntary Sunday-schools has grown up in their wake, and in these schools denominational teaching is abundantly supplied. Every religious denomination has largely availed itself

---

[62] A most remarkable series of testimonies to this effect will be found in a pamphlet published in 1855, by the Hon. Edward Twisleton, called *Evidence as to the Religious Working in the Common Schools in Massachusetts*. Among those who gave evidence were Webster, Bancroft, Everett, Bishop Eastburn, Winthrop, Prescott, Sparks, Ticknor, and Longfellow.

of the common schools; and although of late years the Catholic priests, in accordance with their usual policy, have been bitterly opposed to them, public opinion in America seems far too sensible of the transcendent value of this system of education to allow it to be tampered with.

With some slight modifications, the same system prevails in nearly all the great British colonies, though it is everywhere bitterly opposed by the Catholic priesthood, and sometimes by a portion of the Anglican clergy. In North America, Newfoundland is the only complete exception, for there the system of education is denominational; and in some parts of the Canadian Dominion and the North-West Territories in America the Catholics have succeeded in obtaining grants for the denominational schools which they have set up in opposition to the unsectarian schools. But in general, throughout British North America the system of State-endowed, unsectarian, and common education exists as in the United States. Its purely secular character is usually qualified by the use of the Lord's Prayer at the opening and close of the lessons; by some Bible-reading and moral instruction, which children whose parents object to it are not obliged to attend; and by provisions that the clergy may, at certain times after the school hours, give the children of their own denomination religious instruction in the schoolhouse.

In Australia and New Zealand very large sums have been devoted to education, and the controversy between the denominationalists, who are mainly Catholic, and the unsectarian party has been very keen. Hitherto, however, the former have been almost everywhere completely defeated. In Victoria the system of education is purely and strictly secular, the State leaving the whole field of religious instruction to the voluntary efforts of the different denominations. In spite of the constant pressure exercised by the priests, a large proportion of the Catholic colonists avail themselves of it, and a large number of the teachers are Catholics. In the other Australian colonies, carefully guarded unsectarian religious teaching exists in the State schools, and the excellent unsectarian Scripture lessons which had been drawn up for the Irish National Schools, but which the priests have now succeeded in expelling, are largely used. In nearly all these colonies, education in some form is compulsory, and in many of them it is free. In Western Australia alone denominational schools (which are nearly all Roman Catholic) are assisted by State funds. In the African colonies, however, a different system prevails, and elementary schools of all kinds, provided they submit to a certain amount of Government supervision and control, are assisted from the public funds.[63]

It is still one of the great questions of the future how far a system of education modelled on that of the American common schools is likely to predominate. The old Catholic theory, according to which all education except that which the Church had sanctioned was forbidden, has almost wholly passed away. The old Anglican theory, which only gave State sanction and acknowledgment to an education directed by the Established Church, though it allowed the education of other religious bodies to be carried on by purely voluntary effort, is also rapidly disappearing, and in nearly all countries education is now looked upon as one of the most important functions and charges of the Government. There is no probability that this tendency will be reversed. On the contrary, all the signs of the times point to a continual elevation of the standard of State education and a continual extension of free or State-paid teaching. But opinion, in the most enlightened countries, still floats somewhat indecisively between two types of national education. The one school would only assist by public funds united secular education, or secular education tinged with some entirely undogmatic religious and moral teaching, leaving denominational teaching to the voluntary efforts of the different religious bodies. The adherents of this view maintain that Government is absolutely incompetent to deal with questions of conflicting dogmas; that it is a secular body, repre-

---

[63] A good review of the educational systems in the different colonies will be found in Sir Charles Dilke's *Problems of Greater Britain*, ii. 358–88. See, too, the notices in the *Statesman's Year Book* under the different colonies; Goldwin Smith's *Canada*, pp. 32–35, 36.

senting the whole nation; that it is an object of the first importance that members of all religious persuasions should be well instructed in those secular subjects that are most conducive to their temporal interests; and that it is scarcely less important that on those subjects they should be educated as much as possible together. By such an education the sentiment of nationhood is most powerfully strengthened, and those who differ profoundly on religious questions at least grow up united by common sympathies, interests, and friendships.

In countries, however, where the theological temperature is very high, and where sectarian differences are very profound, this system will hardly work. Parents refuse to allow their children to sit on the same bench with those of another creed. They distrust the neutrality of the religious teaching, suspect the teacher of some subversive or proselytising bias, and demand that definite dogmatic instruction should take a central place in all education.

A powerful party also denounce united religious education on another ground. They contend that great numbers of parents, and especially parents of the poorer classes, are quite content with the amount and kind of religious and moral education their children receive in an English Board school or an American common school, and that the result of this education is the rapid growth of an unsectarian religion, in which the moral element reigns supreme, and in which, if the dogmatic element is not wholly suppressed, it is at least regarded as doubtful, subordinate, and unimportant. They allege, with much truth, that this kind of religion has, in our generation, spread more rapidly than any other, and that the systems of national education prevailing through the English-speaking world are powerfully assisting it. Their own theory is, that the public money which is devoted to national education should be divided in proportion to their numbers between the different denominations, who should be allowed to teach their distinctive doctrines freely, at public expense, subject to Government inspection, to Government tests of efficiency, and, if necessary, to a conscience clause.

This view is not confined to Catholic or to Anglican populations. It prevails largely wherever great stress is laid on dogmatic teaching. One very instructive example of it will be found in the recent educational history of the Netherlands, a country where Evangelical Protestantism is perhaps more fervent and more powerful than in any other part of the Continent. A Dutch law of 1857 established through the country an excellent system of secular national education. Secular teaching alone was to be endowed by public funds. No schoolmaster in the national schools was allowed either to give religious instruction or to say, do, or tolerate anything in school hours that could be disrespectful to the religion of any class of pupils. Religious teaching was left wholly to the different religious bodies, but their ministers were at liberty to give it in the schoolrooms outside the regular hours.

This system of education was at once branded as atheistical. The schools were described as without prayer, without Bible, without faith; every effort was made to prevent devout men from acting as teachers in them, or from sending their children to them, and the stricter clergy absolutely refused to teach religion within their walls. The 'anti-revolutionary party,' which has played an important part in modern Dutch politics, was chiefly formed to abolish this system of neutral education, and it soon became evident that it represented a great mass of earnest and self-sacrificing conviction. For a time the Liberal party steadily supported the national system, and a law of 1878 greatly extended and strengthened it. It provided, among other things, that every commune must establish a public school, even though it was already amply provided with private schools; and it allowed each commune, if it thought fit, to make the education in its national school gratuitous.

It is certain that the majority of the nation readily acquiesced in this national teaching; but a large and earnest minority were violently opposed to it, and they attested their sincerity in the most conclusive of all ways, by setting up at their own expense numerous voluntary schools for the education of their children. Though the Dutch Protestants number only about

2,700,000 souls, there were in 1888 no less than 480 Bible schools supported by voluntary gifts, with 11,000 teachers and 79,000 pupils. These schools had an annual income of three millions of florins; they had a subscribed capital of sixteen millions of florins, or about 1,340,000*l*. During ten years their pupils were steadily increasing; they increased more rapidly than the pupils in the State schools, and in fighting the battle of denominational schools the Evangelical Protestants were supported by the Catholics. It was impossible to be blind to the significance of these facts, and when, in 1887, a lowering of the suffrage at last brought the anti-revolutionary party into power, a considerable section of the Liberals concurred with them in a compromise which was based on a system much like that which exists in England, and which has been very generally accepted. The public secular and neutral schools, which had been so fiercely denounced, were left by general consent undisturbed, except that gratuitous instruction in them might no longer be given, except to paupers. On the other hand, the voluntary schools which had attained certain specified dimensions, and which fulfilled certain specified conditions of efficiency, were subsidised by the State.[64]

The same conflict of principle which existed in the Netherlands existed in a still stronger form in Ireland. If there was a country in the world where a mixed system of education, drawing members of different creeds together, was desirable, it was Ireland, and the National system of education, which was founded in 1834, was intended to establish it. It soon, however, became evident that it did not meet the wishes of the parents, and both the clergy of the Established Church and the Catholic priesthood opposed it. A great Protestant society, called the Church Education Society, was established by voluntary subscriptions for the purpose of founding schools in which it was a first principle that the Bible should be taught

---

[64] An excellent account of this controversy will be found in *Choses de Hollande*, by E. Lacheret, 1893, pp. 59–82.

to all pupils. On the other hand, the Catholic priesthood only consented to work with the National system on the condition of obtaining in the Catholic parts of Ireland an almost complete control over it. By successive steps they have nearly attained their object, and the system in practice differs little from purely denominational education qualified by a Conscience clause. In few countries is the education of the poorer Catholics more completely in the hands of the priests.

The English compromise, as I have said, seems to me to have been signally successful. No one can be blind to the enormous progress which popular education has made under the School Board system, and a million and a half of children are educated in these schools. In a small minority of them the teaching is exclusively secular. In the large majority the Bible is read and some religious teaching is introduced. On the other hand, the voluntary schools, which earn a subsidy from the State, clearly meet the wishes of a vast and very earnest section of the population. The average attendance of children in them nearly doubled in the ten years that followed the Education Act of 1870. Being largely supported by private benevolence, they have greatly lightened the burden of national education to the taxpayer, and the competition between the two systems has been very favourable to the interests of education. Constant efforts are made, sometimes by the enemies of the School Boards, and sometimes by the enemies of the voluntary schools, to disturb the compromise, but on the whole the double system has probably satisfied a wider area of English opinion than any other system that could be devised.

Whether, however, it can permanently subsist is very doubtful. The establishment of free education by the State, and the constant tendency to raise the standard, and therefore the cost, of State education, are profoundly altering the conditions of the problem. Ther ever-increasing burden thrown on the ratepayer for educational purposes is becoming very serious, and is felt as a great grievance by those classes who derive no benefit from it. It is probable that one of its results will be that, sooner or later, a much larger proportion of the wealthier taxpayers will send their children to the free schools, as the corresponding classes appear to do in the United States and in Victoria.[65] Another consequence which appears almost inevitable is the gradual decay of the voluntary schools, if they continue to depend as largely as at present on private contributions and on children's fees. It is scarcely possible that such schools can permanently resist the competition of high-class free schools supported wholly from the rates. In the great centres of population and wealth they may linger on; but in poorer districts this seems impossible, unless the Legislature can be induced to grant them a larger measure of State support. The classes who now chiefly sustain them are too much impoverished by agricultural depression and increasing taxation to bear the double burden, and they are beginning to resent bitterly the obligation. Sooner or later, if the conditions are not altered, great numbers of Church schools will be closed, and the children obliged to resort to the Board Schools. But in the face of the vast multitude of ratepayers who incontestably desire definite dogmatic religious teaching for their children, the demand for a modification of the existing system is likely then to become irresistible. It does not seem to me probable that English opinion will approve of a purely secular education, or that it will in general abandon the unsectarian religious teaching which has proved so salutary and so popular. A very few years ago it appeared at least equally improbable that it would ever consent to endow largely purely denominational schools, but this improbability seems to have recently diminished. The belief that it is criminal for the State to endow the teaching of error, which in the recollection of many of us was so powerful in great portions of the English people, and which was the great obstacle to any system of impartial denominational endowment, has manifestly waned; and the division that has taken place in the Liberal party, and the discredit which the Home Rule policy has cast upon its

---

[65] See the remarks of Mr. Fairfield, in his Essay on 'State Socialism at the Antipodes,' in Mackay's *Plea for Liberty*, p. 151.

larger section, have greatly weakened the forces opposed to
sectarian education. English legislation, however, is peculiarly fertile in compromises, and it is possible that some
arrangement may be made for either strengthening the
denominational schools or giving facilities for the dogmatic
teaching by voluntary agencies in free Board Schools of those
children whose parents desire it. It is a somewhat unfortunate
result of the extreme multiplication of religious services that
has accompanied the High Church movement, that the clergy
have very little time to undertake the duty of teaching religion
in the schools.

Probably the only safe rule that can be laid down in dealing
with questions of this kind is, that the object of the legislators
should be to satisfy, as far as possible, the various phases of
national opinion and wishes. One important consideration,
however, should not be forgotten. The public opinion which
should be really decisive on educational questions is the opinion of the parents, and not that of external bodies. In an age
when agitations are largely organised, and organised for party
purposes, there is always a danger of the silent force of an
unorganised opinion being underrated. The true question to
be asked is, whether parents readily send their children to the
existing schools, and whether they are satisfied with the results. To a statesman, at least, no worse argument could be
directed against the religious teaching of the School Boards
than that it so completely satisfies a great proportion of the
parents that they ask for no other.

In Catholic countries, compromises such as I have described
are almost impossible. Simple Bible-reading is treated rather
as an evil than as a good. Religion is far more intensely dogmatic; and even the conception of morality differs widely from
that of Protestant countries, on account of the infinitely greater
prominence that is given among its elements to distinctively
theological practices and duties. The claims of the priesthood,
in all countries where they have a real ascendency, go far beyond the sphere of purely theological teaching. Apart from all
questions of instruction, they detest mixed education, because

it produces friendship and association between Catholics and dissidents. They, at the same time, claim the most absolute rights of superintendence over all education. The amendment which the French Senate vainly tried to insert in the Ferry law in the interests of the Church, authorising religious teachers to teach religion in the schools after school hours, would have established in France the system which actually existed in Belgium under the ecclesiastical law of 1878. The object of this law was to render the general teaching of the communal schools in Belgium purely secular; but it, at the same time, while placing their control in lay hands, expressly provided for the teaching of religion out of class hours by the priests and in the schools. But no measure ever excited a more violent ecclesiastical opposition. The bishops at once condemned the schools. They refused to permit the priests to teach religion in them; they excommunicated the teachers; they withheld the sacraments from parents who suffered their children to attend them, and they speedily erected a great number of voluntary schools, which, in many parts of Belgium, almost emptied the communal schools. In West Flanders, the children frequenting these schools sank between 1878 and 1881 from 66,000 to less than 20,000.[66] The Government, finding it impossible to induce the priests to teach religion in the schools, threw that duty on the ordinary schoolmaster, and the dominant party broke off diplomatic relations with Rome, abolished the exemption of the clergy from military service, and stopped several State benefactions to the Church. They were, however, totally defeated. It is evident that the Government measures went beyond the wishes of the parents. At the election of 1884 the Catholic party gained a complete triumph, and the ecclesiastical measures were all repealed.

The French legislators were more successful, but their action was, in some respects, extremely tyrannical. It was not merely that no public schools that were not purely secular

---

[66] *Dublin Review*, April 1885. See, too, on this conflict an article of Valbert, in the *Revue des Deux Mondes*, Nov. 1, 1883.

were established. The members of the religious orders were driven out of an immense number which already existed, and which, in many cases, they had themselves founded. It was shown by official statistics that, in 1878, more than a fourth of the primary public schools for boys, and nearly two-thirds of those for girls, were under religious masters and mistresses. They had the confidence of the parents, no serious charge was brought against their efficiency, and they were less costly than the lay schools. The law of 1882, though it severely excluded religious teaching from the public schools, did not prevent the members of the authorised orders from giving secular teaching in them. But the law of October, 1886, went much further. It directed that in all public schools of every kind teaching should be exclusively confided to laymen, and that in five years, in all boys' schools, the substitution of lay for the congregationist element must be complete. The public schools were thus, in the intention of the law, to be wholly disconnected from all religious influence, and as they, and they alone, were endowed and gratuitous, it seemed scarcely possible that in poor districts the free schools could withstand their competition. It was, indeed, the openly expressed hope of the Minister of Instruction that the immense majority of children would thus be forced into the purely lay schools.[67]

Nor were these schools devoted to a merely colourless secular teaching. The programme of literary studies provided in the law of 1881 was very ambitious in the range of its subjects, and among the first was 'moral and civil instruction,' which was to be given without any relation to religion. I do not believe that distinct attacks on religion are to be found in the school-books employed in the public schools, but catechisms depreciating all French history and institutions before the Revolution, and glorifying without qualification the acts of the Revolution, were now generally taught. The attitude of the new Government towards religion was sufficiently shown by the well-attested fact that functionaries have been dis-

---

[67] Simon, *Dieu, Patrie et Liberté*, pp. 324, 330.

missed because they, or even because their families, had attended Mass; and it was a well-understood fact that few acts were more unfavourable to the prospects of a Government official than that he should be seen attending the religious worship which, according to the Catholic faith, it was a mortal sin to neglect.[68] Paul Bert, who represented the most active and proselytising type of atheism, was for some time Minister of Instruction, and, still more strangely, Minister for Public Worship, in France. He chiefly organised the new schools; he himself wrote one of the first manuals of moral and civil instruction, and he made the saying of Gambetta, that 'Clericalism was the enemy,' the inspiring motive of his policy. On

---

[68] One of the best political writers in France says: 'En France, depuis une douzaine d'années, le joug que l'Etat fait peser sur les employés est on ne peut plus lourd. Dans bien des localités on demande la destitution des petits fonctionnaires parce que leurs femmes vont à la Messe, à plus forte raison quand ils y vont eux-mêmes. Presque partout on les force à mettre leurs enfants aux écoles laïques publiques, leur enlevant la liberté de les envoyer aux écoles congréganistes privées' (Leroy-Beaulieu, *L'Etat Moderne et ses Fonctions*, p. 81). A traveller who visited Corsica in 1880, speaking of the small attendance at High Mass, says: 'Officials were conspicuous by their absence. For a prefect or a mayor to attend Mass would have set the world talking for days together; and as for the tribe of smaller functionaries, if any of them harboured an inclination for church-going, they had not the courage to carry it out, for they would have had to face the ridicule of their friends, and might also have been exposed to the machinations of their enemies. "We dare not be seen inside of a church," officials in Corsica have sometimes said to me, "for fear lest some one should report us to Government." ' The author, however, adds this significant note: 'I learn from my kind reviser, Mrs. Lucas, in 1889, that the reaction about religion which has taken place in France has, since my departure, penetrated to Corsica, and that a change for the better has taken place in churchgoing, the dread of Government wrath having been, to a large extent, removed. Mrs. Lucas informs me further, that during the time I was myself in Corsica a few officials went to church at dawn in order to worship without being publicly seen, and that one official (a Frenchman) of their acquaintance attended both Vespers and High Mass. Mrs. Lucas, however, here adds that this official, though most hardworking and honest, did not receive, as is customary, a pension when he came to retire from the appointment that he had held' (Barry's *Studies in Corsica* (1893), pp. 151–52).

the occasion of the annual distribution of prizes, presidents were appointed at the nomination of the minister, who delivered addresses in the presence of the children, and some of these addresses were of a kind which had scarcely been heard in France in the worst days of the Revolution. 'It is pretended,' said one of these presidents, addressing a number of young children, 'that we wish schools without God. You cannot turn over a page of your books without finding the name of a god—that is, of a man of genius, of a benefactor, of a hero of humanity. In this point of view we are true pagans, for our gods are numberless.' 'Scientific teaching,' said another, 'is the only true teaching, for it gives man the certainty of his own value, and impels him towards progress and light, whereas religious teaching plunges him fatally into an obscure night and into an abyss of deadly superstitions.' 'It is said,' declared a third, 'that we have expelled God from schools. It is an error. One can only expel that which exists, and God does not exist.'[69]

It is idle to speak of a system under which such things were tolerated as mere secular education, as we should understand the term in England and the United States. It was a deliberate attempt on the part of the Government of a country to de-christianise the nation, to substitute for religion devotion to a particular form of government, to teach the children of the poor to despise and repudiate what they learnt in the church. The partisans of the new schools had many arguments to adduce which, as arguments of recrimination directed against the Catholics, were very powerful. They cited numerous examples of the grossly superstitious and grossly intolerant teaching that was contained in the old manuals of instruction. They showed that the clergy, wherever they had the power, claimed

---

[69] Simon, *Dieu, Patrie et Liberté*, pp. 350–51. These addresses were delivered in 1882. Of Paul Bert himself the reader may obtain a clear conception if he will read his *Morale des Jésuites* and the speeches appended to it. In addition to his *Manual of Moral and Civil Instruction*, he wrote two little scientific books for the schools, but, as far as I have observed, they were very harmless.

and exercised an absolute authority over schools; that they had expelled all teachers who were not subservient to them, and who were not regular attendants at their worship; that they were educating the French youth in principles directly opposed to those on which the French Republic rested; that they had done their best to overthrow the Republic in 1873 and in 1877. They were, probably, not at all wrong in believing that it is a great misfortune to a nation when the secular education of its youth is controlled by Catholic priests, nor yet in their conviction that it was very necessary to assert the superiority of the State as against the claims of the Church. The importance of education to the well-being of nations was at last clearly felt, and if this work was to be done, it was quite necessary for the State to undertake it. All over the world the Catholic priests claimed to control it, and all over the world the level of education was far lower, and the number of illiterates was far greater, in Catholic than in Protestant countries. The French clergy were strongly opposed to compulsory and gratuitous national education, and, when it was established, it would have been little less than madness to place it in their hands.

These considerations have much weight, and they were reinforced by others of a different kind. A great proportion of the modern controversies on education resolve themselves into one great difference: Ought national education to be regulated by the representatives of the nation, with a view to what they believe to be the interests of the State as a whole, or ought it to be a matter on which the will of the parents should be supreme? In France much more than in England, in the latter half of the nineteenth century much more than in the first half, the former view naturally predominated. The old Greek and Roman notion, according to which it is the duty of the State to mould its citizens in accordance with its civic and moral ideal, has largely revived. It was the doctrine of Danton, who emphatically declared that children belong to the Republic before belonging to their parents. It is equally the doctrine of a powerful school of new German economists. It is the doctrine of the Socialist party in every country. In dealing with national education in a Catholic country this theory of State direction seemed peculiarly applicable. National education, it is argued, is intended mainly for the most ignorant and neglected classes of the community, and in such classes the opinions of the parents are not likely to be either valuable or independent. Perfectly illiterate men will never appreciate the value of education, and if both parents have been educated by a superstitious priesthood, and if one parent is habitually subservient to clerical influence, it is not difficult to predict the course which education will take unless the State intervenes. It is its duty, it is said, to do so in the interests of the nation at large.

These arguments go far to justify the State in establishing a system of good secular education. They do not, however, affect the fact that the system established in France was both intolerant and demoralising, and that it in a great degree defeated its own end. Secular education is not a demoralising thing; but an education which is intended to discredit in the eyes of the young the chief religious and moral organisation of the country can hardly fail to be so, and the lamentable increase of juvenile crime in France is probably largely due to the new system of teaching. 'The moral unity of France,' which the education laws were intended to establish, was never further from being attained. In the face of French Catholic opinion, it was not in the power of the legislators to suppress religious teaching, though they did all they could to discourage it; and the result of their policy was, that in two years after the secularisation of schools had been decreed free schools had been established in every quarter of Paris, and fourteen millions of francs had been subscribed for their support. The official examination of children who were educated at home was so unpopular that this portion of the law was scarcely ever enforced.[70] The Christian Brothers, who had played a great part in French education, still continued their work. They

---

[70] Lefebvre, *La Renaissance Religieuse en France*, pp. 30–32.

were driven from the public schools, but they opened innumerable private ones, which were enthusiastically supported by the parents, and great establishments for higher education on Catholic principles were established by private munificence at Lille, Lyons, Angers, and Toulouse.[71] Under the influence of persecution and of combat the strongest fanaticism was aroused, and all over the country the distinction between Catholic and freethinking France was accentuated.

The movement, indeed, in favour of religious education was by no means confined to orthodox believers. Every one who knows France knows that great numbers of Frenchmen who are profoundly sceptical about the distinctive doctrines of the Catholic faith are extremely desirous that their children should receive a religious education. Men of this type seldom enter a church, and never a confessional, and they have much more sympathy with Voltaire than with Bossuet, but they believe that some form of positive religious teaching is essential to the stability of society; they look with alarm on the coarse materialism, the revolutionary doctrines, the demoralising literature around them, and they wish their children to grow up believing in God and in the Divine foundations of morality, and under the restraining and ennobling influence of a future life. If teaching of this kind could be obtained without priestcraft and superstition, they would be abundantly satisfied; but if they are obliged to choose between schools that teach superstition and schools that are hostile to all religious ideas, they will undoubtedly accept the former.

The religious war was much intensified by other measures. To cut down the income of an opponent is the meanest of all the forms of controversy; and the very moderate ecclesiastical budget, which was originally given in place of the ecclesiastical property that had been taken at the Revolution, has seemed too large to the modern Republican. Between 1883

---

[71] See Hurlbert's *France*, pp. 355–59. Mr. Hurlbert has collected a great deal of curious information about the Catholic revival in France. See, too, the work of M. Léon Lefebvre.

and 1889 the stipends were reduced to the smallest limits.[72] Few positions, indeed, are more isolated and more depressing than that of a country priest in the many parts of France where the anti-clerical spirit predominates. The mayor, the municipality, the national schoolmaster, the village doctor, are all commonly hostile to him. Most of the men, and many of the women, have given up all religious practices. There are no sufficient funds to keep his church in repair. His own salary from the State does not in general touch the 40*l.* a year of Goldsmith's village clergyman, and it is only slightly augmented by a few Low Masses and small ecclesiastical fees. He commonly lives an isolated life, with one poor servant, in the midst of hostile influences, and with no prospect before him.[73] In everything relating to the Church the bias of the Government is displayed. The salaries of the bishops have been cut down to four hundred pounds a year—the sum at which they had stood in 1801—though the expenses of living have nearly doubled since then. The usual funds for the support of the chapters have been withheld.[74] Many small grants, which had for generations been made for assisting the education of poor clergy and for various forms of clerical charity, have been ruthlessly suppressed. Sisters of Charity have been driven from the hospitals. Priests have been impeded or discouraged in ministering to the sick or dying in the hospitals. No Catholic chaplains are permitted in the regiments. The Paris Municipality, which in 1879 actually voted 100,000 francs for the relief of the returned Communists,[75] has always signalised itself by the violence of its attacks on all religious teaching. In 1882 it passed a resolution asking for the suppression of all theological instruction in 'all primary schools.' 'No one,' said one of

---

[72] Hurlbert, pp. 406–408.

[73] A striking picture of the position of the country clergy in France will be found in an anonymous book called *Pressant Appel du Clergé à l'Episcopat par un Catholique* (1893). See especially pp. 78–80.

[74] Duc de Broglie, *Le Concordat*, pp. 140–41.

[75] *Annual Register*, 1879, p. 134.

the members, 'can prove the existence of God, and our teachers must not be permitted to affirm the existence of an imaginary being.'[76] On another occasion, in order to vary the food in certain establishments under its control, they ordered that there should be one day of fast in the week, but added a special provision that it must never be Friday. [77]

Another measure, which is likely to have far-reaching consequences, is that taking away from all divinity students and Christian Brothers their exemption from military service. Some years must elapse before its full effects can be felt, and the French law on this subject presents a most curious contrast to the policy of the Protestant Government of Great Britain. Here the priests succeeded in persuading, first of all the Irish Protestant Parliament of the eighteenth century, and then the Imperial Parliament, that, with their celibacy and their confessions, they were a class so distinct from all other men that it was a matter of the first necessity that they should be educated in the strictest separation, and that the fine flower of their sanctity should never be exposed to the contagion of mixing in a national university with lay students. In France, the future priesthood will have served in the ranks, and spent a portion of the most susceptible period of their life in the not very saintly atmosphere of a French regiment.

It is remarkable how little agitation this great revolution has produced, and very Catholic voices are sometimes heard defending it. It is said that, by removing an old reproach and invidious exemption, it has done much to diminish the unpopularity of the priesthood; that it is giving them a knowledge of the real world they could never have acquired in an ecclesiastical seminary; that it at least secures that those who are binding themselves irrevocably to a life of celibacy and separation will do so with their eyes open, and with a clear knowledge of the world they are leaving.[78] In practice, I be-

---

[76] Hurlbert, p. 486.

[77] Leroy-Beaulieu, *L'Etat et ses Fonctions*, p. 249.

[78] *Appel du Clergé à l'Episcopat*, pp. 106–8, 303–19.

lieve the measure is often mitigated by sending the seminarist
conscripts to serve in the hospitals. Another portion of the
French law goes much further, and makes an ordained priest
liable to be called from the altar for twenty-eight days' service
in the year. Catholic writers justly say that such a service is
utterly inconsistent with the Catholic notion of the priesthood, and that it produces an irritation which is out of all
proportion to its military advantage.

It is too soon to speak with any confidence of the ultimate
results of the new French policy. In this, as in all similar cases,
perhaps less depends upon the letter of the law than upon the
spirit in which it is administered. It is certain that in the field
of education the tension of conflict has been greatly relaxed,
and it is very possible that the public schools have, in most
places, assumed a really neutral character, and are giving the
great mass of the French people an excellent secular education,
without interfering with their religious belief. The spirit that
prevailed in the French Government in the days of Gambetta
and of Paul Bert has greatly changed. A new spirit of compromise and conciliation seems abroad; and although there is
much aggressive atheism in France,[79] this does not appear, as
far as a stranger can judge, to be encouraged in the public
schools. The manuals of 'civic and moral instruction' that are
in greatest use in these schools are, no doubt, in the eyes of
Catholics, very defective, as they establish moral teaching
without any reference to Catholic doctrines, and accentuate
strongly the political improvement since government was established on the principles of 1789. It is, however, grossly untrue to represent them as irreligious. In one of the principal of
them the existence of God, of the immortality of the soul, of
the eternal distinction between right and wrong, is strongly
maintained. The duty of self-examination is enforced, and a

---

[79] Some striking illustrations of the extent to which atheism is taught in
popular catechisms will be found in Mr. Lilly's *Great Enigma*, pp. 41–66;
but the works Mr. Lilly quotes were not intended for or used in the public
schools.

great deal of very excellent and detailed moral teaching is given, in a form that is adapted with singular skill to the comprehension of the young.[80] How far the actual *vivâ voce* teaching is conducted in accordance with this admirable model it is not possible for any one who has not a large practical experience in French education to say.

The stringency of the French laws against priestly interference with politics is very great, and no disposition has hitherto been shown to relax it. The proceedings which are of almost daily occurrence in Ireland would not be tolerated for an hour by a French Government. The law of 1801, forbidding national councils and diocesan synods, and confining the action of each bishop to his own diocese, has been so strictly interpreted that five bishops were prosecuted in 1892 because they jointly signed an episcopal manifesto. A law of 1810, reviving an edict of Louis XIV., peremptorily forbids all interference of the Church with temporal affairs. An article of the penal code makes it an offence punishable by from two months' to two years' imprisonment for any ecclesiastic in the course of his ministry to censure or to criticise a law of the Government. In less than a year the salaries of a cardinal, an archbishop, five bishops, and a great number of curés were stopped by the Government in order to punish them for offences against these laws. The usual charges were that they condemned divorce from the pulpit; that they had enjoined their parishioners not to send their children to the secular schools; that they had refused absolution to penitents; that they had exhorted the faithful to vote at elections for Catholic candidates. In three cases which occurred in 1892 diocesan catechisms were brought before the law courts because they contained articles declaring

---

[80] See the *Eléments d'Instruction morale et civique*, par Gabriel Compayré, 108ᵐᵉ édition. See, too, the excellent manuals of G. Bruno, which are furnished gratuitously by the town of Paris to its communal schools:— *Instruction morale et civique pour les petits enfants; Les enfants de Marcel, instruction morale et civique en action;* Francinet, *Principes élémentaires de morale, &c.*

that it was a sin to vote badly; that marriage without a religious ceremony was no true marriage, but a criminal connection; that parents must not send their children to bad schools. The tribunal pronounced that the bishops who sanctioned these catechisms had attempted 'to trace out for the faithful of their dioceses, on the subject of civil duties, a line of conduct under a religious sanction,' and they accordingly ordered the incriminated passages in the catechisms to be suppressed. It is said on good authority, that in 1892 more ecclesiastics were persecuted on such grounds before the Council of State than in the forty last years of the two monarchies.[81]

The foregoing pages will, I hope, have given a clear, though by no means an exhaustive, account of the religious conflict which, contrary to the anticipation of the best thinkers of the beginning of the century, divides Catholic countries. It has arisen partly from the reaction against the *laisser faire* system which has led the State all over Europe to claim higher powers of moulding the characters of its members, and has greatly increased the sense of the importance of national education. It has arisen partly also from the increased sacerdotalism and centralisation of the Church, and from the peculiar facilities it possesses of influencing the new conditions of European politics. In an age when the world is governed by mere numbers, and therefore mainly by the most ignorant, who are necessarily the most numerous, any organisation that has the power of combining for its own purposes great masses of ignorant voters acquires a formidable influence. The facilities the Catholic Church possesses for this purpose are great and

---

[81] *Le Concordat*, par le Duc de Broglie (1893), pp. 142–60, 172–84, 218–33. See, too, M. Georges Picot, *La Pacification religieuse et les suspensions de traitements* (1892). It is, however, a complete error to suppose that stringent measures against recalcitrant priests took place only under the Republic. The hand of Napoleon I. was at least as heavy. M. Picot observes in his very interesting book, 'qu'en 1812 les prisons d'état de Vincennes, de Fenestrelles et de Ham renfermaient 4 cardinaux, 4 évêques, 2 supérieurs généraux, 1 vicaire général, 9 chanoines, et 38 curés desservants et vicaires' (p. 77).

manifest, and its interests may easily, in the minds of its de-
votees, not only dominate over, but supersede, the interests
of the State.

Patriotism is at bottom, to most men, a moral necessity. It
meets and satisfies that desire for a strong, disinterested enthusiasm in life which is deeply implanted in our nature. It
may, however, be extinguished in different ways. Sometimes
it is destroyed by the excessive growth in a nation of material
and selfish interests. Sometimes it perishes by a kind of atro-
phy when the fields in which it naturally expatiates are no
longer open. This was the case in the despotism of the later
Roman Empire, when, the paths of honourable public duty
being for the most part closed, the best men ceased to interest
themselves in public concerns, and a new ideal type of excellence arose, in which the civic virtues were almost wholly
displaced by the virtues of the ascetic, contemplative and religious life. In our own day, the complete political impotence
to which the upper and more intelligent classes are reduced
in an unqualified democracy is evidently tending, in many
countries, to detach them from all interest in public affairs.
Often, too, the love of country decays by the substitution of
other objects of enthusiasm. Women are, on the whole, more
unselfish than men, but in many ages and countries their
unselfish enthusiasm has been almost wholly unconnected
with national interests. In the periods of the religious wars
the true country of the devotee was usually the country of his
religion, and not the country of his birth. In modern times,
the devout Catholic is very apt to look upon the Church as
his true and his higher country, and he accordingly subordinates all his political action to the furtherance of its interests.

There are many signs that Catholicism will in the future
tend more and more to an alliance with democracy. It has in
most countries lost the dignities and privileges on which its
power largely depended. The powers with which it was once
closely allied no longer govern the world, and it has always
sought to connect itself with what is strongest among mankind. In its early history it will find ample justification for a

democratic policy. The election in the early Church of bishops by universal suffrage; the many passages in which the Fathers, in language very like that of modern Socialism, denounced the rich and advocated a community of goods; the Councils, which formed one of the first great experiments in representative government; the essentially democratic character of a worship which brings together on a common plane members of all classes, and of an organisation which enables men of the humblest birth to attain to a dignity far transcending all mere human greatness; the long war waged by the Church against slavery; the great place in the history of liberty which may be claimed for St. Thomas Aquinas and the early Jesuits, as the precursors of the doctrine of the Social contract, may all be appealed to. Even Bossuet, in the days of Louis XIV., had proclaimed that the Church was pre-eminently and originally the city of the poor; that the rich were only admitted into it by tolerance, and on the condition of serving the poor; that the poor had great reason to complain of the inequality of conditions in the world.[82] It is impossible not to see that the whole system of mediæval industry, with its highly organised and protected guilds, which grew up in an eminently Catholic society, has far more affinity to the modern Socialistic ideals than the system of unrestricted and inexorable competition, with a survival of the fittest, which Adam Smith and his followers proclaimed, which Malthus pushed to its most unpopular consequences, which Darwin showed to be the great principle of progress in the world. Even the cosmopolitan character of working-class politics, which is doing much to weaken the exclusive sympathies of nationality, has some tendency to harmonise with the spirit of a cosmopolitan Church.

In Belgium, in England, and perhaps to a still greater degree in the United States, the priesthood are learning—somewhat to their own surprise—how much better the Church can flourish in countries where it has no privileges but perfect freedom

---

[82] See his sermon, 'Sur l'éminente dignité des pauvres dans l'Eglise.'

than in countries where the whole system of government seems framed on the model of the Syllabus; and a large number of the more intelligent Catholics have come to the conclusion that the Church has much more to fear than to hope from Government interference. Among the many points of interest which Rome presented in the year of the Council, few were greater than the appearance there of a large body of bishops from the United States who were at once intensely Catholic and intensely American, and who were quite accustomed to hold their own amid the stormy freedom of American life. I can remember the course of sermons they preached, in which examples from American history were usually put forward, in a foremost place, among the moral landmarks of the world. I can remember still more vividly the bewilderment of one very eminent American divine, who had long been accustomed to represent Catholicism as the natural ally of democracy and freedom, at the political ideas and the system of government which he found predominating around him. 'If the Pope only could be made to see,' I once heard him say, 'how much better he would get on with public meetings and a free press!'

The downfall of the termporal power, by giving the Papacy a greater independency of secular interests, will probably accelerate this movement. In most countries there now is a strong and growing tendency among Catholic divines to throw themselves ardently into the social question, and, discarding old alliances, to seek new elements of power in connection with the questions that most interest the working classes. This was the policy which Lamennais long since preached with consummate eloquence. This has been, in our day, the policy of Bishop Ketteler in Germany, of Cardinal Gibbons in America, of Cardinal Manning in England, of Father Curci in Italy, of the Comte de Mun in France. In Germany, the Catholic party has more than once shown sympathies with the Socialist party; and both in Germany and Belgium the movement known as 'Christian Socialism' has assumed a very considerable importance. Questions of the international regulation of labour; of the legal restriction of hours of labour; of the possibility of placing wages on a wholly different basis from supply and demand; of the establishment by law of a minimum wage; of the extension of co-operative industry, and of associations much like the mediæval guilds for strengthening the working-class interest and diminishing the stress of competition are now constantly discussed in societies presided over by ardent Catholics. The industrial system as at present existing is denounced as essentially unjust. The demand for a Sunday rest naturally forms a leading part of the programme, and the movement has been usually blended with the anti-Semitic crusade, which is represented as a crusade against usury and capital.[83]

It would be unjust to deny that much very genuine conviction and earnest sympathy with the poor have inspired this movement, though it is, I think, equally certain that questions of ecclesiastical policy and power have entered largely into it. The able and enlightened man who now presides over the Catholic Church has issued a long and remarkable Encyclical 'On the Condition of the Working Man,' dealing with the great social questions of the time. I do not think that it has done much to solve them. Questions of this kind cannot be profitably discussed by wide propositions and vague generalities, without entering into controverted details and grappling with concrete difficulties, and it is impossible for a personage whose words are accepted as inspired and infallible to deal with such questions, except in the most general manner. The Encyclical, however, has had an undoubted effect in accentuating the movement which is giving social questions a foremost place in Catholic politics.

It was a prediction of Count Cavour that, sooner or later,

---

[83] A great deal of information about this movement will be found in the chapter on Catholic Socialists in Laveleye's *Le Socialisme Contemporain;* in Kannengeisen's *Catholiques Allemands*, pp. 115–214; and in Leroy-Beaulieu's *La Papauté, le Socialisme et la Démocratie.*

Ultramontanism and Socialism would be allied.[88] Much that has happened since the death of the great Italian statesman tends to strengthen the probability of his prediction. But, whatever may be thought of the chances of this alliance, it is at least certain that there are real dangers to be feared from the exercise of the spiritual power of the Catholic priests for political purposes over an ignorant population, and with a democratic suffrage. I do not think that this danger has been wisely met either in Germany or France; but I think also that the Catholic Governments of the world are well justified in their belief that the danger is not one that can be neglected by a wise legislator. The most effectual remedy is probably to be found in the withdrawal, as far as public opinion will admit, of secular education from ecclesiastical control, and the establishment of such systems of education as bring together members of different creeds. But those who are aware of the enormous, scandalous, ostentatious clerical coercion that is in the present day practised in Ireland, will probably arrive at the conclusion that the Catholic Governments are quite right in their belief that some further legislation is required. It is true, indeed, that elections may be, and have been, invalidated on the ground of religious intimidation, but this remedy is a very insufficient one. The most crushing intimidation is the most successful, for it scares the witness from the witness-box. The men who are really guilty are altogether unpunished; and even when the election is pronounced void, they usually succeed at the next election in returning their candidates. As long as it remains possible to turn the chapel into an electioneering agency, and to blend politics with religious rites; as long as priests are allowed to overawe the electors at the polling-places, to stand by the ballot-boxes, and take a leading part as personation agents or agents in counting votes, so long clerical intimidation will continue. Two laws, at least, are imperatively needed to meet the evil.

---

[84] Laveleye, *Le Socialisme Contemporain*, p. 134.

The one is a law making the introduction of politics into the chapels, and the actual or threatened deprivation of religious rites on account of a political vote, a criminal offence punishable by severe penalties. The other is a law putting an end to all personal interference or participation of priests at elections, except as simple voters.

CHAPTER 7

In the discussion of legal limitations of natural liberty some confusion is due to the fact that theological, moral and utilitarian considerations often enter in combination among the reasons for legislation, and the proportionate weight which is attached to these several elements varies greatly in different ages and with different classes. A conspicuous instance of this kind is furnished by the laws prohibiting Sunday labour and Sunday amusements. It is now, indeed, very generally recognised by competent authorities that a profound misconception underlies a great part of the popular English religious sentiment on the subject. Sunday is not the Sabbath, and its obligation does not rest upon the Fourth Commandment. It is a Church holiday, enacted in the earliest days of Christianity in commemoration of a great Christian event, and for the purpose of Christian worship, and the same authority which enjoined the festival prescribed the conditions of its observance. In the early Church many Jewish converts considered the Fourth Commandment still binding upon them, and they accordingly observed the Jewish Sabbath as well as the Christian Lord's Day. The Gentile converts, however, in accordance with the express language of St. Paul,[1] considered the former

---

[1] Colossians ii. 16.

day no longer obligatory, though they were bound on other than Old Testament grounds to observe the Christian festival. The early Fathers, with one voice and in the clearest language, recognised the distinction between the two days, and declared that the Jewish Sabbath had been abrogated with the Jewish dispensation, though the observance of the Lord's Day was obligatory on Christians.[2]

Legislation soon confirmed this obligation. A law of Constantine enacted that 'on the venerable day of the Sun' all workshops should be closed, and magistrates, and people residing in cities, should rest; but he at the same time expressly authorised agricultural labour, he placed no restriction on public amusements, and he afterwards permitted the law courts to be open on that day for the purpose of emancipating slaves and freeing sons from the paternal power. The legislation of the elder and younger Theodosius went further. It not only forbade business, but also suppressed the public games and theatrical exhibitions on the Lord's Day. It must, however, be added that these amusements had always been looked on with disfavour by the Church, and there is reason to believe that the Theodosian laws on the subject were very imperfectly executed.

During the Dark Ages several provincial Councils enjoined a more Judaical observance of Sunday: it became customary to draw parallels between the Jewish ordinances and the Christian holidays; the Sabbath was represented as at least prefiguring the Sunday rest, and the Fourth Commandment was sometimes quoted in its support. But though the Judaical element in Sabbath observances undoubtedly increased during the Middle Ages, the Catholic Church has, as a whole, never committed itself to the confusion of the two days. The

---

[2] The whole history of Sunday observance, and of the doctrine connected with it, is treated with an admirable and almost exhaustive fulness in Hessey's Bampton Lectures on *Sunday, its Origin and History*. The reader will find in this book nearly all the authorities I have cited. See also Bingham's *Christian Antiquities*, Book XVI. c. 8, Book XX. c. 2.

term Sabbath was scarcely ever applied to the Christian festival, and many of the chief authorities in the Church continued, up to the time of the Reformation, clearly to testify to
the distinction between the two days. Attendance on a religious service on the Lord's Day was enjoined under pain of
mortal sin. Work, as a general rule, was prohibited, though
there were various exceptions. On the other hand, innocent
amusements, if they did not clash with religious services,
were not only permitted, but encouraged. On Friday public
amusements were suppressed, for that day had very early
been accounted as a fast day; and it was observed with such
stringency that there have been instances of men having been
put to death for having eaten meat on Friday.[3] An English law
of Henry VI. forbade fairs and markets to be held on Sunday.[4]
Four Sundays in harvest-time, however, were excepted, and
this exception was only taken away in the present reign.[5]

If we pass to the Reformation, we shall find that all the
leading Reformers maintained, in clear and decisive terms,
that the Lord's Day was an institution wholly distinct from
the Jewish Sabbath. The 'larger Catechism' of Luther, and the
Confession of Augsburg, which was drawn up by Melanch-
thon and Luther, and which was accepted by the main body
of Protestants, laid down that, while it was highly desirable
for edification that a day should be set apart for Christian
worship and rest, it was a grave error to believe that this was
the Jewish Sabbath, or a substitute for the Jewish Sabbath.
'Scripture abrogated the Sabbath;' 'it is a false persuasion that
the Church's worship ought to be like the Levitical.' 'Those
who judge that in the place of the Sabbath the Lord's Day
was instituted as a day to be necessarily observed are greatly

---

[3] Celui qui avoit mangé de la chair au vendredi estoit bruslé tout vif,
comme il fut faict en la ville d'Angers, l'an 1539, s'il ne s'en repentoit, et
jaçoit qu'il se repentist, si estoit il pendu par compassion' (Bodin,
Démonomanie des Sorciers, p. 216).
[4] 27 Henry VI. c. 5.
[5] 13 & 14 Vict. c. 23.

mistaken.' It is right that a day should be appointed on which
men should rest from their labours, and have leisure and time
to assemble together for Divine worship, but under the dispensation of Christian liberty the observance of days is 'not
a matter of necessity.' 'If any one,' Luther once said, 'sets up
the observance of the day on a Jewish foundation, then I order
you to work on it, to ride on it, to dance on it, to feast on it,
to do anything that shall remove this encroachment on Christian liberty.' 'To think that working on the Lord's Day,' said
Bucer, 'is in itself a sin, is a superstition and a denying of the
Grace of Christ.'

Modern Puritanism is largely traced to Calvin, but in its
views of the nature of Sunday it can derive no countenance
from his writings and example. He stated that the Sabbath
was totally abrogated; that it was a typical and shadowy ordinance, no longer required; and that it was a gross and carnal
error to believe that, although the day of the Sabbath was
changed, its obligation remains. Men should, indeed, devote
a certain portion of their time to the public worship of God
and to resting from their work. The seventh of our time is a
convenient proportion, but the proportion and the special
portion so assigned are alike matters of indifference. He complains that 'Jewish ideas' had been imported into this subject,
and he certainly never intended that Sunday should be kept
by the suppression of all amusements. John Knox once found
him engaged in playing a game of bowls on Sunday. Knox
himself had no scruples about supping in company on that
day, and there is no reason to believe that his views about
Sunday were in any way different from those of the Continental Reformers.

The Helvetic Confession, representing Zwingli and the
other Swiss Reformers, is very clear on the subject. 'In the
Churches of old, from the very times of the Apostles, not
merely are certain days in each week appointed for religious
assemblies, but the Lord's Day itself was consecrated to that
purpose and to holy rest. This practice our Churches retain
for worship's sake and for charity's sake. But we do not

thereby give countenance to Judaic observances and to superstition. We do not believe, either, that one day is more
sacred than another, and that mere rest is in itself pleasing to
God. We keep a Lord's Day, not a Sabbath Day, by an uncon-
strained observance.[6]

Such were the views of the chief Protestant leaders on the
Continent. Those of the Anglican Church up to the time of
the Commonwealth were very similar. Cranmer described
Sunday as resting for its authority on the Church and on the
magistrates, and he drew no distinction between it and other
holidays. Attendance on the Anglican service on Sunday was
enforced by law; but in the first year of her reign Elizabeth
ordered all clergymen to teach their parishioners 'that they
may with a safe and quiet conscience, after their Common
Prayer in time of harvest, labour upon the holy and festival
days over that thing which God had sent; and if from any
scrupulosity or qualms of conscience men should supersti-
tiously abstain from working upon those days, that then they
should grievously offend and displease God.' The theatres
during her whole reign were open on that day, and the afternoons, after Church service, were commonly spent in rustic
sports.

Before the close of her reign, however, a different spirit had
arisen, and the Puritan section of the English people had begun to adopt the Sabbatarian views which, in the following
century, so rapidly spread. In the second volume of Homilies
which was issued by order of Convocation in 1563, there is a
'Homily on the Place and Time of Prayer,' which bases Sunday
observance on the Fourth Commandment. 'Albeit this commandment of God doth not bind Christian people so straitly
to observe and keep the utter ceremonies of the Sabbath Day
as it was given unto the Jews, as touching the forbidding of
work and labour in time of great necessity, and as touching
the precise keeping of the seventh day after the manner of
the Jews . . . yet, notwithstanding, whatsoever is found in

---

[6] See Hessey, Lect. VI.

the Commandments appertaining to the law of Nature . . . ought to be retained and kept of all good Christian people. And therefore by this Commandment we ought to have a time on one day in the week wherein we ought to rest, yea, from our lawful and needful work.' 'God's obedient children,' the homily continues, 'should use Sunday holily, and rest from their common and daily business, and also give themselves wholly to heavenly exercises.[7] Sunday is described as the Christian Sabbath day, and the writer complains bitterly that 'God is more dishonoured and the devil better served upon Sunday than upon all the days of the week beside.' Of 'those that will be counted God's people,' he says, many have given up all thought of keeping Sunday. They ride, journey, buy, sell, keep markets and fairs on that day and on all days alike, while others make Sunday a day of drunken, turbulent, and gluttonous revelry. An admonition which was read from the churches after the earthquake of 1580 complains that 'the Sabbath days and holy days . . . are spent full heathenishly in taverning, tippling, gaming, playing, and beholding of bear-baiting and stage-plays, to the utter dishonour of God, impeachment of all godliness, and unnecessary consuming of men's substance. . . . The want of orderly discipline and catechising hath either sent great numbers, both young and old, back again to Papistry, or let them run loose into godless atheism.'[8]

This disorder contributed largely to the reaction towards a Sabbatarian observance of Sunday that grew up among the

---

[7] This language is very like that of one of the articles for the Irish Church drawn up under the direction of Archbishop Usher in 1615. 'The first day of the week, which is the Lord's Day, is wholly to be dedicated to the service of God; and therefore we are bound therein to rest from our common and daily business, and to bestow that leisure upon holy exercises, both public and private' (see Hessey, Lect. VII.).

[8] Strype, *Annals of the Reformation*, ii. 669. 'The Sundays set apart for the public and solemn worship of God were nowadays much profaned in riot and intemperance, chiefly caused by interludes and sports practised on the eves of those days, and the afternoons also' (iii. 340).

English Puritans, who represented in general the most religious class in England. They felt strongly the necessity of giving a more religious character to the Lord's Day; but they were precluded by their theology from admitting the obligation of any observance resting on mere ecclesiastical authority, and their whole teaching had taken a very Old Testament cast. In 1580, the London magistracy obtained from the Queen an interdiction of Sunday plays and games within the liberties of the City. Two years later an accident which occurred near London, from the falling of a scaffold during some Sunday games at Paris Garden, at Southwark, was represented as a Divine judgment, and in 1585 a measure passed through Parliament 'for the better and more reverend observance of the Sabbath,' but was vetoed by the Queen.[9] The doctrine that the Lord's Day was the Sabbath, that Christians were as much bound as the ancient Jews to abstain from all work and pleasure on that day, was now constantly preached. A work by Dr. Bownd, which first appeared in 1595, and which, having been repressed by authority, was republished in 1606, advocated this view in its extreme form, and met with a very wide acceptance. Strype tells us how, in many parts of England, preachers were maintaining in the first part of the seventeenth century that to work, to play bowls, to make a feast or wedding-dinner on the Sabbath day, or to ring on that day more bells than a single one which was to summon worshippers to prayers, was as great a sin as the most atrocious act of murder or adultery. Before the death of James I. the Jewish Sabbath appears to have been accepted by the whole body of the English Puritans.[10]

It met with great resistance. Whitgift, who was Archbishop of Canterbury when the book of Dr. Bownd appeared, formally condemned it as heretical, and some of the more extreme and aggressive Sabbatarians were molested by authority. James I. consented to the closing of theatres on Sunday, but when he found that Puritan magistrates in Lancashire were

---

[9] Ibid. iii. 140, 295–96.
[10] Strype's *Life of Whitgift*, p. 530.

suppressing all Sunday games, he issued, in 1618, a Declaration, which he ordered all clergymen to read from the pulpit, directing that after Divine service his subjects should not be prevented or discouraged from lawful and harmless recreations, such as dancing, leaping, vaulting, morris-dances and maypoles, provided such sports were held 'in due and convenient time, without impediment or neglect of Divine service;' though bear and bull baiting, interludes and bowling, were still prohibited on Sunday. The opposition, however, which this Declaration produced among the Puritan party was so great that the King wisely withdrew the order for reading it.[11]

The Puritan party were now rising rapidly to the ascendant. The first Parliament of Charles I. passed a law forbidding any assembly of people out of their own parish on the Lord's Day, or any bull-baiting, bear-baiting, interludes, common plays, or other unlawful exercises on the same.[12] In the third Parliament of Charles I. it was enacted that no carriers, waggoners or packmen should be allowed to travel on that day, and that no butcher should kill or sell meat upon it.[13] Soon after some Puritan judges began to forbid the celebration of village feasts and wakes on Sunday, and especially certain 'feasts of dedication' which it was the custom to hold on the Sunday before or after the day of the saint to whom the village church was dedicated, and they also of their own authority ordered the clergy to publish this decree in the time of service, and inflicted punishments on those who refused to do so.[14] Great discontent was aroused by these measures, and it induced Charles, at the advice of Laud, to publish in 1633 the 'Book of Sports,' which fills such a conspicuous and disastrous place in the history of the English rebellion. It was simply a repro-

---

[11] Gardiner's *History of England from the Accession of James I.*, iii. 247–52.
[12] 1 Car. I. c. i.
[13] 3 Car. I. c. 1.
[14] Perry's *Hist. of the Church of England*, i. 259–61, 464–70. See, too, Govett's *King's Book of Sports*.

duction of the Declaration of James I., with a short addition formally authorising the dedication feasts and other village festivals, as long as they were celebrated without disorder; the judges of assize were commanded 'to see that no man do trouble or molest any of our loyal and dutiful people in or for their lawful recreations, having first done their duty to God and continuing in obedience to us and to our laws,' and it was ordered that this Declaration should be read in every parish church. At the subsequent trial of Archbishop Laud, one of the charges brought against him was that he 'held that Sunday is no Sabbath.'

There are few things in ecclesiastical history more remarkable than the speed and power with which the Puritan doctrine of the Sabbath pervaded British Protestantism. It supplied a large portion of the religious fanaticism of the Rebellion. It was supreme in England during the Commonwealth. It moulded by its influence the whole religious life and character, both of Scotland and New England, and it affected, though much less powerfully, the Calvinistic Churches of the Continent. In England, the advantage of a more religious mode of spending Sunday than had hitherto been common was felt by numbers who rejected the doctrinal system of the Puritans, and the Restoration, which brought back many things, did not bring back the Sunday of Elizabeth and the early Stuarts. The 'Book of Sports' never revived. The village dedication festivals were not restored. The theatres and all other places of public amusement remained closed. Among the Dissenting bodies, Sabbatarian views still continued to prevail. In the Church of England, the great majority of divines between the Restoration and the rise of the Evangelical movement were not Sabbatarians, but they cordially supported an observance of Sunday which, though much less strict than that of Scotland and New England, was very different from that which had once prevailed in England, and which still existed on the Continent.

By a law of Charles II. all Sunday labour was forbidden; no article except milk could on that day be exposed for sale, no

hackney coaches and other public conveyances were allowed
to ply their trade, and no legal process could be executed,
except for treason, felony, or breach of the peace.[15] The restrictions on public conveyances were gradually relaxed in
the eighteenth century, as roads were improved and as towns
and travelling increased; but in the first quarter of that century
we find the Chancellor, Lord Harcourt, stopped by a con-
stable for driving through Abingdon at a time of public service. In the higher ranks, the observance of Sunday was
probably less strict than among the middle class. The Lu-
theran education of many members of the Royal Family, and
the foreign travelling and general religious indifference of the
upper classes, contributed to mitigate it. Cabinet Councils,
Cabinet dinners, Court entertainments, and fashionable card-
parties and receptions, were frequent on Sunday during the
first half of the eighteenth century, and by the end of the
century Sunday travelling and Sunday excursions had become very common. Sunday newspapers had arisen, and
Hyde Park was thronged on that day with the carriages and
horses of the rich. The Methodist and Evangelical movement,
however, was intensely Sabbatarian, and it deeply influenced
both the teaching of the Anglican Church and the customs of
society.[16]

There can, I think, be little doubt that this reaction towards
Sabbatarianism, which was very perceptible during the last
years of the eighteenth century and during the first thirty or
forty years of the nineteenth century, has now spent its force.
Public opinion in England, and still more in Scotland, has on
this subject greatly changed. In most classes and districts an
amount of Sunday relaxation has become habitual which
would once have been severely reprobated, and the changed

---

[15] 29 Car. II. c. 7. A law of William III. (10 & 11 Will. III. c. 24, s. 14)
authorised the sale of mackerel on Sunday. An Act of Anne (5 Anne, c.
9, s. 3) allowed the apprehension of persons on certain escape-warrants.
[16] For the history of Sunday observance in the eighteenth century, see
Abbey and Overton's *English Church in the Eighteenth Century*, ii. 513–19,
and my own *Hist. of England in the Eighteenth Century*, iii. 14–18, vi. 12–14
(Cabinet Ed.).

views about Sunday will probably, sooner or later, affect legislation.

It is certain that the legal prohibition of all Sunday labour had a religious origin, and, according to modern principles, no restriction based solely on a contested theological doctrine should be generally enforced by law. The restriction is imposed on multitudes who feel no religious obligation to observe it, and it falls with special hardship upon the Jews, who, in addition to their own Sabbath, are compelled to observe another day of rest, imposed by a religion which they repudiate, in commemoration of an event which they deny, and in the place of an ordinance which they believe to be of eternal obligation. If these considerations remained alone, they would have an irresistible force. But another set of considerations, which had either no part, or only a very subsidiary part, among the motives of the original legislators, have come rapidly into the foreground. It is now very generally recognised that a periodical and complete suspension of severe work is in the highest degree necessary to the happiness, to the health, to the full moral and intellectual development of men, and that one day in seven is the smallest proportion of rest which meets this want. Of all the failures of the French Revolution, none was more complete than the substitution of a tenth for a seventh day of rest, which they established and attempted to enforce by law. The innovation passed away without a protest or a regret, and the proportion which the Jewish and Christian Churches had assigned was resumed. One of the first measures of the Government of the Restoration was a severe law enforcing the observance of Sunday, which is remarkable, among other things, for closing all drink-shops and refreshment-rooms during the hours of Mass in towns of less than 50,000 inhabitants. After the Revolution of 1830 it fell into almost complete desuetude.[17] In 1880 it was formally repealed.[18]

If a man, by working on Sunday, affected himself alone, I do

---

[17] See Chevalier, *Organisation du Travail*, p. 74.
[18] Béchaux, *Revendications ouvrières en France*, p. 73.

not think that the law would have any right to interfere with him, but in the keen competition of industry this is impossible. A shop or a manufactory which was open on Sunday would naturally distance its competitors, and a small minority would thus always have it in their power to enforce Sunday labour on a large majority. It is on this ground that the law is justified in imposing the restriction on all; and when this general pro- hibition is found to be on the whole a great advantage, legis- lators naturally hesitate to admit exceptions which, though plausible or justifiable in themselves, might tend to weaken its force. The foundation of the law, however, is being changed. It was originally enacted mainly or exclusively on religious grounds. It is now defended by its best supporters on secular and utilitarian grounds, though it still derives a great additional weight and popularity from the fact that a strong religious sentiment is behind it.

In Continental countries, and especially in France, the ad- vantages of the Sunday rest are being more and more felt; and not the less so since the French Government has completely dissociated itself from Catholicism. In Germany, a new law came into force in 1893 which closed all shops except for a few hours on Sunday.[19] The Catholic Socialists make a Sunday rest enforced by law one of their leading demands; but the same demand has been included in the programmes of most of the Socialist bodies, which are hostile to religion. It is part of the general movement for shortening by law the hours of labour. In the Berlin Labour Conference of 1890 the represen- tatives of the different Powers were almost equally divided on this subject, though the majority were in favour of the prohibition on Sunday of the labour of women and children.[20] Some pressure has been put upon Governments to set the example by discontinuing on that day manual labour on pub- lic works. In 1874, five great railway companies in France

---

[19] See on this law a report from the English Consul at Mannheim, quoted in the *Times*, July 7, 1893.
[20] Béchaux, pp. 73–74.

petitioned the Government to close the services of 'petite vi-
tesse,' but the Minister of Public Works refused the permission.[21]

As might be expected, in countries where the Sunday rest
is unsupported either by law or by strong religious sentiment
the demand for it varies much with industrial conditions. It
is strongest in large towns and manufactories, where the pressure and competition of labour throughout the year are greatest. It is much weaker in districts where life moves slowly,
where labour is never either intense or incessant or keenly
competitive, and where the distractions of amusement are
very few. It is scarcely probable that a law preventing a farmer
from working on his own land could be enforced in any country where it has not been long since established on religious
grounds, and a new law enforcing cessation of labour would
also be very unpopular in places of pleasure-resort, where
both hard work and large profits are restricted to the few
weeks or months of a fashionable season.

In its broad lines, however, the prohibition of Sunday labour among the Anglo-Saxon race has met with almost universal acceptance, and there are only a few very minor
questions that might be raised. It is, in my opinion, an exaggerated thing to prohibit harvest-work in the critical weeks
during which the prosperity of the farmer so largely depends
on the prompt use of every hour of fine weather. Work that
is in no sense competitive, such as the work of a man in his
own garden, stands on a different footing from competitive
labour; and a wise tolerance is accorded to various small industries, chiefly for the comfort and benefit of the very poor,
or of those who are enjoying a holiday in the country. On the
whole, however, the general legislative prohibition of Sunday
labour secures a great blessing to the community, and a blessing which could not in any other way be attained. Looking at
the question from a merely physical and industrial point of
view, it cannot be doubted that the average health, strength,

---

[21] Castellane, *La Politique Conservatrice*, p. 171.

and working power of the race are immensely increased by
the fresh air and exercise and rest which the Sunday holiday
secures. The addition it makes to human happiness, the benefits it bestows on those large classes whose whole weekday
lives are spent in labour too jading and incessant to leave any
margin or disposition for mental culture, can hardly be overestimated. These, however, are not its only advantages.
Though an enlightened modern legislator will refrain from
basing any restrictive law on a contested theological dogma,
and will hesitate much before undertaking to make men
moral by law, he cannot be indifferent to the moral results of
his legislation. No one who knows England will doubt that
the existence of an enforced holiday primarily devoted to religious worship has contributed enormously to strengthen
the moral fibre of the nation, to give depth, seriousness, and
sobriety to the national character, to save it from being wholly
sunk in selfish pursuits and material aims.

On the whole, the prohibition of Sunday labour has been
at once the earliest and most successful of the small and dangerous class of measures that are intended to regulate and
restrict the labour of men. The question, however, of Sunday
amusements is wholly different from that of Sunday labour,
and there can, I think, be little doubt that great evils have
followed from Sabbatarian notions on the subject. Only a very
small minority of the human race have the character and the
disposition that render it possible for them to spend a whole
day in devotional exercises, and an attempt to force men of
another type into such a life seldom fails to produce a dangerous rebound. All religion becomes distasteful and discredited, and the sense of moral perspective is fatally impaired.
It is no exaggeration to say that there have been periods and
districts in Scotland in which to dance, to play the piano, or
even to walk in the fields for pleasure on Sundays, would
have excited as much scandal as some grave act of commercial
fraud or of sexual immorality. It has often been noticed how
commonly children brought up with great strictness in severely religious families fall into evil ways, and the explana-

tion of the fact is very obvious. They have come to associate the whole religious side of their teaching with a repelling gloom, with irksome and unnatural restraint. Being taught to aim perpetually at a temperament and an ideal wholly unsuited to their characters, they fail to attain the type of excellence which was well within their reach. The multiplication of unreal duties and the confusion of harmless pleasures with vice, destroy the moral proportion and balance of their natures, and as soon as the restraining hand is withdrawn a complete moral anarchy ensues. A severe Sabbatarian legislation has a similar effect upon a nation. Depriving the people of innocent means of enjoyment, and preventing the growth of some of the tastes that do most to civilise them, it has often a distinctly demoralising influence. Men who have not the disposition to spend the day in a constant round of religious exercises, not unnaturally learn to spend it in absolute torpor or in drunken vice. Those have, indeed, much to answer for who have for generations deprived the poor of all means of innocent recreation and mental improvement on their only holiday.

Of all the changes that have taken place in our time, few, I think, are more gratifying than the growth of a more rational conception of Sunday. In dealing with Sunday amusements, much consideration must be paid to public opinion, and also to the amount of labour they entail. There is a wise and general consensus of opinion that they should be, in the main, restricted to the afternoons, and that the mornings should be reserved for religious exercises. Many forms of amusement, such as those of the pedestrian, the fisherman, and the cricketer, involve no addition to Sunday labour; while others, such as country excursions and the opening of museums and libraries, involve an amount of labour that is infinitesimal in proportion to the great benefits they produce. The value of a country excursion to the denizens of our crowded towns can hardly be overrated, and with the growth of towns and the increasing stress and competition of labour it is continually increasing. To secure a weekly holiday for the comparatively

Democracy and Liberty

small number of men whose Sunday labour is necessary for the attainment of this inestimable blessing is a mere question of organisation and money, and it is rendered peculiarly easy by the large profit which the Sunday holidays always produce. One effect of opening on Sunday museums and galleries which are now open only on weekdays, would probably be a reduction of the labour of the attendants from six days in the week to five and a half. Public requirements would be amply satisfied with admission to these museums of Sunday afternoon, and there would not be the smallest difficulty in closing them on one whole weekday, as is done in, I believe, every continental capital.

No way of spending a Sunday afternoon can be more harmless, and not many are more profitable, than in a museum or picture-gallery, and there is a peculiar wrong in closing institutions which are supported by public money against the classes who have most labour and fewest enjoyments on the one day on which they could avail themselves of them. In England, the educational advantages of such institutions are peculiarly needed. Protestantism has many merits, but it does nothing for the æsthetic education of the people; while the eminently pictorial worship and the highly ornamented churches of Catholicism bring men in constant contact with images and ceremonies that appeal to the imagination, and, in some degree, refine the taste. From the days of the Stuarts, and even of the Tudors, England has been full of masterpieces of ancient art, but very few poor men who did not happen to have been servants in some great man's house can have had an opportunity of seeing a good picture before the opening of Dulwich Gallery in 1817, and of the National Gallery in 1824. The taste for public gardens, as a really popular taste, is very modern. The liberality of great noblemen who commonly throw open their parks to public enjoyment, the opening of the first English Zoological Garden in London in 1828, the opening of Kew and Hampton Court on Sunday, the great movement which has been so conspicuous in our day for forming people's parks, throwing open squares and gardens that had formerly been the exclusive possession of a few, admitting all classes to botanical and other gardens on Sunday, and permitting bands to play in parks and gardens on that day, have all contributed to its formation. It has been an unmixed benefit. All good judges have noticed the improvement of manners and the increased power of harmless and decorous enjoyment among the English poor during the nineteenth century, and it is probably largely due to the more rational employment of Sunday. The great provincial towns have, with scarcely an exception, supported the movement, and, while endowing with great liberality museums and public libraries, they have generally opened them on Sundays. In a remarkable petition which was presented to Convocation in 1892, it was stated that thirty-four museums, art galleries, and libraries in the kingdom were open on that day.

It can hardly be doubted that the movement is destined to extend, though probably by gradual steps, and not without some opposition. The Saturday half-holiday, it has been truly said, has mitigated, though it has certainly not removed, the grievance of the Sunday closing of public institutions. In most constituencies there are probably electors holding strong Methodist and Evangelical views of Sunday with such an intensity of religious conviction that they are prepared to subordinate all party questions to their enforcement; and, under our present system of party government, such men have naturally a far greater political influence than a much larger body of men who are in favour of Sunday opening, but who do not attach such transcendent importance to the question as to make it the decisive question on which their votes at an election will depend. There is, also, among the great body of the working classes much indifference on the subject. A taste for art or antiquity is an acquired taste, and although it is extremely desirable that the poor should acquire it, they are not likely to do so until they have had some means of gratifying it. The question is too commonly regarded as if it were merely a question for those who are commonly called 'the working classes.' It concerns at least equally the many thousands of

hard-working men and women who are employed in shops—
often in small shops, where a Saturday half-holiday does not
exist. In this class the taste for music and art is stronger than
among the so-called working classes; but they are not an organising and agitating class, and their political weight, under
the influence of modern democratic changes, has sensibly diminished.

In the trade unions, also, there is some division of opinion
on the subject totally unconnected with religion. Paris is the
continental city with which Englishmen are most familiar,
and many persons are accustomed to speak of the Parisian
Sunday as the one alternative to the English one; though, in
truth, over a great part of the Continent the Sunday in which
shops are shut and labour suspended, while amusement is
encouraged, is very familiar. The limitation of hours of labour
is one of the strongest present enthusiasms of the working
classes, and it has led some of them to look with suspicion
and dislike on the opening of institutions that would imply
some labour. They fear that it would lead to general Sunday
labour, and they very justly believe that, if they worked generally for seven instead of six days in the week, the market
rate of their wages would not be higher than at present.

Apprehensions of this kind appear to me wholly chimeri-
cal, and they are, I believe, only entertained by a small minority of the working classes. The distinction between the
opening of places of amusement and the continuance of ordinary labour on Sunday is so clear and intelligible that it
could hardly be overlooked. The opening of museums and
galleries on that day, as I have said, would probably rather
tend to diminish than to increase labour; it would be an es-
pecial benefit to the labouring classes, and it might, perhaps,
give some employment to the Jews, who have a peculiar
grievance under our present Sunday laws,[22] though that

---

[22] In a reply to a deputation in favour of Sunday opening of museums,
December 14, 1892, Mr. Acland, the Vice-President of the Council of
Education, said: 'I understand that in Birmingham certain persons of the

grievance has been much mitigated by Acts of 1871 and 1878, which gave them some considerable rights of Sunday labour.[23] No one who has realised the immense strength and organisation which the operatives have acquired in dealing with their employers, and the commanding influence they now exercise on legislation, can believe that general Sunday labour could possibly be forced upon them contrary to their will. At the same time, these various forms of suspicion, apathy, and opposition have retarded the movement, and alone prevent its complete attainment. If those who would be most benefited by the Sunday opening of museums and galleries demanded it with real earnestness, no one can doubt that they could obtain it without the smallest difficulty. The opposition to it is certainly not in the upper classes, and the great majority of members of Parliament would be quite ready to vote for it if they believed that by doing so they would not lose more votes than they gained. Governments justly believe that on such matters they must follow, and not precede, public opinion.

The arguments that apply to the opening of museums and picture galleries on Sunday may be extended to some other forms of amusement, such as Sunday lectures and Sunday concerts; and the rule forbidding the taking of money has no real value or meaning. The opening of theatres on Sunday would, however, in my opinion, in the present state of English public feeling, be exceedingly inexpedient. It may, indeed, be argued with plausibility that the fact that some persons object to a particular amusement is an excellent reason why they should not participate in it, but is no reason why others should be deprived of it. This, however, is rather an argument of the school than of the senate. It may be urged with great force against the imposition of a new restriction, but it has much less weight when it is a question of removing

---

Jewish denomination, who have their Sabbath on the Saturday, are willing to, and do, give their services on what to them is a week-day, for the purpose of assisting in the museum and library.'

[23] See Jevons's *State in relation to Labour,* pp. 61, 65.

a restriction which has existed with general acceptance for centuries, and which is deeply rooted in the habits, traditions and feelings of the nation. No wise legislator will needlessly offend or scandalise the great body of the people, and the opening of theatres on Sunday, which scarcely excited a remonstrance under Elizabeth, would undoubtedly be bitterly resented under Victoria.

With Sunday amusements in private life the legislator should have no concern. Hardly any law upon the Statute Book seems to me a more silly or unjustifiable infringement of liberty than that which still makes it criminal for a man to shoot a pheasant or partridge on his own grounds upon Sunday or Christmas Day,[24] though he may shoot wildfowl, or woodcock, or snipe, as these birds are not included under the legal definition of game, and though no restriction is imposed on Sunday fishing.

The duty and the expediency of watching closely the currents of public opinion, and abstaining from all unnecessary changes in customs and traditions, introduce into all wise systems of legislation a large amount of inconsistency and incoherence, and are very unfavourable to any systematic and strictly logical treatment of the subject. One bad thing will be forbidden, and suppressed by law; another thing, which is equally bad, will be forbidden by law, but generally tolerated. A third, which the moralist will regard as equally blamable, will be perfectly legal. Concessions will be made in one direction, while restrictions that are in argument incompatible with them are maintained: and different principles and motives of action are admitted in legislation, no one of which is pushed consistently to its full logical consequences. Thus, for example, it is well understood that the sphere of criminal legislation and the sphere of morals are not coextensive, but at the same time they are closely and manifestly connected. In graduating penalties, in admitting circumstances of extenuation and aggravation, every legislator and administrator of

---

[24] 1 and 2 Will. IV. c. 32, s. 3.

law must necessarily consider moral guilt. No system of law which failed to do so could subsist, for public opinion would refuse to ratify its sentences. Except in some rare cases of political offenses, which fall rather under the category of acts of war than of acts of crime, it would be impossible to inflict the highest legal penalty upon acts, however disastrous to society, if they were felt to involve little or no moral guilt.

On the other hand, no consistent attempt can be successfully made to make the degrees of guilt and the degrees of punishment coincide. Many acts that are grossly immoral lie wholly beyond the domain of the law. Many acts which the law treats as misdemeanors involve as much moral turpitude as acts which the law pronounces to be felonies. Murder is, undoubtedly, morally as well as legally, a worse crime than fraud, yet it would not be difficult to point to particular instances of fraud which imply greater moral turpitude than particular instances of murder. The moral guilt of a man who fires at another with the intention of murdering him is precisely the same whether he misses his victim or simply wounds or kills him, though to each of these cases a different penalty would be assigned. Many a criminal has escaped the gallows because a good constitution has enabled his victim to survive an injury under which a weaker constitution would have succumbed. A man may make himself so mad with drink that he has no more power of judging or controlling his acts than a somnambulist or a lunatic. If in this state he commits a crime, his drunkenness is the true essence and measure of his guilt. Yet the law will only punish extreme drunkenness by the lightest of penalties, while it will punish with perpetual servitude, and perhaps death, acts that may be blindly committed under its influence. The penalties attached to a crime are constantly increased, not because there is a deeper sense of its immorality, but because it has become more frequent, more easy, more dangerous. External provocations are largely considered in extenuating crime, but the law can take no cognisance of the equally real palliating circumstances of a nature which was originally perverted or debilitated by hereditary influences, and which has grown from childhood to maturity in hopeless ignorance and poverty, amid all the associations and contagion of vice.

All that can be safely done is to lay down certain general principles on which the legislator should proceed, admitting at the same time that there are cases in which, under the stress of some strong expediency, these principles may be overborne. The enforcement of theological doctrines, or of obligations resting solely on theological doctrine, is now generally recognised as beyond the sphere of the criminal law, and in dealing with the immorality of adult men it should mainly, if not exclusively, regard its effects on the general wellbeing of society. If a man's bad acts affect himself alone, or if they only affect adult men who voluntarily share in them, there is a strong presumption that they ought not to be brought within the coercive province of law. They may be matters for argument, remonstrance, reprobation, but they are not subjects for legislative penalties.

Those who are acquainted with the writings of the more advanced thinkers of the first half of the present century, and with the writings of at least one of the most illustrious thinkers of our own generation, will probably regard this as a timid, hesitating, and imperfect statement of a great principle. The lines of right and wrong in these matters may, according to these thinkers, be much more firmly and inflexibly drawn. 'Every one,' says Kant, 'may seek his own happiness in the way that seems good to himself, provided that he infringe not such freedom of others to strive after a similar end as is consistent with the freedom of all according to a possible general law.' 'If my action or my condition generally can coexist with the freedom of every other according to a universal law, any one does me a wrong who hinders me in the performance of this action or in the maintenance of this condition.' 'Every man,' writes Mr. Herbert Spencer, 'is free to do that which he wills, provided he infringes not the equal freedom of any other man.' 'The liberty of each is limited only by the like liberties of all.'

The subject was discussed with much elaboration by Mill in his treatise on 'Liberty,' and a few lines from this work express very clearly the conslusion of the most liberal thinkers of that school. 'The sole end for which mankind are warranted, individually or collectively, in interfering with the liberty of action of any of their number is self-protection. The only purpose for which power can be rightfully exercised over any member of a civilised community against his will is to prevent harm to others. His own good, either physical or moral, is not a sufficient warrant. . . . The only part of the conduct of any one for which he is amenable to society is that which concerns others. In the part which merely concerns himself, his independence is of right, absolute.' This doctrine, Mill explains, applies only to human beings 'in the maturity of their faculties,' and to societies which have attained some measure of civilisation. 'But as soon as mankind have attained the capacity of being guided to their own improvement by conviction or persuasion (a period long since reached in all nations with whom we need here concern ourselves), compulsion, either in the direct form, or in that of pains and penalties for non-compliance, is no longer admissible as a means to their own good, and justifiable only for the security of others.' We should all have liberty 'of doing as we like, subject to such consequences as may follow, without impediment from our fellow-creatures, so long as what we do does not harm them, even though they should think our conduct foolish, perverse, or wrong; and from this liberty of each individual follows the liberty, within the same limits, of combination among individuals—freedom to unite for any purpose not involving harm to others; the persons combining being supposed to be of full age, and not forced or deceived.'[25]

In carrying out this principle, Mill argues that the only injuries to society which the law should punish are clear, direct, definite injuries. It is not sufficient to show that a man, by depraving his own nature, makes himself less fitted to do

---

[25] Mill's *Liberty*, pp. 21–23, 26—27.

good and more likely to do harm to the community, and that the example of his vice may create scandal, or prove contagious. There must be 'a definite damage, or a definite risk of damage, either to an individual or the public.' No one, for instance, should be punished simply for being drunk, but he may be rightly punished if, when he is drunk, he impedes or molests his neighbour, or if, being a soldier or a policeman, he is drunk on duty.

This doctrine about the relation of legislation to morals corresponds closely with the doctrine about the relation of industry and legislation which was taught by Adam Smith and his followers. It is defended by many powerful arguments. It is urged that the judgment of the community about right and wrong is by no means infallibly correct; that the tendency of Government to encroach upon the sphere of individual action and domestic life is an exceedingly dangerous one; that the limits which may be at first assigned to such interference will almost always eventually be overpassed, and that to place the private actions of men of ripe years under constant Government supervision and control is the surest way to emasculate the character and to withdraw from it the power of moral resistance. To extend into manhood the restrictive system which is appropriate to childhood seldom fails to stunt and to enfeeble, and, as the sphere of Government interference dilates, the robust, self-reliant elements and spontaneous energies of character naturally decline. Yet it is these qualities that are most essential to national freedom and to a masculine morality. Men seldom realise how much more important the indirect and distant consequences of their acts often are than those which are direct and immediate, and it is in its indirect and ultimate effects that excessive Government regulation is especially pernicious. It is added that Government interference constantly defeats its own ends. Compression produces reaction, which often goes much further than the original vice. Evil things driven from publicity and placed under the ban of the law take in secret more dangerous and insidious forms.

Even when it is in the power of the Government completely to suppress some habit or amusement which in itself produces more evil than good, it by no means follows that this suppression is a real or an unmixed gain. It will often be found that this habit, or amusement, springs from a craving for some strong excitement which is deeply planted in human nature, and which in some periods and with some classes has an altogether abnormal strength, and the extirpation of one more or less vicious excitement is often followed by the growth of another. The real cure for the vices of society must go to their roots, and is to be found in moral and intellectual changes affecting habits, interests and tastes, which the hand of power can never produce.

As far as the question is confined to the criminal law, it appears to me that Mill is right in maintaining that its coercive power should, in the case of adult men, be confined as a general rule to acts which are directly injurious to others. Where an exception is made, the *onus probandi* rests with those who make it, and the case for suppression ought to be very strong. In this, however, as in the economical field, the tendency in the present generation has been to increase the number of the exceptions, and to dwell rather on the exceptions than on the rule. We are far, no doubt, from the paternal supervision of some branches of morals which the Greek philosophers advocated, and which the Roman censors in a great degree attained. We are far from the sumptuary laws, and from the minute moral regulations that have prevailed in some Catholic countries, and among the Puritans of the Commonwealth, of Scotland, and of New England; but British legislation is also far from confining itself within the limits assigned to it in the system of Mill. It condemns prize-fights, and duels, and suicides, though these are purely voluntary acts of adult men. If a man, through some religious scruple, suffers members of his family to die for want of medical aid, he is punishable by law, though all parties concerned may fully share in the superstition. Theatrical amusements are placed under legal censorship; games that are played for money in licensed houses, and some forms of gambling in private houses or involuntary societies, as well as in public places, are criminal offences; and under the guise of the Licensing Acts an increasingly severe censorship is exercised on many other forms of public amusement. There are many persons among us who would forcibly suppress all amusements which are coarse or grossly vulgar, or which cause any kind of suffering to animals, or which can possibly awake evil passions, or which bring together, even for innocent purposes, persons of immoral lives. The sale of obscene literature or pictures, even in a back room and to adult purchasers, is criminal; and although unchastity, and even adultery, are untouched by the criminal law, some forms of gross private immorality are severely punished and some purely voluntary organisations for practising and propagating vice are penal.

Sometimes laws of this kind are in a great degree obsolete. They are left on the Statute Book, and form a kind of reserve power in the hands of legislators in case some private vice which experience shows to be very injurious to society should grow and extend. They are, however, rarely put in force, either because they deal with subjects on which evidence is apt to be peculiarly uncertain and deceptive, or because the scandal and the advertisement of publicity would increase the evil, or because they are unsupported by public opinion, or because their strict execution would bring into clear relief the anomalies and inequalities under which equally bad things can be done with impunity. It is contended that the sentence of law strengthens the weight and authority of moral censure; that a law may throw serious obstacles in the way of the introduction of some new and little-practised vice; that, when public opinion has undermined an evil habit, a coercive law will both hasten its downfall and prevent its recurrence. The suppression of duelling in England was much more due to a change in public opinion than to law, but the existence of a law contributed to make it universal and to prevent the probability of its revival.

There may be great differences of opinion about the expediency or inexpediency of some of these laws, and in some respects they diverge considerably from other legislations. Thus, suicide or attempted suicide is not recognised as a legal crime either in France or Germany. The English law about obscene pictures and books would, if consistently applied, drive not a few masterpieces from our picture galleries and many classical works from our libraries and, as I have already observed, English law regulates the manner in which grown-up men and women may amuse themselves in a manner that would be thought childish and intolerable in many continental countries. The arguments on which such laws will be chiefly defended or impugned are utilitarian arguments, turning upon their influence on the wellbeing of society. These, however, are not the grounds on which this kind of legislation was, in most cases, originally based. During long periods of the world's history it was considered the duty of the legislator to punish immoral acts because they were immoral and offensive to the Deity, altogether irrespective of their effects upon society. A utilitarian basis, however, was at the same time provided, in the belief that immoral acts drew down upon a nation Divine judgments. The story of Sodom and Gomorrah, and many other stories, both in Jewish and Pagan antiquity, clearly illustrate this belief. Nor was it an irrational one. It simply translated into theological terms the great truth that, when a nation becomes thoroughly corrupt, all the elements of its strength and wellbeing will decay and the period of its ruin is at hand. In Pagan antiquity, also, the distinction between the temporal and spiritual power was scarcely known: much of what, in Christian times, is considered the peculiar duty of the Church devolved upon the State, and one of the first aims of legislation was to maintain and realise a moral ideal.

The foregoing remarks will show the great difficulty and complexity of these questions about the connection between legislation and morals. Perhaps the most important and most difficult is the attitude the law should assume towards voluntary habits which are the cause of great and widespread misery in the community. One of the most conspicuous of these is gambling. It is not in itself a crime. Few moralists will pretend that a man is committing an immoral act if he stakes a few pence or shillings on a game of whist, or if, on the chance of obtaining an unusually large return, he invests a sum which he can well afford in some highly fluctuating security, or some undeveloped mine, or in some insurance or tontine investment. Yet no one will doubt that gambling may easily become a passion scarcely less irresistible and less injurious than drink, and it is a passion which is common to all latitudes and to all stages of civilisation. The tranquil Oriental and the Indian savage are as much under its influence as the modern European.

Probably its chief root is that craving for excitement to which I have just referred as one of the deepest and strongest springs of human action. Man is so constituted that tranquil pleasure rarely suffices him. There are chords in his being which must be touched in another way, and he imperiously needs the thrill of intense emotion, even when that emotion is far from being exclusively pleasurable. It was this craving which, in antiquity, found one of its chief vents in the fierce joys of the amphitheatre. In modern Europe it is seldom more impressively displayed than in the white heat of passionate and almost breathless excitement with which ten or twelve thousand spectators at Seville or Madrid will watch some critical moment in the bull-fight. Suspense, and uncertainty, and the mingling of strong hopes and fears, contribute largely to it; it finds a keen satisfaction in some kinds of field sports; it is probably the chief element in that strangely mingled pleasure with which men watch a painful tragedy on the state; it is certainly, in all times and countries, one of the chief sources of the popularity of war; it gives a spur to many noble forms of heroism and adventure, and much vice is due to the want of harmless and sufficient occasion for its gratification. To this element in human nature gambling powerfully and directly appeals. It is curious to observe how men will connect it with amusements that are in themselves purely pleasurable, in order to stimulate languid or jaded interest, to add a touch or sting of passion, even at the price of a large admixture of fear and pain.

The subject becomes especially serious from the fact that there is great reason to believe that gambling is an increasing evil. In some continental countries, and especially, I think, in French watering-places, the increase is very manifest. In England it rages wildly in many different spheres. It flourishes on a gigantic scale on the Stock Exchange, and in all the many fields of speculation. The racecourse is almost wholly under its empire, and the vast place which racing occupies among English amusements, and the great multiplication of small races, have contributed largely to disseminate the taste for betting through all classes of the community. All competent judges seem agreed that during the second half, or at least during the last third of the nineteenth century, it has much increased in a large section of the upper classes in England. During the eighteenth century its prevalence was a matter of constant complaint; but the taste for gambling among this class, like some other things, seems to have greatly passed away during the long French war, and it is not until our own generation that there is much evidence of its serious revival. It is, I think, a still more melancholy feature of our time that among the poor in many parts of England gambling has of late come to be closely connected with innocent and healthy forms of amusement, such as football, and, it is said, cricket, with which it had formerly no relation.

The same fact has been observed in America, where betting at athletic sports has of late years become exceedingly popular, and where the great increase of gambling appears to be quite as conspicuous as in England. During the last few years Connecticut, New Jersey, and New York have enacted State laws suppressing different forms which it has assumed, and a measure has passed through Congress, which it must, I should think, be extremely difficult to enforce, prohibiting the transmission of gambling matter from State to State by mail express or other agencies.[26] On both sides of the Atlantic a vast extension of gambling has been a melancholy and un-looked-for consequence of the enormous multiplication of newspapers and newspaper-readers. The most casual obser-vation is sufficient to show that the results of races and the odds of betting form the most exciting part of the newspaper-reading of multitudes who can seldom or never be present on a racecourse. It is said that domestic servants, who lead very sedentary lives, have through such channels been deeply in-fected with this passion.

English law deals with the subject in an extremely capri-cious manner. Speculative gambling can be carried on in in-numerable forms and to almost any possible extent, and no serious attempt is made to suppress the enormous gambling that is notoriously connected with the racecourse. No form of amusement in England is more popular than this, and there is also no form of amusement which receives so large a mea-sure both of aristocratic and of parliamentary favour. Lotter-ies, on the other hand, have been prohibited by several laws, and Parliament has wholly ceased to make use of public lot-teries as a financial resource. A curious illustration, both of the extreme popularity which a small, and, it might be sup-posed, not very attractive form of gambling can attain, and of the capricious stringency of English law, was furnished in 1892 and 1893 by the sudden growth and rapid suppression of what was called 'the missing-word competition.' The com-petitor paid a shilling and bought a copy of the newspaper which offered the puzzle, in the shape of a printed sentence with an omitted word, which the reader was invited to sup-ply. The proprietor of the newspaper was said to be contented with the increased sale, and the shillings of the unsuccessful competitors went to the successful ones. It was shown that success in this and in some analogous puzzles was altogether

---

[26] See an interesting article on the suppression of the lottery and other gambling in America in *The Forum*, April 1895.

a matter of chance, and not of skill, and, under a judicial interpretation of one of the old Acts against gambling, the practice
was suppressed. It had acquired during its short existence an
astonishing popularity. In the majority of cases it was probably a source of perfectly harmless amusement; and no description of gambling is, on the whole, less dangerous than
that in which the gambler is restricted to a small and defined
stake. Various illegal forms, however, or gambling connected
with charities are tacitly permitted. Indirectly, gambling is
discouraged by the law withdrawing legal protection from
gambling debts; and there are some curious distinctions between particular games of chance that are forbidden while
others are permitted. Gambling in the privacy of the family
circle is in practice unmolested, but voluntary societies of
grown-up men who meet with this object, and who, as they
carefully screen themselves from observation, can hardly be
said to exercise any pernicious influence by example or contagion, have of late years been made the subjects of much
espionage and of many prosecutions, the gamblers in these
cases being usually almost or altogether unpunished, while
the owners of the house are severely punished. The wisdom
of such measures, in the face of the enormous amount and
variety of gambling which is notoriously practised with impunity, seems to me extremely doubtful.

There will be less difference of opinion about the expediency of forbidding by law public gambling such as exists at
Monte Carlo and in the 'cercles' and casinos of many continental watering-places. These establishments, it is true, have
not been without their defenders. On the principle of Mill it
is not easy to condemn them, for no one is under the slightest
compulsion to take part in the game, nor is there any con-
cealment or deception connected with them. It has been argued, too, by some who are not disciples of Mill, that public
gambling houses do not make gambling, but only concentrate
it in particular places, and in some measure regulate and even
restrict it. The inveterate gambler will always find occasion
for play. Public play, it is said, is at least conducted with a

fairness which is not always found in secret gambling; and the taxes levied upon it minister largely to the pleasure and the advantage of those who never take part in the game. It is impossible to put down gambling. If it exists, it should at least contribute something to the useful purposes of the State. This can only be effected if it is openly recognised; and a country which derives a large revenue from the sale of spirits in Great Britain, and of opium in India, has not much right to object to such a tax.

These considerations, however, go but a small way as a counterpoise to the vast and terrible sum of ruin, misery and suicide for which the public gaming establishments are responsible. The man to whom gambling is a master passion will, no doubt, always find opportunities for gratifying it, but the gaming establishment attracts thousands of casual gamblers, who would never have sought out a secret haunt. Experience shows that it is among this class that the catastrophes of the gaming-table are most frequent. The habitual gambler, who plays with coolness and with method, usually in some degree succeeds in balancing his losses and his gains. It is the inexperienced, impulsive, uncalculating gambler whose reckless and ignorant play ends most frequently in ruin and suicide. Most, too, of those who are inveterate gamblers were at first only casual gamblers, and imbibed the passion, which gradually became incurable, at the public gambling table. The suppression by law of public gambling establishments may not be as unmixed a benefit, or as great a benefit, as has sometimes been supposed; but when it has been carried out, it has extinguished great centres of highly contagious evil, and, in my opinion, the certain advantages of the measure enormously overbalance its possible evils.

The most difficult of this class of questions, and among the most difficult in the whole range of practical politics, are those connected with the sale of intoxicating drink. They affect in the highest degree the pleasures, the comforts, the liberty, the morals, and the fortunes of the poor, and they affect, in very different ways, vast material as well as moral interests. Immense sums are invested in public-houses. An immense revenue derived from the sale of intoxicating liquors pours into the coffers of the State; while, on the other hand, the mass of improvidence and ruin, of disorder and crime, of depreciation of property, and of police and prison expenditure, which is clearly traceable to excessive drinking, is so great that many persons would shrink from scarcely any measure, however drastic, to prevent it. The most serious questions of principle are involved. Ought the Legislature of a free country to prevent grown-up men from doing what they wish to do, and what they have a perfect natural right to do, because some of them do not use that right with moderation? The public-house is much more to the poor man than his club is to the rich man. Has the State a right to close it against him, either wholly or during the workman's holiday, because a large minority of those who frequent it indulge in excess? If it has such a right, by what authority ought it to be exercised? Ought a majority of ratepayers, consisting largely of men who have never entered a public-house, to impose their will upon the minority who habitually use it? How far has the State, which has an undoubted right to protect itself against actual crime and against wasteful expenditure of public money, a right to wage war against the sources of crime and of the expenditure that springs from crime? What are the legal, and what the moral, claims of the owner of the public-house? and how far and in what direction is the character of the nation likely to be affected by a great measure of forcible repression?

Libraries of no small dimensions might be formed out of the debates, reports, pamphlets, articles, and books relating to this subject. At each succeeding election it assumes a great, and probably an increasing, importance. It has passed very far beyond the region of calm and impartial inquiry. The immense weight both of the public-house vote and of the teetotal vote in every part of the British Isles has placed the question in the very centre of the maëlstrom of party conflict, and vast selfish interests, as well as furious gusts of genuine but often very ignorant fanaticism, contribute to obscure the issue.

It will hardly be expected in a work like the present that I should attempt any exhaustive examination of it, but a few hints and distinctions may perhaps be of use towards forming sound opinions upon it. It must, in the first place, be noticed that the greatly increasing sensitiveness of public opinion to questions of drink is very far from implying that the evil itself is an increasing one. There is strong reason to believe that the exact opposite is the case. A hundred years ago drunkenness was rather the rule than the exception among the upper classes; but with changed habits, and under the stress of public opinion, it has in this section of society almost disappeared. There are, no doubt, still some dissipated circles where it may be found, and most physicians can point to cases among the upper classes of secret drinking, which is perhaps usually of the nature of a disease; yet it is probable that many of my readers may have moved widely and constantly through good society, mingling with men of various tastes, habits, and professions, without having ever seen at a dinner-table a case of positive drunkenness. This vast change in the social life of the nation has not been effected by law, or by restriction, or even by religion, but by the simple change of habits, tastes, and ideals. The thing which was once supposed to be manly or venial has come to be looked on as ungentle-manly and contemptible.

There can be little doubt that a similar change has also taken place, though not to so great an extent, among the poor. The picture which Hogarth drew of Gin Lane, and the pictures which may be constantly found in descriptions of working-class life at the end of the last century and in the early years of the present century, would certainly not be true of our own day. There have, no doubt, been many fluctuations, due to many causes. In France, the hardships of the great war of 1870 are said to have had in this respect a very bad effect, and there have been alarming signs that since that period absinthe, which is one of the most deleterious of intoxicating drinks, has been, with great numbers, superseding wine. In Ireland, the extraordinary improvement that was effected by the noble work and truly saintly character of Father Mathew has not altogether endured, and constant political agitation and an enormous multiplication of grocers' licenses to sell spirits have not been favourable to the cause of temperance. Sudden changes in the rate of wages, in the hours of work, in the system of licensing, have often had a considerable, though usually only a temporary, influence; but, on the whole, there can be little doubt that there has been, during the present century, a marked and progressive improvement in temperance among the working classes. Francis Place, when describing, in 1829, the changes which had taken place among them in the course of his long life, mentioned as one of the most remarkable, that the most skilled and best paid workmen were, in general, the most dissolute when he was young, and had become the most thrifty and sober when he was old.

There is every reason to believe that the change has continued; that the area as well as the amount of habitual drunkenness in proportion to the population has diminished. The better class of workmen are usually a sober class. The improvement in the army has been enormous. Temperance and total abstinence movements have spread far and wide, and the English working classes have learnt the art of sober and tranquil amusement to a degree which, a few decades ago, would have seemed almost incredible. The great increase in the number of committals for drunkenness that sometimes takes place will be usually found to be chiefly due to a stronger sense of the evil, which makes the police and magistrates more stringent in suppressing it. The fact that, after a rise in wages, the consumption of beer and spirits usually increases is no certain proof of the increase of drunkenness. Hardly any one would make this inference from an increased sale of wine; and in the case of the poor, as well as of the rich, increased consumption often mainly means a greater number of moderate drinkers or a greater use of spirits in more diluted forms. No one can question that the working classes of England, in proportion to their numbers, have much more money at their disposal than in the last century, or in the early years of the present century, but very few persons will question that, as a class, they have become much less intemperate. The evil of drunkenness is still a great and a terrible one, but no good purpose is attained by describing it with exaggeration.

Pushing our inquiry further, we shall find that among its causes there are several which may be at least greatly mitigated without any heroic legislation. Miserable homes, and, perhaps to an equal degree, wretched cooking, are responsible for very much; and the great improvement in working-men's dwellings which has taken place in the present generation is one of the best forces on the side of temperance. Much may also be done to diffuse through the British working-classes something of that skill and economy in cookery, and especially in the use of vegetables, in which they are in general so lamentably deficient. If the wives of the poor in Great Britain and Ireland could cook as they can cook in France and in Holland, a much smaller proportion of the husbands would seek a refuge in the public-house. Of all the forms of popular education, this very homely one is perhaps that which is most needed in England, though of late years considerable efforts have been made to promote it.

A large amount of the drunkenness in the community is due to the want of a sufficient amount of nourishing and well-cooked food; and something is also due, in our great towns, to an insufficient supply of pure water. Conditions of labour have also an immense influence. Incessant toil, prolonged for an excessive period, in a close and unhealthy atmosphere, inevitably produces a craving for drink; and it is surely not surprising that men and women growing up from childhood under such influences should seek some short cut to happiness, some moments of emancipating excitement, during which they can throw off the thraldom and the burden of a dreary life.

In England, the great work of placing labour under healthy conditions has been for the most part effected, and factory laws and sanitary reforms have done much to cut off some of the chief sources of intemperance. Another danger, however, has arisen. A people who have few tastes and amusements, and who live in a gloomy, depressing, inclement climate, are not likely to be sober if they have many long hours of leisure at their disposal. The Puritan conception of Sunday, as I have already said, has much to answer for. It has made the one day of rest from toil a very dreary one, and has deprived the poor of the means of acquiring a healthy variety of tastes. A multiplication of such tastes, and of corresponding amusements, is one of the best ways of combating intemperance. If men find other pleasures that satisfy them, they will be much less likely to turn to drink. This is one of the ways in which popular education, even apart from all direct moral teaching, has a moralising effect.

Every institution which cultivates habits of forethought and saving, and stimulates ambition among the working-classes, acts in the same direction. One of the evils to be feared from the modern tendency of trades unions to discourage unusual industry and ability, and to preserve a dead-level of production, is increasing intemperance among the best workmen when they find that superior industry and superior skill lead to no exceptional rewards. Apart from the purely idle and vicious, the classes in England most addicted to drink are those who pursue callings in which work and wages fluctuate violently. Having little habit of providence, they spend in drink the rewards of the days of prosperity.

Turning to another branch of the subject, it is certain that a large amount of drunkenness is due to noxious adulterations. To protect the subject from the sale of adulterated articles is, it appears to me, a most proper, and most important, function of government. It can command the best expert ability, and it can make use of it with complete disinterestedness. To repress fraud is surely one of its most legitimate tasks. It is especially necessary when the fraud is of a kind which the ordinary customer is unable to detect; and no fraud can be more mischievous than that which adulterates beer or spirits for the purpose of making them more intoxicating and deleterious, or of producing a morbid thirst.

The State can also do much to encourage and regulate the trade by the direction it gives to taxation. It is a well-understood and recognised policy that taxes on noxious spirits find their natural limitation in the danger of encouraging illicit distillation or smuggling. In the plain interest of public order there is a necessity for making public-houses licensed bodies, and in licensing legislation there are some obvious distinctions to be borne in mind. The public-house is not merely valued as a place for drinking. It is the poor man's club and hotel, a place for social meeting and enjoyment, a place for business, a place for general refreshment. Coffee-houses deserve the highest encouragement the State can give, for they fulfil many of these purposes without any attendant evil, and if the taste for them spreads widely, the advantages can hardly be overestimated. There is a distinction also to be drawn between places which are simply drink-shops, and places which are also eating-houses and places of general refreshment. One of the mischievous results of the outcry against the recognition of any right of compensation in cases where well-conducted public-houses are suppressed is, that it directly tends to encourage the former class at the expense of the latter. The small drink-shop, which does nothing except sell gin, or whisky, or absinthe, which is usually drunk standing at the counter, represents little outlay of captital, while great sums are expended on the superior house, which has something of the character of an hotel or a club. No one will expend money in this way if he knows that, owing to the condition of the law or of public opinion, he is likely, without any fault or imprudence of his own, to be deprived not only of his profits, but of his capital. Measures which make money invested in public-houses precarious are likely in this way to give these establishments a more pernicious character.

There ought also, it appears to me, to be a broad distinction drawn between beer and spirits. Beer in England, like wine in France, produces much drunkenness; but in each case the use is vastly more common than the abuse, and the existence of these beverages is, on the whole, a blessing, and not an evil, to humanity. This cannot be said of those intoxicating spirits which are most largely drunk. If their abuse is not more common than their use, it is at least so common, and its consequences are so fatal, that the balance is clearly on the side of evil. If a spirit-drinking population could acquire a taste for light and unadulterated beers, this might not be all that a temperance reformer would desire, but it would be at least a great and incontestable improvement. One of the evil results that are found to flow from the indiscriminate prohibition of intoxicating liquors is, that men learn to drink whisky rather than beer, as it is more and more easily smuggled.[27] It was the policy of the Irish Parliament of the eighteenth century to endeavour to discourage the use of spirits by encouraging breweries. It cannot be said that it met with great success; and the well-meant efforts of the imperial Parliament, in 1830, to diminish the consumption of spirits by multiplying beershops appear to have wholly failed.[28] But, in considering the very drastic legislation which is now advocated for restricting or preventing the sale of intoxicating liquors, this distinction between beer and spirits ought not to be forgotten. It would perhaps be carrying refinement too far to distinguish in legislation between spirits which have a direct and powerful influence in stimulating to violence, and intoxicating drugs which, though they may be equally noxious to those who take them, simply stupefy and calm.

It has not been in general usual in England to treat simple drunkenness, which leads to no disorder or violence, as a crime. By two old laws of James I., it is true, it might be punished with a fine of five shillings,[29] and the Licensing Act

---

[27] McKenzie's *Sober by Act of Parliament*, p. 81.

[28] Ibid. p. 142.

[29] 4 Jac. I. c. 5; 21 Jac. I. c. 7. The first Act and part of the second were repealed by 9 George IV. c. 61, s. 35.

of 1872 made all persons found drunk 'on any highway or public place, or on any licensed premises,' liable to a penalty of ten shillings, to be increased on two subsequent convictions.[30] But in England mere drunkards are commonly simply shut up for the night, until they become sober, and then released, though in Scotland the law has been much more stringently enforced.[31] Opinions on this subject are much divided, but it may be noticed that the eminent jurists from many countries who assembled at the Prison Congress at St. Petersburg in 1889, agreed with Mill and Bentham, that mere drunkenness should not be treated as an offence, and that the law should only take cognisance of it when it assumes the form of disorder and violence.[32]

Drunkenness is, indeed, a thing which springs from many different sources, and the first condition of treating it is to form a just estimate of its origin and nature. In many cases, as we have seen, it arises from causes that are partly or wholly preventible. In other, and perhaps more numerous, cases it grows out of a weak, idle, vicious, and degraded nature, and it strengthens every evil tendency that produces it. In not a few cases, too, it is deserving of more pity than of blame, for it is associated with the saddest tragedies of human life. Every clergyman, every parish visitor who has had much contact with the poor, has known such cases. This man, he will tell us, was once a hardworking and sober labourer: he never took to drink till his wife died; till his child went to the bad; till his health broke down; till the long strike or the great commercial depression deprived him of his employment and plunged him into debt; till the savings bank or the building society failed, and swept away the savings of his life. When passing through the zone of deep depression, when life had lost all its colour and its hope, he sought, as men in all ages have done, to escape from his desolation and forget his misery

---

[30] 35 and 36 Vict. c. 94.

[31] See evidence on this subject collected by the Inebriates Committee, 1893.

[32] Ibid. § 1548.

through the fatal power of strong drink. 'It maketh the mind of the king and of the fatherless child to be all one: of the bondman and of the freeman; of the poor man and of the rich. It turneth also every thought into jollity and mirth, so that a man remembereth neither sorrow nor debt; and it maketh every heart rich.'[33]

For this, saddest of all the sources of temptation to drink, there is no effectual remedy; but there is one element in the question which has recently come into great prominence, and is probably destined to colour a good deal of future legislation. I mean the medical aspect of drunkenness. It is now clearly recognised that drunkenness, though it begins as a vice, may soon become a disease—a morbid physical craving which is susceptible of medical treatment. It is a still more startling fact that this disease is hereditary, the children of drunken parents being often born with it. It is probable that in the future history of the world the medical treatment of vice considered as disease will occupy a much larger place than in the past; and restrictions on the sale of spirits will assume a new aspect in the minds of many if the spirit-shop is regarded as the centre and the seed-plot of a serious malady. In one conspicuous instance, indeed, Parliament has been induced by agitation to abandon all attempts to regulate and diminish a terrible disease which is the consequence of vice, but which is at the same time eminently contagious, and spreads its ravages over multitudes who are absolutely innocent. There is, however, less scruple about treating the disease of drunkenness. It was chiefly in the United States that this mode of looking at the subject grew up, and shortly after the middle of the century a large number of inebriate asylums were established, many of them supported by public funds. New York even made a State law empowering certain authorities to commit drunkards to the State inebriate asylum; but the Supreme Court pronounced the measure to be unconstitutional, on the ground that no citizen could be de-

---

[33] 1 Esdras iii. 19–21.

prived of his liberty except for the commission of crime, and that simple drunkenness could not be treated as such.[34]

It is not surprising that the new movement should have produced some exaggeration and much difference of opinion. There have been complaints that a certain school of doctors treat drunkenness as so purely a disease that they wholly fail to recognise its immoral nature, and the hopes of many cures, that were at first held out, appear often to have been too sanguine. But, on the whole, the idea is a true and a fruitful one, and it has rapidly spread.

In 1879 and in 1888 Parliament, adopting, but only to a very partial extent, the recommendations of a Commission which sat in 1872, provided for the detention in retreats for inebriates, for a period not exceeding twelve months, of habitual drunkards who 'make an application for admission.' As might be expected, this measure, though successful within its limits, had no wide application; but a Commission appointed in 1893 has urged upon the Legislature a policy of a much more drastic kind. Supported by a great mass of medical and other expert evidence, it recommends that habitual drunkards, even if they have not committed any actual offence, should be treated as temporary lunatics, and should, on the application of relations and on the sentence of a judge or magistrate, be subjected to compulsory confinement and treatment in State-regulated and State-inspected retreats for a period not exceeding two years. It is proposed that all right of managing their properties should be taken from them during this period; that their property should be made liable for their maintenance; and that, in cases where neither this source of

---

[34] Much evidence on this subject will be found in the parliamentary inquiries of 1872 and of 1893, and in the work on *Habitual Drunkenness* of Dr. Bucknill, who is opposed to this policy. As is well known, it is claimed for hypnotism that it can for long periods make drink distasteful to the drunkard, and, by changing desires, break the power of habit. It is manifest that, if this claim should ultimately prove well established, it may lead to consequences of the highest importance, especially as the habitual drunkard is commonly a person of very feeble will, and therefore peculiarly susceptible of hypnotic influences.

income nor voluntary contributions proved sufficient, the re-treats should be supported by the public rates.[35]

Such recommendations have not yet become law, but they represent a new and startling departure in the history of the question. In dealing also with the numerous cases of drunkenness which actually come before the magistrates, a great change is gradually being effected. The system of short sentences frequently repeated has been emphatically condemned by the best medical, legal, and prison authorities as perfectly useless, and the method of treatment which has been so successfully adopted in dealing with juvenile crime is coming rapidly into favour. Instead of sending a youthful offender for a short period to a prison, he is now generally sent for a much longer period to a reformatory or industrial school; and while the former treatment proved usually useless or pernicious, the latter treatment has effected, in very numerous cases, a real reformation. The Commission of 1893, to which I have referred, proposed that the police should have power to bring before the magistrates all persons found drunk and incapable in public places; that the magistrates should have additional power of binding them for long periods in sureties and recognisances; that reformatory institutions similar in character to those for juvenile offenders should be established, at public expense, in which habitual drunkards may 'be subjected to less rigorous discipline than in existing prisons, and to the performance of such labour as may be prescribed.' It proposed that the magistrates should have the power of sending to such reformatories for lengthened periods, and with or without previous imprisonment, habitual drunkards 'who (*a*) come within the action of the criminal law, (*b*) who fail to find required sureties and recognisances, (*c*) who have been brought up for breach of such recognisances, (*d*) who are proved guilty of ill-treatment or neglect of their wives and families, (*e*) who

---

[35] Report of the Committee of Inebriates (1893). Part of these recommendations bear an evident analogy to the legislation which exists in many continental countries for taking the management of the property of a confirmed spendthrift out of his hands.

have been convicted of drunkenness three or more times within the previous twelve months.'

A legislation of this kind exists in Massachusetts, where isolated cases of drunkenness are generally unpunished, except by a night's imprisonment in the lock-up; but where persistent offenders, who have been repeatedly brought before the magistrate, may be sent to prison for a year, or to a reformatory for a still longer time, or, by the order of the court, to a State hospital for dipsomaniacs.[36] To English ideas, so long a period of imprisonment, in cases where no actual injury was done by the drunkard, would probably at first appear excessive. The reformatory treatment is also open to the objection that it throws a new and considerable expenditure on the public, and is in the last resort a compulsory payment extracted from the sober, primarily at least, for the benefit of the drunk. On the other hand, it is argued that national resources are never better and more fruitfully expended than in restricting or eradicating some great social disease, especially when that disease is productive of an immense amount of crime and of disorder. The proposals of the Commission of 1893 at least rest upon a true view of the evil to be dealt with. They recognise that habitual drunkenness is a disease, a dangerous form of temporary insanity, and that a prolonged treatment is the only rational chance of its cure.

In estimating the connection between crime and drunkenness there are, no doubt, some prevalent exaggerations. It might easily be imagined that England would have almost attained a moral millennium if the whole amount of crime which is, directly or indirectly, traceable to drink were simply subtracted from her criminal records. But those who will compare the crime of England with that of countries where spirit-drinking is almost unknown, and where drunkenness in any form is very rare, will probably suspect that there is some fallacy in this view. They will suspect that, though the extinction of drunkenness would be a vast benefit to England, that

---

[36] See on this law a paper on 'Drink Laws, American or English' (*Times*, August 20, 1895).

benefit would not be quite so great or unalloyed as is sometimes supposed, for it would, probably, often merely lead to a change of vices. In our age, more than in most others, drunkenness prevails chiefly among the incorrigibly idle, worthless, and morally weak. It is from these classes that criminals in all countries naturally spring, and, although the relation between their drunkenness and their crime is often that of cause and effect, it is also very often that of mere coincidence. Still, when all due allowance has been made for such considerations, it is impossible to resist the evidence that the large majority of the crimes of violence and brutality in England are committed by those who are under the influence of drink, and that a great proportion of other crimes, as well as of improvidence, ruin, disease, and insanity, may be clearly traced to the same source. It is this fact that mainly justifies the legislator in dealing with this subject in a very exceptional manner.

The most popular remedy is the partial or total prohibition of the sale of intoxicating liquors, either by a local veto or by a general enactment. I have already indicated some of the arguments against such a policy. It is an attempt to prevent all men from using drink because some men use it in excess. It means, as has been well said, that whenever two men out of three agree to drink no alcohol, they have a right to prevent the third man from doing so. Such coercion must not be confounded with that which is sometimes found necessary in industrial life for the purpose of carrying out the wishes of a majority. If the great majority of shopkeepers desire to shut their shops on a particular day, or if the great majority of workmen wish to leave the factory at a particular hour, they may plausibly argue that the rule should be made universal, as a dissentient minority pursuing a different course would frustrate their desires. But the man who wishes to go to a public-house does not in any degree interfere with the liberty of those who desire to abstain. In practice, too, the restriction is a measure of extreme partiality. The rich man has his private cellar and his club. The poor man only is restrained.

To attempt to guard adult men by law against temptation,

and to place them under a moral tutelage, may, no doubt, in particular instances prevent grave evils, but it is a dangerous precedent and a bad education for the battle of life. There is a specious aspect of liberalism in a proposal to submit such questions to a popular vote; but in truth this is a pure delusion. The essence of real liberty is that every adult and sane man should have the right to pursue his own life and gratify his own tastes without molestation, provided he does not injure his neighbours, and provided he fulfils the duties which the State exacts from its citizens. If, under these conditions, he mismanages his life, the responsibility and the penalty will fall upon himself; but in a perfectly free State the law has no right to coerce him. Violations of liberty do not lose their character because they are the acts, not of kings or aristocracies, but of majorities of electors. It is possible, as many are coming to think, that unqualified freedom is a less good thing than our fathers imagined; that other things may be more really important, and that it is needful and expedient in many ways to restrain and curtail it. But at least men should do so with their eyes open, without sophistry, and without disguise. The strong tendency to coercive laws on all matters relating to intoxicating liquors, to the restriction of freedom of contract, to the authoritative regulation of industry in all its branches, which is so apparent in modern democracy, may be a good or a bad thing, but it is certainly not a tendency in the direction of liberty.

As I have already said, it is manifest that local option may mean the restriction of the liberty of the classes who use public-houses by the classes who never use them, and never need to use them. It is sometimes said, that it only means a transfer of the power of control from a small oligarchy of magistrates to a democratic vote. But this argument is more plausible than just. Magistrates act in this matter in a judicial capacity, with a judicial sense of responsibility, under the restrictions of well-defined precedent, under the supervision and control of the central government. No such restraints are likely to be observed in a popular vote. In questions, also, in which religious passions are strongly enlisted on one side, popular votes are peculiarly apt to be deceptive. Those who are urged by a genuine religious fanaticism will all vote, while great numbers of electors, who themselves never enter a public-house, but who have no wish to suppress it, will be indifferent, and will abstain. On the other hand, the districts where drunkenness is most prevalent, and the spirit interest most inordinately strong, are precisely those in which the local veto can never be obtained.

But for good or for evil, the tendency of opinion throughout the English-speaking world is evidently in favour of increased restriction in this field. It is remarkable, however, that this tendency is much less strong in England than in the other portions of the British Isles, or in the English-speaking communities beyond the water. The long discipline of Puritan Sabbatarianism in Scotland, and the complete empire of the Catholic priesthood over their congregations in Ireland, have made those portions of the Empire more tolerant of coercive laws in the interests of sobriety than England. In the general election of 1895 the temperance question was only one of several questions that were at issue, but there can be little doubt that the support which the Government of Lord Rosebery had given to local veto contributed materially to the result. The restriction of the hours of public-houses, however, both in England and elsewhere, has been generally acquiesced in, and appears to have had a real and beneficial influence; and Irish and Scotch opinion unquestionably supports the more extensive measure of closing public-houses absolutely on Sunday. This policy was introduced into Scotland in 1854, into Ireland in 1877, and into Wales in 1882, and it prevails in nearly all the Colonies. Few men will now agree with Robert Lowe and the more rigid school of Free-traders, that the drink trade should be left to the simple operation of supply and demand. The disorder, the adulteration, the enormous drunkenness growing out of such freedom, have persuaded nearly every one that stringent regulation and inspection are imperatively needed. Very numerous public-houses do not simply satisfy an existing want. They also stimulate and increase it; and men who are certainly not fanatics believe that the number of drink-shops in Great Britain, and still more in Ireland, is now enormously excessive, and that few more demoralising measures have been carried than that which brought the grocers' shops into the number. But in England, as in most other countries, the difficulties in remedying the evil are very great, and they are complicated, on the one hand by the presence of colossal vested interests wielding an immense political power, and on the other by a fierce fanaticism which will admit no compromise, and which is supported by all the power of great religious organisations.

In the United States, the most various experiments in restricting or prohibiting the sale of intoxicating liquors have been tried, but the extreme fluctuations of legislation and the great conflict of testimony seem to show that no very clear success has been attained. The separate States have an almost absolute power of dealing with the question, and they have adopted widely different policies. The problem in America is, in some respects, different from what it is in England. In the American climate, according to the best medical authorities, the moderate use of alcoholic and fermenting liquors is less beneficial than in England, and the abuse is more rapidly attained and is more gravely deleterious. Drunkenness, too, arises specially from spirits. Except among German immigrants, beer is much less drunk than in England, and wine is much less drunk than on the Continent of Europe. There is also a widespread custom of excluding all strong drinks from repasts, and the greater part of drinking takes place separately at the drinking-bar of the saloon.

The Prohibitionist party is large and powerful, it is ardently supported by the ministers of the chief religious denominations, and most of these ministers are themselves total abstainers. The policy of absolutely prohibiting the sale of intoxicating liquors used to be generally known in England as the Maine Law, it having been enacted in that State in 1851, extended in its operations in 1877, and made a portion of the State Constitution in 1884. It has, however, been much more

widely adopted, but has also, after trial, been frequently abandoned. At the close of 1894 there were seven States in which
the manufacture and sale of spirituous and malt beverages
were forbidden, though the citizens of those States may obtain
them for their own private use from other States. Nine or ten
other States had tried prohibition and abandoned it, and they
include some of the most important and populous States of the
Union—among others, Massachusetts and Rhode Island.

In general, it appears evident that the prohibitory system
can only work, with any approximation to success, in thinly
populated territories. Wherever it is tried it is followed by an
enormous amount of evasion and smuggling, and the spirits
that are smuggled are usually of the worst and most intoxicating description; but many good authorities think
that, under favourable circumstances, it has, on the whole,
diminished the amount of intoxication. In the great centres of
population, however, the system produces so much opposition, unpopularity, and riot, that it has been nearly everywhere abandoned. The system which has there been generally
adopted has been what is called high licensing, usually coupled with some measure of local option. Very much higher fees
than in England are charged for licensing public-houses, and
the number is usually limited in a defined proportion to the
population. It is contended that this system produces a better
class of houses, and gives their owners stronger reasons for
abstaining from any act that might forfeit the license. In Massachusetts there is an annual vote in every township and city
on the question whether licenses should be granted. There are
also in America many laws closing public-houses on Sundays
and on election days, prohibiting the sale of intoxicating liquors to particular classes of persons and the employment of
women at drinking-bars, and even, in some States, making the
seller of intoxicating liquors liable for damages on account of
injurious acts committed by drunkards. In some States the
magistrates, or even private friends, may prohibit the saloon-
keepers under penalty from serving a confirmed drunkard
with drink. Political motives and interests play a gigantic part

in all American legislation on this subject. The 'saloon-keeper' is a great personage, both in local and general politics, and the great variety and complexity of the laws in the different States, the frequent changes they undergo, the enormous extent to which they are evaded, and the extreme conflict of testimony about their results, make it very difficult to arrive at any definite conclusion. On the whole, the consumption of intoxicating liquors per head seems to have increased since the era of repressive legislation began; but this is probably much more due to the number and the habits of the foreign immigrants than to any influence of the law.[37]

The British colonies in America have followed very much in the same lines as the United States. They are said to be, on the whole, more sober than any other portion of the English-speaking world, and the Prohibitionist party is unusually strong. An Act known as the Scott Act, which was carried in 1878, provided that, on the petition of a quarter of the electors of any town or city, a direct vote should be taken on the question whether it should be placed under the provisions of the Act. If a bare majority of the voters desired it, the question was decided for three years. In that case all public-house licenses lapsed at the end of the year without compensation to the owners, and the ordinary manufacture and sale of intoxicating liquors as a beverage were absolutely prohibited. At first this law was adopted very widely and by large majorities; but in a few years the amount of smuggling and the amount of unpopularity produced a reaction, and over the greater part of the country the old licensing system was resumed. Grave questions arose about the relative rights of the Dominion Parliament and the provincial Parliaments to deal with this question. In the North-Western Territory of Canada the dissension

---

[37] See Fanshawe, *Liquor Legislation in the United States*; McKenzie's *Sober by Act of Parliament*; the Foreign Office report (1894) on Liquor Traffic Legislation in the United States since 1889; and excellent article by Dr. Gould in the *Forum*, March 1894; and two papers on 'Drink Laws, American and English,' in the *Times*, August 16 and 20, 1895. See, too, Bryce's *American Constitution*, ii. 350, iii. 280–81.

was especially formidable. A prohibitory law had been imposed on this vast territory by the Dominion Parliament, in the first instance, it is said, chiefly for the benefit of the Indians, but when the white population increased it became exceedingly unpopular. Smuggling and evasion of every kind took enormous proportions; and here, as elsewhere, it was observed that the smuggled drink was usually of the most noxious and intoxicating description. This state of things continued for nearly ten years. At last the Dominion Parliament, after repeated memorials from the territorial Legislature, gave that body the power of dealing with the question, and the immediate result was that the prohibitory system was swept away, and replaced by the system of licenses.[38] During the last few years, however, the Prohibitionist party is said to have increased in Canada, and extensive petitions have been set on foot in many districts petitioning for severer enactments.[39]

In New Zealand, much drastic legislation on the drink question had been carried. It falls in with the strong tendency to State Socialism which is there so conspicuous, and it is especially easy of enforcement in a well-to-do colony where there

---

[38] An interesting article on this struggle, by Mr. T. C. Doon, will be found in the *Nineteenth Century*, May 1895.

[39] McKenzie's *Sober by Act of Parliament*, pp. 75–91. See, too, Dilke's *Problems of Greater Britain*, ii. 430–40.

In a speech delivered at Bath, May 28, 1895, Lord Lansdowne gave the following account of the working of the Scott Act during his Administration:—'In Canada, while he had the honour of being connected with the Government of that country, a very strong temperance Act, known as the Scott Act, was in operation. In 1886, no fewer than sixty-three counties had adopted it, but by the year 1893 forty-three of them had abandoned it; whilst in the great province of Ontario, out of forty-one counties, twenty-five had adopted it by the year 1885, and the whole of them had abandoned it four years afterwards. In the meantime there had been bitter animosities, constant evasion of the law, contraband dealing, and the substitution of dangerous intoxicants for more harmless and bulky fluids; the spy and the informer had plied their trade, and there was corruption among the officials and perjury in the law courts, until at last the people rose as one man and emancipated themselves from the tyranny which had been imposed upon them' (*The Times*, May 30, 1895).

are no great cities, and where the whole population but slightly exceeds 700,000 souls. The principle of local option, making the issue and increase of licenses dependent on a popular vote, is here stringently carried out. It was introduced by a law of 1873, and has taken new forms, which it is not necessary to describe in detail, by Acts which were carried in 1881, in 1889, and 1893. Three questions are submitted to the electors in each district at the local option poll: whether the present number of licenses is to continue, whether the number is to be reduced, whether any licenses are to be granted. Nearly the whole adult population, male and female, have votes; but there is a provision, which is proved to have considerable importance as a safeguard against sudden change, that unless half the voters on the roll record are present the poll is void, and matters continue as they were. If the requisite number of voters is attained, a bare majority can carry the first two questions, and if a reduction of the number of licenses is voted, and elected committee have the right to carry it out to the extent of one-fourth. The third question, which involves the absolute prohibition of licenses in a given district, can only be carried in the affirmative by a three-fifths vote. No increase in the number of licenses is to be allowed until after the next census, or then unless the population has increased twenty-five per cent., and unless the voters of the district desire it by a three-fifths vote. In that case one license may be granted for every increase of 700 inhabitants. In New Zealand, as in several other colonies, Sunday closing and the prohibition of the sale of drink to young persons, and to persons who have been found guilty of intoxication, are stringently enforced.[40]

One fact which is very apparent in New Zealand is, that the enfranchisement of women which has lately taken place is likely to have a great importance on this question. It is ob-

---

[40] A good account of the New Zealand legislation up to the end of 1893 (beyond which I do not go) will be found in an essay by Mr. Hazelden, Under-Secretary for Justice, in the *New Zealand Official Year Book*, 1894, pp. 256–60; see, too, McKenzie, pp. 92–103, and Dilke's *Problems of Greater Britain*, ii. 441–42.

served that the overwhelming majority of female votes is given in favour of repressive measures, some desiring a reduction of the number of licenses, but the very large majority demanding their absolute suppression. The increase which they have given to the Prohibitionist vote, and the vehemence with which women have thrown themselves into this cause, appear to have considerably altered its prospects. In Canada the same thing has been observed. Plebiscites which have no legal force, but which are intended to influence the Legislature, have been lately taken in numerous districts upon the question whether a law should be passed prohibiting throughout Canada the importation, manufacture, and sale of all intoxicating liquors as a beverage. It is stated that the female votes were six to one for prohibition.[41] Those who have observed the attitude taken on this subject by most female political organisations and conferences in England, will scarcely doubt that the same spirit exists at home. On the drink question, as well as on several others affecting amusements, industries, and the habits of social life, the increasing political influence of women is likely to be followed by a greatly increased tendency towards legislative interference and coercion.

I do not propose to examine in detail the legislation of the other colonies, but the importance of the Australian ones is so great that their treatment of the drink question may be briefly referred to. No serious attempt has been made to carry out the policy of prohibition, though in some of these colonies it may be accomplished by a local veto; but the principle of local option, limiting the number of licenses in a given district, generally prevails, though with considerable variations of detail and with different degrees of stringency. Nearly all these local option laws are of very recent origin, having grown up since 1880. Victoria differs from the other colonies in giving compensation in cases where a license is withdrawn. This compensation is derived exclusively from the trade, and is

---

[41] McKenzie's *Sober by Act of Parliament*, pp. 87, 92, 98.

raised by increasing licensing fees and penalties for breaches of the liquor law, and, where this is not sufficient, by a special tax on spirits. As the reader will remember, this policy is sub-stantially the same as that which Mr. Goschen attempted in 1890, without success, to carry in England. Several minor measures against intoxication, imitated from American and New Zealand legislation, exist in Australia; but the main defence against excessive drinking is found in the limitation of the number of licenses and in the enforcement of Sunday closing.[42]

In the Scandinavian countries, where drinking habits had attained an appalling height, the evil has of late years been dealt with by some very instructive and, on the whole, successful legislation. Before 1855 almost complete practical free trade in spirits existed in Sweden; but in that year it was abol-ished, private distilleries were forbidden, and the sale of spir-its was put under strict municipal and parochial control. Ten years later a new policy was adopted in the town of Gothen-burg, which was speedily imitated in other towns. Its object was to put an end both to the competition and the adulteration in the spirit trade, by depriving the retailer of all interest in the spread in intemperance. As the licenses of public-houses fell in, many of them were suppressed, and those which the mu-nicipality considered it desirable to maintain were placed in the hands of a limited liability company, consisting of the most respectable members of the community, who bound them-selves by their charter not to derive any profit to themselves from the sale of spirits, and to pay the whole profits beyond the ordinary rate of interest on the paid-up capital to the town treasury. All persons entrusted by the company with the man-agement of public-houses are strictly bound to sell no spirits and wines that do not come from the company's stores, and therefore none that are not unadulterated, and to sell them solely for account of the company and without any profit to themselves. They are, at the same time, permitted to sell in

---

[42] See Dilke and McKenzie.

these establishments malt liquors, coffee, tea, soda and seltzer waters, cigars and food, for their private profit. The object of the system is to make it the interest of the manager to induce his customers to abstain from spirits, and to consume non-intoxicating or only slightly intoxicating drinks. Malt liquors and wine were left untaxed, and until 1874 they were exempt from the local control under which spirits were placed.

Such are the outlines of this remarkable system, which has very justly attracted the attention of all serious moderate reformers. In the words of an American writer who has studied it with peculiar care: 'If liquor must be sold—and few, even of the most ardent Prohibitionists, will deny that it will continue to be for some time yet—is it not vastly better to take the traffic from the control of the present lower element of society, who conduct it for private gain, and place it in the hands of reputable men with no economic interests to serve, and whose dominating purpose will be its restriction to the lowest possible minimum?'[43]

I cannot now undertake to enter at length into the controversies that have gathered around the Gothenburg plan. It is certain that its adoption was followed by an immense decrease of drunkenness, which continued for some years. The system, however, does not pretend to prevent those from drinking who desire to do so, and, when condition of wages and work tended strongly in the direction of intemperance, the old habit in some degree resumed its sway. It seems to be admitted that the great and sudden improvement effected in Sweden has not wholly been maintained, and the number of convictions for drunkenness has of late increased. How far this is due to a real increase of drunkenness, or to the increased activity of the police, it is difficult to say. It is certain, however, that intemperance is vastly less than before the Gothenburg system was introduced; that the consumption of spirits has shrunk to a mere fraction of its former amount;

---

[43] Dr. E. R. L. Gould in the *Forum*, March 1894. This able writer has also written a report for the American Government on the Gothenburg system.

and that the drunkenness which exists comes mainly from the increased consumption of beer, which lies in a great degree outside the system, though a measure has very recently been enacted limiting its free sale. The general substitution of beer for spirits has been one of the most marked results of the Gothenburg system. The local testimonies recognising it as a great mitigating and regulating agency are overwhelmingly strong, and it was adopted, with some slight modifications, by Norway in 1871.[44]

In Switzerland, intemperance had risen to an enormous height, and a very drastic measure was enacted for the purpose of checking it in 1887. It gave the Federal Government complete control over the production and importation of spirits. Private distilling, which had before been largely carried on, was forbidden, and the State became the one wholesale spirit-merchant. The drinking-shops were untouched by the Federal law, except that they were obliged to receive their spirits from the State and to sell a pure quality at an enhanced price. It was provided that a fourth part of the spirits should be distilled in Switzerland; that the profits of the monopoly should be distributed among the different cantons; and that at least one-tenth of the surplus revenue should be employed in some way calculated to counteract the evil effects of alcohol. It is usually employed in educational and charitable institutions, and some part of it in support of institutions for the cure of intoxication. Another part of the same policy was

---

[44] There is a large literature on this subject, but the reader will find all essential facts in the very full evidence that was given before the Commission on Intemperance in 1877, and in the writings of Dr. Gould. Among the writings in opposition to the scheme I may mention Dr. Wilson Turnbull's *Law and Liquor*, a lecture delivered at Edinburgh in 1873, and *The Gothenburg Licensing System*, by Bailie Lewis. An interesting series of articles on the Norwegian legislation about intemperance appeared in the *Saturday Review* of June 1893. This legislation has very recently been somewhat modified and extended. The most important difference between the Swedish and Norwegian systems seems to be, that in the former the profits of the drink traffic go to the municipal treasury, and in the latter to works of charity and public utility.

the abolition of the cantonal and communal duties on wine and beer.

In accordance with the provisions of the Swiss Constitution, this policy was submitted at two different stages of its progress to popular approbation by the Referendum, and in each case it was sanctioned by an overwhelming majority. The chief opposition naturally came from the native distillers; but they were compensated for the diminished value of their buildings and plant, though not for the loss of profits. It was alleged, however, that not more than one fourth part of the spirits consumed in Switzerland before the new law was enacted was of home manufacture, and the provision in the law guaranteeing that this proportion should be still maintained protected the native distillers from very serious loss. It is claimed for this measure that it has been a great success. The monopoly has produced to the State a large revenue, the quality of spirits sold is more pure, and it is stated that, on account of the enhanced price, the consumption has been reduced by from twenty to twenty-five per cent.[45]

In South Carolina, a law was carried in December 1892 which belongs to the same class of legislation as the Scandinavian and Swiss laws. It gave the State a monopoly of the sale of spirits, which were analysed by a State analyst, and sold under rigid conditions, in State dispensaries, by State officials who derived no personal profit from an increased sale. The sale was restricted to the daytime. The spirits were not to be drunk on the premises, and ample precautions were taken to prevent the dispensaries from being unduly numerous and becoming, like the old drinking-saloons, centres of gambling and immorality. The measure appears to have been,

---

[45] A full and interesting account of the working of the Swiss law will be found in an article by Mr. King in the *Economic Review,* April 1893. See, also, an essay on *The Alcohol Question in Switzerland,* by W. Milliet, published by the American Academy of Political and Social Science, and *Le Monopole de l'Alcohol en Suisse,* par Henri Ascaud, reprinted from the *Bulletin de la Société de Législation Comparée.* This last writer disapproves of the Swiss policy.

in the first instance, designed as a means to raising an additional State revenue, but its bearing on the temperance question is very obvious. It did not, however, exist long enough for us to form any clear judgment of its effects, for it was declared unconstitutional by the Supreme Court.[46]

Legislation of this type, providing that intoxicating liquors should be pure in quality, reducing their sale to moderate limits, and eliminating at once the motive of personal interest on the part of the seller and many concomitant evils that usually accompany the sale, may do very much to diminish the evil of intemperance. Such legislation conflicts far less than measures of prohibition and severe repression with vested rights and with individual liberty, and experience seems to show that it would, from an economical point of view, be very profitable to the State. In addition, however, to the considerable but not insuperable difficulties of applying it to our exisiting system, and in addition to the opposition it would meet from great property interests, it would have to encounter a kind of religious fanaticism which is peculiarly strong in England, and especially strong among the more extreme advocates of temperance. It is no exaggeration to say that a large number of these would rather see all the evils springing from alcohol unchecked and unmitigated than see the Government directly concerned in the trade; and, by a curious anomaly, this feeling will be found among multitudes who are always prepared to support the imposition for public purposes of heavy taxation on spirituous liquors. Few persons who watch the signs of the times will doubt that further legislation on this subject will soon be made. It is probable that licensing will pass from the hands of the magistrates to those of county and town councils, or of boards elected for this purpose, and that districts will obtain a greater power of limiting the number of public-houses.

Whether the policy of absolutely suppressing the liquor

---

[46] Foreign Office report on Liquor Legislation in the United States since 1889 (1894). See, too, Dr. Gould's essay in the *Forum*, November 1894, pp. 342–45.

trade, which is advocated by the United Kingdom Alliance, will receive any measure of legislative sanction is more doubtful. It is a policy, as it seems to me, fraught with danger. If it is in any degree adopted, it should be applied solely to those spirituous drinks which are so plainly pernicious that they may be looked upon as having some affinity to poison, and even in these cases it should be applied with much caution. Unless supported by an overwhelming preponderance of public opinion, it is certain to fail. The majority required should be much more than a simple majority, and gradual, experimental, temporary legislation should precede measures of a wide and permanent character. The indirect influences diminishing intemperance are likely to be more efficacious than direct measures, and a law is only really successful when it acts in harmony with a prevailing tendency of habits and opinions.

Public opinion, and especially working-class public opinion, in Great Britain seems on the whole, and to an increasing degree, to approve of the policy of gradually diminishing by legislative measures the temptation to drink. To this kind of legislation belong the various laws restricting its sale on Sundays, on holidays or half-holidays, and in the late hours of the night, and also the Act of 1883 prohibiting the payment of wages in public-houses. A recent and characteristic example will be found in the Act of 1894 establishing parish councils in England. Every one knows how large a proportion of the public business of the upper and middle classes in England is transacted in hotels. But in the Parish Councils Act, which conferred on electors who are chiefly very poor men enormous powers of taxation, administration, and control, a special clause was inserted to prevent these councils from meeting, except in case of absolute necessity, in premises licensed to sell intoxicating liquors. The provision was probably a wise one, but it illustrates curiously the position which modern democracy assigns to the working classes—so largely trusted to govern others, so little trusted to govern themselves.

The connection between morals and religion on the one

side, and legislation and administration on the other, is a wide subject, leading to many different fields. Difficult questions constantly arise about the attitude Government should assume towards spectacles, amusements, and customs which, though they may not be absolutely vicious in themselves, have a debasing tendency, and easily or generally become occasions of vice. It is impossible, I think, to lay down any inflexible rule on the subject. Each case must be judged according to its particular circumstances, and one of the most important of these circumstances is the state of public opinion. The presumption in favour of repression is strongest where these things are obtruded on those who never sought them. I have stated in the last chapter my belief that placards assailing any form of religious belief ought not to be permitted in the public streets. On the same principle, solicitations to vice, indecent pictures and advertisements or spectacles in such places, call for a more stringent repression than they always receive. The State cannot undertake to guarantee the morals of its citizens, but it ought at least to enable them to pass through the streets without being scandalised, tempted, or molested. The same rule applies to improper advertisements in public journals which are the common reading of all classes and the general channels of information, and also to vicious writings when they are hawked through the streets, thrust prominently into public notice, or sent unasked to private houses. It applies also to some things which have no connection with morals: to unnecessary street noises which are the occasion of acute annoyance to numbers; to buildings which destroy the symmetry and deface the beauty of a quarter, or darken the atmosphere by floods of unconsumed smoke; to the gigantic advertisements by which private firms and vendors of quack remedies are now suffered to disfigure our public buildings, to destroy the beauty both of town and country, and to pursue the traveller with a hideous eyesore for hundreds of miles from the metropolis. This great evil has vastly increased in our day, and it urgently requires the interposition of the Legislature.

But while in all these fields the presumption in favour of legislative interference and repression is very strong, it becomes weaker in the case of things which are done in buildings which no one need enter unless he pleases; and it becomes still weaker in the case of things that are withdrawn from publicity and confined to private houses or associations. In such cases the individual citizen has a *primâ facie* right to judge for himself, as long as he abstains from injuring or molesting his neighbours. This right may be overridden by the law, but there must be strong reasons to justify it.

Another important group of questions connected with our present subject relate to the marriage law, which has been passing during the last century, to a remarkable degree, from a theological to a secular basis. It would lead me too far to enter here into the very curious and instructive history of the growth of the Christian conception of marriage, in which Roman law and German customs have borne perhaps quite as large a part as purely theological influence, and of the great fluctuations, both of principles and practice, which it presents.[47] It will here be sufficient to say that it was only very slowly that the Church acquired a complete control over this field. The civil law of the early Christian emperors and of the early period of the Middle Ages diverges widely from the ecclesiastical conception of marriage, and for a long period of Christian history no religious ceremony of any kind was deemed by the Church necessary for its validity. At an early period of the Church's history it was customary for the priest to give his blessing to a marriage, but it was not pretended that this was essential, and it was far from being universal. According to the doctrine of the Church, the simple consent of the two parties, without any ceremony, constituted a valid marriage.

In the Middle Ages a religious ceremony appears to have been made obligatory by law, and marriages without the in-

---

[47] I have examined this subject in some detail in the concluding chapter of my *History of European Morals.*

tervention of a priest were considered clandestine and irregular; but they frequently occurred, and their validity was perfectly undisputed. In order to put an end to the very numerous abuses growing out of clandestine marriages, the Council of Trent, for the first time, made the celebration of marriage by a priest essential to its validity, and introduced various other regulations connected with it. Its decree did not apply to marriages that had already been contracted, and, in countries where the discipline of the Council had not been formally promulgated, the old doctrine still prevailed, according to which the simple consent of the two parties established a marriage. It still survives in the marriage law of Scotland, where a simple, well-attested declaration of the two parties in each other's presence, or a promise to marry proved by writing and followed by cohabitation, constituted a valid marriage. By an Act of 1856 the further condition was added that one of the parties must have resided, immediately before the marriage, at least twenty-one days in Scotland. In the United States, also, where the marriage law is determined independently by the different States, the same principle is widely adopted. Marriage rests on the English common law, which, in its turn, rests on the canon law, and no ceremony, religious or civil, is necessary to its validity, though certain civil formalities are enjoined by law, and though religious ceremonies are almost always performed.[48]

From a very early period there was a distinction, and in some degree a conflict, between the ecclesiastical and the civil views of marriage. The Church proclaimed marriage to be a sacrament, and therefore wholly within its domain. It declared it to be absolutely indissoluble. It claimed the right of determining the conditions of its validity, and of varying those conditions by Papal dispensations; and from the period of the Council of Trent it made, as a general rule, its direct participation essential to the existence of a valid marriage among Catholics. Nor, indeed, is it at all certain that this doctrine

---

[48] See *Revue de Droit International*, ii. 69–71, 243–50.

applied only to Catholics. It is the opinion of a powerful school of Catholic theologians, that in countries like France, in which the discipline of the Council of Trent has been duly promulgated, all marriages of Protestants are simple concubinage; that they are completely destitute of validity; and that, if one of the parties becomes a Catholic, the pretended marriage may be broken, and the convert may be allowed to contract a new marriage.[49] An exception must be made in the case of Holland, for Benedict XIV., in 1741, in order to avoid 'greater evils,' decreed that in that country marriages not celebrated according to the provisions of the Council of Trent should be deemed valid.[50] This, however, appears to be the only clear exception. In other countries where the discipline of the Council has been promulgated it is a widely received doctrine that Protestant marriages are simple concubinage.[51]

The Church, however, is acknowledged by one of its most accredited expositors to have used 'dissimulation and tolerance' in this matter, and the doctrine is rarely put forward, except when the prospect of breaking a marriage may be made

---

[49] This subject is treated at length by Perrone, who is, I believe, the most accredited Ultramontane writer on the subject (*De Matrimonio Christiano*, in a chapter on the power of the Church over the marriage of heretics, ii. pp. 199–274).

[50] Perrone, ii. pp. 205–6, 223.

[51] 'Possem alia non pauca documenta ejusmodi proferre . . . quæ omnia in unam eamdemque sententiam conspirant, nimirum nulla esse conjugia, quæ in Galliis quovis tempore ab hæreticis inter se celebrata sunt, sive obtinuerint sive non obtinuerint statum quem civilem vocant. Apostolica sedes semper sibi constans fuit in rejiciendis uti nullis ac invalidis ejusmodi hæreticorum connubiis, eo quod ex una parte illi constiterit ab initio in universis provinciis decretum tridentinum *Tametsi* publicatum fuisse; ex altera vero benedictinam decretalem an. 1741 pro Hollandia statibusque fœderatis Belgii datam, sine speciali ejuscem sedis extensione ad alias regiones ius commune non immutare. . . . Quæ de Galliis diximus, eadem de aliis regionibus sive catholicis sive acatholicis sive mixtis dici debent, adeo ut generale sit principium, conjugia sive hæreticorum sive mixta, ubi publicatum fuit decretum tridentinum *Tametsi* et quo benedictina constitutio pro Hollandia speciali ratione ab apostolica sede extensa non est, esse irrita ac nulla' (Ibid. ii. 225–26).

an inducement to or a reward of conversion, or a favour to
the Catholic partner in a mixed marriage. Two remarkable
cases of this kind occurred in Brazil in 1847 and about 1856.
In the first case a Catholic woman had been married to a
Protestant in Paris. They had been married civilly, and also
before a Protestant minister, and they afterwards emigrated
to Brazil. Six or seven years later the woman conceived a
desire to marry a Catholic, and, having consulted the ecclesiastical authorities, they pronounced that she had full liberty
to do so, as her marriage with her present reputed husband
was null and void.[52] In the other case, which led to a change
in the marriage law of Brazil, a Swiss Protestant and a German
Protestant had been, as they imagined, duly married by the
Evangelical pastor at Rio Janeiro. The woman was converted
to Catholicism. Twelve years after her marriage she desired
to take another husband, and the Bishop of Rio Janeiro pronounced that, her former marriage being null, she had a right
to do so.[53] Other examples of the same kind have been cited;
but the theologian who is supposed to represent with the
highest authority the true Ultramontane doctrine in its sanctity and purity, acknowledges that opinions are not agreed on
the subject, and he dilates upon the moderation of the Church
and the discriminating manner in which she has used her
power to break unpleasant marriages as a special instance of
her benevolence.[54]

---

[52] Ibid. ii. 229.

[53] *Revue de Droit International*, ii. 252. Perrone does not mention this case,
but he gives some other curious instances. See also much evidence on
the subject in Mr. Oscar Watkins's treatise on *Holy Matrimony*, chap. viii.

[54] Ecclesia mitissima se cum hæreticis ratione se gessit ac gerit. Nullam
unquam iis hac de causa molestiam intulit aut infert. Dissimulatione
passim ac tolerantia utitur, ac si quid ex hac doctrina et praxi provenit,
vertitur demum in bonum ipsorum acatholicorum, si quando contingat
eos in ecclesiæ catholicæ sinum redire, dum ipsis indulgetur, ita poscen-
tibus rerum adjunctis, vel ob mutua dissidia, vel ob separationem ab
invicem, aliaque ejusmodi, novas inire nuptias, uti ex non paucis reso-
lutionibus liquet, aut proprium instaurare conjugium si ambo conver-
tantur conjuges' (Perrone, ii. 245). Mr. Gladstone has made some
remarks on this passage which seem to me just (*Vaticanism*, pp. 28–29).

While however, the Church claims a complete control over the conditions of a valid marriage, as distinguished from the civil consequences that may flow from it, the State, even in Catholic countries, has rarely admitted this claim to its full extent. Marriage, according to the legislators, in its legal aspect, is essentially a civil contract, and as such it falls within their dominion. The State claims for itself the power of determining the conditions on which it alone can be recognised and these conditions are not always those of the Church.

In most countries a compromise was made between these views. Thus, in France before the Revolution, Pothier proclaimed marriage to be in the eyes of the law a civil contract just as emphatically as Blackstone did in England. He declared that the form of marriage prescribed by the Council of Trent was very wise, and was accordingly adopted and confirmed by the ordinances of the kings, but that, 'nevertheless, the Council exceeded its power in declaring null by its sole authority contracts of marriage in which that form was not observed; for marriages, in as far as they are contracts, belong, like all other contracts, to the political order, and they are therefore within the competence of the secular power, and not in that of the Council, and it does not belong to the latter to decree about their validity or invalidity.'[55] Marriage, however, by the law of France could only be celebrated by a priest, though this provision was not introduced into French law till sixteen years after the decree of the Council of Trent. Divorce was absolutely prohibited. Canonical impediments to marriage were fully recognised. The religious ceremony became a civil act. The care of the official registers of marriages was confided by the civil powers to the clergy; and between the repeal of the Edict of Nantes and the reign of Louis XVI. the only Protestants whose marriages were fully recognised by law were those of Alsace, who had special privileges granted to them by the Treaty of Munster. On the other hand, the priests, in all the civil parts of marriage, were regarded by the law as delegates of the civil power. Papal dispensations in

---

[55] Pothier, *Du Contrat de Mariage*, Part iv. c. 1, s. 4.

matrimonial cases were not recognised unless they were confirmed by the King. There was in some cases a right of appeal
to the Parliament. The State insisted upon conditions of its
own. It especially required the consent of parents, following
in this respect the Roman law, though the Council of Trent
had anathematised those who maintained that marriages
without such consent are invalid.[56]

In most Protestant countries, also, the strong feeling that
marriage should be an indissoluble and a religious contract
maintained the old Catholic conception. Marriage, it is true,
ceased to be a sacrament; while, on the other hand, the slur
which was thrown on it by the celibacy of the priests and by
the superior sanctity ascribed to virginity was abolished. Usually marriages were celebrated by the ministers of the different
denominations. In England, a law of Henry VIII. declared that
all persons may lawfully marry who are not prohibited by
God's law; it settled the degrees in which marriage is permitted
in accordance with the Levitical law, and it pronounced full
and perfect marriage to be indissoluble. Before the Marriage
Act of 1753, and in accordance with the common law, marriages contracted by simple consent and followed by cohabitation were deemed valid without any religious ceremony,
though they did not bring with them all the civil consequences
of marriages celebrated in the church, and exposed those who
contracted them to some ecclesiastical censure and penalties.
During the Commonwealth marriages were purely civil, being
celebrated by the justices of the peace; and a law of Charles II.
pronounced these marriages to be valid without any fresh
solemnisation.[57] Divorce, even in cases of adultery, was not
permitted by law. Much discussion on the subject had arisen
in the reign of Edward VI. The wife of the Marquis of Northampton having been convicted of adultery, her husband obtained a separation *a mensa et thoro,* and he claimed the right
of remarriage. The question was submitted to a commission
of ten bishops, presided over by the Archbishop of Canter-

---

[56] Glasson, *Le Mariage Civil et le Divorce* (1879), pp. 34–37.

[57] 12 Car. II. c. 33.

bury, who proceeded to examine at great length the ecclesiastical precedents on the subject. While the examination was still unfinished Lord Northampton married. After much discussion the commission confirmed this marriage, and he was permitted to live with his wife, but four years later he was advised to have a special Act of Parliament confirming the marriage. When the Catholic power was restored under Mary this Act was repealed.[58]

This was not the only occasion on which the question of divorce was considered by the early English reformers. Most of the continental Protestants admitted divorce, at least in the case of adultery; and Bucer, whose influence in the English Church was very great, had written with much power on the subject. In the reign of Edward VI. a commission of thirty-two learned men, including Cranmer and Peter Martyr, was appointed by the King, under an Act of Parliament, to make a reformation of the ecclesiastical law, and it agreed, among other things, that divorce should be permitted in cases of adultery, desertion, long absence, capital enmities where either party was in hazard of life, and 'the constant perverseness or fierceness of a husband to his wife.'[59] If the life of Edward had been prolonged, this would probably have become the law of England; but his untimely death prevented it, and the proposal was not revived under Elizabeth.

A curious compromise was gradually adopted. Divorce, even in case of adultery, was not admitted by law, but special Acts of Parliament granted it in particular cases. These Acts were at first very rare; but they became a more settled practice in the chancellorship of Lord Somers,[60] and they multiplied greatly in the second half of the eighteenth century. Up to the present day the same system exists in Ireland, to which country the English law of divorce does not extend, and where divorces can only be obtained by special Acts of Parliament.

---

[58] Burnet's *Hist. of the Reformation*, ii. 89–93, 305, 306, 397.
[59] Burnet's *Hist. of the Reformation*, ii. 313–17; see, too, Milton's 'Tetrachordon.'
[60] Campbell's *Lives of the Chancellors*, v. 101–2.

The famous Marriage Act of 1753 completely reorganised the English law of marriage. It was intended to put an end to the great and growing evil of clandestine marriages, and it provided that all marriages, except those of Jews and Quakers, 'should be null and void to all intents and purposes' unless they had been celebrated by a priest in orders according to the Anglican liturgy, and after the due publication of banns in the parish church or in a public chapel, or else under a special license from the Archbishop of Canterbury. This law fully recognised the religious character of marriage. It made a religious ceremony necessary for its validity, and it placed it very directly under the authority of the Church. It did for Anglican marriages much what the Council of Trent had done for Catholic marriages, but it did it by lay, and not by ecclesiastical authority, and English legislators claimed and exercised the power of treating as null and void marriages which, from an ecclesiastical point of view, were undoubtedly valid. The Royal Marriage Act pronounced all marriages of the descendants of George II., other than the issue of princesses married into foreign families, absolutely void if they were contracted without the assent of the King.[61] One of the Irish penal laws dealt in the same way with mixed or Protestant marriages celebrated only by a Catholic priest, and the Marriage Act of 1753 greatly extended the same policy. It also produced a new grievance, as the members of other religious denominations naturally objected to being married in an Anglican church and by an Anglican clergyman.

After many abortive attempts, this grievance was remedied by the great Act of 1836, which is remarkable, among other things, for introducing the principle of purely civil marriage once more into English legislation. The marriages of members of the Church of England were unaffected, except by the nec-

---

[61] It is a curious, and, I believe, little known fact that the French Church claimed the right of pronouncing marriages of the members of the French royal family celebrated without the king's consent null and void. It appears to be disputed among Catholics whether this action of a portion of the Catholic Church was valid. See Migne, *Encyclopédie: Dict. Théol. Morale*, i. 1004.

essary addition of a civil registry. Dissenters from the Church were allowed to celebrate their marriages in their own chapels, which were registered for the purpose, after giving due notice to the registrar of the district, and those who disliked a religious ceremony were enabled to contract a perfectly valid marriage before the registrar.

The English law on the subject of civil marriage is much less rigorous than that of most other countries, and it is marked to a high degree by the characteristic that distinguishes most English from much foreign legislation. Its object is to satisfy many scruples, to attain many ends, to gratify many parties, rather than to establish the clear ascendency of one logical doctrine. The French law of the Revolution, which was enacted in 1792, which passed with some modification into the Civil Code, and which has been the parent of much of the legislation of Europe, provided that the civil contract should be clearly disengaged in matrimony from all theological accessories, and that it should alone be recognised and confirmed by law. Purely civil marriage, in the French code, is at once obligatory and sufficient, though as soon as it has been celebrated the married persons are left at perfect liberty to go through any religious ceremony they please. Two things only are clearly laid down. One is, that an ecclesiastical marriage in the eyes of the law is merely a religious ceremony, and has absolutely no legal validity. The other is, that it is a criminal offence for any priest to perform such a ceremony until after the accomplishment of the civil marriage.

It is claimed, with much justice, for the French law of marriage that it is clear, simple, and uniform, and that, by laying down the principle that marriage is a natural right of all men, irrespective of all considerations of creed and rank; it has swept away a vast mass of unjust disabilities, inequalities, and irregular connections.[62]

---

[62] It should be added, however, that the expense and the complexity of the legal forms and proofs required in a French marriage are much complained of, and are said to be a cause why many of the poor content themselves with connections unsanctioned by law (see *Revue de Droit International*, ii. 259).

One of the most curious chapters connected with this subject is the great number of imperfect, partial, or approximate marriages which have existed in the world, growing for the most part out of aristocratic or theological exclusiveness. In the earlier periods of the Roman Republic no valid marriage could be contracted between a patrician and a plebeian, and the acquisition of this right of marriage was one of the great objects of plebeian politics. This object was at last attained, but a number of other disabilities to marriage had been established by Augustus. In later times, side by side with the 'justæ nuptiæ' was the connection called 'concubinatus.' It was not an illicit connection, for it was clearly recognised and protected by law, and a man who, having one concubine, formed any other relation was guilty of adultery. Its object was to regulate connections between men and women of very different ranks and fortunes. Like the simpler kinds of Roman marriage, it was formed by mere consent, and dissoluble at will. Its principal characteristics were that it might be contracted between persons who could not legally marry; that the woman brought with her no dowry; that she retained her own civil position, and did not share that of the man; and that the children bore her name, held her rank, and succeeded to her property, and not to the property of the father.[63]

There are some curious examples of irregular or semiregular connections during the Middle Ages which were either authorised or notoriously tolerated. The most important were those connected with the doctrine of clerical celibacy. There was a time when clerical marriage was fully permitted. There was another time when a married priest was recognised, but when the marriage relationship was looked on in his case as in some degree shameful, and husband and wife were expected to separate; and there was a time when clerical marriage was forbidden, but when connections that were not formally legitimate were generally tolerated and recognised, were

---

[63] Troplong, *Influence du Christianisme sur le Droit*, pp. 241–45; see, too, an essay by Professor Lawrence, *Revue de Droit International,*, ii. 55.

sometimes even enforced by parishioners in the interests of public morals, and probably brought with them no sense of moral guilt. This subject is a very curious one, and a careful examination of it is much to be commended to those who would seriously study the influence of the Roman Church on the morals of the world.[64]

In more modern times, in Prussia and some other German States, we find what are called 'morganatic marriages,' or marriages 'of the left hand,' which were contracted between princes and nobles of high rank and persons of inferior position. They bore a strong resemblance to the Roman *concubinatus*, being legitimate but inferior connections, which did not give the wife the rank of her husband, or the children the title or succession of the father. They were frequently celebrated between nobles and women of the peasant rank or of the lower-middle classes, but in order to be fully recognised they required the authorisation of the sovereign, and also most of the formalities that were demanded in a regular marriage. They might, under certain circumstances and conditions, be turned into regular marriages.[65]

Up to very recent times German law contained a multitude of disabilities on marriage, most of which have never been known in England. Marriages between nobles and women of inferior classes were illegal without a special dispensation. The consent of superiors to the marriage of functionaries of different orders was very generally required; and in the marriage of the poor there were many curious provisions requiring the assent of the commune, of the feudal lord, of magistrates, or of administrators of poor laws.[66] The marriages of persons in actual receipt of poor-law relief were constantly forbidden, and in many cases the legislators went further, and prohibited all marriages until the contracting parties could prove that they possessed the means of supporting a family. The strin-

---

[64] See that excellent work, Lea's *Sacerdotal Celibacy*.
[65] *Revue de Droit International*, ii. 84–5, xix. 592.
[66] *Revue de Droit International*, ii. 83–86.

gent Bavarian law on this subject is well known; far into the nineteenth century very similar enactments existed in Norway, Mecklenburg, Saxony, Württemberg, and the canton of Berne,[67] and I believe the same system may still be found in the communal legislation of some parts of the Austrian Empire.

It may be defended by powerful arguments. It is an attempt to enforce by law a real though a much neglected moral duty. It was urged that it lay within the legitimate province of the commune, for the pauper children of improvident marriages will naturally become a charge upon them, and that in districts where this provision is enforced there will usually be found a well-to-do peasantry and a high level of comfort, order, and civilisation. But these advantages, it is truly said, have usually been purchased at the price of an increase of extra-matrimonial connections and of illegitimate births. In this case we have one of those conflicts between advantages and disadvantages differing in kind which form perhaps the greatest difficulty of moral philosophy. It is a curious fact that this system of retarding marriages and prohibiting them when improvident has existed in some of the most Catholic parts of Europe, while in Ireland and in Canada priests, in the professed interests of morality, have usually been ardent advocates of early marriage.

Religious intolerance in its different forms had produced great numbers of imperfect marriages. In France, as I have said, Protestant marriages for a considerable period of time carried with them no civil rights; and great evils have arisen from the laws that long made English marriages that were not celebrated by an Anglican clergyman, and Irish marriages between Protestants and Catholics, or between two Protestants, that were celebrated only by a Catholic priest, null and void. There have always been large numbers of women who would never enter into a connection which they believed to be mor-

---

[67] Senior's *Provision for the Poor and Condition of the Labouring Classes in America and Europe* (1835), pp. 71, 74, 82, 88–90.

ally wrong, but whose consciences were fully satisfied by a religious ceremony which their Church pronounced to be sufficient, although it left them wholly unprotected by law, and liable at any time to be discarded or displaced. Connections of this kind, sanctioned by religion, but unsanctioned by law, have been very common, and they have had effects upon titles and property that are felt to the present generation.

In our own day, the same evil assumed formidable proportions in Italy after the introduction of civil marriage in 1865. The law made civil marriage alone valid, but it did not follow the wise example of the French law in making it a criminal offence to celebrate the religious ceremony till the civil marriage was accomplished, and the result was that great numbers of couples, especially of the poorer class, contented themselves with a religious ceremony, and were never married in the eyes of the law. A similar evil was very common in Spain between 1870 and 1875, when a law like that of Italy was in force. In countries, too, where the clergy presided over and regulated marriages, differences of religion were usually obstacles to legitimate marriages. The marriage of a Christian with a Jew was for a long period deemed one of the gravest of criminal offences, and is even now in some countries forbidden by law. The marriage of a Christian and an unbeliever stood in the same category. Marriages between the orthodox and the heretic were either absolutely forbidden or only permitted on the condition that all the children were brought up in the dominant creed. One infamous ecclesiastical law, for which, however, there was a precedent in Roman legislation, deprived actors and actresses of the right of marriage; and the Catholic Church introduced a new kind of disability by pronouncing that persons who were wholly unconnected with one another, if they became sponsors at baptism to the same child, acquired a relationship which made it criminal for them to marry. In most Catholic countries vows of celibacy have constituted a disability, even when those who took them have abandoned their profession and their religion; and, through other motives, there have been in the United States strict laws against the marriage of whites with negroes or Indians.

There is hardly any change in modern legislation which is more important or more significant than the gradual transformation of the legal character of marriage. The first country on the Continent which adopted the principle of civil marriage was the Netherlands; but in 1787 Louis XVI. introduced it for the benefit of Protestants, but of Protestants alone. The French Revolution in 1792 made it universal in France. The conquests of Napoleon greatly extended its area; and it has since spread with extraordinary rapidity through the principal legislations of the world. While civil marriages have been usually made obligatory and legally sufficient, the parties are left at full liberty to celebrate, in addition, any religious ceremony they desire; but the French system, which has been adopted in Holland, Belgium, Germany, and Switzerland, guards against the existence of religious marriages that are not legal marriages by strictly forbidding the religious ceremony till after the civil one has been performed.

The introduction of civil marriage into the legislations of Catholic countries is especially significant, for it has been accomplished in the face of the most strenuous ecclesiastical opposition. It is true, indeed, that it is little more than a reversion to the state of things that was at least acquiesced in before the Council of Trent, but there is no system which the modern Church has more bitterly denounced. Civil marriage was declared by Pius IX. to be 'a filthy concubinage.'[68] Perrone, the chief Ultramontane expounder of the Catholic doctrines on matrimony, declares that 'civil marriage, wherever the Council of Trent has been published, is in its nature a base concubinage, and all who pass their lives united only by a civil marriage are obnoxious to the penalties decreed by the Church against those who are living in public concubinage,' and he pronounces the legislation of those countries which have admitted civil marriage to be utterly opposed to the doc-

---

[68] See the passage cited by Mr. Gladstone in his *Vaticanism*, p. 27.

trines of the Church.[69] Pius VII., in 1809, ordered the Italian bishops to insist that in all cases the religious marriage should precede the civil one.[70] In a letter of Pius IX. to Victor Emanuel the true Catholic doctrine of the respective functions of the Church and of the State in marriage were very tersely expressed: 'Let the civil power determine the civil consequences that flow from marriage, but let it leave it to the Church to regulate the validity of marriage among Christians. Let the civil law take as its starting-point the validity or invalidity of a marriage as the Church has determined it, and, starting from this fact, which lies beyond its power and its sphere, let it regulate its civil effects.[71]

The introduction into the legislation of so many countries of a principle so fundamentally opposed to the teaching of the Church is a proof, only less striking than the general establishment of religious liberty by law, of the declining influence of Catholicism in the government of the world. That decline has not been uniform. There have been many temporary reactions, many unexpected recrudescences, but on the whole, those who will study the broad lines of recent legislation can, I think, have little doubt of the direction in which the stream is moving. In England and some other countries the establishment of civil marriage has been mainly a measure of relief granted as an alternative system to small sections of the community, but leaving the great mass of marriages unaffected. In some countries it is restricted to dissenters from the established creed. In other countries it has had a wider influence, and, among other results, has put an end to a great number of disabilities growing out of theological ascendencies and feudal restrictions. Thus, in Germany, until a very recent period, religious marriages in most States were alone recognised, though divorce was allowed with great facility. Civil marriage, however, existed in the free town of

---

[69] 'Lex civilis quæ omnino pugnat cum ecclesiæ doctrina,' i. 214.
[70] Migne, *Encyclopédie: Dict. de Jurisprudence*, art. 'Mariage.'
[71] Glasson, *Le Mariage Civil et le Divorce*, p. 228.

Frankfort. It existed in the provinces of the Rhine, which, like Belgium, still retained, under another rule, the marriage law they had received when they were a portion of the French Empire. It existed also, in some States, for the benefit of dissenters from the National Church. In 1868 and 1869 nearly all the feudal disabilities I have enumerated were abolished in Prussia and in the whole North German Confederation, and in 1875 civil marriage on the French model was made obligatory and universal through the German Empire.[72] A clause was inserted in the law directing the registrar to inform the newly married couples that nothing stood in the way of their afterwards asking the blessing of their Church.

In Italy, civil marriage was introduced in 1865; but, as I have already mentioned, no step was taken to prevent religious marriages which had no legal validity from being substituted for them. In Switzerland the marriage laws were for a long time varied in the different cantons, but in 1875 a Federal law established a uniform system of obligatory civil marriage through the whole of Switzerland, and at the same time abolished all the surviving disabilities founded on theological doctrines or on poverty.[73]

In Spain the history has been a somewhat different one. For three centuries the decrees of the Council of Trent governed all Spanish marriages, but on the downfall of Isabella, in 1868, a new spirit passed over Spanish government. In 1870 and 1871 laws were passed establishing civil marriage as alone valid, but leaving the priests at liberty to celebrate religious marriages before or after. The result in a very Catholic country where the peasantry were scarcely touched by new ideas, and where the empire of custom was very strong, could hardly be doubtful, and great numbers of persons refused to recognise the new law, contented themselves with the bene-

---

[72] See *Revue de Droit International*, ii. 79–86, xix. 592–94; Glasson, *Le Mariage Civil et le Divorce*, pp. 104–33.

[73] See Glasson, pp. 155–60. Some papers on the Swiss laws of marriage will be found in the twelfth and thirteenth volumes of the *Revue de Droit International*.

diction of the Church, and lived in a state of legal concubinage. The law was so unpopular and produced such bad effects that in 1875, when the monarchy was re-established, the legislators retraced their steps. A retrospective law legitimised marriages and the offspring of marriages which had been celebrated only by a religious ceremony since 1870, and restored the system of purely religious marriages for Catholics. Civil marriages, however, as provided by the law of 1870, continued for non-Catholics and for 'bad Catholics' who, owing either to the failure of their faith or to ecclesiastical censures, could not sanctify their union by a sacrament. This double system was ratified, but also modified, by a marriage law of 1889. The two kinds of marriage were both recognised—canonical marriage, which all who profess the Catholic faith ought to contract, with all the conditions prescribed by the Council of Trent; and civil marriage, for those who could not or would not conform to the religious ceremony. It was provided that a civil magistrate must always be present at a religious marriage, and must register it, and the priest was forbidden to celebrate it without his presence. Secret canonical marriages, however, are recognised, but they must be civilly registered in a secret register kept specially for this purpose. A Portuguese law of 1868 in the same spirit recognised two kinds of marriage— religious marriage for Catholics, civil marriage for non-Catholics.[74]

In the Austrian Empire the marriage legislations have been very various, and have undergone many vicissitudes. In 1856, when, under the influence of the Concordat with Rome, the Empire passed through a dark cloud of superstition and intolerance, the State abdicated nearly all the control it had previously exercised on marriages, and placed them entirely in ecclesiastical hands and under the decrees of the Council of Trent. Marriages between Christians and non-Christians were absolutely forbidden. Marriages between Catholics and non-Catholics were only tolerated on the condition that all

---

[74] *Revue de Droit International*, xix. 601–2, xxiii. 30–42; Glasson, pp. 78–85.

children should be brought up in the Catholic faith. Austria at this period seemed one of the most backward nations in Europe; but its reactionary legislation was no true reflex of the spirit of its people, and when the hour of resurrection arrived it rose speedily to the light.

I have already described in some of its parts that long course of singularly enlightened, moderate, and successful legislation which began in 1868, and which has made Austria one of the best-governed countries in Europe. I have here to deal only with a single department. The legislator did not introduce any violent revolution into the marriage law. He contented himself, in 1868, with a law about mixed marriages, providing that the parents might make any arrangement they pleased about the religion of the children; that in the absence of any such arrangement the boys should be brought up in the religion of the father, and the daughters in the religion of the mother; and that every person above the age of fourteen should have the right to choose his or her religion. By another law of the same year the ecclesiastical courts, which had been established for matrimonial cases under the Concordat, were replaced by civil courts; the civil power regained the right it had previously possessed of concurring independently with the religious power in the regulation of marriage, and it was provided that, in cases in which the priest refused to marry on account of some disabilities which were not recognised by the civil law, civil marriage could be celebrated. A strong party, which had for a time an ascendency in the Lower House, demanded the establishment of universal and obligatory civil marriage as in France; but the Upper Chamber has hitherto steadily resisted, and this system is only in force for members of religions not recognised by the State.[75] In Hungary, after a long and desperate struggle with Papal influence, a great reform has very recently been accomplished. Before it was carried there were no less than seven different legislations regulating the marriage conditions of different kinds of dissenters; but in 1894 all these complex-

---

[75] Glasson, pp. 170–75.

ities were swept away, compulsory civil marriage was established for all creeds, leaving its members afterwards free to ask
the blessing of their respective Churches; and at the same time
marriages between Jews and Christians became legal, and the
principle was recognised that, in mixed marriages, the boys
should follow the religion of the father, and the girls that of
the mother.[76]

The tendency to emancipate marriage from the control of
the Church, which is so apparent in Europe, has spread to
the Catholic States in the New World. A law of 1873 makes
marriage in Mexico a purely civil contract, within 'the exclusive competence of functionaries and authorities of the civil
order,' and the Brazilian Constitution of 1891 recognises only
civil marriages.[77] In the republics, however, of Peru, Bolivia,
and Ecuador, intolerance still reigns supreme. Marriage is altogether in the hands of the Church, and all legal recognition
of Protestant marriages is refused.

In the Protestant Scandinavian countries, and in the countries under the dominion of the Greek Church, the religious
character of marriage is, on the whole, more strongly maintained. In Denmark, Sweden, and Norway, marriage is in its
form a religious ceremony, though the civil power undertakes
to regulate its effects, and on occasions to dissolve it. Civil
marriage also exists in Sweden and Norway, but only for
those who dissent from the Established Church.

In Russia it was introduced in 1874, but only for the benefit
of dissenters. In the small Slavonic States of Southern Europe
the purely religious marriage type still prevails. Roumania
has in most respects copied the French Civil Code, but with
this remarkable difference, that civil marriage, except in some
special cases, only becomes valid when it is followed by a
religious benediction.[78]

This brief sketch will, I hope, be sufficient to give the reader

---

[76] *Annual Register*, 1894.
[77] Dareste, ii. 491–92, 648.
[78] Glasson, pp. 87, 193–204; Dareste, ii. 216.

a clear conception of the character and the tendencies of the chief contemporary legislations on the subject of marriage. The permission of divorce is closely connected with the introduction of civil marriage, but it does not follow it strictly. Civil marriage has sometimes existed without the permission of divorce, and divorce has been sometimes permitted in countries where marriage has been strictly religious.

Looking at the question *prima facie*, it might appear evident that a doctrine which regards marriage merely as a civil contract entered into by adult persons for the furtherance of their happiness, would necessarily imply the liberty of divorce if the two parties to the contract mutually desired it; if the conditions on which they entered into it are not fulfilled; if it is found to result, not in the happiness, but in the misery of the contracting parties. Promises and engagements exchanged between two persons may be dissolved if both parties agree to do so; and although the law is bound to prevent one party from violating a contract to the detriment of the other, it is naturally silent when both parties are consenting. The burden of proof rests upon those who make the marriage contract an exception. Of all contracts, it is that which is most frequently entered into under the influence of blinding passion, and at an age when experience and knowledge of life are immature, and it is a contract in which happiness and misery mainly depend upon conditions of character and temper that are often most imperfectly disclosed. It is the most intimate of all relations. It is that which affects most closely and most constantly the daily happiness of life; and as its natural end is a complete identification of feelings and interests, as it brings with it a far ampler knowledge of the circumstances of a life than any other relation, it may, if it fails in its purpose, become in the highest degree calamitous, and it gives either party an extraordinary power of injuring the other.

If considerations of this kind stood alone they would appear invincible. But another order of considerations has at all times, though in different degrees, weighed powerfully with legislators and moralists. The stability of the family is more essential than any other single element to the moral, social, and even political well-being of a nation. It is of vital importance to the education of the young. It is the special seed-plot and condition of the best virtues of the community, the foundation-stone on which the whole social system must rest. Few greater misfortunes can happen to a nation than that the domestic virtues should have ceased to be prized; that family life, with all its momentous interests, should have become the sport of passion and of caprice.

It is contended, with much reason, that this would inevitably be the case if unlimited license of divorce were granted, and especially if the idea of permanent separation and new marriage were constantly present to the minds of either party. Marriage, beyond all other relations, depends upon a slow and steady formation of habits. When men and women look upon certain conditions as permanent and inevitable, their feelings and habits will gradually accommodate themselves to them. But if the tie is a very lax one, separate interests will soon grow up; passing differences will deepen into aversion; vagrant caprices will be indulged; prolonged sacrifice will be impatiently borne when an alternative is easy; and the repose, the confidence, and the security that are essential to happy marriages will be fatally impaired.

Another important consideration is the inequality that subsists between the two parties. The woman is the weaker; she is commonly the poorer; her happiness is usually much more bound up with domestic life than that of the man; and the strength of passion may subsist in one sex when the power of gratifying and inspiring it has departed from the other. Every one who is acquainted with moral history knows how many divorces in the past have been due to this cause, and what grave injuries they have inflicted on the weaker partner. At the same time, this argument is one which may be easily pressed too far. The injuries for which, in most countries, divorce is granted affect women more than men, and in the countries where divorces are most frequent women form the larger number of the petitioners.

On the whole, however, the considerations I have alleged have convinced the great majority of legislators and moralists that marriage cannot be treated as an ordinary contract, and that its dissolution should only be permitted on very serious grounds. But contemporary legislations differ widely about the number and the nature of those grounds.

The Council of Trent, settling finally, for the Catholic Church, a question which from a very early period of Church history divided its chief authorities, pronounced adultery not to be a justification of divorce, and duly consummated marriage to be absolutely indissoluble. Separation 'from bed and board' may, under certain circumstances, be judicially pronounced; but divorce, involving the liberty of remarriage, is absolutely condemned. At the same time, the Catholic doctrine is not, in fact, quite as inflexible as it appears, for the Church recognises many grounds on which marriage may be pronounced null from the beginning; and some of these grounds are so obscure, technical, and remote, that they have given ecclesiastics a large practical power of dissolving marriages which had appeared perfectly valid. I have already cited the opinion of Perrone about the marriage of Protestants in countries where the discipline of the Council of Trent has been promulgated, and about the reserved, though concealed, power which, in the opinion of that eminent divine, the Church possesses of breaking these marriages if one party becomes a Catholic. Pre-contracts, or earlier engagements of marriage, and very remote affinities extending to the fourth degree and far beyond the Levitical limits, have been made, in the absence of the proper dispensations, causes for dissolving marriages. Affinities might be constituted, not merely by lawful marriages, but even by adulterous connections; and they might also be constituted by spiritual relationship. Coke mentions a case in which a marriage was pronounced null because the husband had stood godfather to the cousin of his wife. Catholic theologians enumerate no less than fourteen classes of impediments to marriage.[79] The statute of Henry VIII. regulating English marriage complains bitterly of the uncertainty and instability which the Church had introduced into this relation. 'Many persons,' it said, 'after long continuance together in matrimony, without any allegation of either of the parties, or any other, at their marriage why the same matrimony should not be good,' had been divorced, contrary to God's law, on the pretext of pre-contract, or by reason of 'other prohibitions than God's law permitteth.' 'Marriages have been brought into such an uncertainty thereby that no marriage could be so surely knit or bounden but it should lie in either of the parties' power . . . to prove a pre-contract, a kindred and alliance, or a carnal knowledge to defeat the same.'[80]

A curious modern instance of the manner in which, when some great personal or political interest is in question, the doctrine of the Church may be found to harmonise with the wishes of worldly politicians is furnished by the divorce of the Empress Josephine. When the Pope agreed to crown Napoleon and Josephine in 1804, the Empress went to him and acknowledged that her marriage had been only a civil one. It was her ardent desire to obtain a religious marriage, and the Pope, by refusing on any other condition to crown her, obtained the consent of Napoleon. The religious ceremony was celebrated secretly the day before the coronation.[81] Cardinal Fesch performed it, with the express authorisation of the Pope. Several eminent persons were present, and it is stated—though on that point there is some dispute—that Talleyrand and Marshal Berthier were the witnesses. The conscience of Josephine was fully satisfied, and she naturally believed that, in the sight of the Church at least, her marriage was holy and indissoluble. Five years later, however, Napoleon determined to divorce her

---

[79] Migne, *Encycl. Dict. de Théologie Morale,* art. 'Empêchements de Mariage.'

[80] 32 Henry VIII. c. 38.

[81] Most accounts say at night, but according to Cardinal Fesch it was at 4 p.m.

and to marry Marie Louise. The reason of the divorce was that Josephine had no children, and, in the eyes of the secular politicians who surrounded Napoleon, the importance of providing a direct heir for the throne justified the step. The dissolution of the civil marriage encountered no difficulty; but it might have been supposed that the Church, which is governed by higher considerations, would have been more difficult.

It must be stated that the Pope was at this time a prisoner at Savona. He was not consulted; and his conduct when Napoleon annulled the marriage of his brother Jerome shows clearly that he would not have consented. The praise of blame of this transaction falls chiefly on a council of seven bishops presided over by Cardinal Maury. The question was brought before the diocesan and the metropolitan authorities, and it was decided that on three distinct grounds the Catholic marriage was void. There had not been a perfect consent, for Napoleon is alleged to have more than once stated that he went through the ceremony only to pacify the conscience of Josephine, and had never intended to bind himself for ever. The marriage was celebrated by a Cardinal, and not, as the Council of Trent prescribed, by the priest of the parish; and although Cardinal Fesch had acted, as he himself stated, under the express direction of the Pope, who had authorised him to dispense with formalities, no document of dispensation had been drawn out. There had also been an informality about the witnesses. On these grounds the religious marriage was pronounced void, and the Emperor was solemnly assured that he would be sinning against the Divine law if he continued to live with Josephine. He was not deaf to this pious exhortation. The same Cardinal who had married him to Josephine performed the ceremony for her successor. Napoleon, in announcing his divorce to the Senate, declared that he was only following the example of thirteen French sovereigns.[82]

---

[82] See Lanfrey, *Napoléon*, v. 188. See, too, the account in Thiers; also Lyonnet, *Le Cardinal Fesch*, i. 364–65, ii. 240–49, 739–53. The whole subject has

The general maxim, however, that divorce is in all cases criminal, has, since the Council of Trent, been steadily maintained by the Catholic Church, and laws permitting it in Catholic countries have always been bitterly opposed. The French legislators in 1792 established it on almost the widest terms. They granted it on the mutual desire of the two parties, and even at the wish of one party on the ground of mere incompatibility of temper, subject only to a short period of delay, and to the necessity of appearing before a family council, who were to endeavour to arrange the dispute. They granted it also for a large number of definite causes, such as judicial condemnations, grave mutual injuries, desertion, notorious immorality, prolonged absence, emigration contrary to the law, and insanity. The law, at the same time, while authorising divorce, of which good Catholics could not avail themselves, put an end to judicial separation, which had hitherto been their only refuge. The result of this law, or, probably much more truly, the result of the utter moral anarchy that then prevailed in France, was an extraordinary multiplication of divorces. In twenty-seven months after the promulgation of the law of 1792, 5,994 divorces were pronounced in Paris; and in the year VI. the number of divorces in the capital actually exceeded the number of marriages.[83]

In that year the 'Civil Code' was drawn up, and one of its most valuable points was the regulation and restriction of divorce. The grounds on which it might be granted were considerably diminished, and mere incompatibility of temper was no longer reckoned among them. Divorce, however, by mutual consent remained, though it was surrounded by serious restrictions, by elaborate, costly, and dilatory forms. A year must elapse in this case between the demand for divorce and the sentence granting it, and three more years must elapse before either party could remarry. Judicial separation,

---

recently been examined with much detail by M. Welschinger, *Le Divorce de Napoléon*.

[83] Glasson, *Le Mariage Civil et le Divorce*, pp. 46–51.

at the same time, was revived, so that the position of good Catholics was unimpaired.[84]

Divorce was abolished in France, in 1816, by the Government of the Restoration, though civil marriage still remained; but it was preserved in Belgium the Rhenish provinces of Prussia, and the Grand Duchy of Baden, which were now severed from French rule. Various attempts were made to re-establish it in France, but, in spite of the many revolutions of power that took place, they were not successful until 1884. The law which was enacted in that year revives, with some modifications, the divorce law of the 'Civil Code,' but divorce by mutual consent is no longer included in it. It provides, among other things, that all couples who have for the space of three years been judicially separated are entitled, without further proceedings, to a divorce, and it renders the simple adultery of a man, as well as of a woman, a sufficient cause. Among the causes of divorce according to the new law are 'bad treatment and grave injuries,'[85] and under the shelter of these vague words the French law courts seem to have included nearly every kind of at all serious provocation.

The movement for establishing divorce, however, has certainly not spread among Catholic nations as rapidly as the movement for the establishment of civil marriage. Italy, Spain, Portugal, and the Catholic States of America, though they have profoundly modified their old marriage laws, still refuse to admit divorce.[86] In the Austrian Empire the marriage of Catholics is indissoluble, but divorce is admitted where the married couples belong to other creeds. The injured party may obtain it for adultery, condemnation to a long period of penal servitude, prolonged desertion, and some grave acts of injury or violence; it is also granted in case of 'invincible aversion,' but only after long delay and several successive separations

---

[84] Ibid. pp. 51–53.

[85] 'Les sévices et injures graves.'

[86] That is, real divorce. In some Catholic countries this term is applied to judicial separations, which do not dissolve the marriage-tie or aurthorise remarriage.

and reunions; and there are some special provisions, into which it is needless for us to enter, about the divorce of Jews.[87]

The measures of 1874 and 1875 giving Switzerland and Germany uniform marriage laws dealt in different ways with the question of divorce. The Swiss law extended it to all the cantons, but the German law left it substantially to the separate legislations of the different States, though it introduced some general regulations about subsequent marriages.[88] In Europe, as in the United States, sincere Catholics refrain from availing themselves of the privilege accorded by law. In France, however, the divorce law of 1884 has been largely used. Divorces are found to be far more numerous than judicial separations, and their rapid increase, especially among the working classes and the very poor, has seriously alarmed many politicians who are far from being bigoted Catholics.[89] Some interesting statistics on the subject have been given in a recent report to the British Foreign Office. It appears that between July, 1884, and the end of December, 1891, 45,822 divorce cases had been brought before the civil tribunals, and that in 40,300 cases the divorce had been granted. The proportion of divorces to marriages, which in 1885 was fourteen to 1,000, had risen in 1890 and 1891 to twenty-four to 1,000. These divorces are mainly

---

[87] Glasson, p. 176. A fuller account of the Austrian legislation about divorce will be found in an *Etude sur le Divorce en Autriche* by Lyon-Coen, reprinted from the *Bulletin de la Société de Législation Comparée*. Statistics about Austrian divorces and about the number of marriages among Catholics that were annulled will be found in a Foreign Office report on the number of divorces in foreign countries during the last ten years (1895).

[88] Glasson, pp. 135–36, 159.

[89] There is a department in Paris called the 'Assistance Judiciaire,' which assists those who are too poor to pay for legal expenses. A writer in the *Figaro* (July 4, 1892) says: 'Si l'on veut se rendre compte des progrès du divorce dans la seule catégorie des Parisiens et Parisiennes mariés qui ont recours à l'Assistance Judiciaire, il suffit de jeter les yeux sur une pièce officielle que j'ai là devant moi. Le relevé des affaires de divorce portées devant le bureau d'assistance près du tribunal de la Seine pour une période de quatre ans du 1ᵉʳ janvier 1888 au 1ᵉʳ janvier 1892 donne un chiffre de 21,000 demandes. . . . Pendant le même laps de temps il a été formé 2,000 demandes de séparation de corps.'

among the town populations. The peasant class, who form nearly half the population of France, are said not to furnish more than 7 per cent.[90]

French legislation and example have always exercised an enormous influence on the whole Latin race, and it is probable that divorce, having been firmly established in France, will, sooner or later, spread widely through Catholic nations. The Protestant Churches and the Greek Church have never condemned it in the same unqualified manner as the Roman Church. Nearly all the Reformers admitted it for adultery and malicious desertion, and many of them on several other grounds, and it gradually passed into German and Scandinavian legislation.[91] England, however, on this subject hung dubiously between the opposing creeds, and Cranmer and his followers failed, as we have seen, to bring her into line with the Reformed Churches. Divorce remained absolutely forbidden by law, though it was soon granted in particular cases by special Acts of Parliament. It was the custom to pass these Acts only when a separation 'from bed and board' had been first decreed by the ecclesiastical court, and when an action for damages had been brought in the civil court against the offending party. Parliament always granted a man divorce on account of the adultery of his wife, but it was very rarely granted to a woman on account of the adultery of her husband, and then only in cases where there were special causes of aggravation.

This system was manifestly absurd. It gave up the principle of the indissolubility of marriage, and at the same time, by a glaring injustice, it restricted relief to the very rich, as neither poor men nor men of moderate fortunes could avail them-

---

[90] *Return of Number of Divorces in Foreign Countries.*

[91] An examination of the opinions of the Reformers by a strong partisan of divorce will be found in Milton's 'Tetrachordon,' and by a strong opponent of divorce in Woolsey's *Divorce Legislation in the United States.* See also a remarkable book, called *Observations on the Laws of Marriage,* published in 1815, pp. 335–42.

selves of it. The injustice was often felt, but it was never brought out more efficaciously than by Justice Maule in a case which was tried before him in 1845. The culprit was a poor man who had committed bigamy. The defence was that when the prisoner married his second wife he had in reality no wife, for his former wife had first robbed and then deserted him, and was now living with another man. The judge imposed the lightest penalty in his power, but he prefixed it by some ironical remarks which made a deep and lasting impression. Having described the gross provocation under which the prisoner had acted, he continued: 'But, prisoner, you have committed a grave offence in taking the law into your own hands and marrying again. I will now tell you what you should have done. You should have brought an action into the civil court, and obtained damages, which the other side would probably have been unable to pay, and you would have had to pay your own costs—perhaps 100*l.* or 150*l.* You should then have gone to the ecclesiastical court and obtained a divorce *a mensa et thoro*, and then to the House of Lords, where, having proved that these preliminaries had been complied with, you would have been enabled to marry again. The expenses might amount to 500*l.* or 600*l.*, or perhaps 1,000*l.* You say you are a poor man, and you probably do not possess as many pence. But, prisoner, you must know that in England there is not one law for the rich and another for the poor.'

The scandal of this system was remedied by the Divorce Act of 1857, an Act which was furiously opposed, and which is in some respects very defective, but which has undoubtedly brightened many lives and relieved a vast amount of poignant and undeserved suffering. The discussions on the subject were curious as showing how powerfully, even to that late period, theological methods of thought and reasoning prevailed in the British Legislature. There were speeches that would seem more in place in a Church council than in a lay Parliament. An Act, however, was at last passed granting divorce to men on account of the adultery of their wives. A wife, however, could not obtain divorce on account of the simple adultery of her husband. She must be able to prove, in addition to the adultery, cruelty, or some specific and very atrocious aggravation of the crime. The consciences of the clergy who objected to divorce were wisely attended to by a clause providing that no clergyman could be compelled to marry a divorced person, though he was not permitted to refuse the use of his church for the celebration of such marriages. In a country which possesses an established Church less than this could scarcely be demanded, though the mere permission of such marriages in the church has lately been made an ecclesiastical grievance.

Apart from the difference between the rights of the two sexes which was established in the Divorce Act, the Act is a manifestly imperfect one. If divorce is admitted at all, on utilitarian grounds, there are reasons quite as strong as adultery for granting it. It is a scandal to English legislation that it should not be granted when one of the partners has been condemned for some grave criminal offence involving a long period of imprisonment or penal servitude, or for wilful and prolonged desertion,[92] or for cruelty, however atrocious, if it is not coupled with adultery. In all continental legislations which admit divorce a catalogue of grave causes is admitted which justify it. In my own opinion, gross, habitual, and long-continued drunkenness should be among them. Much is said of the injury which the permission of divorce would inflict upon women and upon children; but in most of the cases I have just specified women suffer far more frequently than men from its denial, and few greater curses can be inflicted upon children than that they should be brought up by drunken or criminal parents. Divorce laws drawn substantially on the lines I have indicated were enacted in Victoria in 1889, and in New South Wales in 1891. The general tendency of continental legislations seems to be to make all cases in which judicial separation can be granted causes for divorce. It is obvious that, when such separations have taken place, the puposes of mar-

---

[92] This is, however, a ground for divorce in Scotland.

riage are defeated. It is a more difficult and intricate question whether divorce should be suffered to supersede separation, as is the case in many continental countries, or whether the latter should not still continue for those whose principles prevent them from availing themselves of the former.

I do not believe that there is any real reason to think that the standard of domestic morals in England has been impaired by the strictly limited right of divorce which was granted by the Act of 1857. The scenes of shame and vice and domestic wretchedness that are often disclosed in the Divorce Court are certainly not produced by it, though much misery and wickedness which would otherwise have festered in lifelong secrecy are brought by its action into the light of day. It is, however, true that the exposure of the inmost secrets and of the worst sides of domestic life through the reports of the Divorce Court is a source of real demoralisation. The respectable portion of the press fully recognises it, and does its best by very abridged reports to minimise it; but there is a certain section which finds in these reports a kind of literature which is, unhappily, as popular as it is degrading. It is absurd, however, to contend that this abuse is unavoidable, for the publicity of divorce proceedings is almost peculiar to England. It is, I believe, a nearly unmixed evil. Ample guarantees for the observance of justice could be obtained without it; and, in addition to its effect in fomenting and gratifying an appetite for impure scandal, it seriously obstructs the course of justice, by scaring witnesses from the witness-box. Much complaint has also been made of the large amount of perjury that has taken place in the Divorce Court. This is partly because the law on the subject is very imperfectly enforced, partly because the received code of honour does not enforce or even enjoin truthfulness in cases where a woman's frailty is concerned, and partly also because false evidence in these cases can often not be disclosed without revealing or reviving great scandals, from which all parties shrink.

Some good judges are of opinion that the standard of domestic morals, in a considerable section of the upper classes in England, has in the present generation been lowered, and that principle and practice have alike grown more lax. It is extremely difficult to arrive at any accurate judgment on such a subject, but it may, I think, be confidently asserted that, if such a change has taken place, it has been due to quite other influences than the divorce law. Sudden and enormous increase of wealth brings with it luxury, idleness, and self-indulgence. Cosmopolitan habits of life break down old customs and introduce new manners. The decay of ancient beliefs loosens many ties, and a few bad social influences in high places will affect the tone of large sections of society. On the whole, it seems to me that the signs of increasing moral laxity in England are more apparent in other directions: in increased worldliness and hardness, and craving for wealth and pleasure, among the young; in the increased social influence of dishonestly acquired money; in the frequency, the cynicism, and the success of gross instances of political profligacy.

The multiplication of divorces is often the symptom, but it is rarely, I think, the cause, of a moral decadence. Few things are more difficult than a comparison of the social morality of different countries. The clear and decisive evidence which statistics can throw on comparative criminality is here wanting; the sphere of observation of the best observer must be very limited, and many influences are calculated to mislead. No grosser injustice, for example, could be done to ordinary French life than to judge it by the writings of French novelists or French playwriters; and some Catholic theologians on the Continent are accustomed to draw pictures of domestic life in England and America which are at least equally misleading.[93]

---

[93] *E.g.* 'Si vous alliez à certains jours sur une place de Londres ou d'une autre ville d'Albion, dit le P. Ventura, vous y verriez au milieu d'une foule qui rit et se permet les propos les plus grossiers et les plus insultants, des malheureuses, les yeux baissés, l'air profondément abattu, ayant au cou une corde dont un homme tient dans ses mains les deux bouts; ce sont des femmes que leurs maris ont mises à l'encan et qu'ils cherchent à vendre. Ne croirait-on pas se trouver en quelque ville d'Egypte, de la Chine ou de la Tartarie? Le gouvernement a bien essayé d'abolir cette

On the whole, it seems clear that domestic morals in the past have seldom sunk lower than in some countries and periods when divorce was absolutely impossible; and in the present day, I do not think that those who will compare the domestic morality of countries where divorce is denied with those in which it is admitted will find any real superiority in the former. A comparison from this point of view of Italy, Spain, and Portugal, with the Scandinavian countries, Germany and Switzerland; of Berlin with Vienna; of Belgium and Holland with France as it existed before 1884; of the Catholic with the Protestant populations of the Austrian Empire, will, I think, support this statement. It seems, however, to be a general law that in countries in which divorces are permitted they have a tendency to multiply. Bringing with them the power of re-marriage, they have proved far more popular than simple judicial separations, which they are manifestly tending to replace.[94]

The legislators who have dealt with this question, not on theological, but on purely utilitarian grounds, may be roughly

---

coutume barbare, mais ses efforts sont restés impuissants. Elle est le résultat des doctrines du schisme et de l'hérésie touchant le mariage. . . . On ne s'étonne plus, quand on connaît l'Angleterre, du profond mépris dont John Bull accable la femme. . . . La femme du riche n'est ni plus heureuse ni plus respectée. La possibilité du divorce porte le mari à cacher soigneusement à sa femme tous les secrets de la famille. . . . On se réunit pour les repas et l'on mange comme des étrangers au restaurant sans échanger un sourire affectueux, sans presque se dire un mot. Au dessert il faut que les femmes se retirent, et c'est alors que les conversations s'engagent sur les affaires. . . . La défiance et le mépris de la femme sont poussés au plus haut degré. . . . Humiliée, dégradée, malheureuse comme épouse, la femme en Angleterre, pourrait-elle être honorée comme mère? Les enfants ne lui appartiennent pas. . . . S'ils ont un secret, c'est à leur père qu'ils vont le confier et jamais à leur mère' (*Famille et Divorce*, par l'abbé Vidieu (1879), 6th edit. pp. 105–6). In America, l'abbé Vidieu assures us, 'les mots de foi conjugale, d'adultère n'auront bientôt plus de signification,' and in general 'l'épouse est opprimée, dégradée, avilie chez les peuples hérétiques ou séparés de l'Eglise' (pp. 113–14).

[94] See Glasson, pp. 165–67, 263–66.

said to have adopted two systems. One class, who appear to me to have taken by far the safer course, have restricted divorce to a few serious and well-defined causes which manifestly ruin the happiness of married life. In these cases, they contend, the clear balance of advantage is in favour of a complete severance, and the innocent partner, at least, has a moral right to seek his or her happiness in another union. They consider it, however, a matter of supreme social importance that divorce should be only a rare and very exceptional thing, growing out of some great moral catastrophe, and they take no account of mere divergencies of temper or tastes, of alienated affections or capricious fancies.

Another class of legislators have gone much further. They act upon the principle that whenever marriage is clearly proved to have been a failure, a source of unhappiness and dislike rather than sympathy and union, the law ought not to prevent its dissolution. They have multiplied largely the grounds of divorce, including some that are very trifling. In Denmark, in Norway, in Prussia, and in some other parts of Germany, they grant divorce by mutual consent, subject to certain conditions which are intended to guard against the action of mere caprice, by securing a long period of delay for reconsideration. In Switzerland, under slightly different forms, the same system prevails, and the widest discretion is granted to the tribunals. A power of granting it for reasons not assigned in the law has in many parts of Germany, been vested with princes,[95] and under lax laws and lax administration divorces have, in some parts of Europe, multiplied to an extraordinary degree. In Switzerland, in 1876 there were no less than 1,102 divorces in a population of about 2,800,000; and although Switzerland is one of the few countries where the number of divorces tends slightly to decrease, that number is

---

[95] Glasson, pp. 67–106. In Norway there must also be the consent of the King (ibid. p. 221). In Sweden the King, acting in his Council of State, can grant it for incompatibility of temper, apparently at the demand of one party (ibid. p. 220).

still, I believe, in proportion to the population, higher than in any other European country.[96] Some portions of Germany come next on the list. Divorces appear to have been, during the last ten years, somewhat more frequent in Germany than in France, but in France the rate of increase is more rapid.[97]

It may be doubted, however, whether divorces are anywhere more frequent and more easy than in some parts of the United States, and it is remarkable that among these parts are the New England States, which were the special centres of American Puritanism. It is remarkable also that this great facility of divorce should exist in a country which has long been conspicuous for its high standard of sexual morality and for its deep sense of the sanctity of marriage.[98] There is no general divorce law in the United States; each State, provided it does not establish ploygamy, may make its own marriage laws, and the differences are very great. South Carolina admits no divorce; New York admits it ony for adultery. In Maine, on the other hand, it may be given whenever 'the judge deems it reasonable and proper, and consistent with peace and morality.' In Arizona the same latitude prevails; and in several States, where such provisions do not formally exist, the discretion practically exercised by the courts is scarcely less.[99] Dakota is said to be, of all parts of the United States, the most notorious for its facilities of divorce. Under cover of laws

---

[96] Ibid. p. 164. From the Foreign Office report of 1894 it appears that in 1892 there were 881 divorces in a population of 2,962,098; in Belgium in that year there were 441 in a population of 6,195,355; in the Netherlands, 354 in a population of 4,669,576; in Sweden, 316 in a population of 4,806,865; in Norway, 39 out of a population of 2,022,000.

[97] See the statistics collected in the *Return of the Number of Divorces in Foreign Countries* (Foreign Office, 1895).

[98] Thus Tocqueville observed: 'L'Amérique est assurément le pays du monde où le lien du mariage est le plus respecté et où l'on a conçu l'idée la plus haute et la plus juste du bonheur conjugal' (*La Démocratie en Amérique*, ii. p. 215). In another passage he states that all travellers are agreed that the standard of social morals is higher in the United States than in England or any other country (iii. p. 331).

[99] *Encyclopædia Americana*, art. 'Divorce.'

granting divorce for cruelty and ill-usage it has been frequently accorded on the most frivolous pretexts. In the
twenty years between 1866 and 1886, on this ground alone
45,731 wives and 6,122 husbands are said to have obtained it.
Collusive suits are very common. The increase of divorces has
been proportionately far more rapid than that of population.
In the period from 1867 to 1886 divorces increased in the
United States nearly 157 per cent., while population only increased about 60 per cent. In the Census returns of 1890 we
find 49,101 men and 71,895 women mentioned as divorced,
exclusive of divorced persons who have remarried. In some
States, indeed, the unlimited liberty of divorce which Milton
desired for one sex has been very nearly attained by both.[100]
Hardly any problem affecting the future of humanity is more
important than the type and character which the great Republic of the West is hereafter destined to assume. In the
opinion of many good judges, the possible decay of its family
life through the excessive multiplication of divorces is the
darkest cloud upon its horizon.

It would be scarcely possible, without much personal observation of a society in which such a system exists, to form
any confident estimate of its effects. In 1878, important restrictions were introduced into the marriage law of Connecticut by removing 'general misconduct' from the causes of
divorce, and, in consequence of the change, divorce in this
State greatly diminished.[101] Occasional protests against the

---

[100] The Foreign Office *Report on Divorces in Foreign Countries* (1895); and
see also a curious article on 'Divorce made Easy' in the *North American
Review*, July, 1893. Several examples are given in this article of the extremely frivolous grounds upon which divorce has been granted under
the pretext of cruelty. Woolsey (*Divorce and Divorce Legislation in the United
States*) has collected many statistics about American divorce, but he complains that they have only been published in a few States. According to
the Foreign Office report, divorces are proportionately most numerous
among the negroes, and, next to them, among the native-born whites.
They are rarest among the Irish and Canadian Catholics.

[101] *Encyclopædia Americana*, art. 'Divorce.'

prevailing license are sometimes heard, but they do not appear to be very powerful, and, on the whole, the tendency of recent legislation seems to be rather to enlarge than to restrict the liberty of divorce.[102] Some very serious American writers defend it. They contend that, in spite of these laws, the high moral tone that has long existed in America in the relation of the sexes is unimpaired; that the marriages of respectable Protestants, as well as of Catholics, are quite as pure and stable in the United States under the system of great legal license as they are in Europe; and that the numerous divorces, which so impress a foreigner, take place among other classes, and have the effect of mitigating grave evils. The legislator, in the words of the chief American writer on the subject, must choose between illicit connections and a wide liberty of divorce. The marriage-tie is not likely to be often violated if it may be easily dissolved. Illicit connections are not likely to be formed and persisted in when there is little difficulty in bringing them within the domain of law and of settled rights. A system under which marriages may be very easily contracted and very easily dissolved may not in itself be good, but it is, in the opinion of these writers, the best means of remedying or preventing other, and perhaps greater, evils.[103] Such rea-

---

[102] Mr. Woolsey goes so far as to say: 'Every change of legislation in the United States increases the number of divorces. If there is any principle in our legislation, it is not a moral one of reverence for the most sacred institution of the family and of married life, but it is a desire to afford relief for cases that are nearly as pressing as those that have relief afforded already' (Woolsey, *Divorce and Divorce Legislation in the United States*, 2nd edit. 1882, p. 247).

[103] See Bishop's *Marriage and Divorce*, especially his remarks on the state of South Carolina, i. 38. See, too, the article of Mr. Beech Lawrence, *Revue de Droit International*, ii. 244–59; Glasson, pp. 223–24. M. Glasson protests against the views of American writers. Speaking of the results of the very similar license in Switzerland, he says: 'Le mariage tend à devenir dans certaines classes de la société un simple bail' (p. 160). The article in the *North American Review* which I have cited above maintains that the American facilities of marriage and divorce do not seriously diminish the number of illegitimate births. See also on this subject Car-

sonings appear to me to be very questionable, and not a little dangerous. It is evident, indeed, that in some parts of the United States, as well as in some parts of Europe, under the operation of the divorce laws, a kind of inferior and unstable marriage, much like the Roman *concubinatus*, is growing up.

It is a curious fact that divorce, which was long regarded as the special privilege of the male, and as specially injurious to women, has become most frequent and popular in the country in which the position of women is probably the highest, and that it is most frequently demanded by them. The same phenomenon may be found in Switzerland, which on questions of divorce approximates more nearly than any other country to the American system;[104] and it is also to be found in France.[105] It is not inexplicable. Laws which grant divorce for violence, or cruelty, or habitual intoxication, are a special protection to the sex which is the weaker and the more sober, and the tendency of modern legislation to give women increased rights of property and employment diminishes the inequality between the two parties in the marriage contract. The difference which English law establishes between adultery in a man and adultery in a woman, though it is strenuously defended by English, French, and Italian lawyers, on the ground of the more serious effects of female adultery on the constitution and the property of the family,[106] is not widely adopted. It does not exist in Scotland. It is not recognised by the canon law, and it is not in accordance with the general tenor of modern legislation.[107]

Some of the evils which American legislation professes to

---

lier, *Le Mariage aux Etats-Unis*. Mr. Bryce is of opinion that the average of domestic virtue is higher in the United States than in Europe (*American Commonwealth*, iii. pp. 54–5, 499–500, 515), and Mr. Rhodes strongly maintains the same view (*History of the United States*, iii. 97–100).

[104] Glasson, p. 166.

[105] *Foreign Office Report* (1895).

[106] Montesquieu, *Esprit des Lois*,xxvi. c. 8.

[107] See on this subject *Revue de Droit International*, xv. 367–68.

remedy, by giving great facilities both of marriage and of divorce, have been dealt with in other countries by special legislation in favour of illegitimate children. The kind of moral or quasi-moral stigma which the public opinion of most countries attaches to persons who are known to be born out of wedlock, is a curious instance of the way in which considerations of public interest and considerations of morals become confused and intermingled. Few things can seem more irrational than to blame a man for one of the few circumstances of life which can by no possibility be in any degree his fault. The sentiment is a kind of correlative to the aristocratic sentiment which transfers to a living man something of the merits of his ancestors, and it is supported by a strong feeling of the expediency of defending, by the whole weight of public opinion, the inviolability of the family. The French Revolutionists, in 1793, attempted to break down this sentiment by decreeing that legitimate and illegitimate children should have equal rights. The Roman law and the canon law, which is followed in Scotland and in all, or nearly all, the legislations of the Continent, humanely, and, I think, wisely, mitigates the injustice to the children and promotes the marriage of the parents by providing that illegitimate children become legitimate through the subsequent marriage of their parents.[108] English law refuses them this remedy, though it recognises as legitimate all children born in marriage, even when the marriage immediately precedes the birth. It is remarkable that the United States have, for the most part, followed in this respect the English law.[109] In England, also, illegitimate children have, as such, no rights of heritage. Many continental legislations, following the Roman rule, which is also the Germanic rule, give them equal

---

[108] Ibid. ii. 70.

[109] Compare Blackstone, Book i. c. 16, and Carlier, *Le Mariage aux Etats-Unis*, pp. 178–82. M. Carlier says that Ohio is the only exception. The English law on the subject is very ancient. The Statute of Merton (20 Henry III. c. 9) decreed that bastards were not to be rendered legitimate by marriage of parents.

rights with legitimate children in the succession of their mothers and of their relatives in the maternal line, and some of them, under certain circumstances, give them rights, though usually in a less degree, to the paternal succession.[110] The provisions which exist in many continental legislations, making it a less crime for a mother to kill her illegitimate than her legitimate child, spring from another order of ideas—from the belief that in the former case the act is more likely to be perpetrated in an ungovernable paroxysm of shame and of remorse.[111]

The secularisation of marriage legislation is an evident accompaniment, if it is not a consequence, of the progress of democracy. One of its necessary consequences is, that the natural liberty of marriage should never be withheld, except on the ground of evident and considerable physical, moral, or social danger. Under this head falls the question, which has been so much debated in England, about the lawfulness of marrying a deceased wife's sister.

There can be little doubt that the opposition to these marriages rests mainly upon theological grounds.[112] It is said that they are forbidden in the Levitical law, and the belief in their impropriety was adopted by the canon law, and has passed through the canon law into English legislation, into one of the canons of the English Church, and into the Table of Affinities in the English Prayer Book. The Catholic and Anglican views on this subject are, however, not the same. The Catholic regards the prohibition as resting, not on direct Divine or natural law, but merely on an ecclesiastical command, and his Church therefore claims and constantly exercises the right of dispensing with it. English divines and legislators under Henry VIII. and Elizabeth treated these marriages as 'incestuous,' and maintained that they are condemned by the Old

---

[110] See *Revue de Droit International*, ix. 259–63.

[111] Ibid. vii. p. 234.

[112] See the very candid confession of the Bishop of Winchester (*Hansard*, cclxxx. 1671).

Testament. It is by no means irrelevant to observe that the conflict of Henry VIII. with the Pope grew out of the refusal of the Pope to dissolve, at the wish of the king, a marriage of affinity, and that the title of Elizabeth to the throne rested upon the position that this marriage was invalid.

The interpretation of the Old Testament adopted by the Anglican authorities is, to say the least of it, very disputable. The Jews themselves maintain that this kind of marriage is not forbidden in the Old Testament, and great numbers of the most eminent Christian divines concur in their opinion.[113] It is said, on the one side, that with one important exception, the corresponding relation of marriage with a deceased brother's widow is forbidden in the Levitical law,[114] and that some of the other Levitical prohibitions rest on the notion of affinity, and seem to imply that the Jews regarded relations acquired through marriage like blood relations. On the other hand, it is quite clear that the single passage in the Bible which directly forbids marriage with a wife's sister forbids it only during the lifetime of the first wife, and therefore, as far as it has any bearing on the controversy, implies that the prohibition would terminate on her death.[115] It was intended in this one respect to restrict the latitude of polygamy which was then conceded to the Jews; to forbid in the future marriages like that of Jacob, who, apparently with the full approbation of the Old Testament writer, had at the same time two sisters as wives.

Some distinguished commentators maintain that, 'according to the Hebrew law, a man was more nearly related to the house of his brother (that is, the family of his own father)

---

[113] A great mass of evidence upon this subject, from divines and scholars in various countries, will be found in a pamphlet called *Opinions of Hebrew and Greek Professors of the European Universities, &c., on the subject of the Marriage with a Deceased Wife's Sister*, edited by T. Paynter Allen for the Marriage Law Reform Asssociation.

[114] Lev. xviii. 16.

[115] 'Thou shalt not take a woman to her sister, to be a rival to her, to uncover her nakedness beside the other in her lifetime' (Lev. xviii. 18, Revised Version).

than to the family of his wife's parents,' and that this accounts for the fact that marriage with a deceased brother's wife is expressly forbidden, while there is no corresponding prohibition of marriage with a deceased wife's sister.[116] It is certain that the Old Testament does not directly condemn such marriages, and it is very doubtful whether it condemns them even by inference. It is not at all doubtful that it sanctions, and sometimes eminently blesses, polygamy;[117] that it strictly enjoins that, in every case of adultery, both parties should be put to death,[118] that it makes it a capital offence for a man to have intercourse with a woman who, though unmarried, was betrothed to another;[119] that it commands that a man who had defiled an unbetrothed virgin should be compelled to marry her;[120] that it forbids marriage with aliens in religion;[121] that it not only permits, but enjoins, a man to marry the widow of his deceased brother if she had no children, or only daughters,[122] which could scarcely be the case if such marriages of affinity were in their own nature incestuous. It is not easy to understand the process of mind which, among all these provisions of the Jewish code, selects a very doubtful inference condemnatory of marriage with the deceased wife's sister as alone binding on the conscience of the Imperial Parliament.

The other Scriptural argument which has been adduced is based upon a metaphor, which is treated and argued from as if it were a literal fact. Because man and wife are spoken of as being 'one flesh,' it is inferred that they are literally so, and that it is, therefore, as incestuous for a man to marry his wife's sister as to marry his own nearest relative. This mode of treat-

---

[116] See the views of Professor Dillman, of Berlin, in Paynter Allen's pamphlet, pp. 14–16.

[117] Gen. xvi. 7–16, xxx. 16–18, xxxi. 50, xxxiii. 1–5; Exod. xxi. 10; Deut. xxi. 15; Judges viii. 30; 1 Sam. i. 2; 2 Sam. xxi. 8; 2 Chron. xxiv. 2, 3.

[118] Lev. xx. 10; Deut. xxii. 22.

[119] Deut. xxii. 23, 24.

[120] Deut. xxii. 28, 29.

[121] Exod. xxxiv. 14–16; Deut. vii. 3; Ezra ix., x. 1–14; Neh. xiii 23–31.

[122] Deut. xxv. 5, 6.

ing metaphors has played a great part in the history of the Church. The whole doctrine of transubstantiation is based on such a method of interpretation; and it was also largely used by the many theologians who, in the early Church, condemned second marriages on the ground that they were inferentially forbidden by St. Paul's comparison of marriage to the union of Christ with his Church.[123]

But, however important these theological considerations may be for the guidance of individuals in their own personal conduct, they are considerations which ought to have no weight in legislation. The question, and the only question, for the legislator is, whether these marriages produce such a clear preponderance of evil as to justify him in restraining the natural liberty of marriage by forbidding them. Of the physical evils which accompany and stamp really incestuous marriages there can here be no question. Many marriages, indeed, which take place without legal impediment are on such grounds liable to very great objection. Few persons can be insensible to the evils that have been brought into the royal families of Europe by frequent intermarriages within a small circle, and similar evils, due to either social or geographical causes, may be found in other societies. The marriages of near cousins are of very doubtful expediency; and arguments immeasurably stronger than any brought against marriage with the deceased wife's sister might be advanced to justify a legislative prohibition of the marriage of persons afflicted with some grave hereditary disease. Of this class of evils there is

---

[123] I have collected much evidence on this subject in my *History of Morals* (ii. 326–28). It is curious to observe how these kinds of ideas go together. The Council of Illiberis, in the fourth century, is the first council that condemned marriage with a deceased wife's sister. This Council permitted in some cases laymen to baptise, but specially excluded from this right laymen who had been twice married. St. Basil (about a.d. 370) is the first of the Fathers who denounces marriage with a deceased wife's sister, and he is also (as Dr. McCaul observes) one of the most vehement assertors of the impurity and sinfulness of second marriages. See Allen's *Opinions*, p. 167.

nothing in the marriage we are considering, and the sole real question is its social effects.

Of all the social effects of matrimony, that which most concerns the legislator is the interest of the children, and Montesquieu has justly remarked that, in one large class of cases, those interests are peculiarly consulted by this kind of marriage.[124] It frequently happens that a mother dies leaving a young and busy husband and very young children, and in such cases a second marriage will almost certainly take place. No marriage can, in general, be so much in the interest of the children; no marriage can be, in general, so congenial to the feelings of the first wife as a marriage which makes the sister of the dead woman the mother of her children. Such cases form a large proportion of the marriages with a deceased wife's sister, and they frequently take place in obedience to the wishes of the dying wife. They are not unusual among the rich; they are very common among the poor; and it is not too much to say that they stand conspicuous among marriages for the purity of their motives and for the beneficence of their effects.[125]

It is argued, however, that the permission of marriage with

---

[124] Aux Indes . . . si un mari a perdu sa femme, il ne manque pas d'en épouser la sœur, et cela est très naturel; car la nouvelle épouse devient la mère des enfants de sa sœur, et il n'y a point d'injuste marâtre' (*Esprit des Lois*, xxvi. c. 15). Montesquieu seems, however, to think that, where it is customary for brothers-in-law and sisters-in law to live together in the same house, their marriage should not be permitted.

[125] This, *e.g.*, is the report of the Ministry of Ecclesiastical Affairs in Saxony: 'Marriages with the sister of a deceased wife are not rare in Saxony, and occur most frequently among the labouring classes and the agricultural population, where mostly the support of such near relations of the survivor precedes marriage. Public opinion, for a very long time past, takes no umbrage at such marriages, which often have their foundation in a wish expressed by the deceased wife upon the deathbed that her sister should be a careful mother to the children she leaves behind; and when such purposes are fulfilled these marriages enjoy a general approval' (Paynter Allen's *Opinions on Marriage with a Deceased Wife's Sister*, pp. 180–81).

a deceased wife's sister would destroy all familiar intercourse with sisters-in-law during the lifetime of a wife; would make it impossible for the widower to have his sister-in-law in his house after the death of his wife; would even make it difficult for her to attend his wife on her bed of sickness; and that it would thus introduce revolution and suspicion into the constitution of the family. Undoubtedly, if all this were true it would form a real argument, well deserving of the consideration of a legislator. The best answer to such statements is that these marriages exist over a great proportion of the civilised globe without the smallest question, or producing the smallest family disturbance. It is the custom of some of their opponents to declaim on this subject as if the family were a peculiarly English institution, not known in other countries. In all, or nearly all, of the United States these marriages are legal and common, and though a modern school of High Churchmen have raised some objections to them on ecclesiastical grounds, no question has been raised about their domestic consequences. Lowell, while dilating on the earnest protest of thoughtful men in the United States against the demoralising consequences of too lax laws about divorce, contrasts it with the complete absence of any complaint of bad consequences arising from marriage with a deceased wife's sister. 'Nothing,' wrote Chief Justice Story, 'is more common in almost all the States of America than second marriages of this sort, and, so far from being doubtful as to their moral tendency, they are among us deemed the very best sort of marriages. In my whole life I have never heard the slightest suggestion against them founded on moral or domestic considerations.'

In all the chief Protestant countries on the Continent these marriages have long been legal and common, and are perfectly accepted by opinion. In the Catholic Church, it is true, like the marriages of cousins, they require a dispensation, but such dispensations are frequently, in some countries I believe

---

[126] Allen, pp. 177–78. See, too, the Letters of Dr. Woolsey, p. 153.

almost invariably, granted.[127] By the French law of 1832 a dispensation from the civil power is required, but this dispensation is regularly accorded.[128] The great British colonies have nearly all taken the course of expressly legalising these marriages, though their legislation has been much retarded by a frequent and unrighteous exercise of the royal veto. These marriages, however, are now perfectly legal in Canada, in the three Australian colonies, in Tasmania, and in South Africa.[129]

It would be difficult to overstate the extravagance of the language which has been sometimes employed in England by their opponents. One gentleman, who had been Lord Chancellor of England, more than once declared that if marriage with a deceased wife's sister ever became legal 'the decadence of England was inevitable,' and that, for his part, he would rather see 300,000 Frenchmen landed on the English coasts.[130] Pictures have been drawn of the moral anarchy such marriages must produce, which are read by American, colonial, and continental observers with a bewilderment that is not unmixed with disgust, and are, indeed, a curious illustration of the

---

[127] 'As every one knows, marriage with a deceased wife's sister very often occurs among Catholics, the Roman Pontiff readily dispensing in such a case of affinity; since, as there is no Divine precept or positive law opposed to these unions, it is within his power to permit them, and he does always permit them, especially when there exists some motive of convenience, or necessity for re-establishing an injured reputation or of compensating, as far as possible, irreparable wrongs' (Manuel Ribero, Professor at Salamanca, Madrid, and Granada. Allen, p. 36). See, too, the *Revue de Droit International*, ii. 65.

[128] Garin, *Conditions pour la Validité du Mariage*, pp. 237–328. A report from the First Minister of Justice in 1882 states that, in the preceding year, 841 widowers in France were authorised to contract marriage with their late wives' sisters (Allen, p. 174). See, too, pp. 179–80.

[129] In South Australia the royal assent was refused no less than four times. It was refused once in New Zealand, and once in Natal. In Canada the measure was introduced by a Catholic, and supported by the Catholic clergy. In Mauritius, which is mainly Catholic, it was also passed. See *Proceedings of the Colonial Conference*, April 14, 1887, pp. 4–5, 15, 25–26.

[130] *Hansard*, cclxxx. 1675. See, too, a speech of Lord Hatherley (Marriage Law Defence Union Tracts, No. xxx. p. 20).

extreme insularity of the English mind. The truth seems to be that there are cases in which the presence of a young and attractive sister-in-law in a widower's house would, under any system of law, produce scandal. There are others where, in all countries, a sister-in-law's care and presence would seem natural. There are cases where every murmur is silenced by the simple consideration that the two parties are at perfect liberty to marry if they please. Experience—the one sure guide in politics—conclusively shows how quickly the best public opinion of a country accommodates itself to these marriages; how easy, natural, and beneficent they prove; how little disturbance of any kind they introduce into domestic relations. They will long be opposed on the ground of ecclesiastical traditions, and apart from all consideration of consequences, by a section of theologians in England, in America, and in the Colonies. Those who consider them wrong should abstain from contracting them, and a wise legislature will deal gently with the scruples of objecting clergymen, as it has done in the case of the marriage of divorced persons. But the law of the land should rest on other than ecclesiastical grounds, and a prohibition that has no foundation in nature or in reason is both unjust and oppressive. It is not for the true interests of morals or of family life that the law should brand as immoral, unions which those who contract them feel and know to be perfectly innocent, and which are fully sanctioned by the general voice of the civilised world, by an overwhelming majority of the English race, by a great and steadily increasing weight of public opinion at home, and by repeated majorities in the House of Commons. In an age when most wise and patriotic men desire that the influence and character of the Upper House should be upheld and strengthened, few things can be more deplorable than that this House should have suffered itself to be made the representative of a swiftly vanishing superstition, the chief instrument in perpetuating a paltry and an ignoble persecution.

CHAPTER 8

Socialism

In any forecast that may be attempted of the probable influence of democracy in the world, a foremost place must be given to its relations to labour questions, and especially to those socialist theories which, during the last twenty years, have acquired a vastly extended influence on political speculation and political action. These theories, it is true, are by no means new. Few things are more curious to observe in the extreme Radical speculation of our times than the revival of beliefs which had been supposed to have been long since finally exploded—the aspirations to customs belonging to early and rudimentary stages of society.

The doctrine of common property in the soil, which, under the title of the nationalisation of land, has of late years obtained so much popularity, is avowedly based on the remote ages, when a few hunters or shepherds roved in common over an unappropriated land, and on the tribal and communal properties which existed in the barbarous or semi-barbarous stages of national development, and everywhere disappeared with increasing population, increasing industry, and increasing civilisation.

The old doctrine of the criminality of lending money at interest, however moderate, for the purpose of deriving profit from the loan, has had a long and memorable history. It was held alike byAristotle and the Fathers of the Church. It was authoritatively taught by a long succession of Popes and Councils, and it played a great part in impeding the industrial development of Europe.[1] But for about two centuries it had almost wholly vanished among laymen. It was slowly abandoned even by the Church, which had so persistently taught it, and all the governments and all the great industries of the civilised world depend, and long have depended, on loans

---

[1] I have treated this subject at length in my *History of the Rise and Influence of the Spirit of Rationalism,* ii. 250–70 (Cab. ed.) The canons of many different Councils condemning usury will be found in the *Analyse des Conciles,* par le rév. Père Richard: art. 'Usure.' This distinguished ecclesiastic gives the following clear summary of the teaching of the Church: 'On ne peut lire ces canons sans être persuadé qu'ils condamnent l'usure comme mauvaise en soi; qu'ils la condamnent dans toutes sortes de personnes, soit ecclésiastiques, soit laïques; qu'ils la condamnent à l'egard de quelque personne qu'on l'exerce, riche ou pauvre, négociant ou non; qu'ils mettent les usuriers au nombre des séditieux, des vindicatifs, des concubinaires, &c.; qu'ils parlent de l'usure comme d'un crime détestable, défendu par toutes les lois divines et humaines; qu'ils déclarent hérétiques ceux qui soutiendroient avec obstination que l'usure n'est point un péché; qu'ils décident qu'il n'est pas permis de prêter à usure lors même qu'il s'agit de faire valoir les biens des veuves, des pupiles ou des lieux-pies; qu'ils assurent que le prêt doit toujours être purement gratuit, hors le cas du lucre cessant ou du dommage naissant; et enfin qu'ils définissent et caractérisent l'usure par le gain ou le profit quelconque exigé ou espéré au-delà du sort principal, de quelque part qu'il vienne, riche ou pauvre, commerçant ou autre; de quelque espèce qu'il soit, argent, denrée, service, et lorsqu'il est perçu en vertu du prêt ou comme le prix de l'argent prêté. Lucrum ex mutuo, pretium pecuniæ mutuatæ. Tel est le caractère distinctif de l'usure selon les conciles, la surabondance du prêt, our l'excédant, le surcroît ajouté au sort principal, l'addition au capital, le profit qu'on tire des choses prêtées et en vertu du prêt qu'on en a fait.' So also Bossuet: 'La tradition constante des conciles, à commencer par les plus anciens, celle des papes, des pères, des interprètes, et de l'Eglise romaine est d'interpréter ce verset, "Mutuum date nihil inde sperantes," comme prohibitif du profit qu'on tire du prêt' ('*Seconde instruction sur la version du Nouveau Testament imprimée à Trévoux,*' *Œuvres de Bossuet* (1815), tom. iv. p. 544. See, too, his treatise, *Sur l'Usure*).

made for the sake of profit, on borrowed money, and punctually paid interest. But the old superstition has not perished. It will be found repeatedly put forward in the writings of Mr. Ruskin, and the abolition of all interest on money is a favourite doctrine in advanced modern Socialist programmes.[2]

The system of making different forms of industry monopolies in the hands of different corporations, of restricting each labourer to one kind of labour, of regulating minutely by authority the hours, the wages, and all the other conditions of labour, has been abundantly tried in the past. It may be seen in the castes of the East, which descend from a period beyond the range of authentic history, and it was equally apparent in the mediæval guilds and other corporations that were abolished at the French Revolution, and in the restrictive Tudor legislation which lingered in England till the first decade of the nineteenth century. All these ideas of restriction and control are once more in full activity among us, and many of them are rapidly passing into legislation.

Probably the oldest and most important phase of the long battle for human liberty is the struggle to maintain individual rights of property and bequest against the inordinate claims of the ruling power. The very essence of unqualified despotism is the claim of the supreme power of the State, whatever it may be, to absolute power over the property of all its subjects. 'As the Brahmana sprang from Brahman's mouth,' said the laws of Manu, 'as he is the firstborn, and as he possesses the Veda, he is by right the Lord of this whole creation.' 'Whatever exists in the world is the property of the Brahmana; on account of the excellence of his origin the Brahmana is, indeed, entitled to it all. The Brahmana eats but his own food, wears but his own apparel, bestows but his own in alms. Other mortals subsist through the benevolence of the Brah-

---

[2] Thus Mr. George says: 'The feeling that interest is the robbery of industry is widespread and growing, and on both sides of the Atlantic shows itself more and more in popular literature and in popular movements' (*Progress and Poverty*, p. 157).

mana.[3] The Oriental despot claimed a similar right of ownership over the property of his subjects; and such a claim has
descended far into modern history. It was asserted in the
strongest terms by the supporters of the Divine rights of kings.
In the brilliant days of Louis XIV., the Sorbonne formally declared 'that all the goods of his subjects belonged to the King
in person, and that in taking of them he took only what belonged to him.' 'The King,' said Louis XIV., 'represents the
whole nation. All power is in his hands. . . . Kings are absolute
rulers, and have naturally a full and entire right of disposing
of all the goods both of Churchmen and laymen.[4]

In opposition to this claim, the rights of the individual and
the rights of the family to property have from the very dawn
of civilisation been opposed, and they form the first great
foundation of human liberty. They rest on the strongest and
deepest instinct of human nature—the love of the individual
for his family; and the most powerful of all the springs of
human progress is the desire of men to labour and to save for
the benefit of those who will follow them. Through countless
ages, religion and long-established custom have consecrated
and fortified these nobler elements of human nature, and in
all free countries the preservation of property is deemed the
first end of government. It has been a main object of law to
secure it.[5] The right of testamentary bequest passed into
Roman legislation as early as the Twelve Tables, and into
Athenian legislation as early as the laws of Solon; but the
primitive will, though it gave some new power to the individual proprietor, only modified in a small degree the inalienable reversionary rights which, under slightly varying
conditions, had been long before possessed by his children
and other blood relations.[6]

---

[3] *Laws of Manu*, i. 93, 100, 101.
[4] See Guyot, *Les Principes de '89 et le Socialisme*, pp. 50, 159, 160; Garet,
Les Bienfaits de la Révolution, pp. 4–5.
[5] Locke *On Civil Government*.
[6] See on this subject Sir H. Maine on *Ancient Law*, chapters vi. and vii.
and the remarks of Grote, *Hist. of Greece*, iii. 138–40.

In modern Socialism such rights are wholly ignored, and the most extreme power over property ever claimed by an Oriental tyrant is attributed to a majority told by the head. There are men among us who teach that this majority, if they can obtain the power, should take away, absolutely and without compensation, from the rich man his land and capital, either by an act of direct confiscation or by the imposition of a tax absorbing all their profits; should abolish all rights of heritage, or at least restrict them within the narrowest limits; and should in this way mould the society of the future.

This tendency in the midst of the many and violent agitations of modern life, to revert to archaic types of thought and custom, will hereafter be considered one of the most remarkable characteristics of the nineteenth century. It may be traced in more than one department of European literature; in Tractarian theology, which seeks its ideals in the Church as it existed before the Reformation; in pre-Raphaelite art, which regards Raphael and Michael Angelo as a decadence, and seeks its models among their predecessors. These two last movements, at least, have in a great degree spent their force; but we are living in the centre of a reaction towards Tudor regulation of industry and an almost Oriental exaggeration of the powers of the State, though there are already, I think, some signs of the inevitable revolt which is to come.

Schemes for remodelling society on a communistic basis, banishing from it all inequalities of fortune, and by the strong force of law giving it a type and character wholly different from that which it would have spontaneously assumed, have had a great fascination for many minds. In ancient Greece, it is sufficient to mention the system of common property which was established by law in Crete, and the very similar institutions which Lycurgus is said to have given to Sparta; and the 'Republic' of Plato, which is largely based on this example, is the precursor of a great literature of Utopias. It is worthy of notice that in all these cases the existence of a slave caste was considered indispensable to the working of a communistic society, and that both Lycurgus and Plato were prepared, in the interests of the State, to deal as freely with the relations of the sexes to each other, and with the relations of children to their parents, as with the disposition of property. The Spartan laws on this subject are well known, and Plato, like many of his modern followers, pushed communism to its full logical consequences by advocating community of wives and of children, as well as of property.

Such extravagances never appear in the Hebrew writings: but those writings contain some remarkable provisions intended to prevent or arrest great inequalities of fortune, and give the existing disposition of property, and especially of landed property, a stability which it would not otherwise have possessed. Some modern critics, it is true, have doubted whether the more important of these enactments were ever more than ideals which the prophetic writers threw into the form of precepts and which neither were, nor could have been, fully put in force. The institution of the Sabbatical year provided that in every seventh year all debts owed by Hebrews should be cancelled, and private property in land suspended. The fields and vineyards and olive yards were in that year to remain unsown and uncultivated; the owner was neither to reap the harvest nor gather the grapes; but the poor were to take whatever they could find to eat, and the beasts of the field were to eat what the poor had left.[7] It has been truly said that such a provision, if literally carried out, would naturally have condemned the land to periodical famines;[8] but there was a promise of a miraculous harvest every sixth year, which would provide food sufficient for three years.[9] It was at the same time enacted that every fiftieth year should be consecrated as a jubilee year, in which bondmen were to be emancipated, and all who had sold land were, without purchase,

---

[7] Exod. xxiii. 10, 11; Lev. xxv. 1–7; Deut. xv. 2. There are many allusions to the Sabbatical year and its observances in Josephus; and it is also mentioned by Tacitus, *Hist.* v. 4.

[8] Renan, *Hist. d'Israël,* ii. 375–76. Compare, however, the defence of the Sabbatical year in Ewald's *Antiquities of Israel.*

[9] Lev. xxv. 20–22.

to re-enter into their former possessions. No sale of land in perpetuity was to be permitted. Every alienation of land was to last only till the jubilee year, and the price was to be calculated upon that basis.[10]

In the Jewish sect of the Essenes community of goods appears to have been established, and in the early Christian Church something of the same kind for a time prevailed. 'All that believed,' we are told, 'were together, and had all things common; and they sold their possessions and goods, and parted them to all, according as any man had need.' 'Not one of them said that aught of the things which he possessed was his own; but they had all things common. . . . As many as were possessors of lands or houses sold them, and brought the prices of the things that were sold, and laid them at the Apostles' feet, and distribution was made unto each according as any one had need.[11] Such a state of things was possible in a small society pervaded by an overpowering religious enthusiasm, and by an intense conviction that the end of the world was at hand. At the same time, it is not certain how far this communistic organisation extended.[12] The exhortations in the New Testament to give alms, and the references to rich Christians, show that it was by no means universal. Ideas of common property, however, spread far among the early Christians, and in the second century it was the boast of Tertullian that 'all things are common among us, except our wives.'[13]

There are passages in the New Testament that are undoubtedly extremely hostile to riches and the rich, and the strong movement towards asceticism and voluntary poverty which marked the next stages of the Church's history much strengthened this tendency, while the very rhetorical character of the

---

[10] Lev. xxv. *et seq.* There was an exception in favour of land on which houses were built in towns surrounded by a wall. These houses were not to be surrendered in the jubilee year.

[11] Acts ii. 44, 45; iv. 32, 34, 35.

[12] Acts v. 4.

[13] Apol. xxxix.

patristic writings intensified its expression. Some well-known passages in the writings of the Fathers clearly foreshadow the Christian Socialism which is flourishing in our day. Thus, St. Ambrose, St. Basil, St. Chrysostom, St. Gregory the Great, and even St. Augustine, have gone so far as to maintain that a rich man who does not clothe the naked, and give bread to the hungry, has committed robbery as truly as if he had seized the property of another; that charity is not a free gift, but the payment of a debt and an obligation of strict justice; that all property beyond what is necessary is held in trust for the poor; and that if it is withheld, this is an act of fraud, which may easily become an act of homicide. Pages may be filled with passages to this effect from the most eminent of the Fathers.[14] St. Basil, for example, compares the rich to men who had occupied all the seats in the amphitheatre at a spectacle which was intended for all, and prevented all others from coming in.[15] 'The earth,' he says, 'is given in common to all men. Let no man call that his own which has been taken in excess of his needs from the common store, and which is kept by violence. . . . It is no greater crime to take from him who has, than to refuse to share your abundance with those who want. The bread which you keep back is the bread of the hungry; the garment you shut up belongs to the naked. The money you bury in the earth is the ransom and the freedom of the wretched.'[16] 'Nature,' says St. Ambrose, 'has made all things common, for the use of all. . . . Nature made common right, usurpation made private right.'[17] 'The earth has been formed as the common property of the rich and of the poor. Why, rich men, do you claim property in it for yourselves alone?'[18]

---

[14] See, *e.g.*, Champagny, *La Charité Chrétienne*, pp. 36–42; Janet, *Hist. de la Science Politique*, i. 294–95; Schoelcher, *La Famille, la Propriété et le Christianisme*.

[15] *Opera S. Basilii*, iii. 492.

[16] Ibid. ii. 725–26.

[17] *De Offic.* i. c. 28.

[18] *De Nabuthe Jesraelita*, c. i. §2.

Society could hardly rest permanently on such principles, and as Christianity became dominant in Europe they were in practice much mitigated. The aspirations to a communistic life found their gratification in the monasteries, which at the same time in every country absorbed and disciplined a great proportion of the more morbid, restless, and discontented characters. Among the many services which monasticism rendered to the world, not the least important was that of moderating the extreme passion and reverence for wealth, by setting up among mankind another ideal and scale of dignity. Industry at the same time developed, largely under the influence of the Church, into innumerable corporations. They were all under the patronage of different saints, and coloured deeply by religious elements, and the indirect influence of the Church in strengthening the reverence for tradition and encouraging the habit of organisation contributed perhaps as much as its direct influence to sustain them. Under the combined influence of the mediæval Church and of the feudal system, this process continued till industry in all its forms was organised and disciplined as it had never before been in Europe, while the strong repressive agency of the Church set narrow bounds to all kinds of speculation. If the system of corporations restricted in many ways the production of wealth, if the level of material comfort was very low, industry at least acquired an extraordinary measure of stability, and, except in times of war and famine, fluctuations of employment and wages were probably rare and inconsiderable. Class tyranny, or abuse of property, or economical causes affecting injuriously many interests, no doubt from time to time produced communistic or semi-communistic explosions, like the Jacqueries in France or the rebellions of Wat Tyler and Jack Cade in England, and there were a few teachers, like John Ball, who proclaimed that 'things will never be well in England so long as goods be not in common, and so long as there be villeins and gentlemen.'[19] But such movements were very rare.

---

[19] Green's *Hist. of the English People*, i. 440.

Gradually, however, from many sides and under many influences, the old mediæval structure began to break up. The monasteries, which in their own day had performed many useful services, had become grossly and hideously corrupt, while the enormous amount of property that flowed into them, the multitude of strong arms that they withdrew from productive labour, and their encouragement of mendicancy and idleness, made them an economical evil of the first magnitude. The old beliefs on which the edifice of Christendom rested were giving way. The learning of the Renaissance and the strong and independent industrial spirit that had arisen in the great towns of Europe were alike hostile to it. Industry began to outgrow the frameworks that had been made for it. The doctrine of the Church about lending money at interest proved utterly incompatible with the more advanced stages of material progress,[20] and when the Reformation broke out, it everywhere found its most ardent adherents in the intelligent industrial classes. The persecution and exile of such men contributed largely to scatter different industries over Europe and determine the comparative industrial position of different nations.

Great fluctuations in industry had also, from other causes, taken place. The discovery of the Cape passage by Vasco de Gama had given a new course to commerce, and the discovery of America produced effects that were still wider and far more deeply felt. The produce of the American mines created, in

---

[20] 'Il est faux que les conciles ne condamnent l'usure que dans les clercs et non dans les laïques, ou seulement quand elle est excessive et immodérée; ou lorsqu'on la prend sur le pauvre et non pas sur le riche et le commerçant; ou quand on l'exerce par un motif d'avarice et de cupidité; ou quand elle est accompagnée de fraudes et de rapines; ou lorsque ce sont des usuriers publics et de profession qui l'exercent. Toutes ces explications que l'on donne aux canons des conciles qui condamnent l'usure ne sont autres choses que de vaines subtilités et d'artificieuses chicanes.' 'Le prêt de commerce est vraiment un prêt simple et à jour qui doit être gratuit comme tous les autres prêts de la même manière et dont le prêteur ne peut exiger aucun intérêt, même modique . . . on ose défier les plus subtils et les plus artificieux sophistes de se tirer de là' (*Analyse des Conciles*, par le rev. Père Richard, art. 'Usure').

the most extreme form ever known in Europe, the change which beyond all others affects most deeply and universally the material wellbeing of men: it revolutionised the value of the precious metals, and, in consequence, the price of all articles, the effects of all contracts, the burden of all debts. In England, vast changes from arable land to pasture land took place, which involved the displacement of great populations, and became one of the most serious preoccupations of statesmen. To these things must be added the convulsions produced by the long religious wars that followed the Reformation, and the very serious change in the position of the poor produced by the suppression of the monasteries and the confiscation of their property. Ultimately, no doubt, the economical effect of this measure was beneficial to all classes, but its immediate consequence was to throw a vast multitude of poor and very helpless men unprotected upon the world, and to deprive another great multitude of the alms on which they mainly depended. The terrible Tudor laws about vagrancy, and the Elizabethan poor law, sufficiently indicate the acuteness of the crisis, and the sermons of Latimer and the writings of More enable us to see clearly the manner in which it arose.

Social, economical, and political causes bear a large part in the Reformation of the sixteenth century; and communism also had its representatives in the Anabaptists of Munster, who, under the leadership of Jan Matthys and John of Leyden, were for a time so formidable. 'Death to all priests and kings and nobles!' was their rallying-cry, and, while preaching some extravagant theological doctrines, they waged an implacable war against the rich. All these were ordered on pain of death to deliver up their gold and silver for common consumption, and it was proclaimed that everything was to be in common among those who had undergone the second baptism, and that meat and drink were to be provided at the common cost, though each man was to continue to work at his own craft. The movement, after desolating large districts in Germany and producing terrible crimes, at last perished in fire and blood. A few years later the theological doctrines of the Anabaptists spread widely, but the communistic side of their teaching died rapidly away.[21]

A considerable literature of Utopias, however, pointing to ideal states of society, arose. The 'Utopia' of More, which appeared at the end of 1515, led the way. It was obviously suggested by the 'Republic' of Plato, and, in addition to its great literary merits, it is remarkable for many incidental remarks exhibiting a rare political acumen, and anticipating reforms of a later age. It was in the main a picture of a purely ideal community resting upon unqualified communism. Money was no longer to exist. All private property was to be suppressed. The magistrates were to determine how much of this world's goods each man might possess, and how long he might hold it. No town was to be permitted to have more than 6,000 families, besides those of the country around it. No family must consist of less than ten or more than sixteen persons, the balance being maintained by transferring children from large to small families. Houses were to be selected by lot, and to change owners every ten years. Every one was to work, but to work only six hours a day. All authority was to rest on election. Like Plato, More considered a slave class essential to the working of his scheme, and convicts were to be made use of for that purpose.

Many other writers followed the example of More in drawing up ideal schemes of life and government, but they were much more exercises of the imagination than serious projects intended to be put in force. They formed a new and attractive department of imaginative literature, and they enabled writers to throw out suggestions to which they did not wish formally and definitely to commit themselves, or which could not be so easily or so safely expressed in direct terms. Bacon, Harrington, and Fénelon have all contributed to this literature, and traces of the communistic theories of More may be found in the great romance of Swift.[22] About a century after

---

[21] See Ranke's *Hist. of the Reformation in Germany*, iii. 583–610.

[22] See in *Gulliver's Travels*, part iv. ch. vi.

the appearance of the 'Utopia' of More the Dominican monk Campanella published his 'City of the Sun,' which was an elaborate picture of a purely communistic society, governed with absolute authority by a few magistrates, and from which every idea of individual property was banished. Like Plato, however, Campanella made community of wives an essential part of his scheme; for he clearly saw, and fully stated, that the spirit of property would never be extirpated as long as family life and family affection remained.

It is not probable that a literature of this kind exercised much real influence over the world; nor need we lay great stress upon the small religious communities which in Europe, and still more in America, have endeavoured to realise their desire for a common life. In the vast mass of political speculation that broke out in the eighteenth century there were elements of a more serious portent. 'The Spirit of the Laws,' which appeared in 1748, was by far the most important political work of the first half of this century; and in the general drift of his teaching Montesquieu was certainly very much opposed to the communistic spirit. He was eminently a constitutional writer, valuing highly liberty in all its forms, and convinced that this liberty could only be obtained by jealously restricting and dividing power, and introducing strong balances into constitutions. He was, however, a great admirer of the ancient writers, and passages in his teaching embody and foreshadow doctrines which afterwards pushed to extremes from which he would assuredly have recoiled. He maintained that, under democratic governments, it should be a main object of the legislator to promote equality of fortunes; that with this object he should impose restrictions on heritages, donations, and dowries; that not only should the goods of the father be divided equally among his children, but that there should also be special laws 'to equalise, so to speak, inequalities by imposing burdens on the rich and granting relief to the poor.'[23] He looked with considerable favour on sumptuary

---

[23] *Esprit des Lois,* livre v. ch. v.–vi.

laws, and he formally laid down the socialistic doctrine that every citizen has a right to claim work and support from the State. 'Whatever alms may be given to a man who is naked in the streets, this will not fulfil the obligations of the State, which owes to all the citizens an assured subsistence, food, and proper clothing, and a mode of life which is not contrary to health.' 'A well-organised State . . . gives work to those who are capable of it, and teaches the others to work.'[24]

Rousseau is more commonly connected with modern communism, but the connection does not appear to me to be very close. It is true that in his early Discourse on inequality he assailed private property, and especially landed property, as founded on usurpation and as productive of countless evils to mankind; but the significance of this treatise is much diminished when it is remembered that it was an elaborate defense of savage as opposed to civilised life. In his later and more mature works he strenuously maintained that 'the right of property is the most sacred of the rights of citizens, in some respects even more important than liberty itself;' that the great problem of government is 'to provide for public needs without impairing the private property of those who are forced to contribute to them;' that 'the foundation of the social compact is property, and that its first condition is that every individual should be protected in the peaceful enjoyment of that which belongs to him.'[25] In the 'Contrat Social,' however, he maintains that by the social contract man surrenders everything he possesses into the hands of the community; the State becomes the bases of property, and turns usurpation into right; it guarantees to each man his right of property in everything he possesses, but the right of each man to his own possessions is always subordinate to the right of the community over the whole.[26]

Rousseau, though one of the most fascinating, is one of the

---

[24] Ibid. livre xxiii. ch. xxix.
[25] *Discours sur l'Economie Politique.*
[26] *Contrat Social,* livre i. ch. viii.–ix.

most inconsistent of political writers, and he continually lays down broad general principles, but recoils from their legitimate consequences. He certainly desired a government in which individual property should be strictly protected, but by exaggerating to the highest degree the power of the State over all its members, and by denouncing all those restrictions and varieties of representation that mitigate the despotism of majorities he led the way to worse tyrannies than those which he assailed. He defended strongly the right to bequeath property, maintaining that without this power individual property would be very useless. He claims, however, for the State the right of regulating successions, and maintains that the spirit of their laws should be to prevent, as much as possible, property from passing away from the family.[27] His theory of taxation seems to me open to little real objection. All taxes, he says, should be imposed with the consent of the majority, and they should be imposed 'on a proportionate scale, which leaves nothing arbitrary.' The general rule is, that if one man possesses twice, four times, ten times what is possessed by another, his taxes should rise in the same proportion. But this principle should not be carried out with an inexorable rigidity. There should be a leaning in favour of the poor. That which is strictly necessary should be exempt from taxation. Luxuries and amusements should bear a disproportionate share, and as society naturally develops in the direction of excessive inequality, legislation should tend to equalise. Education should be a national concern. Rousseau did not desire to abolish private riches, and he has written some excellent, though not always very practical, pages on the way in which rich men should employ their fortunes. At the same time he strongly maintains that work is a duty for all. 'He who eats in idleness what he has not gained himself is a robber. . . . To work is an indispensable duty of social man. Rich and poor, strong and weak, each idle citizen is a thief.'[28]

---

[27] *Discours sur l'Economie Politique.*
[28] *Discours sur l'Economie Politique.* See, too, the views expressed in *Émile.* I have examined the opinions and influence of Rousseau more fully in my *History of England,* vol. vi. pp. 240–68 (Cab. ed.).

The really communistic element in this period of French speculation is to be found in very inferior writers. Mably is perhaps the most conspicuous. With that gross ignorance of human nature which characterises the writers of his school, he maintains that the faculties and characters of men are naturally but little different, and that all men are born virtuous. 'I am persuaded,' he says, 'that if men are wicked, it is the fault of the laws.' Inequalities of fortune and condition are the root of all evil. They produce ambition and avarice, two passions which he imagines that it is in the power of the legislator to banish from human nature. The true remedy would be the abolition of private property and the establishment of community of goods. Mably, however, with a gleam of unwonted good sense, perceived that in the France of the eighteenth century this was impossible, and he contented himself, accordingly, with urging that the State should enormously increase its power over successions, should appropriate the succession of all but near relations, and should especially very strictly limit the amount of land possessed by each citizen. 'Good legislation should be continually decomposing and dividing the fortunes which avarice and ambition are continually labouring to accumulate.' If the result is diminished production, this signifies little, 'provided there are no longer patricians and plebeians in the State.' The State must act as a general and highly coercive providence. There must be a system of universal, common, and obligatory education, imitated from that of Sparta. Art should be proscribed, for statues, pictures, and vases are very useless things. They are of the nature of luxuries, and have been the source of great evils in the world. The State must also strictly regulate religion, tolerating existing creeds, but not permitting the introduction of any new religions, and punishing atheists, Epicureans, and materialists with imprisonment for life.

Doctrines of substantially the same kind were maintained by Morelly, who desired all private property to be abolished, every citizen to be reduced to the position of a functionary in the State, and all the affairs of private and domestic life to be minutely regulated by law; and also by Brissot de Warville,

whose special title to remembrance is that he is the true author
of the saying, 'Property is robbery,' which Proudhon afterwards made so popular. Very consistently with this principle
he defended stealing, as correcting the injustice of the institution of property.[29]

These doctrines, however, did not play any considerable
part in the Revolution, and in the first stages of that great
explosion they were altogether repudiated. There is a distinction to be drawn between the confiscation of great masses
of property and the establishment of principles essentially
inconsistent with the existence of property. There was much
confiscation in the abolition of feudal rights, and gigantic confiscations followed the political proscriptions and the emigra-
tions; but it was the object of the legislator to divide the
confiscated land as much as possible, and the abolition of the
feudal laws gave to the greatly increased number of small
proprietors, both in fact and in law, an unrestricted and undivided ownership. In this way the Revolution multiplied a
class who clung with extreme tenacity to the idea of private
property in land. At the same time, in the spheres of industry
its great work was the abolition of the monopolies, privileges,
and restrictions which still existed in the mediæval system of
corporations. Before the Revolution, in nearly every town all
the more important trades were concentrated in the hand of
closely organised corporations, with exclusive rights of making and selling particular articles. Free competition was unknown. Every man who desired to practise a trade or industry
was obliged to enter as an apprentice into one of these corporations, to pass through its grades, to submit to its rules.
It is a form of industry curiously like that which would again
exist if the supremacy of trade unions became complete. The
abolition of this system and the establishment of complete
freedom of labour had long been one of the chief objects of
the party of innovation in France. The 'Essay on the Liberty

---

[29] *Recherches Philosophiques sur le droit de propriété et sur le vol.* An analysis
of this book will be found in Janet, *Hist. de la science politique,* ii. 662–65.

of Commerce and Industry,' by the President Bigot de Sainte-Croix, and the famous introduction by Turgot to his law for the suppression of 'jurandes' and 'communautés,' state in the fullest and clearest terms the evils of the system.

The subject was one in which Turgot took a keen interest, and perhaps the most memorable act of his memorable ministry was the abolition of these corporations, which has existed for probably at least 1,000 years, and the reestablishment of freedom of labour. It was a cause in which all the philosophical party, all the men whom we should now call 'advanced thinkers,' were fully agreed. In the words of the admirable biographer of Turgot, 'an odious and ridiculous slavery was abolished. The inhabitants of the towns acquired at last the right of disposing as they pleased of their own arms and their own labour. It was a right which at that time was enjoyed in no nation, not even in those which boasted most loudly of their liberty. This right, one of the first which Nature has given us, and which may be deemed a necessary consequence of the right to live, seemed blotted out of the memory and the heart of man. It is one of the title-deeds of humanity which had been lost in the night of the ages of barbarism, and which it has been the glory of our century to rediscover.'[30]

The edict abolishing these corporations was issued in February 1776. It was natural that so great a change should not have been effected without producing a profound convulsion, and it gave a new force and a rallying-cry to the many reactionary influences which were directed against Turgot. The Parliament of Paris, supported by a large number of provincial Parliaments, took a leading part in opposing it. A very remarkable memoir was published, entitled 'Mémoire à consulter sur l'existence actuelle des six corps et la conservation de leurs priviléges,' in which the case of the corporations was argued with much skill. Two points in it may be especially noted. One is the prediction that, if the restrictions which the corporate system introduced into industry were abolished,

---

[30] Condorcet, *Vie de Turgot*, p. 84.

there would be a dangerous and excessive migration of labour from the country to the towns. The other is a very strong assertion that the mass of the working classes preferred the corporate system, which gives industry a stability it could not otherwise have, to the system of unlimited liberty and uncontrolled competition.[31]

The opponents of Turgot triumphed. The great minister fell, and a few months later the old system of industrial corporations was, with some slight modifications, restored. But the whole force of the philosophical and innovating spirit in France was running against them. What we should now call Radical opinion at the close of the eighteenth century flowed as strongly against the monopolies and restrictions of corporate industry, and in favour of a complete freedom of individual industry, as it is now flowing in the opposite direction. The words which Turgot had introduced into his famous law were often repeated. 'The right to labour is the property of every man, and this property is the first, the most sacred, the most inalienable of all.' The Constitution of 1791 asserted it in the clearest terms, sweeping away the whole system of 'jurandes' and 'maîtrises,' apprenticeships and industrial corporations, and proclaiming the full right of all Frenchmen to practise, with a few specified exceptions, any form of art, or profession, or industry, on the sole condition of purchasing from the State.[32]

No portion of the work of the French Revolution has been more lasting or more widely followed than this emancipation of industry, which enabled every man to carry his labour whither he pleased, to make his own terms, and enjoy the full fruits of his own industry. The Declaration of the Rights of Man and the Constitution of 1791 asserted and guaranteed in the clearest terms the rights of acquired property. 'Property is an inviolable and sacred right. No one may be deprived of

---

[31] Léon Gautier, *Hist. des Corporations Ouvrières*, pp. 105–20.
[32] See on the effects of this law Du Ceillier, *Hist. Des Classes Laborieuses en France*, pp. 318–20.

it unless public necessity, legally established, evidently requires it, and then only on the condition of a just indemnity paid beforehand.' The same principle descended through succeeding codes. Even the Convention decreed the pain of death against any one who proposed a law 'subverting territorial, commercial, or industrial properties.' 'Property,' according to the Constitution of the year III., 'is the right of a man to enjoy and to dispose of his goods, his revenues, the fruit of his labour and industry.' The Code Napoléon described it as 'the right of enjoying and disposing of possessions in the most absolute manner, provided only that the owner does not make a use of them prohibited by law.'[33]

Extreme jealousy of all corporations and combinations within the State was one of the most marked characteristics of the French Revolution. A decree of June 17, 1791, contains the following remarkable article: 'The annihilation of all kinds of corporations of citizens of the same station or profession being one of the fundamental bases of the French Constitution, it is forbidden to re-establish them under any pretext or in any form. Citizens of the same station or profession, contractors, shopkeepers, workmen or apprentices in any art, are forbidden, if they come together, to elect a president, or a secretary, or a syndic to keep registers, to pass any resolutions or to form any rules about their pretended common interests.[34] It would be impossible to show more clearly how emphatically the spirit of the French Revolution is opposed to the organisation of labour, which is an indispensable ingredient of modern Socialism, and in no legislation were the rights of property more clearly defined or the obligations of contract more strictly enforced than in that which grew out of the Revolution.

There was, it is true, one short period in the movement when Socialist theories seemed for a time to prevail. During the Reign of Terror, in 1793, the Convention was in the hands

---

[33] See Guyot, *Les Principes de '89,* p. 162.
[34] Chevalier, *Organisation du Travail,* p. 180.

of the most extreme party, and, in the desperate circumstances in which France then found herself through the utter
disorganisation of industry and property, and through the
pressure of a gigantic war, these theories were acted on with
a feverish energy. War was openly declared against the rich.
No one, Robespierre said, should have more than 3,000 livres
of revenue.[35] Vast sums, raised chiefly by confiscation, were
voted for the relief of the poor. The price of all articles was
strictly regulated by law. It was made death for any merchant
to withhold corn or other articles of first necessity from the
market, for any private person to keep more corn in his house
than was required for his subsistence.[36] The rich were crushed
by requisitions ordering them to give up all precious metals
and jewellery; by an enormously graduated taxation; by a
forced loan imposed exclusively upon them; by the forced
circulation of depreciated paper. At the same time the Convention formally recognised the right of all members of society to obtain work from the State, or, if unable to labour,
assured means of subsistence.

The state of society that at this time existed in France could
not possibly last, and this tyranny—the most odious that
modern Europe has known—soon passed away. Even the
Convention, in spite of its savage energy, was unable to enforce all its decrees; and it is remarkable that it rejected the
proposition of Robespierre to limit the right of property to
'the portion of goods which the law had guaranteed;' to pronounce formally that it was a limited right, and to exempt
formally all the poorer classes from contributing anything to
the public expenses.[37]

---

[35] Taine, *La Révolution*, iii. 92.
[36] Ibid. iii. 103–4.
[37] See Janet, *Origines du Socialisme*, p. 111. A modern English Socialist
pretends that Robespierre and Saint-Just had undue middle-class lean-
ings. 'One leader only can be named at this time who clearly grasped the
situation, and deservedly won the confidence of the people, alike for his
political insight and his honesty of purpose—and this man was Jean Paul
Marat' (Bax, *Religion of Socialism*, p. 74).

With the Convention the immediate danger of communism passed, though the conspiracy of Babeuf under the Directory was intended to accomplish this end. Babeuf had been one of the most ardent and extreme disciples of Morelly and Mably. He taught that all land should be common property, that all debts should be blotted out and all private heritages forbidden, that private property should cease, and that every individual should be made a functionary, or, if old and infirm, a pensioner, of the State. Such doctrines, if simply preached, would probably have proved sufficiently innocent from their absurdity, but Babeuf organised a conspiracy for seizing the government and carrying them into practice. An elaborate system was devised for seducing the soldiers; the poor were to be instigated by a promise that they should be allowed to plunder the rich; and political assassinations were to be largely practised. The conspiracy was betrayed, and after a long trial Babeuf and one fellow-conspirator were condemned to death, and a few others to deportation.

From this time, for a considerable period, the communistic spirit took a purely academic form. In 1793, while the French Revolution was at its height, Godwin published in England his 'Political Justice,' in which, in the name of that much-abused principle, he proposed a general plunder of property and a general levelling of all inequalities. All accumulated, and especially all hereditary wealth, he maintained, is a criminal thing; every expenditure on'a superfluity is a vice. The true owner of each loaf of bread is the man who most needs it, and, 'great as are the evils that are produced by monarchies and Courts, by the imposture of priests and the iniquity of criminal law, they are imbecile and impotent compared with the evils that arise out of the established system of property.' With a profusion of grandiloquent phrases about virtue, and reason, and philosophy, and exalted morality, he sketched a society from which all ideas of authority, subordination, reverence, and gratitude were to be excluded, and in which absolute equality was to be maintained.

Like so many of the writers of his school, he clearly saw

that this could only be accomplished by the subversion of the family, and on this subject his statements bear no ambiguity. 'All attachments to individuals, except as to their merits, are plainly unjust. We should be the friends of man rather than of particular men.' 'I ought to prefer no human being to another because that being is my father, my wife, or my son, but because, for reasons equally apparent to all understandings, that being is entitled to preference. One among the measures which will successively be dictated by the spirit of democracy, and that probably at no great distance, is the abolition of surnames.' 'The institution of marriage is a system of fraud.' 'It is absurd to expect that the inclinations and wishes of two human beings should coincide through any long period of life.' 'The supposition that I must have a companion for life is the result of a complication of vices.' 'So long as I seek to engross one woman to myself, and to prohibit my neighbour from proving his superior desert and reaping the fruits, I am guilty of the most odious of all monopolies.'

Godwin hoped that 'these interesting improvements of human society' might be carried out pacifically by 'a mere change of ideas,' leading men to a higher level of morality, but he acknowledged that 'massacre was the too possible attendant upon revolution.' He argued, however, that we must not, on account of such a transitory evil, 'shrink from reason, from justice, from virtue, and happiness.' 'We must contrast a moment of horror and distress with ages of felicity. No imagination can sufficiently conceive the mental improvement and the tranquil virtue that would succeed were property once permitted to rest upon its genuine basis.'[38]

These sentences will sufficiently illustrate the doctrines of a curious book which is now seldom opened, though it had its hour of noisy notoriety, and was once the evangel of a small sect of young English enthusiasts. It chanced that the life of Godwin intersected that of one of the greatest of mod-

---

[38] *Political Justice* (1st ed.), Book viii. Some of the more obnoxious passages in this book were modified or omitted in later editions.

ern poets, and the biography of Shelley has thrown a light on Godwin and his surroundings which we should not otherwise have possessed. It reveals the austere philosopher as one of the most insatiable and importunate of beggars, and the picture it furnishes of the domestic life that grew up under his teaching is certainly not calculated to impress ordinary mortals with a sense of the superiority of the new morality.

A more interesting and a more considerable figure in the history we are studying is Saint-Simon. He sprang from one of the most illustrious noble families in France, and was born in Paris in 1760. He served with some distinction in America through five campaigns of the revolutionary war, and was afterwards, for a short time, colonel of a French regiment; but he soon abandoned the army, and began the restless, vagrant, but not unfruitful life which was most congenial to his disposition. He had a plan for uniting Madrid by a canal with the sea, and another for piercing the Panama isthmus, He travelled in many countries, read many books, and studied life in many aspects. Like most men of his temperament, he welcomed the French Revolution, but he took scarcely any active part in its politics. He devoted himself, however, in conjunction with a Prussian diplomatist, to speculating in the confiscated property which was thrown at an enormously depreciated rate upon the market, and he also entered into some manufacturing enterprises. Robespierre threw him into prison, where he remained for eleven months. Shortly after his release he quarrelled with his Prussian colleague, retired from industrial life, having only secured a very small competence, and resolved to devote himself exclusively 'to studying the march of the human mind, and thus contributing to bring civilisation to its full perfection.' In 1801 he married, giving as his reason for this step his desire to enlarge his opportunities of studying mankind; but he soon after, on the mere ground of economy, obtained a divorce. He passed some time in what, in the case of an ordinary man, would be called a very common course of folly, dissipation, and vice; but he assures us that it was merely an experiment in life, intended

to aid him in his research into the lines of demarcation between good and evil, and he describes himself as a man who
'traversed the career of vice in a direction that must lead him
to the highest virtue.' It led him, however, still more rapidly
to abject poverty, and he then began his series of works for
establishing a new religion which was to supersede Christianity, a new philosophy which was to absorb all others, and
a new social organisation which was to include and regen-
erate the human race.

With incontestable ability he very evidently combined colossal vanity and inordinate ambition. Many extravagant instances of these qualities are related. 'Get up, Monsieur le
Comte; you have great things to do,' are the words with which
he says he ordered his servant to wake him when he was
seventeen. In prison he pretends that Charlemagne, who was
supposed to be the progenitor of his family, appeared to him
in a vision, and prophesied that the young soldier would
achieve in the field of philosophy as great things as his mighty
ancestor had done in policy and war. He proffered himself in
marriage to Madame de Staël, and is said—though, very possibly, untruly—to have made his proposal in these terms:
'Madame, you are the most extraordinary woman in the
world—I am the most extraordinary man. Between us we
should, no doubt, make a child more extraordinary still.'

The purely philosophical and religious views of Saint-
Simon need not detain us, though in a work of a different kind
they would well repay examination. He had a great power of
fascinating young men, and some of his disciples afterwards
attained considerable distinction in literature, politics, and
finance. Among them were Augustin Thierry, Michel Chevalier, Hippolyte Carnot, Gustave d'Eichthal, Laurent, and
Laffitte; but for some time his favourite pupil, and the pupil
who enjoyed his closest confidence, was Auguste Comte.
Those who will compare the writings of these two thinkers
will probably be surprised to find how many passages in the
works of Comte, including much of what is valuable and essential in his system, are simply copied from his predecessor;

and they will appreciate the ingratitude of the younger man, who afterwards pretended that he had no obligations to his master, and that 'his unhappy connection with that depraved juggler' had been to him 'an evil without compensation.'[39]

The keynote of the social philosophy of Saint-Simon was that the social organisation of Europe which had existed in the Middle Ages, under the auspices of Catholicism and feudalism, was now hopelessly decayed, and that the reorganisation of Europe on a new basis, and in the interest of the poorest and most numerous class, was the supreme task of the thinkers of our age. Like Comte, he had a great admiration for the Middle Ages. He was impressed by the unity, the completeness, and the harmony of the organisation imposed by the Church on all the spheres of thought and action. The beliefs on which this system rested had irrevocably gone, but he believed that it might be reproduced on another foundation, and that this reproduction would confer incalculable blessings on mankind. 'The golden age,' he said, 'is not, as the poets imagine, in the past, but in the future.'

His ideas, however, about the nature of this reorganisation varied greatly at different periods of his life. In his first scheme, which was propounded in 1803, he urged that society should be divided into three classes, all spiritual power being placed in the hands of the learned, and all temporal power in those of the territorial proprietors, while the right of electing to high offices in humanity should be vested in the masses. In another work, which was published in 1814 in conjunction with Augustin Thierry, he drew up an elaborate scheme for the government of Christendom. There was to be a temporal sovereign presiding over the federation of Europe, elected in the first instance, and afterwards hereditary, who was to fill a po-

---

[39] Littré, in his *Life of Comte*, was evidently startled at the contrast (though he does all he can to extenuate it) between Comte's words and his manifest obligations to Saint-Simon; but for a full demonstration of the extent of these obligations I would refer the reader to the excellent monograph of Mr. Arthur J. Booth on *Saint-Simon and Saint-Simonism*.

sition something like that of a mediæval Pope. He was to be assisted and controlled by an international Parliament, chosen in a manner which was eminently conservative. There was to be a House of Lords and a House of Commons; the former was to consist of persons possessing 20,000*l.* a year in land, and the peerage was to be hereditary; but twenty men who had rendered great services to science and industry were to be added irrespective of their fortune.

The House of Commons was to be composed of commercial men, the learned classes, magistrates, and administrators. They were to sit for ten years, and every million of men who could read and write were to choose one representative out of each of these four groups. No one was to sit in this House of Commons who did not possess landed property of the value of 1,000*l.* a year; but, at each election, twenty eminent men were to be chosen irrespective of property, and they were to receive their property qualification from the Government. This federal Government was to legislate on all the differences that may arise between the different nations of Europe, to superintend their common interests, and to establish a common education and code of morality.

The next scheme was of a different character. It transferred all power from the hands of the territorial aristocracy to those of the representatives of industry. Labour was to be universal; all who lived in idleness were branded as robbers; and society was to be divided into two classes—the learned, who were to be engaged in investigating the laws of Nature, and the industrial, who were to be engaged in different forms of production. 'Everything by industry—everything for industry,' was adopted as the motto. The military system was denounced as an anachronism descending from the days of feudalism; all standing armies were to be abolished, and great public works transforming the material world were to take the place of the military enterprises of the past. Society was to be purely industrial, qualified only by the directing influence of the learned classes, who were to hold in the new society a position analogous to that of the clergy in the past. All hereditary privileges were to be abolished. Education on the largest scale was to be undertaken by the Government; and it was also to be its duty to assure work to all who, without its assistance, were unable to find it.

Practical politicians, who know how easy it is to elaborate large schemes for the government of humanity in the seclusion of a study, and how infinitely difficult it is to frame, and work, and regulate institutions dealing, even in very subordinate departments, with the incalculable varieties and complications of human interests and conditions, will not be greatly impressed with these views. They were propounded by Saint-Simon at a time when he was sunk in extreme poverty. On one occasion he was driven to suicide, and inflicted on himself wounds that left him disfigured for life. He died in 1825. 'All my life,' he said on his deathbed, 'may be summed up in a single idea—to assure to all men the fullest development of their faculties.' 'The party of the labourers will be formed. The future is for us.'

His views were taken up by his disciples, who formed themselves into a society, which soon assumed the character of a Church, and they propagated them during many years with great activity in the press, in pamphlets, and by lectures. The attraction of their teaching lay chiefly in certain broad principles which appealed powerfully to the more generous instincts. They taught 'that it should be the supreme end of society to secure with the greatest rapidity the amelioration of the class who are at once the most numerous and the most poor;' that the legislator should continually seek to depress the idle and to raise the labourer; that he should recognise no inequalities, except those which spring from different degrees of capacity and industry. 'To each man according to his capacity, and to each capacity according to its works,' became the formula of the school.

The Saint-Simonians did not, it is true, preach common property. In the manifesto which they published they explicitly recognised the right of private property, as a necessary consequence of their fundamental doctrine that each man

should be placed in accordance with his capacity and rewarded according to his works. They acknowledged, too, that
men are naturally unequal, and that this inequality is an indispensable condition of social order. But they declared war
against the whole system of hereditary property, describing
the transmission of property, even from a parent to a child,
as an immoral privilege, and they desired the State to confis-
cate all property on the death of its owner. In this way it would
gradually engross all the instruments of labour—land and
capital—and would become a colossal, all-absorbing, all-
controlling industrial corporation, in which individual freedom and initiative would be lost, and each man would be
placed according to his capacity and rewarded according to
his work. As society was not yet ripe for this gigantic servitude, they advocated as preliminary measures that the State
should forbid and appropriate all heritages out of the direct
line; that its revenues should be chiefly raised by a heavy
graduated tax on successions in the direct line; that State
banks should be employed for the purpose of diffusing the
benefits of capital; and that a policy of complete free trade
should prepare the way for the coming federation of nations.

On the subject of the family they were somewhat less revolutionary than their predecessors. They were strenuous
advocates for the emancipation of women; by which they
understood their complete equality with men in all the
spheres of industry, professional life, and political privileges.
Marriage was not to be destroyed, but it was to become a
purely voluntary connection, dissoluble by either party at
pleasure. It was on this side of their teaching that they diverged most widely from the views which were afterwards
put forward by Comte.

In the ferment of new ideas that followed the Revolution
of 1830 the Saint-Simonian Church made some considerable
progress, but it had now fully assumed the form of a grotesque
religion. Saint-Simon was declared to have been a Messiah.
He was not, it is true, the first. Moses, and Orpheus, and
Numa had been the Messiahs in one stage of humanity, and

Christ in another. But the world still awaited a saviour. Saint-Simon appeared, uniting the functions of Moses and Christ, and organising the true religion.[40] His dignity and his inspiration descended to his successor, Enfantin, who was hailed as the Supreme Father, and who claimed and received from his followers absolute obedience as the representative of the Deity. There were elaborate dresses and ceremonies manifestly aping Catholicism, the ususal combination of intoxicating vanity and deliberate imposture, the usual very dubious sexual morality and financial transactions. Much was said about a coming female Messiah—a bisexual divinity, a rehabilitation of the flesh. The Saint-Simonians were accused, though, I believe, untruly, of preaching community of wives, and their Supreme Father and some of their other leading members were prosecuted and imprisoned on the charge of holding illegal meetings and teaching immoral doctrines.

Most of them, however, seem to have been well-meaning enthusiasts, and the society included some young men who had made large sacrifices of fortune and position in the cause, and a few who possessed much more than ordinary ability. There were excellent writers, skilled engineers, and sound economists among them, and on many practical economical questions the articles in the Saint-Simonian newspaper had a real authority. Strange veins of insanity and capacities for enthusiastic folly sometimes flaw the strongest brains, and the impetuous ebullitions of youth which impel some men into extravagancies of vice develop in other natures into not less wild extravagancies of thought. The sect speedily dwindled, partly through the ridicule that attached to it, partly through its own dissensions, and partly through the maturing intellects of the young men who had thrown their crude and youthful energies into its service. Several of the old disciples of Saint-Simon sat in the Constituent Assembly of 1848; and perhaps the best critic of the socialist follies of that period

---

[40] Reybaud, *Etudes sur les Réformateurs*, i. 80.

was Michel Chevalier, who had once been one of the most ardent members of the Saint-Simonian Church.

In the latter days of the Church the Saint-Simonians had one remarkable piece of good fortune. The advocacy of great public works for the material development of the world was one of the chief ends of their society. It grew out of their fundamental doctrine that labour is the first of duties and the true source of all dignity. Among the schemes which the Saint-Simonians adopted most ardently was one for a Suez canal. It was not to them a mere speculation in a Paris newspaper. Enfantin and other leading members of the sect actually established themselves in Egypt. Among the disciples were several young engineers from the Polytechnic School, and they surveyed the line, raised large subscriptions, and endeavoured to form an industrial army for the purpose of accomplishing the enterprise. They were warmly welcomed by Ferdinand Lesseps, who was then French Vice-Consul at Alexandria, and some beginning was actually made. Insufficient resources, cholera, and the indifference of the Egyptian Government made the scheme a failure; but the Saint-Simonian Church may truly claim the merit of having devised, and in some degree initiated, an enterprise which has been one of the greatest and most fruitful of the century.[41]

Whether they have in other respects left permanent traces in the world may be doubted. Some writers have attributed to their ideas much importance in the later developments of society, pointing to the many articles in the Saint-Simonian creed which coincide with strong contemporary tendencies.[42] The political importance they ascribed to labour and the labouring classes; their advocacy of a policy tending mainly to social and material improvement; the stress they laid on national education; their doctrines about the rights of women;

---

[41] Mr. Booth has given an interesting account of this curious and nearly forgotten transaction (*Saint-Simon and Saint-Simonism*, pp. 205–12).
[42] See especially the chapter of Blanqui on 'Saint-Simonism,' *Hist. de l'Economie Politique*, ii. 266–82.

their desire to aggrandise the functions and powers of government, and to make it more and more the initiator of industrial enterprises; their proposal to abolish all taxes on articles of necessity, and to throw the burden of the revenue mainly on succession duties, are all points in which the Saint-Simonians agree with large and active parties in every European country. Many of these doctrines, however, existed before them, and the socialistic tendencies of the nineteenth century grew out of wider causes than the preaching of a single sect, and would probably have existed in equal strength if that sect had never been founded.

It is not necessary to dwell at length upon the system of Fourier, which was contemporaneous with Saint-Simonism. He proposed to divide the world into a vast number of industrial communities, called *Phalanges*, in which each man was to do very much what he liked the best, but in which allurements and incentives were to be so skilfully distributed, education so admirably organised, aptitudes and capacities so wisely consulted, regulated, and employed, that each man would find his highest pleasure in work which was for the benefit of the rest. It is a system which might be applicable to some distant planet inhabited by beings wholly unlike mankind. It may be realised on this planet in a far-off millennium if, as some philosophers think, human nature can be fundamentally transformed by many successive modifications of hereditary characteristics; but in our age and world it is as unreal and fantastic as a sick man's dream.

Robert Owen deserves a more serious consideration. He was in real touch with practical life, having been a large and successful manufacturer in that very critical period of English industry when the great inventions of the close of the eighteenth century had given the deathblow to the domestic industries, and laid the foundations of our present factory system; when the complete command of the sea which England obtained during the long French war had given an unparalleled impulse to her manufactures; and when, at the same time, the new conditions of labour were most imperfectly organised, and scarcely in any degree regulated by law. Frightful abuses, especially in the form of excessive child labour, took place, and the vast masses of wholly uneducated men, women, and children, withdrawn from their country homes and thrown together amid the temptations of great towns and of untried and unaccustomed conditions of industry, presented moral, political, and social dangers of the gravest kind.

The part which was played by Owen in the earlier stages of the great manufacturing development was very important. He was a man of ardently energetic philanthropy and transparent purity of character, and his mind teemed with new suggestions. His management of the vast cotton-mills of New Lanark during a long course of years was a perfect model of what can be done by a great captain of industry who, in the pursuit of gain, never forgets his responsibility for the wellbeing of those he employs, and in the first stage of the factory system such examples were both very rare and peculiarly valuable. He contributed more than perhaps any one else to introduce infant schools into England. He was an early and powerful supporter of the Factory Acts, and as early as 1818 he advocated a legislative restriction of adult labour. He soon, however, extended his views to the formation of great industrial communities, in which co-operation should play a greater part than competition, and by which he hoped that the fluctuations of industry might be abolished and the condition of the poor permanently raised. His first scheme was simply an extension of the poor law, enacting that every union or county should provide by county expenditure a large farm, if possible with a manufactory connected with it, for the employment of the poor, and he believed that these would speedily prove self-supporting. He afterwards advocated the establishment all over the country, by private subscription, of industrial colonies, or communities, in which agriculture, manufacture, and education were all to be carried on, and in which, by common labour, common living, and common expenditure, the cost to each member might be greatly reduced.

This scheme attracted a large share of public attention in England in the second and third decades of the nineteenth century. It was taken up by several wealthy and philanthropic men, it engaged the attention of Parliament, and it found several supporters on the Continent. Owen, however, impaired his cause greatly by the unnecessary vehemence with which he put forward his very heterodox religious opinions. He thus alienated the religious world, and especially the Evangelical party, which was then in the zenith of its influence, and which absorbed and directed a great portion of the benevolence and enthusiasm of England; while at the same time he deprived himself of much Radical support by his indifference to the political questions with which Radicalism was then chiefly occupied. Considerable sums were subscribed, but only sufficient to start co-operative societies on a small scale, and these societies almost invariably proved short-lived. In 1832 there were no less than 700 in Great Britain. In a few years four only remained.[43]

In 1824, Owen went to the United States, where he remained for about three years. In a thinly populated country, where there was much less stress of competition and much less organisation of industry than in Europe, the chances of success seemed greater, and eleven industrial communities were established, either by Owen or by men who were under his influence. They all of them signally failed, and the average duration of the eight principal ones is said to have been only a year and a half.[44] The American historian of the movement justly notices how almost impossible it is to maintain industrial communities, which involve a great sacrifice of individual ambition, interest, and energy in the service of the community, unless the body is held together by some distinctive religious doctrine and the overmastering power of a religious enthusiasm.

In the earlier part of his career Owen was not much more

---

[43] A. J. Booth's *Owen*, pp. 145, 154.
[44] Woolsey's *Communism and Socialism*, p. 52.

than a benevolent and energetic manufacturer who had many schemes for improving the position of those who depended on him. Like most benevolent men, he was much impressed by the poverty, drunkenness, and vice that prevailed in the great manufacturing towns in the early days of the factory system, and he soon persuaded himself that machinery was doing more harm than good, and that consumption no longer kept pace with production. One of his favourite remedies for agricultural distress was that the spade should take the place of the plough in the cultivation of the soil, thus giving employment to a much larger number of hands. With advancing life he adopted many extravagancies, and became the apostle of a complete moral and social revolution. He had always held, with a large class of eighteenth-century thinkers, that there is no such thing as free-will; that men are born, morally and intellectually, substantially equal; that moral responsibility, with its attendant feelings of praise and blame, is a mere illusion of the imagination; and that the whole difference between man and man depends upon his circumstances, and especially his education. He had always disbelieved the Christian religion, but it was only in the latter half of his life that he began to inveigh against it with extravagant violence.

He soon came to view marriage with equal hostility. He did not, it is true, preach community of wives, but he urged that marriage was only moral as long as it rested on affection and was dissoluble at pleasure. His views about private property were equally subversive, and he once described religion, private property, and marriage as 'The Trinity of Evil.'[45] He anticipated George in denying the right of private property in land, and Marx in asserting that all wealth is produced by manual labour, and rightly belongs to labour, and he imagined that it was possible to detain it in the hands of the producers. A general union should be established among the productive classes; all individual competition should cease; all manufactures should be carried on by national organisations. The great

---

[45] Booth, pp. 121–22.

object of his later years was to found and extend such organisations. He believed that the trade union of each particular
trade could in this way obtain a complete monopoly in its own
department, acquire possession of the means of production,
replace the capitalist, and regulate hours of work, prices, and
wages. The workmen should own their own factories, and
elect their managers and foremen. In these ways all wealth
would pass into the hands of the producing class. He had a
scheme for suppressing the precious metals as the instrument
of exchange, and substituting for them notes representing different amounts and periods of labour.

The interest excited among the working classes about the
time of the Reform Bill of 1832 by these speculations, and by
the experiments that grew out of them, was very great. They
were diffused by innumerable pamphlets and lectures, and
they aroused among grave men serious alarm.[46] Amid much
that was mischievous, fallacious, and unpractical, something,
however, remained. It is not altogether an evil thing that social experiments, even of the wildest kind, should be tried,
provided men try them with their own money, or with money
voluntarily contributed, and not with money forcibly taken
from other people in the form of taxes. Owen, unlike many
of his successors, relied mainly upon voluntary association.
He did not urge, nor was it indeed possible in the then existing state of the suffrage to urge with success, that the great
social experiments he advocated in favour of one class should
be made with money levied upon another class. The early
attempts at co-operation, which were largely due to his teaching and promoted by his disciples, were, it is true, in a very
remarkable degree failures. They were generally undertaken
by inexperienced men; they were largely mixed with Utopias
and fantastic and untrue doctrines, and they made the fatal
mistake of granting credit, instead of confining themselves
rigidly to the ready-money system. But the co-operative idea
was a sound one, and it was destined to have a great future.

---

[46] See Webb's *History of Trades Unionism*, pp. 141–42.

The economic production that it made possible, the suppression of the middleman, the harmony of interests established between the different classes of producers, the possibility of raising a great capital by small contributions, the advantage which, in all modern industrial competition, lies with any establishment that can offer large choice and low prices, and secure in consequence large sales and quick returns, all furnish elements of success to those who know how to use them with judgment, enterprise, and skill.

The first very striking success in this department was the Rochdale Pioneers. It was founded, in 1844, by a few poor men who, in a time of great trade depression, clubbed together to purchase their tea and sugar and other necessaries at wholesale prices. There were at first only twenty-eight of them, and each subscribed 1*l.* They proposed, as their association extended, to manufacture such articles as the society might determine, to but land for the employment of unemployed labourers, to promote sobriety by the establishment of a temperance hotel, and generally to assist each other in their social and domestic lives. As they became more successful they assigned a certain proportion of their profits to educational purposes. The society gradually grew into a vast store, which in 1882 counted 10,894 members, sold merchandise of the value of 274,627*l.*, made 32,577*l.* of profits, and paid a dividend of 5 per cent. upon its capital, besides distributing considerable sums among its clients.[47] The example was widely followed, and the progress of the cooperative movement, reconciling many hostile interests, is one of the most hopeful signs of our day. It would be easy to exaggerate, but it would be unjust to deny the part which the teaching of Robert Owen has had in promoting it.

In France, ideas of a socialistic order were at this time perhaps more prevalent than in England. For many years before the Revolution of 1848 they had been manifestly fermenting. Ever since the Revolution of 1830 a number of writers, some

---

[47] See Fawcett, *Work and Wages;* Jones, *Co-operative Production.*

of them now forgotten, some of them distinguished in other fields, had been denouncing the wage system; preaching vague forms of social reorganisation, chiefly based on association; uniting the aspirations of extreme democracy with passionate appeals to the interests of the working classes; painting in the darkest colours the contrast between the luxury of the rich and the misery of the poor, and describing the many evils of society as the result of unjust laws, and as remediable by political revolution. Leroux, Buchez, Cabet, Vidal, Blanqui, Raspail, Villegardelle, and many others, wrote in this strain, though they differed widely in their specific doctrines. Some, like Lamennais and Buchez, wrote under the influence of a strong religious enthusiasm. Others, like Raspail, connected their social schemes with blank materialism, and with a denial of all moral responsibility. Cabet threw his views into the form of a romance[48] modelled after Thomas More and Campanella. All the evils of society, he maintained, sprang from inequality, and could only be remedied by community of goods, which he believed to be the ideal of Christ; and he accordingly painted a society in which all the land was treated as common domain; in which all work was a public function, equally and universally pursued, and equally rewarded; and in which men lived together in an idyllic fashion, without private property, without money, without pauperism, without dissension. Unlike many writers of his school, he fully recognised marriage, though he did not treat it as absolutely indissoluble.

The current of ideas in the direction of Socialism may be traced through much of the higher French literature of the period. It is very perceptible in some of the novels of George Sand, and in some of the songs of Béranger; but the writers who at this time most powerfully affected opinion in the direction I am indicating were Lamennais and Louis Blanc. It would be difficult to find in all literature more fiery, more eloquent, and more uncompromising denunciations of the

---

[48] *Voyage en Icarie.*

existing fabric of society than are contained in the later writings of Lamennais. He described the working class in France as absolute slaves, completely dependent on the capitalist, without individual liberty, without defence against oppression, living under a political and industrial system which rested wholly on injustice. He preached a complete social and political renovation, which should make the labouring classes the rulers of the world, abolish the wage system, as slavery and serfdom had been abolished in the past, and open out a new era, in which competition would cease to be the spring of industry, and property would depend on labour, not labour on property.[49]

Similar views were preached with less eloquence, but with more system, and in a scarcely less declamatory form, by Louis Blanc, whose work on the 'Organisation of Labour' appeared in 1845. He thought that competition was the master-curse of the world and the chief cause of the degradation and slavery of the poor. According to him, modern society was sick even to death. All its chief institutions were gangrened with corruption and egotism. The condition of the poor was intolerable, and under the pressure of competition their wages must inevitably sink till they touch the level of starvation. In the face of the plainest facts he maintained that their situation was everywhere and steadily deteriorating; and while drawing the most harrowing pictures of their misery, he did all in his power to discredit the methods by which practical and unpretending philanthropy has laboured to mitigate it. Savings banks, which have proved of such inestimable benefit to them, are denounced by this great reformer as 'a profound delusion.' They are an encouragement of vice, inducing the 'servant to rob his master and the courtesan to sell her beauty;' they make the people dependent on those who govern them, and induce them, 'by a narrow and factitious interest, to maintain the oppression that weighs them

---

[49] *L'Esclavage Moderne, Paroles d'un Croyant, Une Voix de Prison, Du Peuple, Du Passé et de l'Avenir du Peuple.*

down.' The habit of saving in a communistic society is an excellent thing, but in an individualistic society like ours it ought not to be encouraged. 'Saving engenders egotism.' 'It replaces by a greedy satisfaction the sacred poetry of well-doing.' In the true spirit of the literary Socialist, he maintains that nothing but heroic and revolutionary measures will do good.

The real remedy for the ills of society is to be found in an enormous aggrandisement of the powers and duties of the State. By the expenditure of vast sums of public money it should establish great industrial organisations, which will gradually overshadow, absorb, and crush all private industries. It must supply the capital, give ample wages, quite irrespective of market value, to all who are employed, and forbid all competition, either within or between these different national organisations. The complete change cannot, it is true, be effected at once. During the first year of their existence the Government must assign to every man within these organisations his place and his task, but after that period these bodies may become self-governing and based on the elective principle. 'The false and anti-social education,' also, 'which the present generation has received,' renders it essential that there should be at first a different scale of wages for different kinds of workmen and different degrees of capacity and industry. With a new and better education this will cease. 'Inequality of aptitude will result in inequality of duties, but not of rights.' The same wages will be given to the skilled and the unskilled, the industrious and the idle, the genius who produces much and the fool who produces little or nothing. In the lofty moral altitude which society may be expected to attain when it is organised in a communistic form, the community or identity of feeling will be so strong that each man will do his best.

In the meantime, all collateral successions are to be forbidden, and the money diverted to the coffers of the State. Successions in the direct line, however, must be preserved until society has gone through the process of transformation, when they too will disappear. They are an evil, but at present a necessary, though a transitory, one. 'Heredity is destined to follow the same path as societies which are transformed, and men who die.' Mines, railways, banks, insurance offices, are to be taken over by the State, and a great State bank is to lend money to labourers without interest. Education is to be free and compulsory. A fixed proportion of the product of the national workshops is to be reserved for the support of the old and of the sick. Literary property is to be at once abolished, one of the principal reasons being that it is degrading to a writer. Any one is to be permitted to reprint his works, but a highly democratic Parliament, with the assistance of a commission appointed by itself, is to make itself the supreme censor and adjudicator of literature, and to decide by its vote what authors may receive national rewards. It is characteristic that this beautiful scheme for the enslavement and corruption of literature emanates from the writer who objected to the savings bank on the ground that it gave an undue influence to the governing body in the State. Louis Blanc, it may be added, utterly repudiated the Saint-Simonian formula, 'to each man according to his capacities,' substituting for it, 'to each man according to his wants'—a conveniently elastic phrase, which might be contracted or expanded almost without limit.[50]

These views have not even the merit of originality. They are, for the most part, a medley of the doctrines of Saint-Simon, Fourier, and Morelly; and, seven or eight years before Louis Blanc, a writer named Léon Brothier had published a work contending that the State, and the State alone, should sell all articles of production.[51] It may be noticed that it was about this time that the word 'Socialism' first came to use. It is a word of French origin. Reybaud claims to have been the inventor, and he had first employed it in an article in the

---

[50] *Organisation du Travail*, par Louis Blanc. I have used the fourth edition, which is enlarged by replies to critics.
[51] Chevalier, *Organisation du Travail*, p. 125.

'Revue des Deux Mondes,' which appeared in 1836.[52] It comprises, as we have seen, a great variety of sects, and is applied to many gradations of opinion, and it is therefore not susceptible of perfectly precise and exhaustive definition. It represents the tendency in the fields of industry and property to displace individual ownership, unrestricted competition, and the liberty of independent action, by State ownership and State regulation, continually contracting the sphere of the individual, continually enlarging the sphere and increasing the pressure of the community or the State.

The word and the thing became rapidly popular, and the Revolution of 1848 at once assumed a socialistic character. Tocqueville noticed that this, much more than any purely political doctrine, furnished the movement with its motive force. Louis Blanc and his follower Albert, who sat with him in the Provisional Government, exercised for a time much influence, and one of the first tasks of this Government was to satisfy the new demands. Lamartine and the majority of its members had little or no sympathy with them; but, in the disorganised condition of France, the section which was directed by Ledru Rollin and Louis Blanc carried many measures. The hours of adult labour were for the first time limited by law, being reduced to ten in Paris and eleven in the departments.[53] The system of taking small contracts by a middleman standing between the workman and the employer, which was known under the name of *marchandage*, was forbidden. It was found that the decree was at first treated with contempt, and severe penalties were consequently enacted against those who disobeyed it. The State formally guaranteed work to all who needed it. A working-man's congress assembled, under the presidency of Louis Blanc, in the old House of Peers in the

---

[52] See Block, *Dictionnaire de la Politique*, art. 'Socialisme.' There is, however, I believe, some doubt about the origin of the word.

[53] This law was repealed about six months later, and a new law made enacting that the working-man's day in manufactories and mills should not exceed twelve hours of actual labor (see *Reports on the Hours of Adult Labor from H.M. Representatives*, 1889), pp. 15–16.

Luxembourg. Among the demands put forward most prominently was the abolition of piecework, or task-work, which was peculiarly obnoxious to the Socialist party, as, by paying the worker in strict proportion to the result of his labour, it placed an insuperable obstacle in the way of a uniform rate of wages. The Government, it is true, refused to accede to this demand, nor would they consent to the regulation of wages by law; but in many of the great manufactures, both in Paris and in the provinces, the workmen by an organised movement obliged the manufacturers to raise wages, to abolish piecework, and to expel all foreign workmen. Great multitudes of English, German, and Belgian workmen were compelled to abandon France.[54] In some particular cases the Government interfered to regulate wages, and they undertook to exclude prison work from competition with free labour in the market.[55] Graduated taxation was introduced in the most arbitrary and objectionable form, by a decree of the Provisional Government giving discretionary powers to the mayors of the different communes, and the collectors, to remit or diminish the recently imposed additional taxation in cases where they believed that the smaller proprietors were unable to pay it.[56]

The most remarkable achievement of the Provisional Government in the sphere which we are considering was the foundation of the national workshops, or *ateliers nationaux*. This was in part a fulfilment of the promise that the Government would furnish work to all who needed it, and in part a beginning of the realisation of the dream of Louis Blanc, that the State should be the supreme industrial organ in the community. Louis Blanc has himself declared that when he wrote, in conjunction with Ledru Rollin, the decree guaranteeing work to every citizen, exhorting the workmen to associate in order to enjoy the full benefit of their labour, and appropriating to them the Civil List which had once been enjoyed by

---

[54] See Chevalier's *Lettres sur l'Organisation du Travail*, p. 3.
[55] Sargant, *Social Innovators*, pp. 353–57.
[56] Lord Normanby, *Year of Revolution*, i. 299.

the sovereign, he clearly saw that he was pledging the Government to a course which would ultimately lead to a total revolution of the industrial system of the past;[57] but he, at the same time, disclaims all direct responsibility for the form which the national workshops assumed.

Manual labour was at once provided, or, to speak more correctly, promised, for all idle persons in Paris and the neighbourhood. The workmen were formed into brigades. The leader, who directed the labour and received somewhat higher pay than his fellows, was elected by them—a practice which naturally secured that nothing more than a minimum of work should be exacted. In a few weeks about 120,000 men were in receipt of pay. Those who were actually employed were usually engaged on useless and unproductive works in or about Paris, while additional labourers were constantly streaming in from the country. One of the historians of the movement remarks the resemblance of what was taking place in France to the useless and wasteful public works which were about the same time going on in Ireland.[58] In Ireland, however, this was due to the urgent necessity of employing a starving population during an appalling famine. In France there had been a bad harvest in 1847,[59] but there was nothing approaching national famine, and the terrible distress, which was daily increasing, was mainly due to political causes, and especially to the shock which subversive doctrines had given to all industry, enterprise, and credit. Workshops were established for the employment of destitute shoemakers and tailors, with the very natural consequence of accelerating the ruin of private shops. A great co-operative tailor's establishment set up by the Government in the Hôtel Clichy, though it received large Government orders for the uniforms of the National Guard and the Garde Mobile, ended in a few weeks in a disastrous loss.[60]

---

[57] Louis Blanc, *Pages d'Histoire de la Révolution de 1848*, p. 32.

[58] Sargant, *Social Innovators*.

[59] See Léon Faucher, *Droit de Travail*, p. 16.

[60] See some curious particulars about this experiment, collected by Mr. St. Loe Strachey, in *A Policy of Free Exchange*, edited by T. Mackay, pp. 87–102.

The tide of anarchy was steadily mounting. Some of the principal railways were disorganised. The Northern Railway Company endeavoured to meet the demands of the workers by reducing the time of labour to nine hours, discharging all Englishmen in their employment, and even undertaking to grant the workmen a certain share in their profits.[61] On the Orleans line there were combinations of the most formidable character, and, in addition to a great rise of wages and a participation in the profits of the company, the workmen claimed the right of electing the men who directed and controlled them.[62] Even in Paris great numbers of machines were broken, under the notion that their existence was contrary to the interests of the working class.[63] All steady industry was arrested or dislocated; and the fact that men holding a leading position in the Government were preaching a complete revolution in the conditions of labour and the rights and distribution of property had very naturally destroyed all credit. An excellent economist has computed that at this time the loss on French securities on the Paris Bourse amounted to not less than four milliards of francs, or one hundred and sixty millions of pounds, and he adds that almost every other form of French fortune was depreciated in a very similar proportion.[64] Articles of first necessity rose rapidly in price, and in a city where thousands depended for their subsistence on the scale of articles of luxury and superfluity, nearly all expenditure of this kind had ceased. Every employer of labour restricted his business within the narrowest limits. Those who had money concealed and hoarded it till better times. In the great majority of Parisian workshops the number of persons employed was now only a fraction of what it had been a few months before, and, according to the most moderate calculations, the loss in Paris alone was not less than two millions of francs a day, a

---

[61] Lord Normanby, *Year of Revolution*, i. 212–13.
[62] Chevalier, p. 82.
[63] Ibid. pp. 80–81.
[64] Ibid. p. 90.

loss which fell mainly on the humblest and most industrious class.[65]

The Congress of Workmen at the Luxembourg claimed and exercised a despotic power over industrial contracts. Its leaders boasted loudly that they had in some cases arbitrated successfully between employers and labourers.[66] But the main result of their deliberations was to scare capital and shake the very foundations of industry; and the poison which Louis Blanc and his followers were diffusing was not the less deadly because it was abundantly mixed with sentimentality and coupled with the loftiest professions of virtue and philanthropy.

Socialist clubs were rapidly multiplying. Victor Considérant was publishing his pamphlets declaring the iniquity of all private property, and especially landed property, and his doctrines were promulgated by Ledru Rollin from the Tribune, and they found numerous adherents.[67] The systematic intimidation of ministers and deputies, which was so prominent in the first revolution, was again in full force. The debates of the Chamber were constantly interrupted by menacing cries from the galleries. On May 15 the mob burst into the body of the hall, clamouring for the organisation of labour; for the imposition of a new tax of a milliard on the rich; for a war for the liberation of Poland; for the ascendency of Louis Blanc.[68] Deputations of the most threatening kind were sent to the more moderate section of the Government. Lamartine has given a graphic description of his encounter with one of these leaders, who came to him representing the sentiments of sixty thousand armed men and followed by a vast and angry mob.

---

[65] Ibid. p. 303.

[66] See the Report issued by the Luxembourg Commission in April (Sargant, pp. 380–88).

[67] See especially his *Théorie du Droit de Propriété et du Droit de Travail*, and, on the reception of this doctrine, Léon Faucher, *Droit de Travail*, pp. 17–20.

[68] Tocqueville, who was an eyewitness of the scene, has given an admirable description of it in his *Souvenirs*. See, too, Lord Normanby.

He demanded in imperious terms 'the extermination of property and capitalists; the immediate installation of the proletariat into community of goods; the proscription of the bankers, of the rich, of the manufacturers, of all *bourgeois* whose condition was better than that of salaried workmen; the destruction of all superiorities derived from birth, fortune, heredity, or even labour, and the immediate adoption of the red flag.'[69]

The *ateliers nationaux* were perhaps the most alarming of all the many dangers of the time. They had massed in and about Paris an army of some 120,000 workmen, living for the most part in a demoralising idleness, electing their own chiefs, intoxicated by the subversive doctrines that were industriously disseminated, and including, according to good authority, not less than 2,000 liberated convicts.[70] Their pay—which they bitterly complained was insufficient—it is true, was only one and a half franc a day, but even at this rate the cost was ruinous to Paris. It amounted to about four and a half millions of francs a month. It was found impossible to provide work for more than a fraction of this great multitude, or to enforce any subordination or serious labour, even where employment was given. In spite of the vast diminution of production, workmen in private industries were now demanding higher wages; and when this was refused, they usually poured in great bodies into the national workshops, and subsisted during the struggle on national pay.[71] One of the first effects of the Revolution had been to arm the whole body of the Paris workmen, and great supplies of ammunition were being accumulated.[72] The danger to the peace of Paris had become extreme. It had become plainly impossible to provide much longer the requisite pay, and in the meantime paupers were streaming by thousands from the provinces into Paris.

---

[69] Lamartine, *Révolution de 1848*, livre vii.

[70] Normanby, ii. 3.

[71] See the speeches of Léon Faucher on the *ateliers nationaux*, *Vie Parlementaire*, ii. 109–23; Thomas, *Les Ateliers Nationaux*.

[72] Tocqueville, *Souvenirs*, p. 202.

The problem had become an almost insoluble one. Lamartine had no socialist tendencies. He had a well-merited contempt for the characters of his Socialist colleagues, and he clearly saw the madness of their theories. In the first weeks of the Revolution he had more than once encountered the stormy elements around him with a courage, an eloquence, a clearness of vision that could not be surpassed, and for which history has scarcely given him his full meed of praise. But his popularity was rapidly fading. The weaknesses of his character had become apparent, and the shadow of coming calamity, which he clearly saw, fell darkly upon him.

It was necessary, however, to deal promptly with the question. Orders were given to the mayors throughout France to refuse passports to all labouring men who could not prove that they were certain of obtaining work at Paris, and if such men came to Paris they were to be sent back from the barriers. A decree was issued stating that there were 100,000 workmen in Paris without work, and directing that task-work should be substituted for payment by the day. There were schemes for establishing agricultural colonies on waste land, and great works on railways were decreed for the purpose of employing the workmen and withdrawing them from Paris. But they had no intention of leaving, and the only result of the new measures was to accelerate the inevitable explosion.[73]

The situation, indeed, could have but one issue. In the four short months that had passed since Louis Philippe was expelled from France all industry had been disorganised, all the conservative forces of society had been weakened, and the elements of a ferocious social war had abundantly accumulated. It broke out on June 23, and four days of streetfighting followed, which were among the most terrible in modern history. It was in part an insurrection of men who had been persuaded by Socialist agitators that all the inequalities of fortune were due to extortion and robbery; that the wealth of the

---

[73] Lord Normanby's *Year of Revolution*, i. 444–45; *Vie Parlementaire de Léon Faucher*, ii. 116–23; *Souvenirs de Tocqueville*.

world was by right their own; that nothing was needed but the destruction of the existing order of society to bring about a social millennium. It was in part, also, the revolt of starving men with starving families; of men who were willing to work but who could find no work to do, and who had lost all their means of subsistence through the action of politicians and agitators. It was noticed that women and boys were scarcely less prominent, and not less courageous, than the men. The barricades were defended against cannon and regular troops with a deadly tenacity, an indomitable courage, an utter disregard for life worthy of the most seasoned veterans, and the savage ferocity displayed on both sides has not often been surpassed.[74] But Cavaignac and Lamoricière at last succeeded, and the Socialist revolution was crushed in blood. The British ambassador states that it appeared from authentic sources that in those four days 16,000 men had been killed or wounded in the streets of Paris.[75]

Tocqueville has noticed, as one of the most remarkable features of the time, the dread and hatred of Paris which had grown up in the provinces, and great multitudes of volunteers from the country contributed to the suppression of the Socialist rebellion. The panic and the misery which had been produced aroused classes who had long been indifferent to politics, and after the days of June the course of immediate French history was clearly marked. The Socialist party was not destroyed, but it was broken and discouraged. The national workshops had disappeared, and the insurrection which broke out in the June of 1849 was insignificant in Paris, though it was somewhat more formidable in Lyons. The *bourgeoisie* of the towns and the peasant proprietors now mainly directed the course of French politics, and the guiding motive of these

---

[74] A terrible catalogue of what Lord Normanby believed to be well-authenticated atrocities committed by the insurgents will be found in *A Year of Revolution* (ii. 74–76). His chief authority was the French Minister for Foreign Affairs. For the atrocities ascribed to the soldiers, see Louis Blanc, *La Revolution de 1848*, pp. 173–76.

[75] Lord Normanby, ii. 95.

two great classes was a deep dread and hatred of Socialism, and a determination at all hazards to place the protection of industry and property in secure hands. Even before the insurrection of June the simultaneous election of the exiled Prince Louis Napoleon for Paris and several departments indicated the direction of the stream. After the Socialist rising it became evident to clear-sighted observers that the democratic republic was doomed, and that France was on its way to a dictatorship; though for a short time it was very doubtful into whose hands power would fall. The election of Louis Napoleon as President by an enormous majority in December 1848, and the *Coup d'Etat* of December 1851, solved the question, but it may be confidently asserted that this latter event could never have succeeded if it had not been for Socialism and the dread which it inspired.

After this time the storm-centre of Socialism passed from France to Germany, where it chiefly gathered around two men—Lassalle and Marx. They had, no doubt, some precursors, and, among others, Fichte had thrown out in passing some views very like those of the modern Socialists; but these views had taken no real root in the German mind. The two apostles of German Socialism were very different in their characters, though their doctrines diverged but slightly. Ferdinand Lassalle was born in 1825, and was killed in 1864. He was one of those brilliant, meteoric figures who seem more suited to romance than to sober life. With extraordinary social gifts, with extraordinary powers of eloquence, with a quick and vivid fancy, with boundless energy, vanity, and ambition, and with a total absence of moral principle, he sought above all things and in all forms for pleasure, and he found it especially in constant excitement. Being the son of a tradesman of large means, he never knew the stress of poverty, and his social gifts and his high intellectual promise brought him into contact with some of the most eminent men of his time, among others with Humboldt, Heine, and Bismarck.

He was luxurious and ostentatious in his habits, and very fond of women, and they played a great part in his short life.

He first came in conflict with the law through the part which he appears to have taken in robbing a casket which was believed to contain papers that would be important to one of his Egerias, the well-known Countess of Hatzfeldt, who was then engaged in a lawsuit with her husband. He flung himself vehemently into revolutionary politics in 1848, and was imprisoned for six months. At this period of life he took some part in the socialist propaganda of Marx, but he soon threw it aside for some years. He was an early advocate of the unity of Germany, and when the unity of Italy was accomplished, he foretold as clearly as Montalembert that it would be the inevitable precursor of German unity. Like Louis Blanc, he was a passionate admirer of the French Convention, and especially of Robespierre, and he wrote several books clearly showing his belief that force and revolution, fire and the sword, were the only really efficient methods of accomplishing great social changes.

It was only in the last two or three years of his life that he became a prominent figure in the Socialist movement. In the acute conflicts that were then going on in the Prussian Parliament relating to the army and the budget, the working-class vote had become a matter of special importance. Schulze-Delitzsch at this time was doing much to establish among German working-men co-operative societies, independent of all State help, for the purpose of purchasing necessary articles at the cheapest rate, and conducting work with least cost to the labourer. Though himself a politician, he endeavoured to keep the movement wholly clear of politics, and by long, patient, and disinterested labour he succeeded about 1860 and 1861 in carrying it to a very high level of prosperity. Not less than 200,000 members are said to have been enrolled in these co-operative associations, and nearly two millions sterling was invested in them. Some suspicion, however, that Schulze was in sympathy with the capitalists had thrown a transient unpopularity over this great and truly honourable reformer, and Lassalle, availing himself of it, started a violent opposition to the movement, preaching a less austere gospel than that of self-help. He succeeded in displacing Schulze, and he soon after assailed him with a torrent of scurrilous banter and invective.[76]

Lassalle made it his object to persuade the working classes that political ascendency should be their first object; that the Revolution of 1848 should be their guiding light; and that by steadily pursuing this path the means of production and the wealth of the world would soon be at their disposal. Industry and thrift, he maintained, could never permanently improve their position, for it is a law of political economy that wages always tend to the level needed for the bare subsistence of the workman, and every economy in subsistence, every working-class saving, would in consequence be followed by a corresponding depreciation of wages. This was 'the iron law of wages,' against which industry and thrift would beat in vain until industrial society was completely reorganised. Profit is merely the portion of the produce of the labourer which is confiscated by the employer, and that portion will continually increase. Machinery, bringing the 'great industry' in its train, had vastly aggravated the evil. It has introduced an era of great profits, and great profits simply mean increased spoliation of the producer. It has placed the worker more and more in the hands of the capitalist, establishing a slavery which is not the less grinding because it is maintained, not by law, but by hunger. The wealth of the world may increase, but, unless society is radically revolutionised, the part of the labourer must become continually less. 'The back of the labourer is the green table on which undertakers and speculators play the game of fortune.' 'The produce of his labour strangles the labourer. His labour of yesterday rises against him, strikes him to the ground, and robs him of the produce of to-day.'

These doctrines lie at the root of most of the socialistic speculation of our time; and if the stream of humanity moved

---

[76] Dawson, *German Socialism and F. Lassalle,* pp. 137–38. This excellent book gives ample information about Lassalle. See, too, the very full examination of his views in Bernstein's *Ferdinand Lassalle.*

blindly on, with as little providence or self-restraint as the beasts of the field, a great part of them would be perfectly true. In a thriftless and redundant population, multiplying recklessly in excess of the means of employment, the wages of unskilled labour will undoubtedly sink to the level of a bare subsistence. But this is manifestly untrue of a population which multiplies slowly, and of a country where capital and employment increase more rapidly than population. As Cobden truly said, when two labourers run after one employer, wages will fall. When two employers run after one labourer, they will inevitably rise. As a matter of fact, the general rise of wages in Europe during the nineteenth century, both in nominal value and real value, has been undoubted and conspicuous, and the large and rapidly growing amount of working men's savings had been not less clearly so. In no countries have these things been more marked than in those in which manufactures are most developed and in which machinery is most employed.

Manufacturers, indeed, raise the wages even of those who are not engaged in them. Leroy-Beaulieu has drawn as instructive parallel between the lot of the miners in Silesia and the miners in England, compaing their wages, their food, and their hours of work, and he shows how the immense superiority of the condition of the English miner is simply due to the fact that he works in the centre of a highly industrial and manufacturing population.[77] One of the few satisfactory features in the long and terrible period of depression through which English agriculture has been passing, is that while both the landlord and the farming class have suffered ruinous loss, the position of the agricultural labourer has not seriously deteriorated, and is, in fact, better than in periods when agriculture was flourishing.[78] There can be little doubt that the

---

[77] *Le Collectivisme*, p. 61.

[78] In the Report of Mr. Little summing up the evidence on this subject, brought before the Labour Commission in 1892–3, the following passage occurs: 'Upon one point there is an almost unanimous opinion expressed

explanation of this apparent paradox is, at least to a large extent, to be found in the neighbourhood of manufacturing industry. The attraction of the higher wages of the town operates in two ways. It keeps down the number of the agricultural labourers, and it compels farmers to offer higher wages than the state of agriculture would warrant, in order to prevent their best labourers from deserting them. If it were true, as Lassalle and Marx contended, that the profit of the employer is simply the spoliation of the labourer, the peasant proprietor, who has no landlord, and the small manufacturer, who works on his own account, would gain far more than the most skilled wage-receiving artisan. The most rudimentary knowledge of the economical conditions of different classes will show that this is not the case.

Lassalle was not a man of much inventive genius, but he was eminently fitted to be a great agitator. He possessed in a very high degree eloquence and energy, the power of organising, fascinating, and dazzling men. His craving for applause was insatiable, and he was perpetually seeking and achieving theatrical effects. But his leading doctrines scarcely differed from those of Louis Bland and Marx. The first stage of the industrial revolution he preached was the construction of great co-operative associations, conducting different branches of industry, but equipped and supported out of public money furnished by the State. With such support, he believed that they would prove irresistible, would grow and prosper till they

---

by the Assistant Commissioners, and by every class of persons from whom they received evidence, and that is as to the great improvement which has taken place in the labourer's condition during the last twenty years. If in some parts of the country wages are now lower than they were ten years ago, they are certainly higher than at any period previous to 1873–4; and there is reason to believe that the average earnings within the reach of a willing and capable worker are, in most districts, considerably in excess of what they were twenty years ago. Any comparison of the present conditions with those prevailing thirty and forty years ago would be still more favourable to the present period' (Fifth and final *Report of the Commission of Labour*, p. 216).

absorbed or annihilated all private industry, would so regulate supply as to prevent over-production and commercial crises, and would impose their own terms on the consumer. This, as we have seen, was exactly the French idea, and it had been tried to some extent in 1848. After the suppression of the Socialist rebellion of June the French Chamber had devoted three millions of francs to assisting working-class associations. Many demands were refused, but fifty-six societies received state help. The result was not encouraging: in 1865 only four of these societies were in existence; in 1875 only one remained.[79]

In pursuance of these ideas. Lassalle made it his first task to place himself at the head of a separate working-class party, and he founded a 'Working Men's Association,' which was intended to be its centre, and to include working men from all the German States. The primary object was to attain universal suffrage as the means of attaining political ascendency. 'Universal suffrage,' he said, 'belongs to our social demands, as the handle to the axe.' Though he worked in the cause of democracy, he had decided monarchical sympathies, and a democratic Cæsar, carrying out a socialistic policy, would probably have had his full sympathy. In the distant future he looked forward to the extinction of all private property and all heredity, and the enrolment of the whole human race in one great industrial army. He denounced capital as robbery by the same kind of arguments as his predecessors and successors. We have the usual picture of the man who had invested money in some highly successful speculation, and who, without labour, or thrift, or care, found himself in a few years the possessor of colossal wealth. We have the usual suppression of the fact that, for every fortunate investor of this kind, there were hundreds who had invested money in enterprises that were beneficial to the community without obtaining any return, and whose capital, through no fault of their own, had been wholly lost, or reduced to a mere fraction

---

[79] Laveleye, *Le Socialisme Contemporain*, p. 84.

of its original amount. He desired that, by a heavy graduated tax, all rents of land should be diverted from the owner to the State.[80] Every rhetorical device was employed to persuade the working classes that, where wealth existed, it was not due to honest labour or saving, but to the opportunities of fraud that spring from the unjust organisation of society. To inflame class divisions and class discontent, to turn the energies of the working class from the paths of industry and thrift to those of violent revolution, to stimulate to the highest degree their predatory passions, were the chief objects of his life.

A duel growing out of a discreditable love-story cut short the career of this brilliant Epicurean demagogue. He left behind him many admirers, though, on the whole, the strongest influence in German Socialism was Karl Marx, the founder of what Socialists call 'scientific' Socialism. Marx was in most respects curiously unlike Lassalle. He was a frigid, systematic, pedantic, concentrated, arrogant thinker, working mainly through the press and by conspiracy, and, in conjunction with his chief disciple, Engels, he spent his life in elaborating a scheme of class warfare and universal spoliation, which has made many disciples. His life extended from 1818 to 1883. Like Lassalle, he was of the Jewish race, and, like him, he inherited a moderate competence. He was for some time editor of a Cologne newspaper, which was in opposition to the Government, and which was finally suppressed by authority. He then went to Paris, where he threw himself ardently into the Socialist propaganda which preceded and prepared the Revolution of 1848. The French Government expelled him, and he went to Brussels, where he formed, in co-operation with Engels, 'a German Working Men's Association,' and made himself the centre of an active communistic agitation.

The new body took for its motto the words, 'Proletariats of all countries unite;' and this motto showed one of the most

---

[80] Bernstein, *Ferdinand Lassalle* (English translation), pp. 142–43. Bernstein tries (not, I think, very successfully) to distinguish this doctrine from that of Mr. George.

characteristic divergencies of his policy from that of Lassalle. Lassalle desired a purely German movement, and he was passionately devoted to the idea of a united Germany. It was the great object of Marx to denationalise the working classes, obliterating all feelings of distinctive patriotism, and uniting them by the bond of common interests, common aspirations, and common sympathies in a great league for the overthrow of the capitalist and middle class. According to his view of history, the labouring class had, in all ages, been plundered or 'exploited' by the possessors of property. This tyranny at one time took the form of slavery, at another of serfdom, at another of the 'corvées' and other burdens of feudalism. In modern times it takes the form of the wage system, by which the labourer is compelled to work for the benefit of the rich. But democracy has come, and the most numerous class will soon become the most powerful, if they unite in all countries, and discard the sentiments and the divisions of local patriotism. The event to which the disciples of Marx are accustomed to point as realising the best their denationalising teaching is the Commune, when the French proletariat found their opportunity, in the crushing disaster of their country, to attempt a revolution in the interests of their order. It is an event still much commemorated and honoured in the more uncompromising socialistic circles, and they justly boast that men moulded in their principles took the leading part in accomplishing it.[81]

The Commune, however, was the flower of the new teaching, and we are at present concerned with the seed. On the outbreak of the Revolution of 1848 the Belgian authorities expelled Marx from Brussels, and he gladly went to Paris. The aspect of Europe in this year of revolution seemed very favourable to his designs, and in 1848 he put forward, in conjunction with some of his disciples, a German programme of communism which, although it did not attract much imme-

---

[81] As on of the many examples of the way in which the Commune is regarded by the Socialists, the reader may consult Malon, *Le Socialisme Intégral*, i, 187–88.

diate attention, has a considerable importance, for it is the first clearly formulated exposition of the designs of the party, and the parent of the many programmes that were to come. Marx and his fellow-signatories demanded 'the proclamation of a republic; payment of members of Parliament; the conversion of princely and other feudal estates with mines, &c., into public property; the appropriation by the State of all means of transport, as railways, canals, steamships, roads, and ports; the restriction of the laws of succession; the introduction of heavy progressive taxes, and the abolition of excise duties; the establishment of national workshops; State guarantee to all workmen of an existence, provision for the incapable, universal and free education.' They desired also the immediate expropriation of landed property, and the employment of the rents for State purposes; the centralisation of all credit, by the formation with State capital of a national bank having a complete monopoly; the institution at public expense of great industrial armies working in common. They denounced the existing system of marriage and the family as resting on capital or private gain. They declared that their objects could only be attained by force and by a radical revolution, and they called on the 'proletariat' of all countries to unite, and to support any party of movement that could shake the existing fabric of society.[82]

Marx soon returned to Prussia, resumed his newspaper work, and endeavoured to foment and encourage Socialist risings. But after the restoration of order in Germany his journal was suppressed. He was again expelled from Prussia, and, as he was refused permission to settle in France, he took refuge in London, where he became the London correspondent of the 'New York Tribune,' and where he spent the remainder of his life in writing, and in forming or promoting Socialist leagues.

His great work was in connection with the International Society. This society seems to have been first suggested when

---

[82] Dawson's *German Socialism*, pp. 94–95, 235–37.

some skilled French workmen were sent to London, at the cost of the Imperial Government, in 1862, for the purpose of visiting the great Exhibition of that year, and studying the relative industrial progress of different nations. They employed themselves, among other things, in carefully examining English trade unions; and they were received with much cordiality by English working-class leaders. The International Society was founded at a meeting which was held in St. Martin's Hall, in September 1864, under the presidency of Professor Beesly. Marx, Mazzini, and an English working-class agitator named Odger, whose speeches will probably be in the recollection of many of my readers, bore a large part in its foundation.[83] Mazzini, however, had no sympathy with Marx, and when he found that the new organisation was not likely to be used for purely political objects, he withdrew from it. The French element in the movement acquired about this time a considerable accession of strength owing to the law of 1864, which made working men's coalitions legal in France; but German influence, and especially that of Marx, soon became the most powerful, though in the first manifestoes of the International his distinctive doctrines were either concealed or greatly attenuated.

It was, as its name implied, a central and international society, intended to affiliate workmen's associations in all countries, to bring their members into close correspondence, to hold periodical congresses at which their common interests might be discussed, and to impart a common direction to their policy. It was soon found that it included wide differences of opinion. The German element, and a great portion of the French element, aimed at a total destruction of the existing fabric of society and a complete spoliation of property. The English representatives, for the most part, desired little more than that light should be thrown on the condition of working men in different lands, the problems they had to solve, and the solutions they proposed; and that measures should be

---

[83] See Woolsey's *Communism and Socialism*, p. 133.

taken to prevent the beating down of wages in one country by the importation of labourers from another. It was ultimately decided not to interfere in any way with the different working-class associations that were affiliated to the society, and the manifesto which was issued describing its objects was drawn up in eminently moderate and almost colourless language.

It stated that the emancipation of the working classes must be effected by themselves, and that the end for which they should labour should be equal rights and duties for all, and the annihilation of all class domination; that the economical subjection of the workman to those who possess the means of work, and therefore of livelihood, is the first cause of political, moral, and material servitude; that the economical emancipation of the workman should be the supreme object, to which all political movements should be subordinated; that hitherto the efforts of the working classes had failed owing to the isolation of the different nationalities, and that the time had now come when workmen of all countries should combine to solve a problem which was neither local nor national, but applied to all countries in which modern life exists. In accordance with this preamble the council elected by the assembly in St. Martin's Hall had undertaken to found an International Society of Labourers, in which the workmen of different countries who aspired to mutual assistance, progress, and the complete emancipation of their class, might find a central point of communication and co-operation. They declared that this society, and all the societies and individuals connected with it, acknowledged that truth, morality, and justice, without distinction of colour, creed, or nationality, should be the foundation of their conduct. They deemed it their duty to claim for all the rights of men and of citzenship—'No duties without rights, no rights without duties.'[84]

It is probable that this manifesto represented the genuine

---

[84] See Malon, *Le Socialisme Intégral*, pp. 183–84. I have slightly condensed this manifesto.

opinions of a considerable portion of those who signed it, and it certainly contained nothing that was in any degree dishonest or dishonourable. It seemed to point mainly to the formation of co-operative societies, enabling working men to become their own masters, and, whether this scheme was feasible or not, there was at least no objection to be raised against it on the score of morality. Questions relating to marriage and to religious belief, which were so prominent in continental Socialism, were carefully avoided; confiscation, which was a cardinal point in the schemes of Marx and Lassalle, was never suggested; and although the working classes in different nationalities were invited to communicate and combine, there was nothing in the manifesto that was in any degree inconsistent with a genuine patriotism. The divisions in the Socialist camp were very serious, and it was only by the widest compromise that some imperfect semblance of unity could be preserved. In England, there was then no perceptible body of opinion in favour of the more extreme views of the continental Socialists. In Germany, the followers of Lassalle and the followers of Marx were bitterly opposed. In France, though branches of the International were speedily established in most of the great towns, subscriptions came in very slowly. Personal jealousies and suspicions, and grave dissensions of principle, appeared, and they broke out fiercely in a clandestine meeting of representatives of the chief French industries which was held in Paris. There was a powerful party who wished the French delegation to be essentially and exclusively Republican, and the overthrow of the Empire and the establishment of a democratic republic to be made one of the great objects of the society. There was dissension about whether the emancipation of Poland should be included among the objects of the International; whether female labour and intellectual labour should be recognised. The majority of the French workmen looked with great disfavour on the admission of lawyers, journalists, and professors into their councils: they considered that such men were far too closely connected with the *bourgeoisie,* and they desired that manual labour alone should be represented in the International. On the other hand, it was urged that the men whom it was proposed to exclude were the very men who had chiefly created, organised, and managed the whole Socialist movement, and that without their assistance that movement was very likely to collapse. English and German votes, in opposition to those of the French delegates, at last secured their admission.[85]

The Congress of Geneva, which was held in 1866, and the Congress of Lausanne, which was held in 1867, appear both to have been very inoffensive. Many subjects were discussed. Some crude ideas were thrown out. It was resolved that railways ought to be in the hands of the State, but the congress did not attempt to define the means of acquiring them; there was a strong tendency in favour of a limitation of working hours, but no steps of a really revolutionary character were taken. The society became more popular when it was shown that it could do something to procure international support for local strikes, and to prevent in time of strikes the importation of cheap foreign labour; and it was in this direction that a large proportion of its members wished it chiefly to develop. In 1868 some members were prosecuted and condemned to small fines in France for belonging to an association unauthorised by law; but there was no disposition shown by the Imperial Government to deal harshly with its members.[86]

In the Congress at Brussels, in 1868, signs of a more revolutionary spirit appeared, but it was not until the Congress of Basle, in 1869, that the International definitely identified itself with a policy of spoliation. It was the policy of Marx, but the chief resolution was introduced by a French delegate named

---

[85] An account of these dissensions will be found in *L'Association Internationale des Travailleurs*, par F. Fribourg, l'un de ses Fondateurs. There is a useful little *Histoire de l'Internationale*, by Jacques Populus, published in the *Bibliothèque Populaire* in 1871, which gives the chief documents. See, too, Zacher, *L'Internationale Rouge* (French translation); the chapter on the International in Laveleye, and the accounts of it in Woolsey and in Dawson.

[86] Laveleye, *Le Socialisme Contemporain*, pp. 179–82.

Paepe, who induced the congress to vote that all private property in land should be at once abolished, and that all farmers
should hold their farms in lease from the State, paying their
rents to it alone. As a transitional measure, however, it was
agreed that the peasant proprietor, who cultivated what is
now his own land, might be exempt from rent during his life.
After his death his plot of land was to pass under the same
conditions as the others.[87] A motion was made that all inheritance of property should be abolished; but, although the congress would not reject, it was not prepared to adopt, so radical
a measure. An amendment limiting inheritance, as a transitory
measure, to near kindred met with a large amount of support;
but there were many abstentions, and it accordingly failed to
obtain the assent of a full majority of the congress.[88]

Differences of opinion on other points were very apparent.
One French representative warned his fellows that the course
they were taking would alienate from them the whole body of
the French peasant proprietors, and that it was the opposition
of this class that crushed the Republic of 1848. He added, that
the only result of a collective ownership of the soil would be
that the whole rural population would become a population
of serfs, performing forced labour at the command of the
agents of the State, and that they would gain nothing in material wellbeing that could compensate them for the total destruction of their liberty.[89] The term 'Collectivist' about this
time became common. Like most Socialist terms, it was somewhat vague, or at least covered many subdivisions of opinion;
but its general idea was that all the means of production—
land, machinery, and capital—should be appropriated by the
State, though, subject to this condition, men were to be allowed to own, to save, and even to inherit, provided that they
did not turn what they possessed into capital. The Collectivists

---

[87] Malon, *Le Socialisme Intégral*, i. 186.
[88] Woolsey, pp. 144–45. The numbers were, 32 in favour of the amendment, 23 against it, and 17 abstentions.
[89] See his speech in Laveleye, p. 196.

were opposed to the Communists, who would deny to the individual even this small measure of liberty, and aggrandise still further the power of the State.[90]

It was about this time, also, that the influence of the Russian Nihilist, Bakúnin, became considerable, and it was exerted in strong opposition to Marx. Bakúnin seems to me to be best described by the term *fou furieux*, which Thiers once applied, with less justice, to another politician. He illustrates the mania for destruction which sometimes takes hold of a diseased nature, and is probably a good deal strengthened by a kind of vanity very common in our generation. It makes men feverishly anxious that no one should pass them in the race, holding opinions more 'advanced' than themselves. It must be acknowledged that, in his own path, Bakúnin can hardly be outstripped. He preached, as he said, 'not only the collective ownership of the soil, but also of all riches, to be effected by a complete abolition of the State as a political and juridical entity. . . ; the destruction of all national and territorial States, and on their ruins the construction of an international State consisting of the millions of workmen.'[91] 'It is necessary,' he said, 'to destroy all existing institutions—the State, the Church, the law court, the bank, the university, the army, and the police, all of which are fortresses of privilege against the proletariat. One method, which is particularly efficacious, is to burn all papers, so as to destroy the whole legal basis of family and property. It is a colossal work, but it will be accomplished.'[92] He objected to the Communists, that their theory recognised and strengthened the power of existing States, all of which must be abolished.

It is a melancholy proof of the force of the volcanic elements that underlie civilised society that such a man should have obtained a large following. He represented a great body of French and Italian workmen in the Congress of Basle, and he

---

[90] Leroy-Beaulieu, *Le Collectivisme*, pp. 6–8.
[91] Laveleye, p. 200.
[92] Malon, *Le Socialisme Intégral*, i. 199–200.

set up a rival society, called 'An Alliance of the Social Democracy.' Its programme consisted of atheism; the abolition of all worship; the substitution of science for faith, and human justice for Divine justice; the abolition of marriage as a political, religious, judicial, and civil institution; of all inheritance; of private property in all its forms, and of all existing States and bodies invested with authority. Collective property and industrial associations, and 'universal and international solidarity, discarding all politics founded on so-called patriotism and the rivalry of nations,' were to be the characteristics of the regenerated world.[93]

Socialism in 1869 and 1870, in its different forms, advanced rapidly. The International established branches in nearly every European country, and it had taken some root in America. It was assisted by formidable strikes which broke out in France and Belgium, and by the unbounded latitude of the press which existed in France in the last days of the Empire. Its literature in newspapers and periodicals became very considerable, and its revolutionary tendencies more clearly marked. Laveleye has noticed that while in its earlier days the chief task of the International was to raise wages and assist strikes, it was now mainly concerned with the transformation of society. At the outbreak of the War of 1870 its cosmopolitan character was shown by some addresses of protest and mutual sympathy emanating from working men belonging to each of the belligerent nations; but in the fierce clash of passions that ensued they passed almost unperceived.

Then came the seventy-three terrible days of the Commune, and during this time members of the International bore a conspicuous part in the government of Paris. In the agony of the struggle there was little time for reorganising society, and the ghastly scenes of anarchy, of deliberate and cold-blooded murder, and of gigantic incendiarism that soon took place have diverted all attention from the attempts to realise the programme of Socialism. Nor, indeed, had those attempts much importance. The decrees sweeping away some of the arrears

---

[93] Woolsey, p. 148.

of house-rent, postponing the payment of commercial debts, and suspending the sale of pledged articles, might have been taken in any period of extreme and desperate crisis. Other decrees of the Commune reduced the salaries of all function-aries; forbade employers to punish workmen by levying fines or withholding wages; prohibited night-work in bakeries, and ordered that all workshops which had been abandoned should be reported to the Revolutionary Government, in order that they should be converted into co-operative associations in the hands of the workmen. Priests and monks were treated as wild beasts, and many of them were murdered with every circumstance of deliberate ferocity; and it is therefore not sur-prising that the Commune should have decreed the confis-cation of all property belonging to religious corporations, and the suppression of all State endowments of religion.[94]

There has been some dispute about the part borne by the International in the rising of 1871. The truth seems to be that the central council in London had absolutely nothing to say to it. When the war broke out, no one could have anticipated the Communist revolution, and, when it became possible, Paris was surrounded by a ring of German bayonets, which effectually excluded external interference. Nor, it may be added, had the central council of the International any dis-position to take the initiative in political revolution. On the other hand, it is equally clear that the whole body of the Socialists in Paris threw themselves passionately into the ris-ing; that a large proportion of its ablest, though not its most violent, leaders were drawn from the ranks of the Interna-tional, and that, when the struggle was over, Marx and the council in London, as well as innumerable Socialists in other countries, expressed the warmest sympathy and admiration for the defeated Communists.

The well-known French Socialist, Malon, was one of the members of the Commune, and he illustrates the relation of the International to this revolution by the aloe, which, after

---

[94] Mermeix, *La France Socialiste*, pp. 81–82, 103; Mendes, *Les 73 Journées de la Commune* (3rd ed.), p. 62; Martin's *Histoire de France depuis 1789*, tome vii. 394.

many years, throws out a splendid flower, and then dies away. Its history in the period immediately following the Communist rising was one of constant and bitter dissension, which it is not here necessary to relate. The supreme council was transferred to New York; it lost its influence, and the organisation either ceased to exist or took new forms. But the movement towards Socialism continually spread. Socialist congresses multiplied, and that which was held in Gotha in 1875 had a special importance in drawing together the divergent sections of German Socialism. Its programme was unusually full. It was adopted in its principal parts by Socialist bodies in many countries, and, in the opinion of the best historian of the International, it may be regarded as the fullest and most authentic expression of the views of the whole body of continental Socialists.[95]

It states that all wealth and all civilisation spring from labour, and that the whole fruit of labour belongs to society— that is to say, to all the members. All men under an obligation to work, and each member has a right to receive of the fruit of this work the part reasonably necessary to satisfy all his wants.

In the existing state of society, the means of work are monopolised by the capitalist class, and the dependence of the working class caused by this monopoly is the source of misery and of servitude in all its forms.

The emancipation of labour requires the transfer of all the means of work to society as a whole, the collective regulation of all work, and the equitable distribution of its produce.

The emancipation of labour can only be effected by the labouring class, all other classes being reactionary.

Starting from these principles, the Socialist working party of Germany aims by all legal means at the establishment of a free State in a socialistic society. It undertakes to break 'the brazen law of wages;' to put an end to 'exploitation' in all its forms, and to all political and social inequality

---

[95] Zacher, *L'Internationale Rouge* (French translation), p. 13.

While in the first instance limiting its action to its own country, it recognises the international character of the working-class movement, and will fulfil the duties arising from it so as to realise the fraternity of all men.

As a preliminary step to the solution of the social question it demands the formation of co-operative associations of workmen acting with State help, and at the same time under the democratic control of the workers. These associations must be sufficiently numerous to become the point of departure for the socialistic organisation of collective labour.

The Socialist working party of Germany demand as the foundation of the State equal and direct universal suffrage in all elections, general and local, and including all citizens above the age of twenty. The voting is to take place on a Sunday or other holiday. It is to be secret, and it is also to be obligatory.

They demand also direct legislation by the people; war and peace voted by the people; the substitution of a national militia for permanent armies; the suppression of all restriction on the liberty of the press, of public meeting, and combinations; justice administered by the people and administered gratuitously; free State education in all grades, and the complete disconnection of religion from the Government.

As long as the present constitution of society exists the Socialist workmen of Germany demand the greatest possible extension of political liberties; a single direct and progressive tax upon revenues; unlimited rights of combination; a normal day of labour, regulated according to the needs of society; a prohibition of Sunday work; a limitation in the interests of health and morality of the work of children and women; a severe sanitary inspection of all forms of labour by inspectors named by the workmen; a regulation of prison labour, and a completely free administration of all institutions established for the assistance of the working classes.[96]

This comprehensive programme comprises some articles

---

[96] Zacher, *L'Internationale Rouge*, pp. 236–39.

which are very feasible and reasonable, and others which
could only be carried out by the violent spoliation of all existing property and a total revolution of society. The article
admitting, as a transitional measure, co-operative societies
was due to the followers of Lassalle. In most of the other parts
of the document the influence of Marx prevailed. The sharp
division between the wage-earning class and all other classes
was his cardinal doctrine, and the appropriation without purchase by the community of all the land, machinery, and capital which belongs to private persons, whether they have
received or inherited it from others or whether they have
acquired it through their own industry and saving, is an object which seems common to all the leading sects of continental Socialists.

On the means of attaining this object they are not agreed.
The predominant and, as it seems to me, the more rational
opinion is, that the great multitude of the owners of property
can never be dispossessed except by force. This was evidently
the opinion of Marx, though in a speech which he made at
the congress at The Hague, in 1872, he admitted the possibility in some countries of a peaceful solution. 'We do not
deny,' he said, 'that there are countries, as America, England,
and Holland, where working men can reach their ends by
pacific means. If this is true, we must still acknowledge that
in most continental countries force must be the lever of our
revolution.'[97] Bebel, who is one of the most important of the
later disciples of Marx, has never concealed his opinion. 'We
aim,' he said, 'in the domain of politics, at Republicanism; in
the domain of economics, at Socialism; and in the domain of
what is to-day called religion, at atheism.' 'There are only two
ways of attaining our economic ends. The one is the general
supplanting of the private undertakers by means of legislation when the democratic State has been established. . . . The
other, and decidedly shorter, though also violent way, would
be forcible expropriation—the abolition of private undertakers at one stroke, irrespective of the means to be employed.

---

[97] Dawson, *Lassalle and German Socialism*, p. 243.

. . . There is no need to be horrified at this possible use of force, or to cry 'Murder' at the suppression of rightful existences, at forcible expropriation, and so forth. History teaches that, as a rule, new ideas only assert themselves through a violent struggle between their representatives and the representatives of the past.'[98]

Another school, however, maintain that by the assistance of democratic institutions the whole process can be accomplished by mere force of law. It is only necessary, they say, for the Socialist party to obtain an uncontrolled ascendency in the legislature, and all the rest will easily follow. The repudiation of national debts, which is one leading article of the party, presents no difficulty. It only requires a simple breach of faith—the violation of the promise in virtue of which the money had been lent. Land confiscation does not need even a change of title-deeds. It can be effected by a special tax diverting to the State all that portion of the profit which now takes the form of rent. Private industries can be strangled by the competition of co-operative institutions endowed out of taxation, and out of taxation levied on the very class whose private industry it is desired to crush. A single highly graduated tax on incomes, and a legal prohibition of inheritance, could easily and effectually destroy all private wealth. The agglomeration of industries into large companies, which is so characteristic of our generation, and the rapid growth of a democratic municipal and county government, would, it is maintained, greatly facilitate the process of confiscation and transformation.

There is also an intermediate opinion, which is probably still more widely held. It is that the full ends of Socialism can never be attained without violence, but that constitutional agitation would greatly help by placing all the posts and elements of power in the hands of the Socialists, and thus giving them a commanding 'vantage-ground when the struggle breaks out.

This question for some time greatly occupied and divided

---

[98] Dawson, pp. 286–87.

the Socialist body, especially after the stringent anti-Socialist legislation which was carried in Germany in 1878. Most, the notorious editor of the 'Freiheit,' and a German named Hasselmann, led the more violent, or, as we should now call it, the Anarchist party, which placed all its hope in armed insurrection, and until that insurrection could be effected advocated dynamite, assassination, and all other means of destroying a capitalist society. On the other hand there was the parliamentary party, led by Bebel and Liebknecht, who desired that Socialism should pursue its parliamentary course; though, as has been already seen, they were quite prepared to admit that force was the ultimate solution. After many abortive negotiations, the question was brought before an important Socialist congress which was held at the old castle of Wyden, in Switzerland, in 1880. Most and Hasselmann did not appear, and after much discussion the congress gave a decided victory to the parliamentary party. The Anarchist leaders were severed from the body, on the charge of having undermined its discipline, and the congress expressed its full confidence in its parliamentary leaders. It at the same time revised the programme of Gotha by effacing the word 'legal' from the clause in which that congress described the means by which the Socialists were aiming at their ideal. It formally adopted a Zürich paper, called the 'Sozial-Demokrat,' as the one official organ of their party, and it issued a manifesto which clearly shows that the difference between the moderate and the extreme party was only a difference of expediency, and not of principles or of aims. It was addressed to the workmen's Socialist party in Germany, and to their co-religionists and sympathisers in all countries; and a few condensed extracts will sufficiently show its purport.

The Social Democratic party of Germany, it said, will continue to the end what it has been at the beginning—the champion of the emancipation of a crushed and exploited people. It will continue to struggle courageously, perseveringly, and deliberately for the annihilation of the insensate and criminal order of things, both political and social, which now exists. The persecutions of an infamous Government and a not less infamous *bourgeoisie* have not bent the democracy: it remains faithful to its principle and its revolutionary courage.

The immense majority of the German Social Democrats never indulged in the illusion that democracy would succeed by purely legal means in effecting the triumph of their principles; or, in other words, that the privileged classes would of their own accord renounce their privileges.

But no German Democrat has ever thought that he should therefore renounce our principles. If the privileged classes close the legal way—the way we should prefer—all means will be good to us. The political and economical masters of Germany wish a war to death. They will have it, and the whole responsibility will rest upon them.

Our party, however, will never lightly risk a criminal revolution, which would greatly compromise our cause. The people are not sufficiently prepared for the struggle; it would throw back for many years the realisation of our ideas, and it would be a great crime, for it would uselessly shed the precious blood of the people.

The first duty of every revolutionist is to prepare insensibly the way for the revolution in its definite and violent form by spreading our principles among the people, strengthening the party which is to lead the coming struggle, weakening and paralysing the enemy.

If, through the force of circumstances, extreme measures some day come, the German Socialists will prove that they know how to do their duty. They will enter into the struggle well prepared, and with the hope of conquest.

This is the spirit that has inspired the decisions of our congress. As a means both of agitation and of propagandism, the Socialists are invited to take an active part in all elections which offer the smallest chance of success, whether they be for the Reichstag, the Landtag, or the commune.

While regulating our internal affairs, we have never for a moment forgotten the bonds that unite our party indissolubly with our brothers in other countries and other tongues—with the socialist proletariat of the whole world.

An office is established for the express purpose of main-

taining a close and uninterrupted communication with Socialists in other countries, and wherever in the world there is
a struggle to emancipate the working classes from political
and social servitude, there the social democracy of Germany
will be found ready to help.[99]

The same views were constantly expressed in the official
paper of the party. Many extracts, both from the 'Sozial-Demokrat,' which represented the so-called Moderate party, and
from the 'Freiheit,' which represented the Anarchist party,
were read in the Bundesrath in the March of 1881, and they
show that no real difference of aim divided them. Both papers
welcomed with enthusiasm the assassination of the Czar Alex-
ander II. Both papers acknowledged that a total revolution of
the existing fabric of society was their ultimate end. Both papers united their dreams of social regeneration with a very
aggressive and virulent atheism. The possibility of a peaceful
revolution was described by the 'Sozial-Demokrat' as 'a pure
Utopia.' 'We know,' it said, 'that the socialistic State will never
be realised except by a violent revolution, and it is our duty to
spread this conviction through all classes.' 'We believe that if
war broke out on our east, or on our west, or from both quarters at once, another enemy would arise far more formidable
than the foreign foe, and that enemy would be the proletariat.
It will then be a war to the death.' 'Sooner or later will come
a famine, or an epidemic, or a great European war. In that day
the cry of anguish of the poor, which has been so long un-
heeded, will turn into a cry of vengeance that will blanch the
cheeks of the great and of the powerful. Then will sound the
hour of judgment, the hour of deliverance.' 'Christianity is
the greatest enemy of Socialism.' 'When God is expelled from
human brains, what is called the Divine Grace will at the same
time be banished; and when the heaven above appears nothing more than an immense falsehood, men will seek to create
for themselves a heaven below.'[100]

---

[99] Zacher, pp. 240–44.
[100] See these extracts in Zacher, pp. 35–38; a number of instructive extracts
from the *Freiheit* follow.

Such extracts, taken from the organ of the main and more moderate section of the German Socialists, will probably help to make the English reader understand why it is that German statesmen regard the Socialists, not as a normal political party, but as the deadly enemies of their country and of civilised society. Marx, towards the end of his life, employed himself in writing his elaborate treatise on Capital, of which the first volume was published by himself, and the conclusion, after his death, by his disciples. It is not probable that a work so long, so obscure, confused, and tortuous in its meanings, and so unspeakably dreary in its style, has had many readers among the working classes, or indeed in any class; but the mere fact that a highly pretentious philosophical treatise, with a great parade of learning, and continually expressing the most arrogant contempt for the most illustrious economical and historical writers of the century, should have been written in defence of plunder and revolution has, no doubt, not been without its effect. It is impossible in a short space to give a complete summary of this book, but a few leading doctrines stand out prominently, and have been widely diffused in more popular forms through many countries.

The work is, as might be expected, a furious attack upon capital. It describes it as wholly due to violence or fraud, extending through the whole past history of the globe. Marx recognises no such thing as prescription. The frauds, the violence, the unjust confiscations of a remote past are brought up against peaceful and industrious men who for many generations have bought, sold, borrowed, and let with perfect security on the faith of titles fully recognised by law, and absolutely undisputed within the memory of man. The most serious vice of capital is, however, not derived from the past. It lies in the present confiscation of labour and its fruits, which, according to Marx, is its essential characteristic. To understand his position it is necessary to consider his law of value. He distinguishes between the 'use value' of a thing and its 'exchange value,' and exchange value, he maintained, can only be created in one way. This way is by labour. All commodities are merely 'masses of congealed labour-time,' and derive their whole exchange value from the labour bestowed on them. 'The value of every commodity is determined by the labour-time necessary to produce it in normal quantity.' 'Commodities in which equal quantities of labour are embodied, or which can be produced in the same time, have the same value.' 'All surplus value, under whatever form it crystallises itself—interest, rent, or profit'—is only the 'materialisation' of a certain amount of unpaid labour-time.[101]

Two startling consequences spring from this doctrine. One is, that commerce can never produce a surplus value, or, in other words, increase wealth. It merely moves from one quarter to another a fixed amount of value, or 'congealed' labour-power. 'A. may be clever enough to get the advantage of B. or C. without their being able to retaliate . . . but the value in circulation has not increased by one iota—it is only distributed differently between A. and B. . . . The same change would have taken place if A., without the formality of an exchange, had directly stolen from B. The sum of the values in circulation can clearly not be augmented by any change in their distribution, any more than the quantity of precious metals in a country by a Jew selling a Queen Anne's farthing for a guinea. . . . If equivalents are exchanged, no surplus value results, and if non-equivalents are exchanged, still no surplus value. Circulation, or the exchange of commodities, begets no value.'[102]

And if money devoted to commerce or the mere exchange of commodities is thus incapable of producing a surplus value, the same thing is true of the money-lender's capital, which is employed in loans. Capital is naturally barren. It has no real power of reproduction, or of creating value. Its power of acquiring wealth lies solely in its power of purchasing labour, and enabling its owner to appropriate the proceeds. Interest of money is an essentially unjust thing. The expen-

---

[101] Marx, *Capital*, p. 6 (Eng. trans.). See, too, the chapter on 'The Labour Process.'

[102] Ibid. p. 141.

diture of labour-time can alone create and measure increase of value, and there is no other way of adding to the wealth of the world. Marx quotes, with complete approbation, the well-known assertion of Aristotle, that 'the usurer is most rightly hated, because money itself is the source of his gain, and is not used for the purpose for which it was invented, for it originated for the exchange of commodities, but interest makes out of money more money. . . . Interest is money of money; so that, of all modes of making a living, this is the most contrary to nature.'[103]

In what way, then, is capital formed? The answer is, that it is simply the unpaid and confiscated labour of the labourer. The capitalist, having obtained command of the means of production and subsistence, is able to buy at the price of a bare subsistence the whole labour-time of the labourer. By right the capitalist has no claim to profit, or to anything beyond the mere sum required for keeping up his machinery. In fact he is able to exact far more. The labourer works, perhaps, for ten hours. In five hours he probably produces an equivalent to his subsistence, and he receives that amount of the produce of his labour in the shape of wages. For the other five hours he receives nothing, and the whole produce of his labour is appropriated by the capitalist. 'Wages by their very nature always imply a certain quantity of unpaid labour of the part of the labourer.'[104] It is an illusion to suppose that the labourer is paid by the capitalist out of his capital. This would, no doubt, be the case if he were paid in advance. As a matter of fact, he is paid only at the end of his day's, or week's, or month's work, and he is paid entirely out of his own earnings. He receives only what he has himself made, or its equivalent. Every shilling that is made by him is merely the equivalent of commodities which he has already produced; but he has produced many commodities besides, for which he obtains no return, and this constitutes the profit of the capitalist.

The doctrine that a capitalist has no right to derive profit

---

[103] Marx, *Capital*, pp. 142–43.
[104] Ibid. p. 632.

from the use of his machinery may obviously be extended further, and some at least of the Collectivists do not at all flinch from their conclusions. They very consistently maintain that, if a man lives in the house of another man, it is an extortion to ask him to pay a rent. All that the owner is entitled to is that his house should be kept in good repair. One distinguished economist of the party, named Briosnes, has gone a step further. He argues that the owner of the house should not only receive nothing , but should pay the lodger for keeping up his house.[105] It may be left to the common sense of the reader to determine how many men would build houses under these conditions for the accommodation of others, and what would be the fate of the houseless poor.

Marx observes that one of the chief abuses of the feudal system was the 'corvée,' or the obligation imposed upon the tenant to labour gratuitously for a certain number of days in every year for the benefit of his landlord, or feudal chief. The same system, he maintains, exists under the capitalist system at the present day, and in a greatly aggravated form. Under the old system the poor man was obliged to give uncompensated labour for a certain number of days in every week, or month, or year. The only difference between the ancient and the modern system is, that the unpaid labour is now exacted daily, in the shape of several hours of uncompensated work. 'The essential difference between a society based on slave labour and one based on wage labour lies only in the mode in which the surplus labour is in each case extracted from the actual producer and labourer.'[106] Machinery has greatly aggravated the servitude. 'Previously the workman sold his own labour-power, which he disposed of nominally as a free agent. Now he sells wife and child. He has become a slave-dealer.'[107] The 'brazen' or 'iron' law of wages prevents the possibility of the workman rising above his slavery. The wealth that is pro-

---

[105] Leroy-Beaulieu, *Le Collectivisme*, pp. 265–66.
[106] Marx, *Capital*, pp. 200–1.
[107] Ibid. p. 393.

duced may increase, but this will only profit the capitalist; and if for a short time wages rise, the pressure of population will become greater, and soon reduce them to their normal level of a bare subsistence. The prices of the articles of first necessity may fall, but to the labourer the only result will be a corresponding fall of wages, as the cost of his subsistence will be diminished. Under the capitalist system the labourer is unable to purchase with his earnings what he has himself produced, and with the progress of machinery the impossibility becomes continually greater. There is but one real remedy. It is to place the land and the instruments of production in the hands of the producers. 'The expropriation of the mass of the people from the soil forms the basis of the capitalist mode of production.'[108]

To sum up the position Marx assures us that 'capital is dead labour, that, vampire-like, only lives by sucking living labour, and lives the more, the more labour it sucks.'[109] It is 'the vampire which will not lose its hold on the labourer so long as there is a muscle, a nerve, a drop of blood to be exploited.'[110] 'In proportion as capital accumulates, the lot of the labourer, be his pay high or low, must grow worse. . . . Accumulation of wealth at one pole is, therefore, at the same time accumulation of misery, agony of toil, slavery, ignorance, brutality, mental degradation at the opposite pole—*i.e.* on the side of the class that produces its own product in the form of capital.'[111] 'As in religion man is governed by the products of his own brain, so in capitalistic production he is governed by the products of his own hand.'[112]

The doctrine of Marx is, in its essential features, the received and recognised doctrine of the great body, not only of German, but of French Socialists. It is the basis of the teaching of Mr. Hyndman and some other Socialist writers in England, and it has a considerable and probably a growing body of

---

[108] Ibid. p. 793.
[109] Ibid. p. 216.
[110] Ibid. p. 288.
[111] Ibid. p. 661.
[112] Ibid. pp. 634–35.

adherents in nearly every country. Marx is described by his followers as the new Adam Smith, another and a greater Darwin, the author of 'The Bible of Socialism.'

Burke has noticed that the weakest reasonings are sometimes the most dangerous, because they are united with the strongest passions, and I do not think that the reasonings of Marx would have received these eulogies if they had not led to conclusions appealing strongly to cupidity and to revolutionary passions. Nor are they, I think, ever likely to take deep root in English soil. That curious Teutonic power of framing a picture of the world out of formulæ and abstract reasonings, to the neglect of some of the most patent facts, is not an English characteristic; and certainly no one who compared the realities of a manufacturing country with the doctrines of Marx would be likely to find much correspondence between them. It is quite true that, both in the present and in the past, large fortunes are often due to fraud and violence, and perhaps still more frequently to some happy chance; but it is also certain that the normal increase of wealth springs from quite other sources. Superior talent, superior industry, superior thrift, lie at the root of the great accumulations of every civilised age. The true source of the enormous disparities of condition lies in the great natural inequality of men, both moral and intellectual and physical, and in the desire of each man to improve his position. It is a desire which is one of the deepest and most indestructible elements of human nature, though it acts in different degrees of force and of efficiency. When a workman shows an ability, an industry, or a thrift that marks him out from his fellows; when he spends in work the time and saves the money which others spend in idleness or dissipation, there may be seen the incipient capitalist. Trace the pedigrees of the great fortunes among us, and in how many instances will it be found that we arrive in one, two, or three generations at the superior workman? It is the characteristic of modern saving that it is scarcely ever hoarded, but is at once thrown into circulation in the form of capital, and made productive of more riches; and it is in the enormous scale of this production, going on year by year over the whole surface of the community, that the growing wealth of the country mainly consists.

We have seen the picture Marx gives of the slavery of a nation which lives under the capitalist system; of the steady decrease of wellbeing and of wages that must follow; of the hopelessness of expecting that any increase of manufacturing wealth, or any cheapening of the articles of first necessity, can improve the condition of the labourer. In 1883, the year when Marx died, one of the greatest of living statisticians published his estimate of the condition of the working classes in England during the fifty preceding years.[113] He was writing of the country and the time in which manufactures had most enormously developed, in which machinery had played the greatest part, in which the capitalist system had been most fully tried. He tells us, as the result of a careful and minute investigation of the industrial statistics of the United Kingdom, that in every class of work in which it is possible to make a comparison the wages of the labourers have in those fifty years risen at least 20 per cent., that in most cases they have risen from 50 to 100 per cent., and in one or two instances more than 100 per cent. 'If,' as he truly says, 'in this interval the average money earnings of the working class have risen between 50 and 100 per cent., there must have been an enormous change for the better in the means of the working man, unless by some wonderful accident it has happened that his special articles have changed in a different way from the general run of prices.'

Have they, then, done so? The answer is, that while the prices of wheat and sugar have immensely decreased; while the price of clothing, and most of the other articles of working men's consumption, have diminished in a less, but still considerable, proportion, the only articles in which the workman is specially interested which have risen are meat and house rent. And at the beginning of this period meat, which now

---

[113] *The Progress of the Working Classes in the Last Half-century*, by Robert Giffen.

enters largely into an English working man's diet, was almost unknown in that capacity, with the exception of bacon, which has not increased sensibly in price; while 'there is reason to believe that the increased house rent is merely the higher price for a superior article which the workman can afford.'

On the whole, Sir Robert Giffen considers it a moderate statement of an incontestable truth to say, that 'the increase of the money wages of the working man in the last fifty years corresponds to a real gain.'

And this increase of wages has coincided with a great diminution in the hours of work. Sir Robert Giffen observes that it is difficult or impossible to state with absolute precision the amount of this reduction in the United Kingdom, but he concludes from the data we possess that it is nearly 20 per cent. 'There has been at least this reduction in the textile, engineering, and house-building trades. The workman gets from 50 to 100 per cent. more money for 20 per cent. less work.'

Other and not less decisive evidence is to be found in the returns of the savings banks, which represent more faithfully than, perhaps, any other test the savings of the wage-earning class. In the fifty years of which we are speaking the depositors in the savings bands of the United Kingdom multiplied nearly tenfold, and the amount of the deposits more than fivefold, while the population had not increased more than 30 per cent. In 1881, which is the last year on the lists of Sir Robert Giffen, the amount deposited in the savings banks amounted to the enormous sum of 80,334,000*l*. And this increase has taken place in spite of a vast multiplication of the kind of investments in which the savings of poor men are chiefly placed. Giffen gives some statistics of the progress of industrial and provident co-operative societies in England and Wales. They extend only over the period from 1862 to 1881. In that short period the members of these societies rose from 90,000 to 525,000, and their capital from 428,000*l*. to 5,881,000*l*.

The reader may refer to the valuable paper I am quoting for further evidence on this subject. He will observe the marked decline in the amount of pauperism in all parts of the United Kingdom during the last fifty years, the reduction in the rate of mortality, and the increased duration of average life. These things do not, it is true, absolutely prove a general increase in material wellbeing, but they are at least wholly inconsistent with generally increasing misery. I shall not here follow Sir Robert Giffen in his very instructive examination of the proportionate share of the different classes in the great increase in national wealth, as shown on the one hand by the Income tax returns and the Probate duties, and on the other by the changes in the rate of wages. His conclusion may be given in his own words. It is that, 'allowing for the increase of population, the growth of capital and income-tax income is really much smaller than the growth of the money income of the working classes; . . . that the number of owners of personal property liable to probate duty has increased in the last fifty years more than the increase of population, and that, on an average, these owners are only about 15 per cent. richer than they were, while the individual income of the working classes has increased from 50 to 100 per cent.'

All this is compatible with the fact that there is still much that is deplorable in the condition of the working classes, especially at the period when their strength has failed. It is compatible with the fact that, in the vast agglomerations of population that grow up around every great manufacture, there is always to be found a broad though, it is hoped, a diminishing fringe of abject poverty, misery, and vice. Drink, and vagrancy, and idle habits, criminal or at least vicious lives, imprudent marriages, and a total absence among great multitudes of all disposition to save, account for much. But much also springs from causes that bring with them no moral blame—from disease and the incapacity for work that follows it; from misfortunes which no human providence could have foreseen dissipating in a few weeks the savings of an industrious life; from the want of employment that too constantly follows great fluctuations in demand, great and sudden changes in the course of industry, or commerce, or population. Millions of human beings exist in the chief manufacturing countries who would never have been called into being if these manufactures had not been established, and in this vast increase of population there will always be too many sunk in misery. How strange it seems, a great writer once wrote, that the sternest sentence pronounced on the traitor of the Gospels was, that it had been better for him if he had never been born! How common, to our finite wisdom, such a lot appears to be!

But though the field which lies open for philanthropic effort and judicious legislation is very large, the plain, palpable facts of English life are abundantly sufficient to prove the gross and enormous falsehood of the estimate which Marx has given of the effects of the growth of capital and the increase of machinery on the wellbeing of the labouring poor. The evidence of all other countries agrees with that of England, though in no other are the phenomena exhibited on so gigantic a scale. M. Leroy-Beaulieu has dealt with the continental aspects of the question with a fulness and a competence that leave little to desire. He shows how, whenever one nation obtains a marked ascendency in any form of industry, whenever an extraordinary proportion of capital is attracted to its development, the invariable result will be that in this particular branch the level of the workmen's wages will be the highest. In a work published in 1881 he examines the history of working men's wages and expenditure in France during a period almost exactly coinciding with that which had been the subject of the inquiry of Sir Robert Giffen in England. France, of all continental countries, most closely rivals England in wealth, but her industrial conditions are widely different. She differs greatly in the proportion which agriculture bears to manufacturing industry; she has not experienced, to the same degree, the revolution in the price of agricultural produce which has taken place in England, and her population increases more slowly than that of any other great continental nation. Leroy-Beaulieu computes that in forty or fifty years the cost of life in a French working man's family has probably increased from

25 to 33 per cent., but that the generality of wages in France have risen at least from 80 to 100 per cent.[114] In Paris, where capital is most largely agglomerated, real wages rose in the short period between 1875 and 1882 from 50 to 60 per cent.[115] Between 1854 ad 1876 the number of members of the Sociétés de Secours Mutuel increased from 315,000 to 901,000, and the sums invested in them rose from thirteen to seventy-six millions of francs.[116] In 1882, the sums placed in the French savings banks are officially stated to have amounted to 1,745 millions of francs. The whole annual saving of France is estimated by the best statisticians at something between one and a half and two milliards of francs—that is, between sixty and eighty millions sterling.[117]

Taking a wide survey of the subject, M. Leroy-Beaulieu shows by a vast accumulation of evidence that the steady tendency in the great industrial centres of Europe is not, as the Socialists aver, towards greater disparity, but towards greater equality, of fortune. The number of colossal fortunes augments slowly, and they bear but an insignificant proportion to the great aggregate of wealth. The fall in the rate of interest; the effect of increased means of locomotion and of telegraphic intercourse in stimulating competition and destroying trade inequalities springing from advantages of situation or priority of knowledge; the rise of the joint-stock company system; the special severity with which periods of depression fall upon the large fortunes, all tend to diminish them, or at least to retard their progress. On the other hand, moderate and small fortunes have in the present century

---

[114] *La Répartition des Richesses,* p. 453.

[115] *Le Collectivisme,* p. 60.

[116] *La Répartition des Richesses,* p. 478.

[117] *Le Collectivisme,* p. 237. If the reader desires later statistics, he will find them in the very remarkable chapter on the division of fortunes in France in *La Tyrannie Socialiste* of M. Guyot, pp. 102–6 (1893). M. Guyot speaks 'des 6 millions de livrets de caisses d'épargne, des 3 milliards qu'ils représentent; des 450 millions de la caisse d'épargne postale'; and he also shows the enormous diffusion of small investments in the national funds and in the shares of the French railways.

enormously multiplied, and in all countries which are in the stream of industrial progress the wages of the labourer have materially risen.[118]

To anyone who looks on the question with a mind undistorted by the sophistries of Socialism this conclusion will seem very natural. There may be much that is obscure, much that is inequitable, in the proportionate distribution of profits between the manufacturer and the labourer, but above all these controversies one great fact is sufficiently apparent: when an industry is flourishing and growing, all classes connected with it will more or less benefit by its prosperity. When an industry is failing and dwindling, all classes connected with it will suffer. It is often said, with truth, that the older political economists confined their attention too much to the accumulation of wealth, and did not sufficiently consider the manner of its distribution. But it is no paradox to say that, to the working man, the question of accumulation is really the more important. With a progressive industry and abundant employment, questions of wages and profits will easily adjust themselves. With a declining industry and a stationary or increasing population no possible change of distribution will prevent all classes from suffering.

In their whole treatment of wages, Marx and his school fall into the grossest fallacies. They announce as a great discovery, that the labourer is not paid out of capital, but out of his own earnings, because he produces the equivalent, or more than the equivalent, of his wages before he receives them. This

---

[118] See, too, a remarkable passage in which Professor Marshall shows how the strongest industrial forces of the time 'are telling on the side of the poorer classes as a whole relatively to the richer,' and how all the best tests that can be applied 'indicate that middle-class incomes are increasing faster than those of the rich; that the earnings of artisans are increasing faster than those of the professional classes; and that the wages of healthy and vigorous unskilled labourers are increasing faster even than those of the average artisan' (Marshall's *Principles of Economics*, i. 735). Mr. Goschen, in an address to the Statistical Society, in 1887, on The Increase of Moderate Incomes,' has collected much additional evidence in support of the same conclusion.

statement is most obviously untrue in a vast proportion of industrial employments. The labourer who is employed in laying down a railway, or building a house or a ship, or constructing a machine, or preparing a field for the harvest of the ensuing year, or contributing his part in the beginning of any one of the countless enterprises which only produce profit in a more or less distant future, is certainly paid from capital, and not out of what he has himself produced. His work may or may not hereafter produce its equivalent, but it has not done so yet. If capital is not there to pay him, his labour will never be required. It is true that the work of a miner who raises daily a given amount of coal, or of the factory labourer who turns out daily a given number of manufactured commodities, rests on a somewhat different basis; but it is not less true that the mine would never have been opened, that the factory would never have been built, if capital had not been threre to do it, and to provide the costly machinery on which the whole of the labour depends. Nor is this a complete statement of the case. The commodities which the workman has produced can pay no wages as long as they are unsold. It is the error of Marx and his school that they treat the question of wages as if it depended only on two parties—the manufacturer and the labourer. A third party—the consumer—must come upon the scene, and wages, profits, and employment will alike fluctuate according to his demand.

Few things in modern industrial life are more wonderful than that parts of England with no great natural advantages have become the emporia from which the most distant countries are provided with articles made out of cotton grown in the far-off plantations of America and India. These hives of prosperous industry are justly regarded as among the most marvellous monuments of skilful and well-directed labour. Yet, if we look to their origin, the fructifying influence of capital is at once seen. A few men found themselves in possession of superfluous wealth. They might have spent it in gambling or dissipation. They might have simply hoarded it, doing neither good nor harm to their neighbours. They might have invested it in the funds of a foreign nation, and it would probably have been wasted in some pernicious war. Instead of this they combined together. They brought over cotton across the ocean, they laid down railways, they established factories, they founded a great industry. It would be absurd to praise them as if they had acted from philanthropic motives, and not through a regard to their own interests; but it is a simple truth that all the wealth that has been created, all the industry that is supported, all the happy families that exist in that spot, may be traced to their action as the flower to the seed. And if some vicissitude of opinion or affairs leads the capitalist to believe that his capital has become insecure; if he makes it his object to contract instead of to expand his business, and to draw his money as much as possible from it, all this industry will gradually wither, wages and profits will sink, and the number of the unemployed will increase, until population, finding no sufficient means of subsistence, has ebbed away.

Capital, indeed, which is denounced as the special enemy of the working man, is mainly that portion of wealth which is diverted from wasteful and unprofitable expenditure to those productive forms which give him permanent employment. The mediæval fallacy that money is not a productive thing, and that interest is therefore an extortion, might have been supposed a few years ago to have been sufficiently exploded. As Bentham long since said, if a man expends a sum of money in the purchase of a bull and of a heifer, and if as the result he finds himself in a few years the possessor of a herd of cattle, it can hardly be said that his money has been 'unproductive.' If he expends it in stocking his lake with salmon or his woods with some valuable wild animal which needs no human care, this increased value may be created without the intervention of any human labour. The wine in a rich man's cellar, the trees upon his mountains, the works of art in his gallery, will often acquire a vastly enhanced value by simple efflux of time. Usually, however, capital and labour are indissolubly united in the creation of wealth, and in all the larger industries each is indispensable to the other. It may be truly said that it is not the steam-engine, but the steam, that propels the train so swiftly over the land; but the statement would be a very misleading one if it were not added that the steam would be as powerless without the engine as the engine without the steam. If a man by the possession of a sum of money is able to start a business which gives a profit of 8 or 10 per cent., and if he borrows this sum at 4 or 5 per cent., can it be denied that the trasaction is a legitimate one, and beneficial to both parties? If a workman is able to produce by the aid of a machine 100, or perhaps 1,000, times as much as he could produce by his unassisted hands, is it unnatural that some part of the profit should go to the capitalist who has supplied the machine, or to the inventor who conceived it? The great evil of the capitalist system, the Socialists say, is that the workman is more and more unable to purchase by his earnings the result of his own labour. The answer is, that by his unassisted labour he could barely have produced the means of living, while by the aid of machinery his powers of production are incalculably multiplied. Commerce, according to Marx, can produce no surplus value, for the labour-time spent on what is exchanged remains unaltered. But if Newcastle coal which is worth 1,000*l*. at the pit's mouth is exchanged for Brazilian coffee which costs 1,000*l*. on the plantation, can it be said that the coalowner and the coffee-planter have gained nothing by a transaction which gives each of them a rare and valuable commodity, instead of one which was cheap and redundant? Can any statement be more palpably untrue than that equal quantities of labour produce equal values—the labour of Raphael, and the labour of a signboard painter; the labour which is employed in the manufacture of some rare and delicate instrument, and that which is employed in carrying bricks or sweeping roads; the labour which taxes the highest faculties of the human mind, and the labour of a plodding fool; the labour which involves grave danger to the labourer, and the labour which asks nothing but patience and brute strength?

Another great fallacy which pervades the teaching of Marx and of his school is to be found in their enormous exaggeration of the proportion of the produce of labour which, in every manufacturing industry, falls to the share of the capitalist.[119] If their estimate was a just one, every manufacture which employs much labour would prove lucrative, and every addition of salaried labour would largely increase profit. It is one of the most patent of facts that this is not the case, and that a vast proportion of the employers of labour end in bankruptcy. If the profits of capital, as distinguished from labour, were what Socialists represent them, co-operative working-men's associations would speedily multiply, for, by placing labour and capital in the same hands, they would almost inevitably succeed. The co-operative movement has, no doubt, largely extended, and it is one of the most hopeful signs of the industrial future. But can any one who has followed its history, who has observed the great multitude of these societies that have totally failed, and has computed the gains of those which have succeeded, conclude that their success has been on such a scale as to show that those who participate in them gain far more than salaried labourers? Perhaps their greatest economical superiority is to be found in the lessened probability of wasteful strikes.

There are two elements which, in estimating the capitalist system, Marx and his followers systematically ignore. One is the many risks that attend industrial enterprise. These risks depend not merely on the misconduct or mistakes of those who conduct them, but also on causes over which they have no possible control. Famines, wars, changes of fashion and demand, new inventions, injudicious legislation, commercial crises, sudden suspensions, or displacements, or expansions of other industries, continually ruin the best conceived and best organised enterprises. If wealth and earnings are often greatly enhanced, they are perhaps quite as often fatally de-

---

[119] See some good remarks on this in Woolsey's *Communism and Socialism,* p. 169.

preciated by surrounding circumstances, and as many fortunes are lost as gained through causes which the owner
could neither influence nor foresee. Too often, also, it is the
very men who have deserved best of the community who
suffer. How often does an original inventor find his great idea
appropriated by another who, by devising some improvement in detail, some simplification and economy of mecha-
nism, is able to drive him ruined from the field? What can be
more melancholy than the history of many industrial enterprises that have proved ultimately most successful and most
beneficial to the world? The original company foresaw the
ultimate advantage; they planned and executed the enterprise, and bore the cost. But profits developed more slowly
than they expected, unforeseen obstacles arose, the expenses
exceeded the first estimate, and before long the company was
overwhelmed and ruined. Other men, who had no part in
the work, then came in. They bought up the works at a fraction of their original cost and real value, and they soon reaped
a vast harvest from their purchase.

Risks of the most multifarious kinds, indeed, surround industrial enterprises, and the path of progress is abundantly
strewn with wrecks. It is the habit of Marx and his followers
to concentrate attention wholly on the few instances of great
gain; to represent them as due to the robbery of the workman
by his employer, and altogether to ignore the plain fact that
great occasional gains are the inevitable accompaniment of
great risks. No one would incur the one who had not at least
a prospect of obtaining the other. They at the same time systematically depreciate or neglect the intellectual element in
industry. They write as if all wealth were produced by mere
manual labour, and as if the men who organised and directed
it had no part in the matter, except that of appropriating its
fruits. It would be as reasonable to refuse to Napoleon and
Moltke all share in the victories of Austerlitz and Sedan, as-
cribing the whole merit to the privates who fought in the
ranks.

In truth, the part which has been played by the great captains of industry in the wealth formation of the world can hardly be exaggerated, and, in most cases, the success or failure of an important industrial enterprise will be found to depend far more on its organisation and its administration than on any difference in the quality of its labour. The man who discovers among a thousand possible paths of industry that which is really profitable; who possesses in a high degree promptitude and tact in seizing opportunities and foreseeing change; who meets most successfully a popular taste or supplies most efficiently a widespread want; who invents a new machine, or a new medicine, or a new comfort or convenience; who discovers and opens out a new field of commerce; who enlarges the bounds of fruitful knowledge; who paints, among a thousand pictures, the one that fascinates the world; who writes, amid a thousand books, the one which finds a multitude of readers, is surely a far greater wealth-producer than the average labourer who is toiling with his hands. It is by such men that, in modern times, great fortunes are most frequently made, and the skill that determines the wise application of labour is as much needed as the labour itself.

The delusion that all wealth is the creation of manual labour may be supported by great names, but it is one of those which a careful analysis most conclusively disproves. The true sources of wealth are to be found in all those conditions which are essential to its production, and in the great and complex industries of modern life these conditions are often very numerous. The Duke of Argyll, in a book which is a valuable contribution to economical science, has examined this subject with much fulness, analysing in many particular instances the elements which contributed, in addition to manual labour, to the production of wealth. There is the conceiving mind that devised the enterprise. There is the capital, without which it never could have been started. There is the administrative and organising talent that renders manual labour really efficient. There is the inventive skill which is embodied in the machinery, without which the enterprise would have been impossible. There is the demand, without which it could never have been profitable; and it is no paradox to place in the same category the political, administrative, and military conditions which are essential to that security of industry, property, and credit on which all great works ultimately depend. All these elements enter into the production of wealth, and some of them to an extraordinary extent. The Duke has hardly exaggerated when he asserts that 'the single brain of James Watt was, and still is, the biggest wage-fund that has ever arisen in the world.'[120]

Considerations of this kind are wholly neglected by Marx. The gross sophisms and the enormous exaggerations he has diffused would probably have had little importance if they had not been found useful to disguise the naked dishonesty of designs for the spoliation of realised and inherited property which have found supporters in many lands. In Germany especially, the progress of the Socialist party had excited great alarm. With one or two exceptions, each succeeding Imperial election since the foundation of the empire has increased the number of Socialist votes and Socialist members. In 1871, two members of the party only were elected to the Reichstag, and the number of Social Democrat votes were 124,655. In 1893, forty-four members were elected, and 1,786,738 votes were given to the party. In nearly every important town in the empire the Socialist vote within the last twenty years had vastly increased, and in Berlin itself the party succeeded, in 1893, in returning five members. Among the many political groups in the Reichstag, it is now the largest. It is said to possess in Germany, besides many minor publications, thirty-one daily and forty-one weekly and semi-weekly newspapers; and in Brandenburg, Pomerania, Mecklenburg, Bavaria, and Alsace-Lorraine, it has grown rapidly in the agricultural districts.[121]

---

[120] *Unseen Foundations of Society*, p. 455.
[121] See some tables in Ely's *Socialism*, pp. 387–89, and compare an article by Liebknecht, on 'The Programme of German Socialism,' in the *Forum*, February 1895.

In France, Socialism was much thrown back by the events of 1848, and in the vast mass of peasant proprietors, imbued with the strongest sense of private property, it encounters the most formidable of obstacles. Some revival of the socialistic spirit appeared in the last days of the Empire; but it was far from adopting the extravagant form it was assuming in Germany. In the congress of the International which met at Basle in 1869 a resolution that it was 'necessary that the soil should be made collective property' was carried in an assembly of seventy-six delegates. Fifty-eight votes supported it, eight votes opposed it, and ten delegates abstained from voting. Of the eight minority votes, seven were French; of the ten absentees, six were French; and out of the fifteen delegates from Paris, four only supported the resolution, while the remainder either opposed it or abstained.[122] During the insurrection of the Commune the Socialist element, as we have seen, bore a prominent part, and nearly all the more active Socialists in France were implicated in the movement. On the defeat of the Commune many of them were killed, and many more driven into exile; and stringent repressive legislation, fully supported by the immense majority of Frenchmen, threw great obstacles in the path of socialistic agitation. It revived, however, about 1876, and was much strengthened by the successive amnesties which brought back to France the more malignant spirits of the Commune. Socialism was chiefly propagated in the form of newspapers, and chiefly under the influence of Jules Guesde and of a newspaper called the 'Égalité.' His doctrine was essentially that of Marx, and he desired that all land, all capital, all means of locomotion, should be taken by the State, thus reducing the whole community into State functionaries working at State orders and receiving State wages.

'The Collectivists,' however, as they were generally called, did not at once or completely dominate among the French Socialists. The certain opposition of the peasant proprietors

---

[122] Mermeix, *La France Socialiste*, p. 45.

threw a shadow on the movement; and, according to some of the best judges, Collectivism, with its complete absorption of individual interests and ambitions in the ruling State is a form of revolution which is exceedingly uncongenial to the ambitious, highly independent, and intelligent Paris workman. Good workmen seldom like a system which, as it is truly said, implies 'equal division of unequal earnings,' and which, by destroying all competition, closes the path of advancement against superior capacity and superior industry. There are no better workmen than the French, and none in whom individual qualities are more strongly marked. At a French working-men's congress which was held at Lyons in 1878, the Collectivist programme was for the first time brought forward, in the form of a resolution that all land and instruments of work should be collective property; but it was rejected by a large majority. The remedies for industrial troubles which the French working-class leaders at this time chiefly advocated were of a much more moderate description. They desired a fuller recognition of the syndicates, or trades unions; an extension of cooperative societies supported by national credit; provision for insuring against accidents and providing for the incapacity that follows disease or old age; shortened hours of work; a fuller regulation of factory work, and especially of the work of women and children.[123] Most of these demands pointed to real defects in French industrial legislation. Profit-sharing industries have been peculiarly popular in France, and, with the excellent business qualities of the French working man, they have attained a large measure of success. They are said to be far more numerous than in any other country, and especially during the last few years they have advanced with great rapidity. At least forty firms, some of them of great magnitude and importance, have adopted this system.[124]

---

[123] See Zacher, *L'Internationale Rouge*, pp. 71–72.
[124] Jevons's *The State in relation to Labour*, pp. 147–50. See, too, an essay by Mr. Samuelson, on German and French Labour Movements (*Subjects of the Day*, August 1890, p. 173).

The contagion, however, of German Socialism has of late years spread widely into France. It became the custom to hold anniversary banquets for the purpose of glorifying the Commune, and it was noticed that at these banquets a strong socialistic spirit was apparent.[125] A few trade syndicates adopted the views of Guesde, and during the International Exhibition of 1878 that party assumed a considerable prominence. In a clandestine congress they met the working-men representatives from other countries, and, though they represented only a small portion of the French workmen, they claimed to be the representatives of the whole. Their first great success, however, was in the Congress of Marseilles in October, 1879, when the party of Guesde succeeded in obtaining a complete ascendency, carrying the programme of Collectivism by seventy-three votes to twenty-seven, and organising a Socialist movement over the whole of France.[126]

The programme which was carried at this congress appears to have been drawn up in London, principally by Marx; it was afterwards ratified by congresses at Havre and Paris, and it gives a very full summary of the aims and opinions of the most important body of the French Socialists. It states that their ultimate object is to place the producer in possession of all the means of production—land, manufactures, ships, banks, credit, &c.—and that, as it is impossible to divide these things among the individuals, they must be held in a collective form. This can only be achieved by the revolutionary action of the producing, or proletariat class, organised as a distinct political party, and subordinating all other ends to its accomplishment. The French Socialist workmen must make use of all the weapons at their disposal, and especially of universal suffrage, in order to effect the political and economical expropriation of the capitalist class and the collective ownership of all the means of production. With a constant view to this end, and with the purpose of organising and strengthening themselves for the struggle, they are directed to take an

---

[125] Mermeix, *La France Socialiste*, p. 88.
[126] Mermeix, pp. 98–100.

active part in every election, and to demand the immediate realisation of the following objects.

The political part is put first. It comprises the abolition of all laws restricting the liberty of the press and the liberty of French workmen to associate among themselves and with the workmen of other countries; of all articles in the Code which place the workman in any way in an inferior position to the master, or the woman to the man.

They must demand, also, the suppression of the Budget of Public Worship; the confiscation of all property belonging to religious corporations, including all industrial and commercial establishments belonging to them; the suppression of the national debt; the abolition of permanent armies, and the arming of the whole people; and, finally, the complete right of the commune to administer its own affairs and to control the police.

The economical demands follow. These comprise a legal day of repose in every seven; the reduction by law of the hours of work for adults to eight hours, the prohibition of the employment in factories of children under fourteen, and the limitation of the work hours of those between fourteen and eighteen; a right of inspection and protection, to be exercised by trade unions over apprentices; a legal minimum of wages, to be fixed by law every year, by a working-class commission, in accordance with the local prices of articles of food; a law forbidding employers to employ foreign workmen at a lower salary than French workmen; equality of salary for equal work between men and women; scientific and professional education for all children at the cost of the State; State provision for the old and the infirm; the complete exclusion of employers from the administration of all institutions for the benefit of the working classes; the obligation of employers to indemnify their workmen for all accidents that take place in their service; the right of the workers to have a controlling voice in all the regulations of a factory; and a law prohibiting employers from imposing fines or withholding salaries from workmen as a punishment.

With these measures, others of a still more sweeping kind

were demanded. All contracts must be cancelled in virtue of which banks, mines, railways, and other things which, according to the Socialist doctrine, should be public property had become private property; the management of all State works should be put in the hands of the workmen who work in them; all indirect taxes should be abolished, and all direct taxation concentrated in one progressive tax, falling on revenues which exceed 3,000 francs; all inheritances in the collateral line should be forbidden, as well as all inheritances in the direct line which exceeded 20,000 francs, or 800*l*.[127]

This programme is perhaps the best authoritative statement of the doctrines of the French Socialist school. It is obvious that, in its leading views, it is identical with German Socialism. It is also obvious that, while some of the minor demands of the party are rational and moderate, the scheme as a whole aims at a spoliation of property, a revolution and subversion of the whole existing framework of civilised society more complete and radical than any the world has ever seen. The French Socialists, it is true, speedily broke into a number of hostile sects, chiefly, as it would seem, due to the mutual jealousies of different leaders and different newspapers, but embodying some faint and ill-defined differences of doctrine or tendency. The Anarchists followed mainly the ideas of Bakúnin, and disdained all methods other than violence for obtaining their ends. The Blanquists took for their motto the phrase, 'Ni Dieu ni Maître'; but, while advocating complete social revolution, they appear to have cared more for its political than its economical aspects, and were not altogether averse to alliances with other parties. The 'Possibilistes' revolted against the personal authority exercised by Guesde, set up a rival administration, were inclined to postpone some of the demands of the programme of Guesde as for the present impracticable, and revived the demand of Louis Blanc for cooperative and municipal industries. But the real differences between the programmes put out by the different sections

---

[127] See the text of this programme in Mermeix, pp. 101–5.

were extremely small, and on the whole the doctrine of Marx clearly dominated. In spite of, or perhaps in consequence of, its divisions the organs of the party considerably multiplied, and they possess an elaborate review, called the 'Revue Socialiste,' which was founded by Malon.

It is difficult for any one, and especially for a stranger, to form a confident opinion about the extent to which Socialism has penetrated into French thought. The artisan class, among whom it is most rife, form only a small fraction of the French nation, and it would be grossly unjust to suppose that they have generally adopted the Socialist creed. A large section of them have openly repudiated the Collectivist doctrine,[128] and it would be easy to exaggerate the significance of the Socialist victories in working-men's congresses. Experience shows how often an active and resolute minority has succeeded in dominating, in such assemblies, over a timid and apathetic majority, and how easily men can be induced to vote for extreme and dangerous courses, which they do not really desire, as a mere weapon of offence, as long as there is no danger of these measures being carried into effect. Much, too, which goes by the name of Socialism is a very different thing from the doctrine of Marx, and indicates little more than a sentimental leaning towards State interference and State philanthropy. It is probable that multitudes who have given their adhesion to the revolutionary programmes are, really, only seriously interested in the minor and subsidiary questions involved in them.

In spite of the many political revolutions it has experienced, France is not a country well adapted for revolutionary Socialism. The clear, simple, sharply defined titles of property that are alone recognised by French law are probably less liable to indirect attacks than the more confused, blended, and complex forms, growing out of long prescription and ancient laws and customs, that still linger largely in England. The great division, not only of the soil, but also of the national

---

[128] Mermeix, p. 106.

debt, of the municipal debt, and even of the shares of the railways, strengthens property, and throws enormous obstacles in the way of the Socialist agitation. Probably in no other country are these forms of investment so widely diffused through all classes of society; and the equal division of property under the Code Napoléon between the different members of the family both intensifies and widens the feeling in favour of heredity. No nation in the world is more industrious and more saving; and when industry and parsimony prevail, the sense of private property is always very strong. It is a certain and a significant fact that the growing political power of a sect which preaches, among other things, the repudiation of all national debts, in the most indebted country in the world, has not yet so seriously alarmed the holders of that debt as to affect the national credit. There exists, I believe, at the bottom of most French minds a conviction that the power of the small owners of property in France is irresistible, and that, if Socialism ever rises to a point which seriously endangers their interests, they will be able to crush it by overthrowing the form of Government under which it has acquired its power.

Still, the growth of revolutionary Socialism in France is great and incontestable. Until about fifteen years ago the Socialists had scarcely any importance in the existing Republic. For some time they had, I believe, only a single avowed representative in the Chamber of Deputies, though the Extreme Left sometimes coquetted with their views. Before 1884, however, it was estimated that there were about six hundred syndicates or groups of Socialists in France,[129] and since then their increase has been very great. In the election of 1893, the Socialists in the Chamber rose at a bound from fifteen to fifty-three; and it is computed that the party received six and a half times as many votes as in the election of 1889. Socialists are very powerful, if not absolutely dominating, in the Municipality of Paris. They are scarcely less powerful at Lyons, and

---

[129.] Zacher, p. 87.

they may be found in greater or smaller proportions in the municipalities of nearly all the principal towns in France.[130] The disintegration of Parliaments into small groups has greatly strengthened their influence, and they have been assisted by the extraordinary weakness and instability of the Governments of the Republic; by the destruction, in large bodies of Frenchmen, of all positive religious beliefs; by the prodigious increase of the national debt, and by a long period of severe commercial and agricultural depression. In many cases the movement has been allied with the glorification of regicide, dynamite, and other forms of political assassination, and the Commune is very habitually held up to admiration as the best recent efflorescence of their principles.[131] Of late years extravagances of language are said to have diminished, and the main object of the party has been, if possible, to seduce the peasant-proprietors. The task is a difficult and, it is to be hoped, an impossible one, but the Socialists have one advantage. The immense majority of the small proprietors have sunk deeply in debt, and long-continued agricultural depression has greatly aggravated their difficulties. When frugal and industrious men find themselves on the brink of undeserved ruin, it is not surprising that their minds should be open to revolutionary ideas, and the Socialists promise that, in a Socialist State, the debts of the peasant proprietors will be cancelled.

One of the ablest members of the French Collectivist party is M. Gabriel Deville. He published in 1883 a French translation of the treatise of Marx on capital, and he prefaced it by a highly instructive introduction, explaining with great fulness and candour the nature of 'Scientific Socialism' and the hopes and the policy of his party. He speaks with much dis-

---

[130] Compare the statistics in Ely's *Socialism*, pp. 62–63, 390–98. M. Guyot estimates the number of Socialist deputies at more than sixty (*Principes de '89 et le Socialisme*, Préface). The difference is accounted for by the fact that many violent Radicals who are not avowed Socialists usually vote with the Socialist party.

[131] See the chapter on Socialism in France in Zacher, *L'Internationale Rouge*.

dain of the Utopianism of the early Socialists, and the cold, measured, reasoning virulence of his own style contrasts remarkably with the effusive sentimentality of Louis Blanc and his contemporaries. Deville declares that the first object of his party is the total overthrow of every class outside that of the wage-earners; that for this purpose the proletariat must keep themselves rigidly separate from every other class, and that they must treat all political and patriotic interests as insignificant, except as far as they aid them in the war of classes. Force alone can effect the Revolution; the occasion for its successful exercise will arise in the inevitable political and economical troubles that are manifestly impending over Europe; and in order to avail themselves of it, the proletariat must make use of all the means of destruction which modern science can furnish.[132] There are traitors in the Socialist camp, who would simply place the great industries in the hands of existing Governments, as railways and telegraphs already are in many countries, and who would encourage and endow working-men's co-operative societies, or extend the system of profit sharing between workmen and their employers. All these schemes are delusive. Co-operative societies would compete with one another, and thus maintain the present system of industry, and the object of the Socialist is not to strengthen, but to destroy, the State. The State is simply the organisation of the 'exploiting' class, for the purposes of guaranteeing their 'exploitation' and keeping the 'exploited' in subjection. The workmen employed by the State are very manifestly no better off than those in the service of private capitalists.

---

[132] Compare the following passage of Mr. Hyndman: 'While these truths are being learnt by the people . . . chemistry has placed at the disposal of the desperate and needy cheap and powerful explosives, the full effects of which are as yet unknown. Every day adds new discoveries in this field. The dynamite of ideas is accompanied in the background by the dynamite of material force. These modern explosives may easily prove to capitalism what gunpowder was to feudalism' (*Historical Basis of Socialism*, p. 443).

Capitalist, society, and the whole system of wages must be overthrown from their foundations. It is a form of slavery which differs chiefly from the ancient slavery in the fact that the capitalist is not obliged, like the slave-owner, to support his slaves. The working-class must seize by force on the power of Government, and make it the instrument of 'the economical expropriation of the *bourgeoisie*' and of 'the collective appropriation of the means of production.' 'We wish to proceed by the way of authority against the caste that is our enemy. We wish to suppress those capitalist liberties which prevent the expansion of the liberty of the workman. . . . We desire the dictatorship, not of an individual, but of a class, . . . and that dictatorship must continue till the day comes when liberty will be possible for all.' All existing laws are intended to maintain intact the economical interests of the class which possesses and directs. They must be swept away; and when the working men have acquired full political power, 'they will, in their turn, make a new legality, and proceed by law to the economical expropriation of those whom they will have already dethroned by force.'

Deville admits that his party is only 'a conscious minority of the proletariat;' but he observes that most revolutions are the work of a daring minority, seconded by the apathy of majorities, and he asks whether France would now be a republic if the adhesion of the majority of the country to the Republican idea had been first asked. At the same time, the basis of the revolution must be broadly laid. 'We celebrate the anniversary of the Commune as that of one of the stages of the Socialist evolution;' but the Commune failed chiefly because it committed the fault of confining its action to Paris, struggling for the bourgeois notion of Federalism, or Communism, and not endeavouring to rouse the working-classes through the whole nation.

The task of Socialism, he says, has been prepared by the great concentration of industries, which is one of the most marked characteristics of our age, and which renders the process of confiscation, or 'expropriation,' comparatively

easy. Thus, the railways can be appropriated by simply confiscating the shares which are now the property of those at
whose risk and cost they had been made. The work has been
done. The machinery for locomotion exists in all its perfection, and a single act of plunder will place it in the hands of
the community as an unencumbered property. But the same
thing applies to all great shops and factories, and to every
kind of industrial corporation. Multitudes of more or less
wealthy men have, in our day, built up, with the accumulated
savings of their lives, gigantic industries, and where these industries have succeeded they are drawing their dividends as
shareholders. All this, Deville observes, will make the task of
the Socialist an easy one. 'The suppression of the shareholders—that is to say, of the proprietors—now become a useless
wheel, will occasion no trouble in the machinery of production.' 'There can be no difficulty in dealing with anything that
is constituted in the form of a society. It is only necessary to
destroy the title-deeds, shares, or obligations, treating these
dirty documents as waste paper. The collective appropriation
of capital will thus be at once realised, without any disturbance in the mode of production.' Deville is careful to add that
all this is to be done without any indemnity to the plundered
parties.

The national debt is, of course, to be dealt with in the same
way. It is to be simply blotted out. The promises of all preceding Governments are to be repudiated, and the creditors,
who, on the faith of these promises, had placed their money
at the service of the State, are to be deprived alike of their
interest and their capital. All banks are, by a similar process,
to be seized and appropriated by the community.

So far the work of 'expropriation' moves—at least on paper—very easily. But there are two classes with which it is
more difficult to deal. The first are the small shopkeepers and
employers of labour. They must cease to exist as a class; but
they are a large and formidable body, and their resistance
might be serious. Fortunately, however, a sharp line of antagonism already divides the small shopkeeper and the small

manufacturer from the gigantic shop or factory, which is overshadowing, underselling, and gradually ruining them. It is impossible they can long resist the competition, and they will gradually discover that it is their interest to join the Socialist party, and obtain the benefits of a Socialist society, rather than await in a hostile attitude a ruin that will have no compensation.

The next class are the peasant proprietors. Deville, like most of the writers of his school, deplores the great division of French soil, but he does not despair of gradually winning over the small proprietors. The Socialist movement, however, must proceed by stages, and the small proprietor and small shopkeeper need not be absorbed or 'expropriated' at once. The peasant proprietor who cultivates what is now his own land, and employs no one, is not an 'exploiter.' He is himself 'exploited' by the money-lender, to whom he is nearly always in debt, and the triumph of Socialism will cancel his debt. When the proletariat have seized power, they are not at once to dispossess the peasant proprietor. On the contrary, they are to shower benefits upon him. With the exception of a moderate sum, which he is to pay to the 'collectivity' as long as he remains a separate proprietor, he is to be at once freed from all his debts. The present tax upon land is to cease, and seeds, manure, and agricultural machinery are to be provided for him gratuitously by the community. In his case no violence, or even persuasion, is to be used; 'but it will be seen whether, if his egotism is in this large measure satisfied, he will not look on with indifference upon the expropriation of the larger proprietors.' The overwhelming competition of these large properties, when administered by the community, and the manifest advantages flowing from the collective ownership of the soil, will do the rest, and the small proprietor will soon exchange his nominal possession of a fraction of the soil for the position of co-proprietor, with a remuneration equivalent to his time of work.

This, then, is the economical scheme of the party as sketched by a most competent and authorised hand. Nothing short of it will be accepted, and all measures of reform that are carried are to be regarded simply as weapons to be used in the struggle, as means for strengthening one class and weakening the other, or for stimulating the appetite for further revolutionary change. Universal suffrage, Deville specially urges, can never prove a substitute for force, or effect the emancipation of the working classes. It has done evil in interesting them in national and political questions, bringing them into alliance with different sections of the possessing classes, and thus diverting them from what ought to be their true and only object. It should be made use of solely for the purpose of accentuating the division and war of classes. No candidate, whether he be a working-man or an employer, should be elected who does not pledge himself to sacrifice habitually all other interests to the triumph of the social revolution. If employed in this way, universal suffrage will prove very useful. But it can never by itself overcome the resistance of the large classes who are interested in maintaining the present constitution of society. Force, and force alone, is the ultimate remedy. As Marx said, 'Force is the midwife of every old society pregnant with a new one.'

There are two other changes which Deville and his party consider essential to the triumph of their ideas. One is the complete suppression, not only of Churches, but of all idea of God and of religion. 'God,' in the words of Deville, 'is dying without posterity.' The true source of the religious sentiment is the misery that grows out of capitalism. 'The emancipation of thought is thus linked to the emancipation of labour. . . . The terrestrial despot, the capitalist, will drag down in his fall the celestial bugbear.[133] Mankind, ruling production, instead of being ruled by it, will at last find their happiness upon earth. . . . The belief in a Supreme Being, sovereign dispenser of happiness and suffering, will univer-

---

[133] *Le Croquemitaine Céleste. Croquemitaine* is defined by Littré: 'Monstre imaginaire qui figure dans quelques contes de fées et dont on fait peur aux petits enfants.'

sally disappear.' Religion he describes as 'an engine of domination,' 'one of the most useful springs in a government of caste.'

The other change is the suppression of marriage and the substitution for it of free love. 'It is marriage which gives to the possessing class its hereditary character, and thus develops its conservative instincts. . . . Marriage is a regulation of property, a business contract before being a union of persons, and its utility grows out of the economic structure of a society which is based upon individual appropriation. By giving guarantees to the legitimate children, and ensuring to them the paternal capital, it perpetuates the domination of the caste which monopolises the productive forces. . . . When property is transformed, and only after that transformation, marriage will lose its reason for existence, and boys and girls may then freely, and without fear of censure, listen to the wants and promptings of their nature; . . . the support of the children will no longer depend on the chance of birth. Like their instruction, it will become a charge of society. There will be no room for prostitution, or for marriage, which is in sum nothing more than prostitution before the mayor.'

These last two considerations mark a great difference between continental Collectivism and that which is held in England and America. English and American opinion would not tolerate such language as I have quoted, and many English Socialists treat questions of religion and marriage as wholly extraneous to their theory. In the opinion of Marx, and of the great body of continental Socialists, they are intimately, and, indeed, necessarily connected with it.[134] In my own judgment,

---

[134] On the violent atheism of continental Socialism, see Woolsey's *Communism and Socialism*, pp. 247–49. The German Socialist, Bebel, has written an elaborate book on *Woman and Socialism*, which has been translated into English under the title of *Woman, her Past, Present, and Future*. His view is that 'the bourgeois marriage is a consequence of bourgeois property. This marriage, standing as it does in the most intimate connection to property and the right of inheritance, demands "legitimate" children as heirs. It is entered into for the purpose of obtaining them, and the

the continental view is the more just. It is perfectly true that marriage and the family form the tap root out of which the whole system of hereditary property grows, and that it would be utterly impossible permanently to extirpate heredity unless family stability and family affection were annihilated. It is not less true that a system which preaches the most wholesale and undisguised robbery will never approve itself to the masses of men, unless all the foundations and sanctions of morality have been effectually destroyed. The sense of right and wrong must be blotted out of the minds of men before the new doctrine can triumph. It is obvious, indeed, that the whole of the scheme which has been described is simply dishonesty carried out and systematised on the most gigantic scale, and accompanied with every aggravation of solemn promises deliberately violated, of great services to the community repaid by the blackest ingratitude, of constant attempts to excite the worst passions of ignorant and suffering men. The true character of the theory is not changed because

---

pressure exercised by society has enabled the ruling classes to enforce it in the case of those who have nothing to bequeath. But as in the new community there will be nothing to bequeath, unless we choose to regard household furniture as a legacy of any importance, compulsory marriage becomes unnecessary from this standpoint, as well as from all others. This also settles the question of the right of inheritance, which Socialism will have no need to abolish formally' (pp. 231, 232). M. Jules Guesde, in his *Catéchisme Socialiste,* has unfolded the same views with much clearness: 'La responsabilité humaine,' he says, 's'évanouit comme un mensonge qu'elle est . . . il y a autant de sottise et d'injustice à le rendre responsable de ce qu'il a pu faire, à le lui reprocher ou à l'en louer, qu'à louer la fleur d'embaumer et qu'à reprocher au feu de brûler' (pp. 28, 29). The family, M. Guesde considers, was useful and indispensable in the past, but is now only an odious form of property. It must be either transformed or totally abolished. He conjectures that the time may come when it will be reduced to the relation of the mother to her child 'à la période de l'allaitement, et que d'autre part les rapports sexuels entre l'homme et la femme, fondés sur l'amour ou la sympathie mutuelle, puissent devenir aussi libres, aussi variables et aussi multiples que les rapports intellectuels ou moraux entre individus du même sexe ou de sexe différent' (pp. 72–79).

its adherents prefer to the homely language of the market-
place a jargon about 'nationalisation' and 'economical expropriation,' and because they are often accustomed to unite
their advocacy of plunder with high-sounding phrases about
justice and ethics, and even religion. Cant is never a beautiful
thing, but, among all the forms that are now current in the
world, this, perhaps, is the most nauseous.

The reader will understand that these remarks are intended
to apply to the clear and definite programme of policy which
I have been describing, and not to many very different proposals for enlarging the sphere of Government influence and
philanthropy, to many vague sentiments, aspirations and
tendencies which are loosely classified under the name of Socialism, and which are often favoured by upright and benevolent men. The theory of Socialism which was taught by Marx
and Lassalle, and which now dominates in continental Socialism, is a perfectly definite one, formulated in a number of
programmes that are at least as clear and precise as the Confession of Westminster or the decrees of the Council of Trent. It
is difficult, I think, to reflect without a shudder on the fact
that, in the two foremost nations on the European continent,
this programme has been accepted by many hundreds of thousands of voters; that it has taken deep root in all the great
centres of German and French civilisation; and that it is represented in the Legislature of each of these great countries by
a powerful parliamentary group. Nor is it by any means confined to France and Germany. 1893 is a memorable year in the
annals of Socialism, but it was nowhere more memorable than
in Belgium. For the first time in history a great Reform Bill,
involving universal suffrage, was then carried by a gigantic
workmen's strike which brought the country to the verge of
revolution. The result of the enormous lowering of the suffrage was in some respects very disappointing to its authors,
but it was not the less significant. In the election which took
place in October 1894 the Moderate Liberals were almost annihilated. An overwhelming Conservative majority, holding
Ultramontane opinions, was returned, but also a Socialist mi-

nority more powerful in proportion to the number of the chamber than in any other country. Out of the 152 members of the Chamber of Deputies, 107 were Clericals and 33 were Socialists, chiefly holding the creed of the Collectivists.[135] The omen is not a good one for constitutional government. It would be difficult to conceive two classes less endowed with that spirit of compromise which is essential to its successful working than Ultramontanes and Socialists.

These three countries are now the special centres of the Socialist movement, but in most other countries a similar tendency may be traced. Thus in Italy a great Labourers' party formally professing the doctrines of the Collectivists was organised in congresses at Milan in 1891, and at Genoa in 1892, and it has already won several seats in the Italian Parliament, and many triumphs in local elections. In Switzerland, a Social Democratic party holding similar views was organised in 1888 and 1890. In Austria, under the guidance of a follower of Marx named Victor Adler, Socialism has manifestly increased. It has for the first time, within the last few years, become an appreciable power in Holland. In Denmark it captured, in 1893, seven seats in the Municipal Council of Copenhagen, and it has some, though apparently feebler, influence in Sweden and Norway. In Spain and Russia also it has appeared, sometimes in the form of Collectivism, and perhaps more frequently in the form of Anarchism. Its teaching has evidently permeated great masses of men with something of the force, and has assumed something of the character, of a new religion, rushing in to fill the vacuum where old beliefs and old traditions have decayed.[136]

---

[135] See an article on Belgian Socialism, *Fortnightly Review*, February 1895. There is, however, some difference in the computations, chiefly owing to the difficulty of discriminating between the Radicals and Socialists. The *Annual Register* (1894, p. 304) gives, as the result of the election, 104 Catholics, 28 Socialists, and 20 Liberals, belonging to the Moderate and Radical groups.

[136] Much information about the recent progress of Socialism on the Continent will be found in the Reports from Foreign Countries laid before the Royal Commission on Labour. See, too, Ely's *Socialism*.

In the United States also it has made some progress, though it would be scarcely possible to conceive a nation where the spirit of individualism is more strongly developed and the spirit of competition more intense. America had long been the refuge of an immense proportion of the banished Anarchies of Europe, and it presents the curious spectacle of a country where the working-class, at least in its lower levels, consists mainly of foreigners or children of foreigners. At the same time, the most prominent type of American Socialism does not appear to have been created by direct foreign propagandism, though its leading doctrine had long since been anticipated on the Continent. The great popularity and influence of the writings of Mr. George, on both sides of the Atlantic, have been a remarkable fact. It is largely due to the eminent literary skill with which he has propounded his views, and described and exaggerated the darkest sides of modern industrial life, and partly also, I think, to the general ignorance of continental Socialist literature, which has given his doctrines something of the fascination of novelty. His fundamental proposition is that, the soil not having been made by man, and having in the beginning of human society been a common property (as it still is in most savage nations), should be taken by the community, without compensation, from its present owners, although it has been recognised as private property for countless generations; although it has been bought, sold, inherited, and mortgaged on the faith of the most undisputed titles; although the earnings and savings and labour of innumerable industrious lives have been sunk in its improvement, and have given it its chief present value; although its existing rent represents, in innumerable cases, nothing more than the lowest, or almost the lowest, rate of interest on the sum actually expended upon it within the memory of living men. It is but a slight circumstance of aggravation that large tracts of the land which Mr. George desires the American Government to take without compensation, had not long since been sold by that very Government to its present owners.

This scheme of plunder, as we have seen, is by no means

original. It had long been a leading article in the Socialist programmes of Germany and France, and the continental Socialists, long before Mr. George, had clearly seen that it could be carried out by the simple process of imposing a special tax on land, equivalent to its full rent value. The doctrine that wages are not paid from capital, but from earnings, on which Mr. George lays so much stress, is merely the doctrine of Marx; nor is there any originality in Mr. George's proposal that nations should still further improve their condition by defrauding their creditors and repudiating their debts. It is 'a preposterous assumption,' he assures us, 'that one generation should be bound by the debts of its predecessors.'[137] That all the profits of production of every kind must ultimately centre in the possessors of land (who must, in consequence, be reaping the most enormous wealth) is a doctrine which belongs more distinctively to Mr. George; but his statements that wages are steadily tending to the minimum of subsistence, the condition of the working-classes steadily deteriorating, and society rapidly dividing into the enormously rich and the abjectly poor, have been abundantly made in Europe, and will, no doubt, long continue to be repeated, in spite of the clearest demonstrations of their falsehood.

It is a somewhat singular fact that the most popular work in favour of the plunder of landed property should come from a country where there is neither primogeniture, nor entail, nor any other form of feudal privilege or restriction; where land is far more abundant than in the Old World, and where the immense majority of the enormous fortunes that have been so rapidly, and often so scandalously, amassed have been acquired in ways quite different from those of the landowner. In no country, in modern times, have abuses of property been greater than in America, and in no country have these abuses been more rarely and more slightly connected with the ownership of land.

In another respect the American authorship of these books

---

[137] *Social Problems*, pp. 213–21.

may excite some surprise. Whatever may have been the nature of the first division and appropriation of the soil when societies passed from their nomadic to their agricultural stage, it is at least incontestably true that the early histories of all nations are full of scenes of savage violence. Exterminating invasions have nearly everywhere been again and again repeated, and again and again followed by vast dispossessions of land. In European countries, it is usually impossible to say whether any particular man is wholly or in part descended from the aboriginal inhabitants, or from one of the many successive races of plundering invaders. All that can be confidently alleged is, that the latter descent is by far the more probable, when we consider that vast period that has elapsed since the aboriginal inhabitants were displaced, and the exterminating character of savage warfare. But in America we may go a step further. It is at least quite certain that the original owners of the soil, whoever they may have been, were not the members of the Anglo-Saxon race. If there is no such thing as prescription in property; if violent dispossession in a remote and even a prehistoric past invalidates all succeeding contracts, the white man has no kind of title, either to an individual or to a joint possession of American soil. The sooner he disappears, the better. Against him, at least, the claim of the Red Indian is invincible.

But, in truth, the principle of Mr. George may be carried still further. If the land of the world is the inalienable possession of the whole human race, no nation has any right to claim one portion of it to the exclusion of the rest. The English people have no more right than Frenchmen to the English soil. The French have no more right to the soil of France than the Germans. Inequalities of fortune are scarcely less among nations than among individuals, and they must be equally unjust. Compare the lot of the Esquimaux in the frozen North, or of the negro in the torrid sands of Africa, with that of the nations inhabiting the fertile soils and the temperate regions of the globe. And what possible right, on the principle of Mr. George, have the younger nations to claim for them-

selves the exclusive possession of vast tracts of fertile and
almost uninhabited land, as against the teeming millions and
the overcrowded centres of the Old World? Mr. George is a
Californian writer. The population of California is about a
fifth of that of Belgium. The area of California is nearly fourteen times as large as that of Belgium.

In some respects the writings of Mr. George differ widely
from those of European Socialists. They contain no aggressive
atheism, and no attacks on marriage. The American writer
knows his public, and there are few books on economical
subjects which are so percolated with religious phraseology
and so profusely adorned with Scriptural quotations. We pass
at once into a region of piety to which continental Socialism
has not accustomed us. Nor are these writings characterised
by that desire to aggrandise the functions of government
which is so general in continental Socialism. Mr. George does
not wish to suppress competition, or individual initiative, or
individual savings, and he desires rather to diminish than to
extend the powers of Government. In these respects, indeed,
he cannot properly be called a Socialist. All he asks from the
Government is, that it should rob two great classes, appropriating the whole rent-value of land by a single tax, which
should supersede all others, and repudiating its national and
municipal debts.

The results to be expected from the confiscation of private
property in land he describes in rapturous terms. 'It is the
golden age of which poets have sung and high-raised seers
have told in metaphor! It is the glorious vision which has
always haunted man with gleams of fitful splendour. It is
what he saw whose eyes at Patmos were closed in a trance.
It is the culmination of Christianity, the City of God on earth,
with its walls of jasper and its gates of pearl! It is the reign of
the Prince of Peace!'[138] In another and more terrestrial passage

---

[138] *Progress and Poverty*, Book x. chap. 5. Compare the boast of a prominent
English Socialist: 'The Churches are turning timidly towards the rising
sun, and the eager reception by Evangelical Christian reformers of Mr.

he describes the promised millennium in the words of an English democrat. It would be 'no taxes at all, and a pension to everybody.'[139]

Mr. George is quite as ready as the German Socialists to plunder the capitalist. He maintains that the first act of the Federal Government, at the beginning of the War of Secession, ought to have been to provide for its expense by confiscating the property of all the richest members in the community who remained loyal to the Union;[140] and no continental writer ever advocated dishonesty to national creditors with a more unblushing cynicism. At the same time, capital, as distinguished from landowning, does not occupy in his system the same position as in the treatise of Marx. In the demonology of Marx the capitalist is the central figure. He is the vampire who sucks the blood of the poor, and absorbs all the wealth which more perfect machinery and more productive labour create. According to Mr. George, he can ultimately absorb none of this wealth, unless he happens to be a landowner. The interest and profits of the capitalist, as well as the wages of the labourer, can never, in the long run, increase while land remains private property. Some of my readers will probably doubt whether such a doctrine could have been seriously propounded, but the language of Mr. George is perfectly clear. 'The ultimate effect of labour-saving machinery or improvements is to increase rents without increasing wages or interest.' 'Every increase in the productive power of labour but increases rent. . . . All the advantages gained by the march of progress go to the owners of land, and wages do not increase. Wages cannot increase.' 'The necessary result of material progress—land being private property—is, no matter what the in-

Henry George as a notable champion of the faith is significant of the change of tone. . . . English Protestantism . . . is coming more and more forward as an active political influence towards the creation of "the Kingdom of God on Earth" ' (Webb's *Socialism in England*, p. 72).

[139] *Protection and Free Trade*, p. 334.

[140] *Social Problems*, p. 216.

crease in population, to force labourers to wages which give but a bare living.' 'Whatever be the increase of productive power, rent steadily tends to swallow up the gains, and more than the gains.' It is a general law, according to Mr. George, that wherever land is cheap wages will be high, and wherever land is dear wages will be low.[141] It is obvious that, according to this law, wages must be far lower in London, in the great provincial towns, and in the country that surrounds them, than in Dorsetshire or Connemara; far lower in England and France than in Hungary, or Poland, or Spain! Mr. George assures us that the whole benefit of the increase of wealth which has taken place in England within the last twenty or thirty years has gone to a single class—the English landowners. It has not alleviated pauperism, but only increased rent.[142]

I can imagine a speculative writer who belonged to one of the more severe monastic Orders, or who wrote, like Campanella, in the profound isolation of a prison-cell, arriving at such conclusions. That sophistry of this kind should deceive anyone who saw, or might have seen, Manchester, or Birmingham, or Leeds; who observed the countless prosperous villas, built out of successful industry, that are growing up around every great manufacturing centre; who had paid the smallest attention to the history of wages in different times and different places, or to the comparative increase of the revenues drawn from personal property and from land, in any of the great countries of the world, is truly amazing. One touch of the reality of things is sufficient to prick the bladder.

---

[141] *Progress and Poverty*, Book iv. chap. 3. 'Wherever you find land relatively low, will you not find wages relatively high? And wherever land is high, will you not find wages low? As land increases in value, poverty deepens and pauperism appears' (Book v. chap. 2). It is obvious that Mr. George merely thought of the high wages in some new countries. It is equally obvious that the explanation of those high wages is, simply, that the labourers are few, and that, if they do not wish to labour for an employer, they have other and easy ways of acquiring a comfortable subsistence.

[142] Ibid. Book vi. chap. 1.

Mr. George devotes a special chapter to repudiating all idea of compensation to the 'expropriated' landowner. In this he is perfectly consistent. I have already examined this point in a former chapter, and need here only repeat that Mr. Fawcett, and several other writers, have shown to absolute demonstration that any attempt to purchase the soil at its market value, by means of a loan raised at the current rate of interest, could only end in a ruinous loss to the nation, while the lot of those who are actually cultivating the soil would become incomparably worse than at present. To pay the interest of the purchase money it would be necessary to raise their rents to the rack-rent level, and to exact them with a stringency which is now only shown by the harshest landlords. The scheme of an honest purchase is, in fact, I believe, now universally abandoned; but some of the English disciples of Mr. George have proposed that, although the land should be taken by the State, an annuity of two lives, equal to its net revenue, should be granted in the form of a pension to the dispossessed owner and to his living heir. It is charitable to assume that this proposal is a serious one; but a man must have a strange conception of human nature if he imagines that a nation which had gone so far in adopting the principles and policy of Mr. George, would consent for a long period of years to burden itself with this enormous tax.

Few things are more difficult than to estimate the real force of dishonest and subversive theories in a great, free nation, where every novelty and every extravagance find an unshackled utterance. In the chaos of vast redundant energies, of crude opinions, of half-assimilated nationalities, of fiercely struggling competitions, paradox and violence rise easily to the surface, for they strike the imagination, and give men the notoriety which, in such a society, is feverishly sought. Notoriety, however, is no measure of power, and the controlling force of the good sense and the sound moral sentiment of the community has, in America as in England, usually proved invincible. The writings of Mr. George are said to have made much more impression in England than in his own country, and few things are more improbable that that his doctrines should triumph. Whatever form land legislation may take in the future, it will never take the form of wholesale spoliation if a country where land is as divided as in America; and a people who so honestly accepted and so courageously reduced their national debt at a time when its burden seemed overwhelming, are certainly not likely to seek their millennium in fraudulent bankruptcy. Nor is the American Constitution one in which the firm fabric of property and contract can be overthrown by any transient ebullition of popular sentiment.

It is, however, impossible to deny that there are signs of grave labour troubles in America, and elements out of which very dangerous opinions might easily grow. In America, no doubt, as in all other civilised countries, most wealth is made by honest industry, and, more than in most countries, it has been expended for public uses. At the same time, there is no country where the struggle for it is fiercer or more unscrupulous, or where vast sums have been more frequently or more rapidly accumulated by evil means. The colossal fortunes built up by the railway-wrecker, by the railway-monopoliser, by the fraudulent manipulator of municipal taxation, by unjust favours extorted from bribed legislators, by great commercial frauds and commercial monopolies under the names of trusts and syndicates, must one day bring a terrible nemesis. These are the things that do most to sap the respect for property in a nation, and they are especially dangerous where no aristocratic or established territorial influence exists to restrict the empire and overshadow the ostentation of ill-got wealth. The vast development of the protective system, and of the system of subsidising great multitudes from the pension list, can scarcely fail to weaken the spirit of self-reliance, and to teach the American people to look more and more to government to create for them artificial conditions of wellbeing. On the other hand, pauperism has appeared, and spread widely through the American cities, where so many turbulent and explosive foreign elements already exist. The unoccupied land, which was once the great safety-valve of dangerous energies, is fast contracting; wages during the last terrible years of depression, probably for the first time in American history, have generally fallen, and, in a country where the cost of living is extremely high, the number of the unemployed has enormously increased.

It is, perhaps, not very surprising that, under these circumstances, more than a million of votes should have been given in the Presidential elections of 1892 in support of a programme embodying a great part of the Socialist creed.[143] The gigantic coal and railway strikes that subsequently broke out almost assumed the character and the dimensions of civil war. The railway strike of June and July 1894 is said to have dislocated for a considerable time the operations of not less than 70,000 miles of railway, and the power and organisation of the labourers completely paralysed and defeated the State Governments. In no less than eight States it was necessary to employ the military force of the Federal Government to move inter-State commerce and the United States mails, and there were signs that even the Supreme Executive Government had lost something of its old controlling power.[144]

Among the forms of the extension of government which have recently been discussed, a prominent place must be assigned to the purchase of railways by the State, and the 'municipalisation' of some of the great corporations of joint-stock industry. Policies of this kind, I need scarcely say, stand on a wholly different basis from that which we have been examining. They involve no necessary spoliation, and there is no reason why they should not be advocated by honest and honourable men. As I have already noticed, the system of unlimited competition in railway construction which exists in the United States is the parent of some of the very worst influences in American life. It has involved an absolute loss and waste of capital that it is impossible to compute. It has

---

[143] The *Forum*, March 1894, p. 90.
[144] Ibid. Jan. 1895, pp. 523–25.

ruined countless families, and broken countless hearts. It has built up and consolidated some of the most colossal frauds that ever were known among mankind. It has spread its demoralising influence through every port of political and municipal life; and as the useless parallel line which is built along an important railway for the purpose of extortion is nearly always, sooner or later, bought up by the older line, it usually ends in a new monopoly. A living American writer has gone so far as to declare that, if every house in the Republic were destroyed, they could all be rebuilt and the whole population comfortably housed for a sum not greater than that which has been lost in competition in railway business in the United States.[145]

How far this evil could now be remedied by State purchase is a question on which I am not competent to pronounce. Railway governments may be broadly divided into three great classes. There is the system of practically unlimited competition, which exists in the United States; there is the system of competition, strictly limited and controlled by parliamentary action, which prevails in England; and there is the system under which the State is the owner of the railways, and either works them through its own agents, or leases them for a term of years to a company. Of these systems, the American one seems to me incomparably the worst. It is more difficult to decide between the two others, and the balance of advantage and disadvantage will probably vary in different countries, according to their special economical conditions. It is, however, one thing to establish the system of an incipient enterprise; it is another and far more difficult thing to change a system which has long been established.

There is also a strong movement for placing telegraphs, telephones, water-supply, tramways, gas and electric light, directly in the hands of the municipal government; and the enormous increase of late years of great industrial monopolies, which has grown out of the American protective system,

---

[145] Ely's *Socialism*, pp. 118–19.

has led many to advocate still further extensions of the industrial functions of municipalities. They contend that every
industry which has become a monopoly should be in the
hands of the State, or of the municipality. In such questions
the three things to be considered are honesty, efficiency, and
economy. Much local knowledge is required, and very much
must depend upon the character of the municipality. Considering the universally acknowledged corruption of American
city government, schemes of this kind would appear to a
stranger more dangerous in America than in almost any other
civilised country. They would inevitably place an enormous
accession of power, influence, and lucrative patronage in the
hands of bodies that are notoriously and scandalously corrupt. Functions that might be excellently discharged by the
municipalities of Birmingham or Liverpool would be very differently managed if they were in the hands of Tammany Hall.
It is argued that independent corporations in America exercise
an overwhelming corrupt influence on municipal government, and that it would, therefore, be better to place them
completely in the hands and under control of the municipalities. 'This reform,' we are told, 'will be favourable to the
purification of politics.'[146] Such reasoning seems to me of that
overrefined character which verges closely on paradox.

I scarcely know whether it is right to include among the
signs of growing Socialism in America the extraordinary popularity which the 'Looking Backward' of Mr. Bellamy has obtained on both sides of the Atlantic. A skilful novel on an
unhackneyed theme naturally strikes the popular fancy, and
Mr. Bellamy has drawn with much skill his picture of a socialistic society. It is a society in which there is no money, no
competition, no pauperism, and no debt; in which all individual ambitions are extinguished; in which each member is
like a soldier in an army, performing in order his appointed
task; and in which, by the expenditure of a mere fraction of

---

[146] Ely's *Socialism*, pp. 282–84. See, too, an essay by Mr. Gladden on Social
Problems in the United States (*Subjects of the Day*, Aug. 1890, pp. 190–91).

the present amount of labour, mankind are to live together in perfect comfort, contentment, and peace. Of all the many readers of this ingenious book, few, I suppose, who have thought seriously on the subject can have persuaded themselves that it would be possible to effect such a radical transformation of society; that, if it were possible, it could be done without a ruinous struggle, which would begin by effectually impoverishing the human race; that, if it were established, it could by any possibility last. The admirable picture which Eugene Richter has drawn of the effects of such a revolution on the different classes of society is, perhaps, the best answer to this picture.

There are, in truth, several grave fallacies which lie at the root of all such Utopian pictures. One of these is, that any possible redistribution of the goods that are in the world can maintain mankind in comfort if production flags and does not, indeed, steadily increase. The mere division of the larger fortunes of the world among the teeming masses of mankind would go but a very small way, and what little might be thus obtained by the poor would be speedily consumed. Wealth perishes swiftly in the usage, and needs to be perpetually replenished; and no reform which impoverishes society as a whole can permanently raise the level of comfort among its members. Socialists dilate, with some truth, on the waste and the over-production which the competitive system continually involves; and it is probable that most of the future industrial progress of the world will consist in co-operative schemes for mitigating these evils. But the Socialist remedies would only bring evils far greater than any they could possibly prevent. The desire of each man to improve his circumstances, to reap the full reward of superior talent, or energy, or thrift, is the very mainspring of the production of the world. Take these motives away; persuade men that by superior work they will obtain no superior reward; cut off all the hopes that stimulate, among ordinary men, ambition, enterprise, invention, and self-sacrifice, and the whole level of production will rapidly and inevitably sink. If industry is greatly diminished in its amount and greatly lowered in its quality, no possible scheme of redistribution or social combination will prevent the material decadence.

The question of increasing population has also to be met. It is one which, under every possible system, is very formidable. The main contention of the school of Marx is, that increased production does not benefit the producer, because it leads to increased population and a corresponding fall of wages. No one can maintain that the wages of a stationary or nearly stationary population would not enormously rise with the great increase of wealth which modern machinery creates. But machinery makes men. The higher wages it produces stimulate early marriages; and if this process is absolutely unrestrained, it is quite true that the working-classes will gain nothing in the shape of wages by the improved production. Fortunately, however, such restraints do exist. The desire to save, the desire to rise, the fear of poverty, the habits of foresight and providence which education produces, the higher standard of comfort which men come to regard as indispensable—all act powerfully in the direction of tardy marriage. That population has not, on the whole, outrun the production of wealth is conclusively proved by the higher average of wages and comfort which has been attained. That there are great multitudes upon whom these restraining influences do not operate is one main cause of the misery which we all deplore. But a Socialist society cannot escape the problem, and the pressure of population on its resources would soon become overwhelming. In a society where there was no motive for saving, and where all children were supported by the community, the strongest natural restraints would be destroyed.

It is also sufficiently obvious that the first condition of the success of a socialistic community is complete isolation. Socialism is essentially opposed to Free Trade and international commerce. It is conceivable that, in some remote island of the Pacific, the whole population might be organised into one great co-operative society, in which each member filled an assigned part and discharged an assigned duty in obedience to the authority of the whole. But this organisation must be stereotyped. It must be kept separate, drilled and disciplined like a regiment of soldiers. It is absolutely inconceivable that such a state of society could exist in a vast, fluctuating, highly locomotive population, spreading over a great part of the globe, deriving its subsistence from many distant countries, bound to them by the closest commercial ties, continually sending out vast streams of emigrants, continually absorbing into itself Indian, colonial, and alien populations. To organise such a people on the plan and in the framework of a Socialist State is the idlest of dreams.

In the future of the world it is, no doubt, possible and probable that the industrial conditions to which we are accustomed may be profoundly modified. There may be great changes in the incidence of taxation, in the regulation of successions, in the part which co-operative industry plays in the world, in the part which Governments and municipalities play in initiating, directing, and subsidising industry, or in providing for the old, the impoverished, and the unemployed. But proposed changes which conflict with the fundamental laws and elements of human nature can never, in the long run, succeed. The sense of right and wrong, which is the basis of the respect for property and for the obligation of contract; the feeling of family affection, on which the continuity of society depends, and out of which the system of heredity grows; the essential difference of men in aptitudes, capacities, and character, are things that never can be changed, and all schemes and policies that ignore them are doomed to ultimate failure.

CHAPTER 9

Labour Questions

It would be hardly possible that the immense extension of Socialism which has taken place, in all parts of the civilised globe, within the last twenty-five years, and the immense change that has been effected in the balance of political power in England by the Acts of 1867 and 1884, should not have powerfully stimulated English Socialism. The whole wealth and greatness of the community lie at the mercy of an electorate in which the poorest and least instructed class have the largest share, and, if it is the will, it is well within the power of the democracy to make taxation the most efficient instrument of confiscation. The temptation is a great one; though it is but justice to observe that the men who have of late years been labouring most zealously to seduce the poorer voters into the paths of plunder have not themselves been of that class. The proposal of George to rob, by means of a confiscating tax, all the owners of land, whether it be purchased or inherited; and the doctrine of Marx, that all capital should be taken possession of by the community, are now often put forward in England, usually in those sonorous phrases by which some men seem able to disguise from others, and perhaps from themselves, the profound dishonesty of their teaching. The policy is described as 'the collective administration of rent

313

and interest, leaving to the individual only the wages of his labour of hand or brain;' as 'the nationalisation of land and organisation of agricultural and industrial armies under State control and co-operative principles;' as 'the emancipation of land and industrial capital from individual and class owner-ship, and the vesting of them in the community for the general benefit.'[1]

There are several small bodies which are at present advo-cating these views, though they are usually divided from one another by much jealousy and antagonsim. The Social and Democratic League, of which Mr. Hyndman is the leading spirit, is, I believe, the oldest. It has published a programme demanding, among other things, nationalisation of the land; the rapid extinction of the National Debt; cumulative taxation upon all incomes above 300*l*. a year; the establishment of national banks 'which shall absorb all private institutions that derive profit from operations in money or credit;' a law pro-hibiting men and women in any trade from working more than eight hours a day; the compulsory erection of dwellings for artisans and agricultural labourers, for which no rent must be paid beyond the bare cost of their building and mainte-nance. In order to attain these objects the State is to be made as democratic as possible. There must be annual Parliaments, adult suffrage, proportional representation. The taxpayers are to pay the members. The ratepayers are to pay for their elec-tion. The House of Lords and all hereditary authorities are to be abolished. All State Churches are to be disestablished and disendowed, and the powers of County Councils are to be enlarged. One article of this programme is ambiguous. The 'rapid extinction of the National Debt' might appear to un-wary readers to point merely to an extension of the admirable efforts which British Governments have made for many years to diminish out of the annual revenue the capital of the debt. The tracts, however, which are issued by this society abun-

---

[1] Programme of the Fabian Society; Sidney Webb's *Socialism in England*, p. 10.

dantly correct the error. The extinction desired is of a far simpler character. It is merely to cheat the national creditors by repudiating the debt.

'The few thousand persons,' they write, 'who own the National Debt, saddled upon the community by a landlord Parliament, exact twenty-eight millions yearly from the labour of their countrymen for nothing. The shareholders who have been allowed to lay hands upon our great railway communications take a still larger sum.' 'The land must be in future a national possession; so must the other means of producing and distributing wealth.' 'The handling of money and credit must necessarily be carried on in future for the community at large. . . . As a stepping-stone to the attainment of this State organisation of production and exchange we advocate the heaviest cumulative taxation, rising upon all incomes derived from trade or business, as well as upon those drawn from the land.' 'The means of production, distribution, and exchange are to be declared and treated as collective or common property.' 'Nor is it reasonable to suppose that any compensation will be given to the landholders, the fundholders, or the railway or water shareholders, when it has been determined to assume administration of all for the public benefit.'[2]

The society is characterised by some other tendencies. It is much opposed, chiefly on lofty moral grounds, to any extension of the Empire, and is generally, within the very moderate limits of its influence, a supporter of any movement within the Empire which tends to weaken the coherence and the power of its central Government. It is also strenuously opposed to both of the great parties in the State, and maintains that its members should never support any politician who does not accept their programme. They have not, however, invariably acted on their principle, and on one memorable occasion, in 1892, a branch of this society interposed, and

---

[2] *Manifesto of the Social Democratic Federation* (1883); Hyndman and Morris, *The Principles of Socialism*, written for the Democratic Federation, p. 59; Hyndman's *Historical Basis of Socialism*, p. 467.

effected by their vote the return of the Indian member, Mr. Naoroji, the official Liberal candidate for Central Finsbury. He was returned by a majority of three.[3]

The Social Democratic Federation seems to have been somewhat unfortunate in losing its members; and there have been several divisions, arising, as far as I can understand, chiefly from personal quarrels. There was a secession in 1883, resulting in the foundation of a 'Socialist League,' under the presidency of the distinguished poet, Mr. W. Morris. There was a secession in 1886, resulting in a new body, called the 'Socialist Union,' which, however, appears to have only lasted for two years;[4] and the society of Mr. Hyndman afterwards quarrelled with at least three of its most active members—Mr. John Burns, Mr. Tom Mann, and Mr. Champion. Members of the party have been concerned in several riots, and some of them have endured 'martyrdom' in the shape of short periods of imprisonment. There is also, I believe, an independent group, called the 'Kropotkin Anarchists,' and there is a separate society for the purpose of bringing about the 'nationalisation of land' and the 'expropriation' of its owners.

Another body, which has of late years made some noise in the world, is the Fabian Society. If the figures it publishes are true, its tracts must have been circulated by tens of thousands, and it contains at least two men of considerable ability. It proposes to work for the extinction of private property in land, and the appropriation of all industrial capital by the community, in order that rent and interest may be added to the reward of labour; and it differs from the Social and Democratic League in urging its members to take an active part in all general and local elections. The creation of a pure Socialist party in Parliament is one of its objects; but until this is possible its members are to endeavour to obtain a place in all local

---

[3] See on this case the postscript to Mr. B. Shaw's lecture, *The Fabian Society, and what it has done.*

[4] *The Fabian Society, and what it has done*, p. 7; Webb's *Socialism in England*, p. 33.

bodies of power and influence, and to support on all occasions, and regardless of all party considerations, those candidates who will go furthest in the direction of Socialism, even though they altogether repudiate its ultimate ends and its guiding principles.

Mr. Bernard Shaw—a writer of plays, and an excellent musical and dramatic critic—who has taken a leading part in the society, has written a very frank and instructive little paper on 'The Fabian Society: what it has done, and how it has done it,' which was published by the society in 1892. He claims that it is eminently practical, and he cannot be accused of taking it too seriously. He says that in 1885 it consisted of forty members, male and female. 'We denounced the capitalists as thieves at the Industrial Remuneration Conference, and among ourselves talked revolution, anarchism, labour notes *versus* pass books, and all the rest of it, on the tacit assumption that the object of our campaign, with its watchwords "Educate, agitate, organise," was to bring about a tremendous smash-up of existing society, to be succeeded by complete Socialism. And this meant that we had no true practical understanding, either of existing society or Socialism. Without being quite definitely aware of this, we yet felt it to a certain extent all along; for it was at this period that we contracted the invaluable habit of freely laughing at ourselves, which has always distinguished us, and which has saved us from being hampered by the gushing enthusiasts who mistake their own emotions for public movements.' There was a Fabian Conference in 1886, which achieved the great success of obtaining a notice in the 'Times.' It had not, Mr. Shaw thinks, much other result, but 'it made us known to the Radical clubs, and proved that we were able to manage a conference in a business-like way. It also showed off our pretty prospectus, with the design by Crane at the top, our stylish-looking blood-red invitation cards, and the other little smartnesses on which we then prided ourselves.'[5]

---

[5] *The Fabian Society: what it has done, and how it has done it*, p. 11.

After this, however, the society took a new departure, chiefly under the influence of Mr. Sidney Webb, a plausible writer and adroit tactician who, on the London County Council and elsewhere, has played a considerable part in contemporary English Socialism.[6] The society clearly saw that they represented only a very small portion of the English working class. 'We have never indulged,' Mr. Shaw writes, 'in any visions of a Fabian army any bigger than a stage army.' 'We have never advanced the smallest pretension to represent the working classes of this country.' 'We know that, for a long time to come, we can only make headway by gaining the confidence of masses of men outside our society, who will have nothing to do with us unless we first prove ourselves safe for all sorts of progressive work.'

They accordingly adopted what they called a policy of 'permeation.' In other words, they made it their object to enter as largely as possible into all the many Radical organisations and movements, and endeavour to add Socialist formulæ to the received Radical programmes; to acquire an influence over municipal and political bodies which had no sympathy with their specific tenets; to help on all revolutionary or subversive tendencies, even though the men who represented those tendencies were far from looking forward to a socialistic State. A few small newspapers had been set up as purely Socialist organs, but most of them proved perfectly insignificant, and soon died away. Many young newspaper writers, however, sympathised with Socialism, and some of them obtained employment on well-established Radical journals, and induced two or three editors to admit into their columns a certain amount of Socialist doctrine and colouring. The vast multiplication of local elections by the legislation of the last few years assisted the movement. A large proportion of them ex-

---

[6] 'The generalship of this movement was undertaken chiefly by Sidney Webb, who played such bewildering conjuring tricks with the Liberal thimbles and the Fabian peas that to this day both the Liberals and the sectarian Socialists stand aghast at him' (Ibid. p. 19).

cited little general interest, and in the face of the numerous abstentions, and by judicious combinations, alliances, and surprises, it was not difficult for a small but well-organised minority to capture occasional seats.

Long before the formation of the Socialist bodies I am describing there had been a tendency, largely illustrated in the present work, to increased extravagance in taxation; an increased disposition to extend the sanctions of Government, both in restraining, initiating and supporting private industries, in dealing by State methods with social evils, in supplanting in many fields the action of the individual by the action of the State and the municipality. Growing democracy had weakened the connection between property and taxing power, and had made it easy for a majority of voters to throw the burden of the taxation they voted, upon other shoulders than their own. It was the object of the Socialists to fall in with these tendencies; to encourage, intensify, and embitter them. They recognised fully that the confiscation of all rent and interest, which was their ultimate object, could only be fully attained in the distant future; but in the meantime they worked with all parties who desired to extend the power of the State or of municipalities over industries, to sap in any form the rights of property and the obligation of contract, to throw taxation more and more upon land and realised property.

Some changes which took place in the character of trade unions assisted in the same direction. Partly through the distress and fluctuations produced by a long period of trade depression, partly through the contagion of the socialistic and anarchical tenets that were circulating through the working classes of the Continent, partly through the wild hopes which the great and sudden lowering of the suffrage had produced, and partly, too, through the natural disposition of young, poor, clever, discontented and ambitious men to revolt against established authorities, and seek a new deal in the good things of the world, there arose a party within the trade unions who were bitterly discontented with the conservative and moderate spirit of the old leaders. They assailed them with the most scurrilous invective, preached a more violent and aggressive policy and a more clearly defined class warfare, and brought the chief objects of Socialism rapidly to the front.

It was about 1885 that this new element became prominent in the trade unions. It increased in the following years, and was much strengthened, not only by the progress of democracy in the State, but also by the introduction into the trade unions of great masses of unskilled labourers, who were much more easily led by agitators than the skilled artisans. Socialists of all kinds and persuasions allied themselves with the new leaders, and by doing so they achieved considerable triumphs. Trade in most of its departments was at this time very bad. Work had become scarce; wages were falling. Some great strikes, rashly undertaken in the midst of a declining demand, created sharp conflicts between capital and labour; while their inevitable failure aggravated the distress, ruined many trade unions, and discredited the old methods in the eyes of great bodies of workmen. The old, stern gospel of thrift and self-reliance was put aside, and the opinion grew rapidly that more was to be hoped from State action and from a great industrial revolution.[7]

Independent Labour candidates, usually preaching socialistic doctrines, were now frequently put forward. In parliamentary elections they had very little success. Their minorities were nearly always infinitesimal; and although a few Socialists entered the House of Commons, they usually did so, much less as Socialists than as advanced Radicals, and the more powerful of them soon sank into regular members of the Radical party. In school-board and municipal elections, however, they were more successful. Mr. Keir Hardie boasted that in 130

---

[7] For the rise of the New Unionism the reader should consult Howell's *Trade Unionism New and Old*, Webb's *History of Trade Unionism*, and the evidence given on the subject before the Labour Commission.

municipal elections, of which he obtained information, the Independent Labour vote exceeded 25 per cent. of the votes.[8] The most remarkable success was in the London County Council, where the Socialist element acquired an undoubted influence, and has given a distinct bias to municipal politics. The party had already achieved a similar success in the Municipality of Paris, and the two largest and wealthiest cities in Europe were thus in a large measure under their influence.

Still more serious is the hold which they have acquired over the Trade Union Congresses. This is a very recent, but surely a very serious, fact, due to the rise of the New Unionism, and it is shown in many forms. Undeterred by the disastrous example of the French national workshops of 1848, the Trade Union Congress of 1890 voted 'that power should at once be granted to each municipality or county council to establish workshops and factories, under municipal control, where destitute persons shall be put to useful employment, and that it be an instruction to the Parliamentary Committee to at once take the matter in hand.'[9]

In a similar spirit, a conpulsory Act limiting the labour of adult men in all trades to eight hours has come to be a leading article of trade-union politics. All parties and classes have agreed that, under the stress of intense competition, the hours of labour have been, and still often are, too long, and that where their reduction can be effected without serious injury to the productive powers of the nation it is a great blessing. Very much has been actually done in this direction, by voluntary effort and combination, both in the way of a reduction of daily labour and in the extension of the Saturday half-holiday; but the law has hitherto shrunk from regulating by a hard and fast line the hours of adult labour, and thus invading what Adam Smith called 'the most sacred and inviolable' of all properties—'the poperty which every man has

---

[8] See an article in the *Nineteenth Century*, January 1895.
[9] Howell's *Trade Unionism New and Old*, p. 166.

in his own labour.' The legal eight hours, however, has long been prominent in the continental Socialist programmes, and it has made great progress in England.

The movement has taken several forms. One demand is, that it should be the rule in the case of all persons employed either by the State, or by municipalities, or by any other public body. If this were established by law, it would become a model which private employers would be soon forced to follow; and if the State and the local bodies lost by the transaction, they had always the purses of the taxpayers and ratepayers as their resource. The possibility of obtaining higher wages and shorter hours is one of the chief grounds for the demand for the municipalisation of industries. Another proposal, which is likely soon to become law, would restrict the legal eight hours to miners. It is very evident that such a period of work is quite as much as can in general be exacted without injury in this kind of labour, and, as a matter of fact, the limitation which it is sought to impose by law is very nearly attained by private arrangement. In Northumberland and Durham the miner's actual working day is, in most cases, less than seven hours. In other parts of England it it generally less than eight and a half hours.[10] Another proposal, which has received a large amount of working-class support, has been that the eight-hour limitation should be introduced into each trade on the vote of the members, the majority binding the minority. In the International Congress of Workmen which was held in London in 1888, a resolution was carried in favour of a general limitation of the hours of all trades to eight hours; and although this policy was defeated in the Congress of 1889, an eight hours day for all trades by Act of Parliament was voted

---

[10] Howell's *Trade Unionism*, p. 171. If the actual working hours 'at the face,' as it is termed, deducting the time for meals and rest, and also the time occupied in going to and fro, be taken, the time of work appears much less. A Government report on thirteen mining districts in Great Britain shows that in no district except South Wales did this kind of work average forty-six hours a week; in all the other districts it was less than forty-four, in six districts less than forty (Ibid. p. 183).

by a large majority in the Congress of 1890, and a Bill was subsequently introduced making it a penal offence to 'cause or suffer any other person to work, on sea or land, in any capacity, under any contract, or agreement, or articles for hire of labour, or for personal service on sea or land (except in case of accident), for more than eight hours in any one day of twenty-four hours, or for more than forty-eight hours in any week.'[11] Sometimes it has been proposed that an eight hours day should be established by law, but that any trade objecting by a formal vote to that standard should be exempted.

Still more significant is the conversion of the New Unionism to the extreme Socialist doctrines of George and Marx. The writings of George, as a Socialist historian observes, 'sounded the dominant note alike of the New Unionism and of the English Socialist movement of to-day,'[12] and demands for the nationalisation of land were soon regularly put forward at Trade Union Congresses. An amendment in this sense was carried, though apparently only by surprise, and in the absence of many delegates, in the Congress of 1882. It was rejected in the five succeeding congresses, but carried in a vague form in 1887, and, more decisively, at Bradford in 1888. It began to take the place of the demand for the creation of peasant proprietors and household enfranchisement, which had formerly been urged.[13] The congress which was held at Bradford in 1893 laid the foundation of an Independent Labour party in Parliament, which was intended to act in complete separation from all other parties in the State, and one of the main articles of its programme was 'the taxation to extinction of all unearned incomes.'[14] In the congress which was held at Norwich in 1894 a delegate moved, 'that in the opinion of this congress it is essential to the maintenance of British industries to nationalise the land, mines, minerals, and royalty rents, and that

---

[11] Ibid. pp. 188, 193–205.
[12] Webb's *History of Trade Unionism*, p. 362.
[13] Webb's *History of Trade Unionism*, pp. 362, 375–76.
[14] Article of Mr. Keir Hardie, *Nineteenth Century*, January 1895.

the Parliamentary Committee be instructed to promote and support legislation with the above object.' The motion was met by an amendment, moved by Mr. Keir Hardie, substituting for the words, 'mines, minerals, and royalty rents,' the words, 'and the whole of the means of production, distribution, and exchange.' He explained that there was no argument in favour of the nationalisation of land and mines which did not apply to the nationalisation of every other form of production; that if the mines from which minerals were taken were nationalised, the same thing should be done to the railways which conveyed these minerals, to the depots where they were deposited, to the works where they were manufactured; that for every 1*l.* taken by the landlord in the form of rent, 2*l.* were taken by the capitalist in the form of interest, and that there was, therefore, no reason why the landlord should be attacked and the capitalist allowed to go free. The amendment was supported, among others, by Mr. John Burns and Mr. Tom Mann, and was carried, amid loud applause, by 219 votes to 61.[15]

This congress consisted of 380 delegates from different trade bodies, and it was the boast of one of its members that it included at least 100 men who were either members of town councils, county councils, school boards, benches of magistrates, or the House of Commons. That such a body should have carried, by a great majority, such a resolution must surely be regarded as a grave portent, even by men who are in no degree disposed to panic or exaggeration.

There are, no doubt, serious deductions to be made from its significance. One of the largest and richest of the trade unions formally seceded from all connection with the Trade Union Congress on account of this resolution; and it has long been asserted, by those who have the best means of information, that these bodies only represent to a very small and imperfect degree the older and larger trade unions, which are

---

[15] *Report of the Twenty-seventh Annual Trade Union Congress* published by the authority of the Congress, pp. 53–55. Very similar resolutions were carried a year later in the congress at Cardiff.

the special organs of the more intelligent members of the working-classes. It is the old story of the active agitators of a new doctrine acquiring for a time a notoriety and prominence out of all proportion to the real weight and number of their adherents. The increasing influence of unskilled labour in the trade unions, and some changes that had been made in the manner of electing delegates, have assisted them. In the separate trade unions voting power is not proportioned to the amount which each member has contributed to its funds, and in the congresses each delegate has one vote, quite irrespectively of the wealth and number of the union he represents. Under such a system the votes of the Trade Union Congresses can only represent in a very imperfect degree the real weight of opinion in the bodies from which they spring. There have been large abstentions, and active minorities have often governed the proceedings.[16]

It is also not surprising that, in the terrible shrinkages of industry that have of late years taken place on all sides around us, wild and revolutionary experiments should have been advocated. The schemes of gigantic plunder which are put forward are relegated to a distant future, and they therefore fail to arouse the full measure of earnest opposition. It is probable that the resolution of the Norwich Congress is far from representing the genuine opinion of trade unions, and it does not even pretend to represent that of the workmen who are outside them. Yet Sir Robert Giffen stated in 1893 that, according to the latest returns, out of a working population of 13,200,000, only 871,000 are members of trade unions.[17] No one who knows England will seriously doubt that, if these

---

[16] See Howell's *Trade Unions*, pp. 192–99; Brook's *Industry and Property*, ii. 362–63, 398–99.

[17] See his evidence before the Labour Commission (*Digest*, p. 43). A well-informed correspondent, in the *Times*, September 7, 1895, gives somewhat different figures. He estimates the branches of labour from which trade unionism seeks its recruits at 11,338,035 persons, and the total membership of the 677 unions at the close of 1893 at 1,270,789. He also collects much evidence to show that the number of the members of trade unions is declining.

schemes of nationalisation were submitted to the English people as a plain issue for immediate action, the overwhelming majority would pronounce them to be a mixture of madness and swindling, certain to ruin any nation that adopted them, and fundamentally opposed to those ideas of right and wrong on which all civilised society must rest. No feature of the general election of 1895 was more remarkable than the invariable defeat of representatives of the New Unionism and of the Socialist party, and the strong conservative tendencies that were dominant in the great working-class centres. The same thing had been shown shortly before, on a smaller scale, by the defeat of the Socialist party in the London County Council. The avowed and exclusively Socialist party, which is so formidable in the Parliaments of Germany, France, and Belgium, can scarcely be said to exist in the British House of Commons. Knots of men holding such views may be found in many constituencies, but they scarcely anywhere predominate. Except in places where political parties are closely balanced, or greatly disintegrated, they have little power, and the sustained market value of the forms of property which they desire to rob shows that the secrurity of this property is not yet greatly shaken.

At the same time, it cannot be an indifferent thing that there is a large number of men in England who look upon Government as an instrument, not for protecting, but for plundering property, and who are exerting all their influence to lead the ruling democracy in this direction. Those who have followed the writings and speeches of the members of this school will scarcely deem these words too strong. 'Thrift,' Mr. John Burns assured the Trade Union Congress at Norwich, 'was invented by capitalistic rogues to beguile fools to destruction, and to deprive honest fools of their diet and their proper comfort.'[18] Mr. Hyndman expressed very similar sentiments before the Labour Commission, and added, that 'to put money into savings banks,' or to accumulate it in any other way, is to accu-

---

[18] *Report*, p. 55.

mulate orders on other men's labours, and is no benefit to the class who so save. All thrift on the part of the working classes which leads to their becoming small capitalists he declared to be an evil. It only intensifies competition, and fortifies the class which they should endeavour to supplant.[19]

The two most successful methods that have ever been employed to mitigate the antagonism of classes, and to give the working classes the full benefit of capital, have been the system of profit-sharing which has been so successful in France, and the system of co-operative industrial undertakings worked by working men. Both of these modes of raising the condition of the working class have been strenuously opposed by the New Unionists.[20] No feature of the Old Trade Unionism is more admirable than the efforts they have made to encourage providence among their members and to assist them to provide for sickness, old age, and the destitution of their families. Mr. Howell has given the statistics of the sums expended by the fourteen largest trade unions in England in sick-pay, superannuation allowances to aged members, funeral allowances, and other benevolent purposes, and he has compared the sum with that expended by these bodies in strikes. For the detailed accounts I must refer the reader to Mr. Howell's valuable book. They clearly show how entirely subordinate is the part which strikes have held in the policy of the most important trade unions; how admirable and conscientious their administration has usually been; what a vast sum of self-help and providence exists among the better class of the English labourers; and what incalculable benefits these trade unions have conferred upon their members. 'The aggregate amount devoted [by these fourteen societies] to what might be called

---

[19] *Minutes of Evidence*, 8406, 8718–9. See, too, *Digest*, p. 23. Mr. Bax observes that the aim of the Socialist 'is radically at variance with thrift.' 'To the Socialist, labour is an evil to be minimised to the utmost. The man who works at his trade or avocation more than necessity compels him, or who accumulates more than he can enjoy, is not a hero, but a fool, from the Socialist's standpoint' (*The Religion of Socialism*, p. 94).
[20] Howell's *Trade Unionism*, p. 233.

the constant and permanent requirements of workmen—namely, pecuniary assistance in cases of need over which they have little control—reaches the grand sum of 7,331,952*l.*, while the total ascertained amount expended solely on strikes was only 462,818*l.*' 'Singularly enough,' Mr. Howell adds, 'the provident side of trade unions is the one mainly attacked by the apostles of the so-called New Trade Unionism, whose objects seem to be to make the unions merely fighting-machines, unencumbered with any sick or accident fund.'[21]

I have mentioned in a former chapter that worst and most dangerous form of corruption, which has shown itself in modern times in England—the combination of workmen in the dockyard towns, and of Civil Servants of different categories, to use their voting power for the purpose of putting political pressure upon their representatives in parliament in order to raise their own salaries and wages, subordinating to this end all national and political considerations. It would be scarcely possible to conceive a habit more calculated to demoralise constituencies to the core, and more certain, if it spreads widely, to destroy all sound patriotic feeling in the nation. It is one of the usual arguments of the Socialist party in favour of the municipalisation of industries, that it enables workmen more easily to exercise their franchise with this object, and Mr. Sidney Webb informed the Labour Commission that he desired an indefinite extension of this practice.[22]

At the same time, the necessity of acting with other sections of the Radical party obliges the Socialist bodies engaged in active politics in some measure to mask their objects, and to throw many of their favourite arguments in the background. The confiscation of mining royalites and of ground rents are the only forms of direct plunder which are now put forward with much persistence. These kinds of property belong chiefly to a few men, and they are, therefore, natural objects of dishonest cupidity. But on the question of the taxation of ground

---

[21] Howell, pp. 96, 127, 137.
[22] *Minutes of Evidence*, 4045, 4046; see, too, 4505.

rents we find an instructive combination of two classes of very different arguments.

The subject is one into which I do not propose to enter at length. There is obviously a great distinction between proposals to break existing contracts, under which householders have engaged to pay all rates and taxes, and a proposal like that of a recent town holdings committee, that in all future contracts rates should be compulsorily divided between the owner and occupier. The point on which I would insist is, that the arguments which are commonly advanced in public in favour of the special taxation of the ground landlords are based on that bourgeois morality which Socialists so much disdain. It is argued that the ground landlord does not pay his fair or due share to the improvements that are rapidly and enormously raising the value of his property; that vast expenses have been imposed on the community which were not anticipated at the time when existing contracts were made. The question is treated as one of equity and degree, and on the principle that all parties should contribute their fair proportion to the common expenditure.

Among the Socialists it is looked on in another light. It is considered simply as a step to the confiscation of the whole value of the ground on which cities are built. 'The movement for the absorption by taxation of the site value of great cities,' Mr. Sidney Webb writes, 'is making enormous strides,' and he congratulates himself upon the fact that when Mr. George propounded his views on these subjects in London, in 1889, his lectures were presided over by Liberal members and candidates, and by ministers and other leaders of the great Nonconformist religious bodies, who would once have regarded his doctrine with horror. 'The accepted method of land nationalisation,' he says, 'is the taxation of rental values;' and he notices how a Committee for the purpose of bringing about the taxation of ground rents and values has enjoyed the presidency of a noble lord who holds a high judicial office under the Crown, 'and has succeeded in enlisting nearly all the Liberal (and some Conservative) members of Parliament in support of the special taxation of urban land values.' The committee does not profess to be a Socialist body, or to aim at the Socialist ideal. At the same time, Mr. Webb remarks, its first important publication 'was, at the request of the committee, written by a Socialist, and the arguments used therein support the complete nationalisation and municipalisation of all rent.'

On the whole, Mr. Webb observes: 'The special rating and taxation of urban land values, the amount being left unspecified, is, indeed, now fully accepted as part of the official Liberal programme; and this fact is the more significant of the popular pressure in that probably not one of the present Liberal leaders really desires or intends any such confiscatory taxation, though they take no trouble to disclaim it.'[23] Mr. Webb's own view is very clearly stated. He has no objection to purchase ground rents, but he would first of all tax them to extinction. He would gladly see a rate of twenty shillings in the pound imposed on ground values, and would then 'take over the reversion of the estate of London of these terms.'[24] It would be difficult to be more completely emancipated from the trammels of a mere *'bourgeois* morality'!

It is instructive to notice the analogy between these views and the agrarian movement which has lately taken place in Ireland. Mr. Parnell was quite prepared to advocate the purchase by the tenants of their farms, but he desired in the first place to beat down their cost to a mere fraction of the natural value. This was to be accomplished by violent conspiracy and intimidation; by systematic breach of contract and repudiation of rent; by throwing the country into a state of anarchy, in which all market transactions in land were paralysed. The English Socialist differs in his means, but not in his end. He seeks by a special and confiscatory taxation to reduce to a mere nominal value the property he desires to appropriate.

The connection, indeed, of Irish agrarianism and the laws that it has produced with English Socialism is very close, and

---

[23] Webb's *Socialism in England*, pp. 58–60.
[24] *Labour Commission: Evidence*, 3887–3891.

it has been clearly seen, not only by Socialists at home, but also by some of the most eminent economists on the Continent.[25] It is a significant fact that one of the earliest and most unqualified advocates of the doctrines of Mr. George was a leading member of the Irish agrarian movement. That movement showed more clearly than any preceding one how possible it was for a class who possessed a predominance of voting power, to use it for the purpose of breaking contracts and confiscating property; and it also showed that we have arrived at a stage of party government in which neither Parliament nor the ministers of the Crown can be trusted to resist the pressure, or to protect the property and legal contracts of any class who have lost political power. The lesson will not be lost upon wise men. The precedents and principles introduced into Irish legislation, and the methods by which that legislation was carried, will have far-reaching results, and have already given a powerful impulse to English Socialism.

One of the immediate objects of the Socialist wing of the Radical party is to advocate on all occasions the absorption of as many great industries as possible by the State or the municipality, with the curious result that the very men who are preaching the repudiation of debts, and the policy of taxing interest out of existence, are the strenuous advocates of enormous national and municipal loans. Thus Mr. Hyndman, who is the leading spirit of an association that desires the 'rapid extinction of the National Debt' by means of repudiation, informed the Labour Commission that the State should immensely enlarge its functions as an employer of labour; that the first industry it should take over is the railways; that the cost of the acquisition would be about 1,100,000,000*l*., and that he would gladly see the State giving this sum, and raising it by State bonds. He acknowledged, indeed, that if he had his way he would take the railways for nothing; but as, in a capitalistic society recognising private property, this is not possible, he urged for the purpose of the purchase an immediate

---

[25] See Vol. i. pp. 163–64.

addition to the National Debt greatly exceeding the whole of that debt when it reached its highest point, at the Peace of 1815. As one of the first duties of the State on taking the railways would be to reduce the cost of transport, and as one of the great advantages of State ownership would be that those who were employed upon them would have the power of exerting political pressure to extort higher wages, the reader may easily foresee the nature of the financial millennium that would ensue. Nor is it difficult to conceive what prospect a Government would have of raising such a loan at the instigation of the party that talks of the 'healthy indifference' which each generation should cultivate to the debts incurred on its behalf by its forefathers, of the facility with which 'veiled repudiations' might be effected 'by a judicious application of the income tax.'[26]

But the railways, though the largest, form only one item in the long list of State acquisitions that are advocated by Socialist leaders, each one of which, in the present condition of society, could only be effected by raising vast loans. Canals, dockyards, tramways, omnibuses, the gas supply, and the water supply, are in like manner to be taken over by the municipalities; which are also to set up municipal workshops, to make large purchases of land, to absorb in succession the great private industrial concerns, and to set up new ones. The hours of work are to be shortened by law; the municipalities are to establish a minimum of wages for all workmen in their employment—which Mr. Hyndman puts at 30s. a week, and which would be, certainly, considerably above the market rate—and they are to guarantee that the advantages in the matter of wages and hours obtained in good times should not be taken from the workmen in bad times without their consent.[27] The enormous additional taxation that would naturally ensue is not a thing to be deprecated, but rejoiced in, for 'the

---

[26] *Fabian Essays*, p. 143.
[27] See the evidence of Mr. Hyndman and Mr. S. Webb before the Labour Commission.

increasing absorption of rent and interest by taxation' is one of the objects the Socialists most desire. They propose, in the words of an academic Socialist,[28] 'to make rent and interest pay for their own extinction.' They hope that the ever-increasing burden of rates may drive the smaller rate-payers in despair into their ranks,[29] and it is only when taxation has reached the point of confiscation that their ideal will be attained.

That this insane and grotesque policy can ever be carried into effect is impossible; but any near approach to it would produce calamities in a country like England which it would be scarcely possible to exaggerate. It would blast as in an hour the whole prosperity of the nation. If a House of Commons were elected which accepted the Socialist programme, long before that Parliament had time to assemble countless millions of capital would have passed out of the land. The whole system of credit, on which the vast and complex edifice of English industry and commerce depends, would inevitably collapse. Every manufacturer, every employer of labour, would make it his object to stop his works and dismiss his workmen, and, in an overcrowded country, nearly every main channel of employment would be at once obstructed. The Cotton Famine of Lancashire during the American Civil War, even the ghastly

---

[28] Hobhouse, *The Labour Movement.*

[29] 'The small tradesmen and ratepayers who are now allying themselves with the Duke of Westminster in a desperate and unavailing struggle against the rising rates entailed by the eight hours day and standard wages for all public servants, besides great extensions of corporate activity in providing accommodation and education at the public expense, must sooner or later see that their interest lies in making common cause with the workers to throw the burden of taxation directly on unearned incomes' (B. Shaw, *The Fabian Society, What it has done*, p. 26). Mr. Hyndman observes: 'It may be reasonably contended that the well-to-do classes are, as a rule, a good deal overhoused, and some have urged that direct expropriation should be resorted to the instant the workers are strong enough to act. . . . The rise in the rates would compel the well-to-do to throw good houses on to the market, thus enlarging the sphere of action' (*Historical Basis of Socialism*, pp. 453–54).

scenes that were witnessed in Ireland during the great Famine of 1847, would only faintly foreshadow the misery that such a state of things must produce. For a juster parallel we should have to go to the last days of the Roman Empire, when the Egyptian corn supplies were cut off, and the population of Italy slowly dwindled by famine to a mere fraction of what it had been. In no age of the world could such a calamity be more easily produced, for never before could capital be so quickly and easily displaced, and in no other country do industry and employment more largely depend upon national credit. In a population like that of England every fluctuation of credit, every diminution of capital, every temporary dislocation or enfeeblement of a great industry, produces deep and wide-spread distress, and adds largely to the number of the unemployed. Who can estimate what would happen if all the elements of national prosperity were convulsed or paralysed by the prospect of a legislative confiscation?

The good sense and the fundamental honesty of the English people may be trusted to guard against such a catastrophe, but measures that are far short of it may produce grave evils. I have already described the effects on national industries when any considerable revolutionary body passes into power, when capital begins to feel itself unprotected and insecure, and when confidence and credit decline. Men cease to undertake great enterprises which can only slowly mature. They contract those in which they are engaged. They diminish their risks. They divide and scatter their investments, and place large portions in other lands. Hitherto every wave of continental trouble has brought large sums of money to England, under the belief that it was the country where property is the most secure. If men whose avowed object is to use their political power for the purpose of confiscating property increase in influence, the stream will flow in the opposite direction. If the belief once grows and strengthens that England has ceased to be a safe country for investment and enterprise, employment in all its branches will speedily wither. Unemployed capital means unemployed labour, and the migration of capital is soon followed by the displacement of industry. In modern times political causes may easily change the course of wealth and industry; and this is especially true of a country which lives not by agriculture, but by manufactures and commerce, and which possesses no natural resources sufficient to support its population.

The increase of taxation has similar effects. No delusion can be greater and more dangerous than to suppose that it is possible to throw great burdens of taxation on the rich without injuring the poor. In a thousand ways employment will be contracted, and the capital from which it is paid will be diminished, or will seek lands where it is less heavily burdened. There are comparatively few homes in London into which the recent increases of rates and taxes have not introduced an increased spirit of economy. Servants are dismissed; charities are cut down; luxuries which give a livelihood to numbers of poor people are given up. The small struggling shop is abandoned for the cheaper store. Contracts are more rigidly enforced. Every article of expense is closely scrutinised, and final remedy is probably found in a period of economy in some cheaper country or some distant watering-place. Every small London shopkeeper knows but too well that the augmenting pressure of taxation is diminishing his custom, as well as absorbing a larger proportion of his profits; that both by its direct and indirect action it is constantly increasing the cost of living; and that it is forcing numbers into the ranks of pauperism who had hitherto maintained an honourable, though struggling, independence. It is perhaps less evident, but not less true, that the great industries, on which so large a proportion of London workmen subsist, are made by the same cause less productive, and therefore less capable of giving employment.

The tendency to place important industries more and more in the hands of municipalities is very evident, and it is not one wholly to be condemned. As I have already said, the municipal government of our provincial towns is one of the most remarkable of English successes, and in several cases great industries which are essential to the town, such as the supply of water or gas, have been taken over by the municipalities, and managed with honesty, efficiency, and economy. At the same time it must be acknowledged that the low franchise which now prevails is too modern to justify us in speaking with much confidence of its results; and certainly, if the principles and methods of the Socialist party were to prevail in English town government, the evils which have been so abundantly displayed in the United States would not be permanently averted. Municipalities are becoming enormous employers of labour. The labourers are at once their servants and their masters, having the power of coercing their employers by their votes; and a strong party is encouraging their very natural temptation to use this power with the object of obtaining higher wages.

In London the number of labourers employed by the Metropolitan Board of Works is said to have been already multiplied fourfold by the County Council, and every effort is made to extend the sphere of municipal employment. Chiefly through the influence of the Socialist members of the County Council, that body, under the plausible pretext of setting an example to other employers, has fixed a minimum rate of wages, irrespective of the value of the work performed, independent of the market rate for similar work, and considerably higher than that for which equally efficient labour could be easily procured. It has thus, in a slightly different form, brought back the system of 'make-wages,' or 'rate in aid of wages,' which had long been regarded by economists as one of the worst abuses of the earlier years of the century. That system also endeavoured to establish a certain standard of comfort, beneath which wages should not fall, and it did so by granting to the poorer labourers an allowance from the rates in addition to the wages they received from their employer.[30] In the present case the whole wage comes from the rates; but

---

[30] There is an instructive account of the working of this system in a pamphlet, by Mr. Montague, on *The Old Poor Law and the New Socialism*, published by the Cobden Club.

it is fixed above its market, or natural value, and the excess is a gift made by the ratepayer to the labourer.

In this way the London County Council has completely abandoned the old notion that a representative body is a trustee for all classes, and that one of its first duties is to obtain the best market value for the money with which it is entrusted. One of the ablest of its members[31] observes that it 'has adopted a policy that would involve a private firm in bankruptcy,' and it only escapes this evil because the purse of the ratepayers is behind it.

Whether a step which must at once injure independent industries and increase the inducement to country workmen to flock to London can be really beneficial to the working classes is surely very doubtful, but it is not doubtful that it opens the door to vast possibilities of corruption. The danger has been greatly aggravated by two other steps which have been taken by the same body. They have made the trade unions arbiters of the wages they give, by resolving that no contractor shall be employed by the municipality who does not sign a declaration declaring that he pays the wages 'recognised, and in practice obtained, by the trade unions in the place or places where the contract is executed.' One of the results of this step has been that contractors have largely increased the sum they demand for executing municipality work. In one case, out of a total of 54,353*l.* in an accepted tender, no less than 5,750*l.* was increased charge due to the rule of the Council that the tendering company must bind itself 'to adopt the rates of wages and hours of labour as fixed by the various trade unions concerned.' Soon after the County Council, moved partly by the increased cost of the contract system which was due to their own rule, and partly also by the desire to realise the Socialist idea of municipal workshops, undertook as far as possible to abolish contractors, and carry out their public works without their intervention. It thus entered into the most direct

---

[31] Evidence of Sir T. Farrer before the Labour Commission.

business relations with great masses of labourers on whose votes its members largely depended for their seats.[32]

The dangers that may spring from such a policy seem to me very obvious. Where democracy reigns, few things are more to be feared than a great increase in the number of those who are in the direct employment of the State and the municipality. If a dominant proportion of the voters in each constituency are in the pay of one or other of those bodies, it is idle to suppose that the relations between the representative and his electors can long be kept distinct from the relations between the employer and the employed. The temptation of the representatives to use public money and public works as a means of electioneering, and the temptation of the electors to use their political power as a means of obtaining trade advantages for themselves, will soon become irresistible, and the floodgates of corruption will be opened. A candidate for election is never likely to appear before an audience of working-class electors advocating either a reduction of wages or a restriction of work. Public works are, in this respect, far more dangerous under a democratic Government than under a despotism. There is a remarkable contrast between the works carried out at public expense in India and in France. In both cases they have largely added to the national debt, and some persons believe that, in India as well as in France, they have been carried to excess. But no one doubts that, under the despotic system in India, public works have been undertaken according to the best Government intelligence, and with the sole view of benefiting the country. No one also doubts that, under the democratic system of France, they have been in a great degree electioneering devices, intended to conciliate a class or a district and to induce them to support the Government. And because this has been the object, an immense proportion of them have proved unremunerative to the State.

---

[32] See on this subject an excellent memorandum, drawn up by Lord Farrer (then Sir T. H. Farrer), on the London County Council's Wages Bill in 1892, and also his later evidence before the Labour Commission.

Many dangerous experiments of this kind are likely to be made in England, and it is probable that there will be many attempts to withdraw great industries or forms of production from private hands, and to place them in the hands of the State—or, in other words, under the management of Government functionaries. The belief in the competence of the State to undertake all kinds of tasks and to deal with all kinds of questions is one of the most curious characteristics of much contemporary political thought. It is difficult to discover on what ground, either of experience or of reasoning, it is based.

One other remark on this subject may not be useless. Experience has shown that Government organisation may be applied, with some success, to such industrial undertakings as can be managed on the system of strict routine, and by rigid and inflexible rules. The State administers very efficiently, on such a system, the Post Office and Telegraph services, and in some countries it undertakes the management of the means of public transport, or the supply of a few great articles of public necessity, such as gas and water. But in all those departments of industry which are not susceptible of this kind of management it is certain to fail. It is, for example, utterly unfit to undertake on a large scale the duties of a landowner. The extreme variety and fluctuation of conditions and circumstances among agricultural tenants; the great place which exceptions and allowances, and special treatments and indulgences, must play in the wise management of land, are quite incompatible with those hard and fast lines of administration which the State can never abandon without the most imminent danger of jobbery and favouritism. Equally hopeless would be the attempt to convert the State into a gigantic shopkeeper, or storekeeper, or manufacturer, providing for the vast and ever-changing variety of human wants and tastes. All the qualities that are needed for success in these fields are qualities that are found in exceptional individuals, acting under the impulse of strong personal interest, but never in the disciplined action of a great public service. The tact and foresight which anticipate changes in the course and conditions of commerce or fashion; the promptitude which seizes the happy moment for contracting or expanding supply, meeting half-disclosed wants, and giving to enterprise new direction and impulses; the rare combination of daring, caution, and insight by which alone these great forms of industry can succeed, will never be found in routine-ridden Government officials.

There is not, I think, any real danger that the vast predatory schemes of George and Marx will ever be carried into effect in England, or indeed in any other great civilised country; though it is probable that the disciples of these men may, in some degree and in more than one direction, modify the action both of the State and of local bodies. The mere presence also in the political world of a group of men openly advocating the confiscation of all interest on public debts, of all rent on land, of all mining royalties, is a portent of some significance. It is a deep-seated conviction of English political life that, where dangerous and subversive opinions exist, it is desirable that they should be brought into light, fully discussed, and adequately represented. Opinions, it is said, are never so dangerous, and their power is never so exaggerated, as when their free expression is suppressed. Discussion brings out any element of truth that underlies them; fanaticisms wither in the atmosphere of free criticism; and contact with the reality of things, and with the various forms of national thought, seldom fails either to convert or moderate the revolutionist, or to reduce him to insignificance, or to lead to some compromise which allays friction and diminishes the area of discontent. In hardly any country in Europe have extreme or revolutionary opinions been so freely propagated as in England. In hardly any country in Europe have they so little power. At the worst, it is said, they only produce strong reactions, unduly frightening moderate men, and delaying for a time inevitable reforms.

There is great truth in this political philosophy, which for several generations has been that of the more sagacious English politicians. There is, however, another side to the question, which in England, I think, is apt to be underrated. Legal toleration is one thing, social and political toleration is another; and, as Burke long since observed, the widest latitude of legal toleration is only harmless where there is a strong restraining moral opinion in the nation. There can be little doubt that this restraint has diminished in England. There has grown up in our day an extreme laxity of opinion in judging men who are advocating courses which are palpably criminal, provided they have not themselves a direct money interest in the issue. It is true that this pretended disinterestedness is often, perhaps usually, a fraud. Money by no means supplies the only selfish motive by which men can be actuated. A desire to enter Parliament; to win votes, or popularity, or power; to obtain the kind of notoriety which the profession of extreme and startling opinions often gives to very commonplace men; the vanity, the discontent, the incapacity for serious and continuous work, the bitter class hatred growing out of a diseased, envious, acidulated nature—all these things lie at the root of much anarchical and socialistic speculation. But, apart from these considerations, it is an evil sign for a nation when those who are preaching open dishonesty are treated by great sections of society as honest men, deserving of no more moral reprobation than if they held extreme or eccentric opinions about vaccination or vivisection, about the nature of the sacraments or the organisation of the Church. It is no real dishonour to a nation that it produces among its teeming millions teachers of dishonesty. It is a far graver thing when such teachers can command the votes of thousands of their fellow-citizens, can rise to positions of power and influence in the State, can move uncensured, or even applauded, through large circles of society. The sense of right and wrong in the sphere of politics is thus gradually dimmed. Success justifies, to most men, the methods and the principles that lead to it. A new standard of judgment and honour is insensibly formed, and the public opinion of the nation too easily accommodates itself to a lower moral level.

I have noticed in the last chapter that English and American

Socialism differs from that of the Continent in the fact that it
is not usually associated either with aggressive atheism or with
attacks on the relation of the sexes. There are, it is true, some
exceptions. Thus Mr. Bax, who is prominent among English
Socialist writers, describes Socialism as an 'atheistic human-
ism,' which 'utterly despises the "other world," with all its
stage properties—that is, the present objects of religion;' and
he tells us that the existing theology 'is so closely entwined
with the current mode of production that the two things must
stand or fall together.'[33] There are also clear signs that a section
of the party contemplate, and desire, great revolutions in the
sphere of family life. I have already quoted the subversive
views of Godwin and of Owen on the subject. The work of
Bebel 'On Woman,' advocating an extreme latitude of free
love, has been translated and published in an English Socialist
library. Mr. Hyndman assures us that the family, 'in the Ger-
man-Christian sense of marriage for life, and responsibility
of the parents for the children born in wedlock, is almost at
an end even now,' and he predicts 'a complete change in all
family relations,' which must issue 'in a widely extended communism.'[34] Mr. William Morris and Mr. Bax, in a joint work
on Socialism, contend that marriage should cease to be a permanent and binding contract, and should be a mere voluntary
association, dissoluble by either party at pleasure.[35] But it
would be unjust to English Socialists to attribute to them in
general such views. A large proportion of them treat questions
of religion and questions of marriage as entirely outside their
system; while another section, who call themselves Christian
Socialists, very earnestly deprecate all attacks upon religion
and upon the Christian conception of the family.

---

[33] Bax's *Religion of Socialism*, pp. 52, 81.

[34] Hyndman's *Historical Basis of Socialism*, p. 452.

[35] *Socialism in its Growth and Outcome*, pp. 299–300. Mr. Grant Allen also,
who has identified himself with extreme Socialism (see *Vox Clamantium*,
pp. 138–61), has in other writings shown himself little less revolutionary
in the domestic sphere.

The denationalising influence of Socialism probably goes deeper. Its very essence is to substitute a class division for the division of nationalities, and to unite the workmen of all countries for the overthrow of the owners of property. Nearly all the institutions that make the distinctive glory and greatness of a nation are bound up with the state of society it desires to overthrow, and the enthusiasm of patriotism is one of the most formidable obstacles to its progress.

Mr. Bax, with his usual uncompromising candour, has expressed the feelings of the genuine Socialist. 'The establishment of Socialism on any national or race basis is out of the question. The foreign policy of the great international Socialist party must be to break up these hideous race monopolies, called empires, beginning in each case at home. Hence anything that makes for the disruption and disintegration of the empire to which he belongs must be welcomed by the Socialist as an ally. It is his duty to urge on any movement tending in any way to dislocate the commercial relations of the world, knowing that every shock the modern complex commercial system suffers weakens it, and brings its destruction nearer.'[36]

Much, however, of the Socialism which we see around us is of a more superficial and less dangerous description. It has little genuineness, and is largely due to transient causes. Prolonged and widespread agricultural and commercial depression has increased the number of the unemployed. By introducing acute suffering and anxiety into many industrious homes, and a new uncertainty and fluctuation into many great industries, it has had the very natural effect of greatly widening the area of restlessness and discontent. Something, too, is due to mere fashion. Around the nucleus of genuine conviction that underlies every great movement there gathers loosely a vast accretion of half-formed, unsifted, unsubstantial assent. The half-educated, the excitable, the great multitude

---

[36] *Religion of Socialism*, p. 126.

who, without seriously formed convictions, desire to show that they are in the van of progress, naturally catch up and exaggerate the dominant enthusiasm and tendency of their time, and when the current changes they will change with it. It is curious to observe how rapidly this may happen. In the early years of the century nearly all the genuine religious enthusiasm of the country flowed in the Evangelical channel; in a few short years it was mainly flowing in the channel of Tractarianism or Rationalism. Fifty years ago nearly all political enthusiasm in England ran in the direction of Free Trade, and the restriction in every form of Government interference. The dominant note in all countries is now a desire to enlarge the sphere of State action and control in nearly all departments of industrial life.

Such considerations are well fitted to prevent us from exaggerating the importance of the movement of the hour. At the same time it is extremely improbable that a tendency which is so widely spread will pass away like a vapour or a dream, and leave no serious legislation behind it. Nearly all working-class movements of late years have assumed something of a socialistic tinge. In the industrial, even more than in the purely political, sphere, many hazardous experiments, many dangerous conflicts, lie before us.

It would be very unjust, however, to classify the many efforts that are made to regulate by Government authority the different forms of industry with the confiscating and dishonest type of Socialism. No legislation of the nineteenth century has been, on the whole, more successful, and certainly none was more clearly called for by great abuses, than the factory legislation which began with the Act of 1802 for regulating the health and morals of apprentices, which was consolidated and codified by the Factory and Workshop Act of 1878, and which has received several important additions within the last few years. Even the history of the African slave trade hardly reveals more horrible abuses than may be found in the early days of the factory system in England, when machinery first introduced child labour on a large scale into industrial employment, when the domestic industries were suddenly broken up, and when multitudes of ignorant peasants were precipitated from their country homes into the great manufacturing towns. The laws dealing with these subjects are very numerous and very intricate, but a brief outline of their leading provisions will here be sufficient.

Their chief object was to protect three classes. The first were children. The factory laws carefully regulated the ages at which they might be introduced into the factories, and the amount and the continuity of work that might be exacted from them; they prohibited their night work, and at the same time provided for them an excellent system of education, running concurrently with their work. Provisions of this kind have met with an almost universal approval. They have been extended by many successive enactments to a great variety of industries, and they have been adopted, in their main lines, in all civilised countries.

The second class to be protected were 'young persons' between thirteen and eighteen—a class who were first made the subjects of distinct legislation in the Act of 1833. They were withdrawn from night work, and the hours of their labour in the many employments which were regulated by this Act were definitely fixed. In 1874, the age at which children were counted as 'young persons' was raised to fourteen, except in cases where a child of thirteen had passed a specified educational test.

On this class of subjects also there has been little serious controversy; but there has been grave difference of opinion, on grounds which will be mentioned in the following chapter, about the provisions limiting and interfering with the right of adult women to work as they please and make their own contracts with their employers. By the Factory Act of 1844 all women in factories or workshops were, for the first time, placed under the same regulations and disabilities as 'young persons.' An earlier Act had absolutely excluded them from underground employment in mines; and in 1891 their employment for four weeks after childbirth in the protected trades was forbidden. This last law is copied from continental precedents. Laws of the same kind, though with different time limits, now exist in Switzerland, Germany, Austria, Hungary, and the Netherlands.[37]

Concurrently with these provisions there are a vast number regulating with extreme minuteness the health conditions of factories and workshops. With the progress of sanitary science laws of this kind have immensely multiplied. An army of inspectors, armed with large powers, and acting sometimes under the central authority, and sometimes under local authorities, control all the details of protected industries. This control is not confined to unhealthy industries, or to industries in which children or young persons are employed. It extends to many which involve no special danger and are carried on by adult men, and there are, at the same time, minute directions about fencing dangerous machinery, and about the ways in which it may be employed. No woman or young person, for example, is permitted by law to clean any mill-gearing in motion, or to work between the fixed and traversing parts of a self-acting machine, though a man has full liberty to do so.[38] No one will question the general utility of sanitary regulations, and of regulations for the prevention of accidents, but many good judges doubt whether it is a wise thing for the State to regulate the industry of adult men in all its details, as if they were children, incapable of taking measures for their own protection, and requiring at every turn to be directed and inspected by authority of the law.

This policy, however, has been largely carried out, and in many different forms. Thus, for example, the truck laws prohibit any arrangements between employers and employed for the payment of wages in goods, or otherwise than in the current coin of the realm. An Act regulating agricultural gangs provides that no females may work in the same gang as men.

---

[37] A good summary of the provisions of the foreign factory acts will be found in an article of M. Emile Stocquart on 'Les restrictions à la liberté' (*Revue de Droit International*, tom. xxvii.).

[38] Cooke Taylor, *The Factory Laws*, p. 170.

An Act of 1883 makes it penal to pay wages in public-houses, lest the workmen should fall into the temptation of spending them in drink. Another Act, intended to protect seamen against fraudulent lodging-house keepers, makes it penal for any person on board a ship, and within twenty-four hours of its arrival, to solicit a seaman to become a lodger.[39] Sometimes the proposals of legislators are curiously infelicitous. Thus, a few years ago, the Sweating Committee was struck by the weight of the hammers used by women in a certain branch of the iron manufacture, and proposed an Act of Parliament for diminishing their size. The project, however, was abandoned in consequence of a deputation of sturdy workwomen to the Home Secretary. They represented to him that the immediate consequences of the proposed Act would be to deprive them of their means of livelihood, by throwing this branch of industry into the hands of men, and they proved very conclusively that, by constant practice, they could wield the customary hammer without the slightest difficulty, while the use of smaller hammers would require a considerably greater muscular effort, as the work could only be accomplished by a much larger number of blows.

The next great restriction involved in the Factory Acts is that of the hours of adult male labourers. For a long period it was universally held that adult men were capable of making their own bargains, and that a restriction of their hours of work was utterly beyond the legitimate province of the law. The Tudor Acts arranging the period of working hours have been often quoted in this connection, but, as Mr. Jevons observes, they were not intended to limit, but to lengthen, work. They established a minimum, but not a maximum, providing that 'the legal day's work was to be twelve hours at the least.'

It is very obvious, however, that in numerous trades habitual work is far too prolonged for the physical wellbeing of the workman, and that it practically reduces his life to a life of continued slavery. Nothing can contribute more to raise the

---

[39] 17 & 18 Vict. cap. 104, sect. 238.

mental, moral, and physical condition of the working classes, to strengthen their domestic happiness, and to lighten lives that are at best toilsome and difficult, than a wise limitation of the hours of work, and no part of modern industrial reforms has been more really beneficial. There are several considerations which have of late years considerably added to its necessity. The Sunday holiday had fallen in a great measure into abeyance in Catholic countries, though its importance is now more generally felt, not so much on religious as on economical grounds. The Church holidays, though often multiplied to excess, secured to past generations frequent intermissions of labour; but they, too, are now little observed. On the other hand, facilities of communication have immensely added to the severity of competition; and the unintermitted action of machinery, though it greatly diminishes physical toil, brings into many forms of labour a vastly increased mental strain through the constant watchfulness and attention it requires.

Another consideration, which is of great importance in judging this question, is the demonstrated fact that the most prolonged work is not the most productive. The greatly increased amount and accuracy of statistical information which has been acquired in the present generation has established this fact beyond dispute. Work which exceeds the healthy physical powers of the average labourer is always inefficient. In employments that require hard and steady work, it may be safely assumed that a work-day of twelve hours will produce less than a work-day of ten hours. It is, of course, obvious that the diminution of the length of labour cannot be carried on indefinitely without leading to a diminution of production. Ten hours will produce more than twelve hours, but it is not certain that eight will produce as much as ten, and it is quite certain that six, or four, or two, will not produce as much as eight. It is also true that shorter hours usually mean a diminished employment of machines, which know no fatigue;[40] but,

---

[40] There are, however, cases in which expensive machinery can be worked with greatly increased profit by the system of 'double shifts,' or relays of labourers working in succession. Sixteen hours' work of such machinery,

on the whole, a widespread and various experience clearly shows that those men will work the best who work well within the limit of their physical capacities, and in this fact we have a groundwork on which we may safely build.

A similar process of reasoning applies to the rate of wages. High wages do not necessarily mean dear labour, or low wages cheap labour. It is bad economy to underfeed the horse that labours in the field, and human labour only attains its full efficiency when the labourer is enabled by good wages to keep his strength at the highest point. A comparison has been made of wages and work in many different countries, and it supplies ample and striking evidence that the efficiency of work usually rises and falls with the rate of wages, underpaid labour producing little, well-paid labour producing much. In most fields of labour there is no labour more remunerative to the employer than that of the Englishman and American, who are usually the most highly paid. One of the best living authorities goes so far as to conclude that, in spite of all the difference of wages, the real price of labour is everywhere much the same; that, on the whole, for the same sum of money, much the same amount of work may be everywhere procured.[41]

Taking these principles as a guide, a great deal has been done within the last half-century to diminish the hours of labour in different industries; but it has been done, for the most part, by voluntary agreement, and not by the action of the law. Indirectly, however, the Acts limiting the work of young persons and women in textile factories to 56½ hours a week, and in a great variety of other industries to 60 hours

carried on by two bodies of workmen, each of them working eight hours, would produce much more than could be produced by a continuous employment of the same men for ten hours. It is found, however, in England that there have been great practical difficulties in establishing this system, and it does not seem to be popular with the workmen. See on this subject Marshall's *Principles of Economics*, i. 741–42.

[41] This subject is treated with great ability, and with ample illustrations, by Lord Brassey in his *Work and Wages;* see especially p. 75 (3rd ed.).

a week, have influenced adult male labour, for it has been found necessary, or advisable, to stop the work of the factory at the time when a great proportion of the workers were obliged to desist. In addition also to Sunday the law has secured some periods of intermission. The Saturday half-holiday, which has spread so widely through all departments of English industry, was first incorporated in the Factory Acts in 1825, and several other holidays and half-holidays have since then been established.[42]

As we have already seen, the demand for a legal limitation of all adult labour has of late years grown and strengthened in many countries, and the form which it has assumed had been a general demand for an eight hours day. In some Socialist programmes it is decreed that overtime should be strictly forbidden, and even the eight hours day is treated as merely an instalment, to be followed at a later period by much greater reduction. In many industries the eight hours limitation has already been effected by voluntary agreements between masters and men; and there can be little doubt that, wherever it is economically harmless, wherever it can be effected without diminishing produce and profit, the same course will be taken.

The interference of the law, however, is a matter of very dubious policy; and the extension of the same legal limitations to all industries would produce numerous evils, injustices, and anomalies. There are forms of work—such as domestic service, or the work of a sailor, or the work of an agricultural labourer during harvest-time—in which the eight hours system would be manifestly impossible, and it would be absurd to apply the same time limit to industries that are utterly dissimilar. Eight hours in a crowded London store is much harder work than twelve hours in a quiet village shop; and there can be no real comparison between the labour of a porter

---

[42] Cooke Taylor, pp. 62, 168. M. Stocquart observes that one of the old Flemish customs (prescribed by law) prohibited most forms of work, not only on Sundays and other religious festivals but also on Saturday afternoons and on the eve of festivals (*Revue de Droit International*, xxvii. 148).

at a country station, or of a servant in a well-to-do household, and the incessant strain of factory labour. One of the most remarkable instances of the curtailment of work hours without the assistance of the law is the early closing and the half-holiday in the great shops, and some persons would extend this system by force of law to the small shops, which are usually open the longest. Hitherto the law has done nothing in this field except providing, by Acts of 1886 and 1892, that persons under eighteen years must not be employed more than seventy-four hours a week, including mealtime.[43] That the hours of the small shops are often far longer than is desirable is incontestable. To the richer classes their curtailment would be a matter of indifference; but it is specially for the convenience of the working classes that a great proportion of these small and poor shops are kept open into the night, and it is solely by these long hours that they are able to hold their own against the crushing competition of the great shops.[44] It would surely be an act of tyranny to prevent a poor man from serving his customers in his own shop as long as he pleased; but it would be very difficult to distinguish by law between the shop where the master served alone, and that in which he served with two or three assistants, leaving the one open, while the other was forcibly closed.

In trades where work is intermittent, and where long periods of depression are followed by brief periods of inflation,

---

[43] Jevons, p. 87.

[44] The same distinction appeared when the question was raised of bringing laundries under the Factory laws. 'The movement was viewed favourably by the larger employers, who could afford to keep a double staff, but was objected to by the smaller ones, who were afraid that they would lose their trade if they were obliged to observe the limited and regular periods of employment ordained by the Acts' (Spyer, *The Labour Question*, p. 118). Mr. Spyer sums up the views of those who advocated before the Labour Commission more stringent shop regulations, and concludes: 'They were, for the most part, viewed not unfavourably by the larger employers; but the smaller shopkeepers complained that, if they were obliged to close early, they would lose the patronage of the working men, for whom they chiefly catered' (p. 125).

the time limit is especially harsh. Take, for example, the common case of a strong girl who is engaged in millinery. For perhaps nine months of the year her life is one of constant struggle, anxiety, and disappointment, owing to the slackness of her work. At last the season comes, bringing with it an abundant harvest of work, which, if she were allowed to reap it, would enable her in a few weeks to pay off the little debts which weigh so heavily upon her, and to save enough to relieve her from all anxiety in the ensuing year. She desires passionately to avail herself of her opportunity. She knows that a few weeks of toil prolonged far into the night will be well within her strength, and not more really injurious to her than the long succession of nights that are spent in the ballroom by the London beauty whom she dresses. But the law interposes, forbids her to work beyond the stated hours, dashes the cup from her thirsty lips, and reduces her to the same old round of poverty and debt. What oppression of the poor can be more real or more galling than this? What consolation can it be to the poor girl who is thus deprived of the liberty which is most vital to her happiness, to be told that she lives in a free country, where men speak and write and vote as they please?

There are other and still larger aspects of the question to be considered. In the keen competition of modern industrial life, knowledge, machinery and opportunities are all greatly equalised, and some of the most important trades are only kept in England with extreme difficulty and by a narrow margin. This is especially the case in the textile manufactures, which support such a vast proportion of our working classes. International competition in this manufacture is now so close that any change which seriously diminishes profit will inevitably lead to a migration of the capital. Any change that, by considerably increasing the cost of production, raises prices, and thus enables other countries to undersell England, must give a death-blow to the industry. In the French factories the workmen are said to work sixty-six hours a week. In England it is proposed that they should be forbidden by law to work more than forty-eight, and it is contended that wages would be undiminished, and even increased, by the change.[45] Is it quite certain that, under these conditions, the ascendency of the English cotton manufacture would long survive?

But French competition is far from being the most formidable. The growth of the cotton manufacture in India, which is one of the most significant facts in modern industrial history, is not likely to be isolated. Japan has swiftly followed in the steps of India, and it already possesses a large, flourishing, and rapidly growing cotton manufacture. In the great awakening which is taking place in the East the same manufacture is likely to spread through other countries, where the manufacturer may have his cotton growing at his door, where the cost of living and the price of labour are a mere fraction of what they are in Europe, where labour is so abundant that machinery might easily be worked during the whole, or nearly the whole, of the twenty-four hours by relays of fresh labourers. If such a system can be made profitable, it is not probable that mere difficulties of organisation and displacement will permanently prevent it. It is far from improbable that, in no very distant future, some of the chief centres of the cotton manufacture may be in these regions; and if the legislative tendencies that now prevail in England increase, it is also probable that the machinery that works them may be largely provided by English capital. The capitalist, discouraged and restricted at home, will find his profit—but what would be the fate of the English workman?

Coal, unlike cotton, is a great English product, and there are some who contend that, as it cannot be driven from the country, it should be the object of the colliers to raise its price. The great strikes in the coal trade that have taken place within the last few years enable us to realise clearly what would be the effects. To the rich man who only consumes coal in his own houses it would be of little consequence. The present wasteful

---

[45] See the evidence of Mr. T. Mann, Mr. Hyndman, and Mr. S. Webb before the Labour Commission.

methods of consumption furnish an ample margin for economy, and, after all, the cost of coal will form but a small item in his budget. To men of moderate income it would be a cause of great inconvenience, sometimes making all the difference between comfort and straitened means. But to the poor it would be a calamity of the first magnitude. In a climate like ours warmth is only second in importance to food, and a change of price that placed it beyond the means of the poor would produce an amount of suffering and illness that it would be difficult to exaggerate. But this is only one part of the question. There is a considerable export trade of coal from England, which may easily be arrested or diminished; and there are also a crowd of important home industries which depend vitally for their profit on cheap coal. Every considerable rise of prices extinguishes furnaces, throws multitudes out of employment, and endangers still further great industries on which tens of thousands depend, and which are already shrinking and tottering before foreign competition.

All this is very elementary, but it is apt to be forgotten or deliberately concealed. It is obvious that, if an English industry be so handicapped by restrictions that it is unable to compete with a foreign industry of the same kind, it must lose its ascendency abroad, and can only in the long run retain its ascendency at home by the help of stringent protective legislation. This fact does not, as I have shown, lead to the necessity of low wages and excessive hours, but it does add immensely to the dangers of the hard and fast lines of legislative restriction.

In nearly all the reforms of industry which seem most desirable we find a painful conflict of poor men's interests. The hardships that may be found in domestic service are certainly not to be found in the houses of the rich, but in the poor and struggling homes, where one overworked servant is all that can be kept. The horrible grinding of the poor that takes place under the name of sweating is not for the benefit of the rich. They buy their clothes or shirts at a price which should amply allow for the proper payment of labour. It is in the struggle to provide clothes of extreme cheapness for the very poor that these evils chiefly arise. The building trade is one of those into which international competition can enter least, and it would therefore appear at first sight to be one of those in which artificial methods may be most easily and most safely employed to raise the price of labour. But, in the words of Mr. Jevons, 'nothing can be more injurious to the poorer classes than any artificial restrictions in the building trades tending to raise the cost of building, or to impede the introduction of improvements in bricklaying and the other building arts. The effect is peculiarly injurious because it places great obstacles in the way of any attempt to produce really good new dwellings for the working classes. There are always quantities of old houses and buildings, of various sorts, which can be let as lodgings at a rate below that at which it is possible to build good new ones. The result is either that very inferior cheap houses must be built, or the more expensive model dwellings fall practically to a better-paid class. The general effect is to make really wholesome houses a luxury for the wealthier classes, while the residuum have to herd together between whatever walls they can find.'[46] It is already observed by those who are connected with societies for building artisans' houses, that the enhanced cost of building is making it necessary to choose between meaner cottages and higher rents.[47]

---

[46] Jevons, *The State in relation to Labour*, pp. 107–8.

[47] The most important of these societies is the Artisans and Labourers' Dwellings Company, which has done a vast beneficent work, and been established on a thoroughly sound economical basis. The following passage from a speech of the chairman (Mr. Noel) at the annual meeting in 1895 seems to me very significant: 'I am bound to point out a third consideration connected with the estates, which is important, namely, that we shall never be able to build so economically in the future as we have built in the past. This naturally arises, in the first place, not from the increase in the price of material—for this has diminished, and we can build more economically, in some respects, as regards such things as iron and wood—but our great bill, which is the wages bill, is larger, and must be larger, owing to the rise in wages. There is also not only the rise in wages, but there are shorter hours of labour. Both these things must produce more costly buildings; but I should rejoice personally in both of

Considerations of this kind are well fitted to preach caution to the legislator, whose efforts to benefit the poor may often be the means of seriously injuring them. One truth should never be forgotten: it is, that no change which renders labour less productive and efficient can permanently benefit the working classes. Short hours in industry are frequently advocated, not only on the sound and proper ground that they are a blessing to the workman, and give him the means of larger instruction and increased happiness in life, but also on the very different ground that, by making it necessary to employ more workmen to produce a given result, they will diminish competition, and give work to the unemployed. This doctrine has of late years obtained a great prominence in trade-union politics, and has evidently taken deep root in the English working-class mind. There can, I think, be little doubt that a grave economical fallacy underlies it. If the shorter hours produce as much as the longer ones, the change will be a great benefit to the actual workman, but it will create no additional demand, and will do nothing for the unemployed. If the produce is diminished, either wages will be reduced so that the same wage fund may be distributed among a larger

---

these, even if we had to find our buildings more costly. I could hardly but rejoice, seeing that the money was thus spent; but I must add another fact, which is, to my mind, not at all satisfactory, and that is an apparently marked desire on the part of the labour leaders, supposing it to be on the principle of doing good to their fellow-workmen, that the men should do less work and less efficient work during the hours of labour. This, gentlemen, seems to me a most suicidal policy. Not only does the rise of wages and the shorter hours of labour increase the expense of building, but it must also increase the rents that the working classes pay for their houses, for, as you know, we work on a very small margin of profit. There will be a perpetually increased rent for workmen's houses owing to this unfortunate action on the part of some of the labour leaders. But there is something more than that. It will tend, I believe, to diminish the capital employed in building—I believe it has already done so—and therefore will certainly cause an ever-increasing number in the building trades to join the ranks of the unemployed' (*Report of the General Meeting,* 1895).

number, or prices will rise, or profits will fall. Against the first
consequence the labouring classes emphatically protest, but
in a large number of cases it would be the inevitable result.
On the other hand, increased prices mean decreased consumption, and smaller profits mean a contraction or a migration of industry; and in all these cases the ultimate result will
be to diminish instead of increase the number of the unemployed. In the long run all who are engaged upon an industry
must be supported out of its profits, and if an industry is
declining, the wellbeing of those who are employed in it cannot permanently be maintained. Law or combination may
compel the capitalist to shorten hours or increase wages, but
they cannot compel him to pursue an industry which has
ceased to be profitable; nor can they compel the consumer to
purchase. Protective laws may, no doubt, exclude foreign articles, but an immense proportion of the purchasers of English goods are foreigners, who are attracted to them mainly
by their cheapness.[48]

It is worthy of notice also that in some important respects
trade-union policy has a tendency to multiply rather than
diminish the number of the unemployed. One of its chief
objects is to maintain the highest rate of wages an industry
can bear, and to make this rate uniform through the trade or
district. The consequence is that the employer is necessarily
driven to employ exclusively the most efficient labour. One
of the saddest features of modern industrial life is the growing
difficulty of the old, the sickly, and the feeble to obtain a
living. It is observed that, since the maximum trade-union
wages have been stringently enforced, men come to the workhouse earlier than before.[49] Formerly, when their powers declined, they could usually find work at reduced wages. Now

---

[48] The effect of a legal eight hours on different kinds of industry is treated,
with much fulness and skill, by Mr. Graham in his *Socialism New and Old*,
pp. 362–76.

[49] The reader will find some remarks on this subject, by Mr. Mackay, in
A Policy of Free Exchange, p. 226. See, too, Marshall's *Principles of Economics*, i. 733.

such wages are prohibited by trade-union rules, and as they cannot be profitably employed at the trade-union wages, they sink rapidly to pauperism. By this process multitudes who are still able to work, but not at the highest average of efficiency, swell the ranks of the unemployed. Not unfrequently an employer, through a feeling of benevolence, keeps on the old worker at a loss to himself; but if a strike is ordered by the union, this worker is obliged to quit his work with the rest, and he very seldom regains his position. Such facts make the problem of dealing with old age especially serious. It is difficult to find any sufficient remedy, except by the large extension of piecework—the form of labour which is the most just, as it proportions the reward of each man rigidly to his production. But piecework can be less easily controlled and managed by trade unions than day labour, and, accordingly, in the New Unionism it is generally opposed. Wherever labour is very highly organised, the tendency is towards industries carried on by the smallest possible number of workmen at the highest possible rate of wages.

There is also a marked tendency, especially among the New Unionists, to establish monopolies, excluding, often by gross violence and tyranny, non-unionists from the trades they can influence, and sometimes even closing their own ranks against new recruits. In a large number of trade unions there are strict rules, much like those of the mediæval guilds, limiting the number of apprentices who may be taught a trade, and maintaining by trade-union action the restrictions on skilled employment which were once enforced by law.[50] One of the most significant strikes of late years has been that which took place in 1890 in the great pottery works of Sir Henry Doulton. There was no question of wages or hours, but the sole point in dispute was the right of the manufacturer to teach new hands the more difficult branches of the work. 'Throwing' on the potter's wheel is an art which requires much skill, and can rarely be attained to perfection except by those who begin it

---

[50] Many particulars about these restrictions will be found in Howell's *Conflicts of Labour* (2nd ed.), pp. 216–50.

early in life. Sir Henry Doulton states that it was only by the careful training and selection of youths in this branch that his works had attained their world-wide fame. When several vacancies had occurred near the close of 1890, he selected three lads, the sons of journeymen employed by the firm, and put them in training; but he was surprised to receive a peremptory demand from the trade union that there should in future be only one apprentice to seven journeymen. Sir Henry Doulton replied that such a rule had never existed in the past; that if it had existed, past progress would have been impossible, and a large proportion of his present workmen could never have received their training; that the number of learners was at this time less than it had been in any period during the last fourteen years; and that it was absolutely essential to the maintenance of the trade that the number of the skilled labourers should be kept up. The only reply was a peremptory order from the trade union that the three boys should be at once dismissed, under pain of a general strike. The manufacturer refused to submit to this dictation, and a desperate strike in the pottery trade ensued, lasted for three months, and ended in the total defeat of the workmen.[51]

Another illustration of the same spirit was shown by the London Dockers' Union. This body aimed at nothing less than a monopoly of the whole riverside industry of London, and in 1890 it passed a resolution that no further members should be admitted without the special sanction of the district committee.[52] It is obvious that such a policy, which has of late years been shown in many quarters and in many forms, has a direct tendency to increase the number of the unemployed.

Some writers, in considering the possibility of a great reduction in the hours of labour, place much stress on international agreements preventing any one country from taking an unfair advantage of its neighbours. In many large departments of human affairs international agreements have proved

---

[51] Brooks's *Industry and Property*, i. 104–6.
[52] Spyer, *The Labour Question*, p. 2; Howell's *Trade Unionism New and Old*, p. 150.

very successful. Telegraphs, the rates of postage, extradition, and copyright have all been regulated in this way; the same system has been efficacious in suppressing the slave trade and introducing several mitigations into war; and a large and growing party are advocating international agreements for regulating the currency and maintaining a fixed ratio between the precious metals.

The prospect, however, of such agreements for regulating the hours of work seems to me exceedingly remote. Nations differ so vastly in their industrial circumstances, in the price of food, in their standard of living, and in their commercial and industrial legislation, that agreements of this kind would meet with almost insuperable difficulties. Free trade has not triumphed, and does not appear likely to triumph, in Europe. If all customs barriers were struck down, the more important forms of manufacture would be concentrated in comparatively few centres, where large capital and a gigantic production and sale would reduce prices to a lower level than could be made profitable in a small manufacturing State. It is the object, however, of each nation by protective legislation to preserve its own industries. There are cases, like those of the carpet manufactures of the Netherlands, where the industry of a small and comparatively poor country is able to hold its own, and in some degree to flourish, in spite of the gigantic manufactures of the greater nations, but it will usually be found that it can only do so by longer hours and lower wages. In most of the countries of Europe, legislation about the hours of adult labour either does not exist, or is drawn in terms that would certainly not be regarded by English workmen as an improvement on their lot. In France the law of 1848, establishing a twelve hours working-day, remains, but it has been interpreted to exclude the time of meals. It is largely evaded where it is nominally in force, and several of the most important industries have, by subsequent measures, been withdrawn from its operation. As a rule, the French labourer is present in the factory for at least fourteen hours out of the twenty-four. In Germany, Russia, Turkey, Spain and Portu-

gal, Sweden and Denmark, and in most of the smaller countries in Europe, there are no laws restricting the hours of adult
work. In Austria mining work is limited to ten hours, actual
working-time, and factory work to eleven hours, exclusive of
meal-time, and there are some special regulations about female labour, which are said to be not generally enforced. In
Belgium and the Netherlands limitations of adult labour are
confined to the case of women. Switzerland, however, has
legislated more stringently on the subject, reducing the working-day to eleven hours on ordinary days and ten hours on
Saturdays and public holidays, and regulating with much
strictness the conditions of female labour.[53]

In most countries it is found that the workers are very ready
to connive at evasions of laws restricting their labour: a large
proportion of adult women resent bitterly laws which injure
them in the competition with men, and deprive them of some
portion of their scanty earnings. Among adult men also there
is a great deal of opposition to limitation of working-hours,
and the legal eight hours is probably intended quite as much
to coerce the workmen as to coerce their employers. The strong
desire of workmen to work longer than the prescribed hours,
if they can by doing so increase their wages, and the impossibility the trade unions find in preventing them, are among
the chief reasons why these bodies advocate a compulsory
eight hours bill. One of the most significant pieces of evidence
laid before the Labour Commission was the case of the En-
ginemen and Firemen's Union, in favour of a legal limitation
of the hours of adult work. 'It would be impossible,' they said,
'to reduce the hours permanently except by Act of Parliament,
since in bad times employers must either reduce wages or
lengthen hours in order to make a profit, and the men always

---

[53] See on this subject the *Reports from Her Majesty's Representatives on the
Hours of Adult Labour in the Countries in which they reside,* published by
Parliament in 1889. It is possible that since these Reports there may have
been some fresh legislation. See, too, Béchaux, *Revendications Ouvrières
en France,* pp. 45–46.

prefer the latter alternative if left to their own devices, thereby increasing the number of unemployed members on the funds of the union.'[54] 'There is really no disguising the fact,' says another good authority, 'that overtime is worked willingly by large bodies of men as a means of increasing their earnings. It is even known as a fact in some trades that men will leave situations in which they can only work their nine hours per day, to go to places in which they can increase their time and earnings by night work.'[55]

It is certain, indeed, that a large proportion of those who desire a fixed eight hours day do not do so for the purpose of diminishing the amount of their work. Their calculation is that, by systematically working overtime at a higher rate, they will add something to their earnings.[56] If this is true of England, we may be sure that it is equally true of other countries, and that a legal eight hours day could only be established by coercing a large number of workmen. If we cross the Atlantic, we find it enacted in some American States, including New York, Connecticut, and California, but it appears to be much evaded, and there is great latitude of altering the hours by agreement and working overtime. In the Australian colonies the legal eight hours generally prevails; but in Australia, in addition to the protective system, the sparseness of the population and the great distance from Europe establish industrial conditions wholly unlike our own.

This survey gives little reason to believe in a general reduction of hours by law, though it is probable that the excessive hours which prevail in many continental countries will be gradually reduced, that the Sunday rest will be more generally secured, and that the Saturday half-holiday will be more frequently adopted.

The idea of an international regulation of labour has of late years spread widely. It has been proposed in several working

---

[54] Spyer's *Labour Question*, p. 80.

[55] See the article on Trade Unions in *Subjects of the Day* (August 1890), 'Socialism,' pp. 119–20.

[56] Howell's *Conflicts of Labour*, pp. 282–84.

men's congresses, and in 1881, and again in 1889, the Swiss Federal Council invited the leading Powers of Europe to join in a conference on the subject. The invitation was not warmly received; but in 1890 the Emperor of Germany took up the subject, and at his invitation the representatives of fourteen States assembled at Berlin. They soon decided that they could do no more than submit some very platonic recommendations to the public, without attempting in any way to enforce their decisions, or even to bind the Governments they represented. They also agreed that it was impossible to come to any conclusion about the normal length of the working day, and this subject was, in consequence, formally excluded from their discussions. On nearly all points there were grave differences of opinion, and nearly all the decisions were only carried by majorities.

Resolutions were passed commending the general adoption of the Sunday rest; the establishment of an age, which the majority fixed at twelve years, before which children should not be admitted into factories; and some special regulations for the labour of children and young persons. The majority of delegates also desired that female labour should be specially regulated. Women, they maintained, should not be allowed to work at night, or in mines, or for more than eleven hours, or for four weeks after confinement. The conference recommended additional sanitary precautions, additional inspectors, additional institutions for encouraging thrift, periodical meetings of the representatives of the European Powers to consult about labour problems. Most of the measures recommended by the Berlin Conference had already been taken in England, and there has been some recent continental legislation in the same direction; but international and simultaneous consultation and legislation about labour seem to have found little favour with the sovereigns and statesmen of the world.[57]

---

[57] Béchaux, *Les Revendications Ouvrières en France*, pp. 66–77; see, too, Reports of Her Majesty's representatives abroad relative to the recommendations of the Berlin Conference (1891).

A few more remarks must be added to those which have been already made about the position and functions of trade unions. These bodies rose naturally when factory industry, carried on by great bodies of workmen, took the place of the domestic industries, which were carried on in independence and isolation in the cottages. No one will now deny their legitimacy, or defend the legislation which for so long a period condemned them. They perform many functions of the highest value, most of them, as we have seen, quite unconnected with any class antagonism. They are friendly societies, discharging efficiently a large number of most useful benevolent purposes. Under this head are included their sick funds, their burial allowances, their superannuation allowance, their funds for assisting their members when out of work or when travelling in search of work, and for rendering to them several minor and occasional services. They are the clubs of the working men. They are class parliaments, representing, organising, and furthering their class interests; and if a trade union is wisely and equitably conducted, it does much to raise the moral level of its members, by sustaining the sentiment of fraternity and association, and extending their range of sympathies and interests.

In dealing with the employers these organisations are also of great value. The workman, if isolated, is in two essential respects at a disadvantage in bargaining with the manufacturer. He has not the same knowledge of the conditions, and profits, and probable future of the trade, and has, therefore, insufficient means of testing the justice or injustice of the terms that are offered him. He has also the great disadvantage of being unable to wait for better times and more favourable terms. His daily work is necessary for his daily subsistence, while the manufacturer can for a time suspend production and forego profits, and fall back on the fortune he has already amassed. In both of these respects the trade union is of inestimable value. It is a great cooperative society for collecting all the available facts relating to its trade, and it has largely accumulated resources which enable the workmen to exist for a considerable period when on strike. It in this manner places the two parties to the bargain on a basis of substantial equality. Politically, too, labour, like other things, has its own special interests, and those interests are likely to be most attended to when labour is powerfully organised and intelligently represented.

On the whole there can be little doubt that the largest, wealthiest, and best-organised trade unions have done much to diminish labour conflicts. They remove these questions from the domain of passion and ignorance, and secure that no strike shall take place without knowledge and without deliberation. The employer, knowing the vast reserve of strength that lies behind a trade-union demand, is not tempted to take any undue advantage of transitory conditions, and is prepared to concede all that can be conceded without seriously or permanently affecting his industry. The trade union, on the other hand, acts only after a careful examination of the conditions of the trade, and under the direction of leaders who have secured the confidence of large numbers of workmen. It knows that the whole complex system of benefits for the class, which it has laboriously built up, depends upon its financial solvency, and may be shattered by imprudent policy; and the very magnitude which organised trade warfare assumes gives a strong sense of responsibility, and prepares the way for compromise and mutual concession. Industry also, it may be added, is now of a very international character, and it is chiefly by means of these great organisations that the labourers of one country are able to come into correspondence with those of another.

These advantages are very great; but it is a fallacy to attribute to trade-union organisation the chief part of that increase of wages which has taken place during the present century. This increase is due to much wider and larger economical causes, relating to the production and interchange of wealth. It has often been noticed, that it has been nowhere more conspicuous than in the case of domestic servants, and in the case of agricultural labourers, though in these cases trade-union or-

ganisation has been absolutely, or almost absolutely, unknown; and the unassisted action of supply and demand has
given great and permanent addition in many forms of mer-
cantile, professional, and government employment.[58] Lord
Brassey has collected conclusive evidence showing that some
of the most considerable and rapid rises of wages in our time
have taken place in foreign countries, without any trade-union
pressure.[59] But although it is impossible that trade-union combinations can permanently raise the general level of wages,
there are doubtful and balanced circumstances where a little
pressure can turn the scale on one side or the other, and a rise
of wages has often been accelerated, or a fall in wages in some
degree delayed, by trade-union action.

The doctrine that the price of labour in the long run and on
a large scale must necessarily be regulated by supply and
demand—the demand for labour in the labour market; the
demand for the things that it produces, and the amount of
capital that is applied to the production—is, in the eyes of
many contemporary writers, a hard doctrine, and much dec-
lamation has been expended on its immorality. Mr. Ruskin,
for example, expresses his regret that he can find no language
'contemptuous enough to attach to the beastly idiotism of the
modern theory that wages are to be measured by competition;'[60] and both within and without trade unions a school
has arisen which believes that wages can be placed on another
foundation. It maintains that the relation of the employer and
the employed should be an ethical relation: that the first duty
of the employer is to give his labourer a 'just wage,' repre-

---

[58] See on this subject Jevons, *The State in relation to Labour*, pp. 120–21.

[59] Brassey's *Work and Wages*.

[60] Ruskin's *Munera Pulveris*; see too, his *Unto this Last*, and the eloquent
chapters denouncing the modern industrial system in Mr. Lilly's *Shibbo-
leths*. Mr. Lilly has recurred to the same subject in several other thoughtful and striking essays. A very able, and at the same time candid and
temperate, criticism of what is called the orthodox school of English
political economy, will be found in a little book by Mr. William Dillon
(the biographer of John Mitchel) called *The Dismal Science* (Dublin, 1882).
It is a book which deserves to be far better known than it is.

senting a 'fair' proportion of the produce of his labour; 'a
living wage,' enabling him to live up to a given standard of
comfort; and that by such considerations the rate of wages
can be, and ought to be, determined.

To me, at least, these writers seem to confuse a desirable
end, which may be largely attained, with the means of attaining it. In a prosperous industry, and with an intelligent and
provident working class, the 'living wage' and the 'just wage'
will be easily reached, but they will be reached through the
improved conditions of the market, and not by any ethical
consideration. It is true, indeed, that modern economists have
shown that the influences acting upon the rate of wages are
both more numerous and more complex than their predecessors had supposed, and that causes which often seem very
remote have sometimes modified them. But these influences
play only a minor and subsidiary part. It is idle to suppose
that the great body of average men will ever consent to purchase an inferior article at a high price in one shop, when they
can purchase a superior article at a lower price in the adjoining
one, because the conditions of production are less favourable
to the labourer in the latter case than in the former. It is no less
idle to suppose that they will pay a high rate of wages for any
given service if a multitude of equally efficient labourers are
willing to perform it at a lower rate.

The phrase 'a living wage,' which has lately come into use,
is a very vague one. It was first, I believe, brought into prominence during a great miners' strike, and it was noticed that
the rate of payment which was then rejected as below 'a living
wage' was about double the agricultural wage over a great part
of the world. And, indeed, in the same trade the same wages
will be opulence to one man and penury to another. One workman is unmarried, and has no one but himself to support, or
he has a strong wife and child, who can fully bear their part
in maintaining the family. Another workman has to support
old and infirm parents, or a dying wife, or a young, numerous,
or sickly family. Can it be supposed that, in the vast competing
industries of the world, the wages of equally efficient labour-

ers can ever be varied according to such considerations? Old age and diminished strength need more than youth, but in manual labour they will always gain less. Winter in a cold climate is more costly to the labourer than summer, but it is also the time of slack work, and therefore of diminished wages.

There is undoubtedly some truth in the doctrine which is now much taught, that a rise in the habitual standard of comfort among the working classes is not only the consequence, but also, in some degree, a cause of higher wages. This is especially the case when it is gradual, normal, and general. Such a rise gives an increased earnestness and steadiness to the pressure of one of the two competing parties in the labour market, and it tends to limit the supply of labour, by making labours more prudent in contracting early marriages, and more ready to abandon callings in which the requisite wages are not given. In this way the share of the labourer is often increased at the cost of diminished profits or enhanced prices. But although this fact is of real importance in the history of industry, its action is restricted to narrow limits. Nothing can be more idle than to suppose that the mere increase of a labourer's wants, without any increase of the produce of his labour, will secure him increased prosperity. If the rise of wages is sufficient to swallow up the profits of the employer, or to make those profits less than he could have obtained in other fields, the industry will inevitably cease, and the capital that supports it will go to other lands or to other employments. If the increased cost be thrown upon prices, the demand will, in most cases, be reduced, and the industry will, in many cases, be annihilated by foreign competition. No trade-union combinations can possibly, in the long run, emancipate industry from this law.

The first step towards establishing the present position of trade unions in England was the repeal of the combination laws in 1824 and 1825, which gave workmen full liberty to combine for the purpose of raising and maintaining wages, and regulating the hours of work. But although from this time trade unions rapidly multiplied, especially after the Reform Bill of 1832, their position was still somewhat precarious. In addition to the very just laws against molestation, obstruction, and intimidation, which were often stringently enforced, they suffered under the great disadvantage that, as far as they were considered corporations 'acting in restraint of trade,' they were still illegal, excluded from the power of protecting their property which was accorded to other corporations by the Friendly Societies Act, and liable to be robbed with impunity by their own officers. The Trade Union Act of 1871 remedied this evil. It enabled all trade unions, even though they were acting in restraint of trade, to obtain full corporate rights of holding land and other kinds of property in the name of trustees, who might sue or be sued in respect to it. The only condition required was that the rules of the society should be registered.

In this manner the trade unions acquired full rights of holding and protecting corporate property. At the same time, by a strange anomaly, which was partly due to the jealousy with which they were regarded, but still more, I believe, to their own desire,[61] they remained in other respects purely voluntary societies, external to, and uncontrolled by, the law. The law took no cognisance of their internal arrangements; they had no power of making binding contracts in their corporate capacity, either with their own members or with other bodies or individuals, and they could neither sue nor be sued. If a trade union made an agreement with an association of employers about the conditions of work, neither party had any power of enforcing it in the law courts. If a member was expelled from the union for some alleged offence against trade-union rules, and was thus deprived of all the benefit of his previous subscriptions, he had no legal redress. If an employer or a non-unionist was injured by a trade-union official

---

[61] See on this controversy Webb's *History of Trade Unionism*, pp. 254–60.

acting as a trade-union agent, his only remedy was to bring an action against the individual who had injured him, who would probably be unable to pay any considerable damages. He could bring no action against the trade union itself, and recover no damages from its collective funds. In this way these great bodies were left in an entirely exceptional, and in some respects privileged, position, quite unlike that of a club, or a joint-stock company, or a railway company, or any other fully legalised corporation.

Such a privilege, granted to bodies which are under manifest temptations to oppress and to coerce; such an immunity from responsibility, granted to bodies which seek to extend to extreme limits the responsibility of others, was, to say the least of it, anomalous, and illustrates clearly the tendency of modern industrial legislation to aggrandise the powers of the corporation at the expense of the liberty of the individual. The enormous wealth, power, and magnitude which these corporations have attained in England make their legal position peculiarly surprising. Thus it appears that in 1889 sixteen trade unions had together a membership of 216,634 and an annual income of 530,755*l*.[62] Sir Robert Giffen stated before the Labour Commission that, according to the latest returns, the aggregate annual income of the trade unions is nearly 1,200,000*l*.[63]

In one of the reports of the Commission, which was signed by the Duke of Devonshire and some other Commissioners, it was contended that this state of things ought to cease; that the trade unions being, in fact, great, powerful, and wealthy corporations, ought in all respects be treated as corporations by the law; that those whom they had injured should have the power of bringing actions against them in their corporate capacity; and that they, in their turn, should have the power to take legal proceedings on behalf of their members, and to make legal contracts with other bodies or with individuals.

---

[62] Howell's *Conflicts of Labour*, p. 153.
[63] *Digest of Evidence*, p. 43.

This suggestion, however, appears to have been very unpopular in trade-union circles.[64]

It was put forward with great moderation, for it was only proposed that those trade unions should acquire a complete legal personality which desired to do so. The trade unions of the workers and the federations of the employers stand in this respect on the same legal basis, and it was urged that English industry on a large scale is coming more and more to rest on collective agreements, made in the most formal way, between these great and highly organised trade associations. Such agreements are constantly made. They are becoming much more than engagements between individual employers and individual workmen, the form into which English industry is manifestly developing. This is perhaps, on the whole, a good thing, and is probably inevitable, but in order that it should work well it is manifestly necessary that each party should have a legal power of enforcing its contracts. Sooner or later this view is certain to prevail.

The growth of trade-unionism all over Europe is perhaps the most marked feature of modern industrial life. It is remarkable, too, that exactly in proportion as these bodies acquire an overwhelming power, that makes them fully competent to make their own bargains, so does the tendency to regulate and restrict industry in all its details by direct legal enactments increase. Scarcely a ministry, scarcely a Parliament, passes over the political scene without adding something to the vast network of restrictions, precautions, and limitations by which the action of men and women in nearly all the branches of industry is now regulated. The law pursues them into the smallest industry, into the humblest workshop, even into their own homes, dictating in minute detail how long they may work, under what conditions they may work, what risks they may incur, what risks they must avoid.

---

[64] See the *Final Report*, Part i. pp. 115–19. Compare the very hostile report brought before the trade union congress at Norwich (Report of its proceedings, pp. 27–28). There is an interesting article, by Mr. B. Holland, on this subject in the *Nineteenth Century*, March 1895.

Public opinion, and especially the public opinion of those who are most directly interested in these questions, is now the supreme arbiter, and it evidently approves of these restrictions. It is, however, a somewhat singular fact that an age in which liberty of worship has been most fully secured and in which the liberty of holding, expressing, and propagating every variety of opinion on religious, moral, social, and political questions has become almost unlimited, should have witnessed this strong disposition to limit in so many forms and in so many spheres the freedom of human action.

That the laws to which I have referred—especially in their sanitary aspects—have done much good cannot reasonably be denied. They have prolonged life, and diminished disease, and blotted out many plague-spots from the world, and given to multitudes healthier, happier, and more rational lives. At the same time, as I have already hinted, it may well be questioned whether their effects have been wholly good, and whether their exaggeration may not lead to very dangerous consequences. It may well be asked whether the old energy, self-reliance, and resourcefulness of the English character will continue unimpaired under this education of perpetual legal regulations; whether it is really advantageous to cripple by rigidly uniform rules the flight of superior industry, capacity, or daring; whether great industries, which are now barely retained in this country, may not easily be regulated or taxed out of existence; whether the growth of a vast bureaucracy of inspectors and other officials, and the constantly increasing mingling of questions of industry with questions of politics, do not foreshadow grave evils to the State; whether it is a genuine kindness to the very poor, the very imcompetent, and the very thriftless, to drive them even out of unhealthy trades, in which they may be overworked and underpaid, when, as is too often the case, the only real alternative is the poorhouse or the street.

The complexity and interdependence of industrial interests are very great, and the effect of laws reach far beyond the intention of the lawgiver. It is possible and easy by improving the conditions of one trade, to injure many others that are dependent on it, and widely different motives blend in the movements for reform. Among the advocates of increased regulation of the work of women and young persons there is always a minority whose real object is to establish a precedent for the increased regulation of the work of adult men, or to drive child labour and female labour out of competition with the labour of adults, or to lay the foundations of a Socialist organisation, which is certainly very alien to the wishes of the majority of the reformers. The regulation of the industrial system is one of the most difficult tasks of statesmanship, and requires beyond most others a judicial and impartial temperament, a rare power of tracing distant consequences and estimating nearly balanced advantages and disadvantages. Whether a Government depending for its existence on a democratic Parliament, and compelled at all times to seek support by conciliating great masses of the most ignorant voters, is likely to deal wisely with so delicate a machine may surely be gravely doubted.

Experiments of organisations and restriction, however, are ardently advocated in many lands. Sometimes the demand is for a legal minimum of wages, and sometimes for a legal maximum of hours. Sometimes it takes the form—which a German law of 1889 has sanctioned—of an obligatory insurance against old age. Sometimes there is a demand for legislation investing conciliation or abritration boards, or trade unions, with increased powers. A considerable working men's party on the Continent, but especially in Austria, Germany, and Switzerland, desires 'obligatory syndicates,' or in other words, corporations for carrying on particular trades, to which all who practice these trades must necessarily belong. It is a system curiously like the guilds, and other trade organisations and monopolies, that flourished in the Middle Ages, and existed till the French Revolution. In Austria, a very remarkable law, enacted in 1883, established compulsory guilds, including all employers and workmen, for the smaller industries, with power of regulating apprenticeships. In these corporations workmen and their employers are brought together; there is a court for arbitration, and there is a trade savings bank and insurance fund. The system is said to be, on the whole, popular with the working men in Austria. In 1893 a working men's congress held at Bienne, in Switzerland, unanimously voted for obligatory corporations; a revision of the Constitution was prepared which would have made it possible to establish such corporations and suppress free labour, but it was defeated by a small majority on a referendum vote.[65]

In countries where there is no legal restriction imposed upon the liberty of industry, much legislation is sometimes required to protect the individual workman against molestation and intimidation from his fellow-workmen. This is one of the many questions which present little or no difficulty as long as we confine ourselves to broad and general principles, but great difficulty when we attempt to apply them in detail. As a general principle, it is clear that when men of their own free will join an association, and retain the liberty of leaving it, they have no right to complain if, while they remain in it, they are obliged to conform to its rules. The most obvious case is that of a great strike which is ordered by the executive of a trade union. A minority of the members, in most cases, would much prefer to continue at work, but they are compelled by the orders of the trade union to desist. As long as this body confines its coercion to threatening recalcitrant members with expulsion, there is no real grievance in the case. Men have sought certain advantages by joining the society, and placing the direction of their industry under the order of its chiefs, and they have no reason to complain that they lose the advantages if they discard the obligations. On the other hand, it is equally plain that any attempt to carry out a strike by force or intimidation ought to be rigidly suppressed by law.

The English law on the subject rested, for many years, on

---

[65] Béchaux, *Les Revendications Ouvrières en France*, pp. 192–200; see also the Report on Austria laid before the Labour Commission.

the enactment of 1825. By this law both workmen and employers had obtained full liberty of meeting, consulting, and combining for the purpose of regulating wages and hours of work, but a summary process was established for the punishment of all those acts of violence which were already indictable, and additional provisions were enacted providing summary punishment for the employment of threats, intimidation, molestation, and obstruction directed to the attainment of trade-union objects.[66] In the early history of trade unions, however, the extreme difficulty of carrying on a labour war without acts of violence and intimidation, directed either against members of the unions who refused to obey the orders of the executive, or against non-unionist workmen who took the place of those who were on strike, was abundantly shown. Every period of depression and distress was accompanied by fierce explosions of crime, which induced some men to regret the authorisation of trade unions in 1824 and 1825. Several trials took place. Several workmen were sentenced to long periods of transportation. In 1830 Nassau Senior drew up, at the request of the Government of Lord Melbourne, a report on the subject, in which he described the 'cowardly ferocity' with which not only innocent and laborious workmen, but also their families, were assailed; the paralysis of industries employing thousands and tens of thousands of workpeople by organised intimidation; and the necessity of strengthening the coercive provisions of the law if the national superiority in industry was to be preserved.

Similar violence was displayed, and similar complaints were made, at many later periods, and the trade outrages that took place in the last years of the sixties in Sheffield and Manchester sent a thrill of indignation through the land. The practice of rattening, or purloining or destroying the tools of recalcitrant workmen, was found to be constantly pursued. Cases of gunpowder were exploded in the houses of workmen who had broken the trade-union rules, and several deliberate murders

---

[66] Stephen's *History of the Criminal Law*, iii. 215–16.

were committed. A searching parliamentary inquiry, assisted by a promise of indemnity to the instigators or perpetrators of these crimes, succeeded in tracing them, for the most part, to the Grinders' Clubs at Sheffield and the Brickmakers' Union at Manchester, and in proving that they had been deliberately organised, and paid for out of the club funds. It was shown that these bodies had succeeded for many years, by systematic and organised crime, in keeping up a reign of terror in these districts and trades as complete as has ever been achieved by agrarian conspiracy in Ireland, or by the Molly Maguires in Pennsylvania.

At the same time the inquiries into these outrages led also to other conclusions, which I have already indicated. They showed that it was the small, the young, the poor trade societies that tried to make their way and to hold their members together by stimulating trade warfare, and establishing through outrage and intimidation their authority over their members. The older, larger, and richer societies were animated by a different spirit. By securing for their members the advantages of a friendly society, they gave them such a strong personal interest in the organisation that the simple threat of expulsion was an amply sufficient instrument of coercion; while in their relations with the employers they usually exerted their influence on the side of peace. Their vast accumulated funds made them very cautious in risking financial disaster by an unnecessary struggle, while the consciousness of their strength and their widely representative character made the employers attend with great deference to their demands. This distinction has steadily prevailed to the present day. It was clearly brought out before the Labour Commission, and it is one of the landmarks that are most useful in guiding us in the future.

One of the results of the disclosure of the gross abuses that had taken place was the Criminal Law Amendment Act of 1871, which inflicted a punishment of three months' imprisonment, with hard labour, on any one who attempts to coerce another for trade purposes by the use of personal violence; by such threats as would justify a magistrate in binding a man to keep the peace; or by persistently following a person about from place to place, hiding his tools, clothes, or other property, watching and besetting his house, or following him along any street or road with two or more other persons in a disorderly manner. These last clauses were directed against the practice of picketing, a practice which was, and still is, constantly employed in strikes. It consists of bodies of workmen on strike surrounding and guarding the places of labour, and the approaches to them, in order that no workmen should be able to take up their work without passing through the midst of them, being observed and reported, and, if possible, persuaded or induced to abandon their purpose. Even when no actual violence is employed, it is idle to suppose that picketing can be carried on by bodies often amounting to some hundreds, and even thousands, of rough and angry workmen, without a great deal of obstruction, insult, intimidation, and molestation.

The Act of 1871, as it seems to me, in its general purpose was a very just one; but in a trial which took place in the following year the term 'coerce' was interpreted from the bench in a wider sense than it was probably meant to bear, and it appears, or was believed to have been held, that a strike was criminal if it forced its terms on an unwilling company under pain of producing a great public inconvenience, or breaking contracts which had been already formed. Magistrates were accused of construing the word 'coerce' as if it were rather a synonym for 'induce' than for 'compel.' Rightly or wrongly, great discontent was produced in trade-union circles, and as it continued unabated the Legislature at last intervened. In 1875 the Act of 1871 was repealed, and a new Act was substituted for it.

This Act specifically protected all combinations in furtherance of trade disputes, and laid down the principle that what one man might do in such disputes without committing an indictable offence did not become criminal because many did it. It followed that the action of hundreds of men assembled to dissuade non-unionists from working was of the same legal nature as if a solitary individual had been sent to remonstrate with them. The other very important portion of the Act was the seventh clause, which dealt with the more subtle forms of coercion, and re-enacted in substance, but in more carefully limited terms, the provisions of the law of 1871. This clause provided that 'every person who, with a view to compel any other persons to abstain from doing, or to do any act which such other person has a legal right to do or abstain from doing, wrongfully and without legal authority (1) uses violence to or intimidates such other person, or his wife and children, or injures his property; or (2) persistently follows such other person about from place to place; or (3) hides any tools, clothes, or other property owned or used by such other person, or deprives him of or hinders him in the use thereof; or (4) watches and besets the house or other place where such other person resides, or works, or carries on business, or happens to be, or the approach to such house or place; or (5) follows such other person, with two or more persons, in a disorderly manner in or through any street or road, shall, on conviction thereof by a court of summary jurisdiction, or on indictment as hereinafter mentioned, be liable either to pay a penalty of 20*l.*, or to be imprisoned for a term not exceeding three months, with or without hard labour.' The same section contains a proviso that 'attending at or near the house where a person resides, or works, or carries on business, or happens to be, or the approach to such house or place, in order merely to obtain or communicate information, shall not be deemed a watching or besetting within the meaning of this section.'[67]

Such is the law which at present governs these matters, and opposite parties have been endeavouring in opposite senses to obtain its revision. It is contended on one side, that the whole system of picketing ought to be made illegal: that

[67] Compare Stephen's *History of the Criminal Law,* iii. 224–27; Spyer's *The Labour Question,* pp. 16–19; Howell's *Conflicts of Capital and Labour* (2nd ed.), p. 293; *Final Report of the Royal Commission of Labour,* pp. 39–41, 106–7.

it is inevitably a system of terrorism, intimidation, and molestation, and is something quite different from merely giving information, or submitting arguments or remonstrances to non-unionist workers. On the other side, it is argued that the workmen on strike have an undoubted right to inform any workmen who are brought from a distance to supply their place that a strike is in existence; to persuade them that they are injuring their class by giving their labour to the employers; to offer on the part of the trade unions to pay their travelling expenses, or even give them a gratuity, if they will return to their homes. They maintain that the right of 'moral suasion,' as distinguished from 'violence' and 'intimidation,' should be fully recognised and widely interpreted, and they endeavour, with no great success, to establish a parallel between picketing and the confidential communications about the circumstances of a strike which often pass between employers, and make it difficult for its leaders and organisers to obtain employment.

In accordance with these antagonistic views, different amendments of the law have been demanded. The employers desire that the term 'intimidation' should apply to the assemblage of more than three men in the neighbourhood of industrial establishments for the purpose of picketing. They maintain that information about the strike can be amply communicated to workmen by public meetings, placards, advertisements in the papers, or canvassing from house to house, and they desire that the penalties under the Act should be increased, and made in all cases imprisonment. The workmen, on the other hand, take two different lines. Some of them wish the term 'intimidation' to be so restricted as to include only threats accompanied by physical violence, and of such a character as to put men in reasonable bodily fear, and they wish the whole of the seventh clause, with its elaborate provision against molestation, to be repealed. Others desire to see the Act so expanded as to include several acts of employers. 'Black-listing' obnoxious workmen, eviction at less than three months' notice, dismissal without assignment of a valid reason, and the engagement of men during a strike without informing them of its existence, ought all, they maintain, to be included.[68]

The majority of the members of the Labour Commission concluded that very little could be done on either side to amend the law. They recommended, however, that the word 'intimidation' should be suppressed as ambiguous, and the phrase 'uses or threatens to use violence to such other person, or his wife or children, or injures his property,' should be inserted in the Act. They also hinted that much of the difficulty of the question would be removed if the full legal personality of trade unions were recognised, and if it were possible to recover damages from them in the case of injury in the civil courts.

In spite of these differences of opinion, the legislation of 1875 appears, on the whole, to have been successful; and though great strikes, sometimes accompanied by great abuses, have since then taken place, there has been certainly, of late years, less open violence and crime in labour disputes in the United States. It has been observed, however, that the New Unionism brought with it a considerable recrudescence of violence and a greatly increased stringency of trade despotism.

That a vast amount of intimidation and coercion prevails in trade-union politics is incontestable. Lists are sometimes put out of shops and other work-places which unionists may not enter. Some unions aim at obtaining a complete monopoly in their respective trades, by depriving non-unionists of all means of livelihood, and thus forcing them into subjection to their rules. Unionists are often forbidden to work the non-unionists, or with any employer who supports nonunionists. They are forbidden to teach non-unionists their trade, to lend them tools, or to assist them to obtain work, and all the weap-

---

[68] Spyer, pp. 18–19. The whole subject of picketing is treated very fully, from the workman's point of view, in Howell's *Conflicts of Labour*, pp. 305–24.

ons of social persecution are often lavishly employed. The word 'boycott,' as is well known, is a recent word, of Irish origin; but the thing has long existed in English trade disputes, and the rapidity with which the new word has been adopted in several languages is itself some evidence of the wide diffusion of the practice. Black-listing, or posting the names of recalcitrant or non-unionist workers during a strike, has been a common device, and has recently been condemned by the law courts. There are rules for excluding from a given neighbourhood all workmen from other parts of the kingdom, thus curiously reproducing the old limitations on the circulation of labour which existed before the laws of settlement were abolished in 1795. There is, indeed, a strong and constant disposition among large bodies of workers to prevent the free circulation of labour, either from one country, or district, or trade to another. A workman who has learnt more than one trade, or who undertakes more than one division of a complex industry, or who in off hours or in times of slackness turns his hand from one trade to another, is severely condemned. 'One man, one job,' is a favourite maxim, and many trade unions desire not only to confine the workmen to one kind of work, but also to limit severely both its amount and its efficiency. Overtime is either forbidden or greatly discouraged. No workman, it is said, ought to work more, or produce more, or earn more than his fellows. There are said to have been rules limiting the number of bricks that a bricklayer may place in a specified time, limiting the output of machinery, prescribing in different trades the amount of work which may be performed. It is curious to observe that these rules measuring the amount of productive work are sometimes found where there is most opposition to piecework when instituted by the employers.

There has been a considerable amount of controversy about the extent to which these different forms of restriction are carried, but there can be no real doubt that they are widely diffused, and that they have been supported by a large amount of persistent persecution. The rules limiting the efficiency of labour are especially dangerous, and they appear of late years to have become very popular in some branches of trade. They rest upon the fallacy that, the less work each man accomplishes, the more there will be for his fellows, and that by raising the cost of work they will benefit the workman; but they strike directly at the superior quality, and therefore superior cheapness, of English well-paid work, on which the whole edifice of our industrial supremacy mainly rests. They belong to the same order of ideas as the attacks upon labour-saving machines, which were once so common, which even now are not wholly extinct, and which are encouraged and applauded by some Socialist writers.[69]

Experience shows that coercion and oppression may exist in extreme severity without actual violence, and in forms which it is very difficult to bring under the direct action of the law. Fortunately, however, in England other and stronger influences than legal penalties usually arise to correct the evil. The abuses of power to which I have referred are not practised by all trade unions, and when they are pushed very far they arouse a healthy reaction. The great organisations of labour that have taken place in our century have been speedily followed by great federations of employers for the purpose of acting in concert, protecting their interests, and resisting unjust demands. This has been one of the most important facts in modern industrial history in England, and it is of very recent date. The earliest of these federations appears to have been the Association of Engineers and Ironfounders in Scotland, which was established in 1865, and in 1894 there were at least seventy associations of this kind in Great Britain.[70] They are very powerful, and when trade unions are despotic

---

[69] Thus Mr. Bax assures us that machinery, 'up to the present time, has proved the greatest curse mankind has ever suffered under' (*The Religion of Socialism*, p. 75). 'The action of the Luddites in destroying machinery, so far from being a mere irrational outburst, the result of popular misapprehension, as the orthodox economists assert, was perfectly reasonable and justifiable' (ibid. pp. 157–58).

[70] *Memorandum on Associations produced before the Labour Commission*, p. xxii.

and oppressive they become the natural protectors of the non-unionists. The war between the trade union and the isolated employer seems to have almost ended. It is being replaced by the far more formidable, but far more equal, struggle between the trade union and the federation. One of the first objects of the latter has been to put down the system, which the New Unionists have endeavoured to establish, of driving non-unionists out of employment, compelling employers to dismiss them on pain of a strike, forbidding unionists to work in conjunction with them. Thus the great Shipping Federation, which had registered no less than 128,000 seamen up to September 1893, employs unionists and non-unionists alike, but on the express condition that they bind themselves to work in harmony together; and a similar policy has been successfully adopted by most of the great dock companies.

Among the workmen also there have been growing signs of reaction against the tyranny of the New Unionism, and a Free Labour Association was founded in 1893 for the purpose of vindicating the right of workmen to sell their labour at the best market, and to make their agreements on their own terms. This society has a central council in London, and it claims to have thrown out many branches and enrolled many thousands of workmen. The fact is one of undoubted significance, though it is too early to forecast its full importance. One of the resolutions of the Free Labour Congress of 1893 is especially significant. It is: 'That this congress, bearing in mind the system of intimidation and coercion practised by union pickets during the recent disastrous strikes, whereby the common law of the land has been practically set aside, most earnestly calls for an amendment of the law relating to unlawful picketing, with a view to secure the just liberty of the subject for a workman to sell his labour in the best market during the internecine warfare arising from labour conflicts.'[71]

---

[71] See on this subject Brooks's *Industry and Property*, ii. 335–46. Mr. Brooks has collected a great amount of material illustrating the coercive measures adopted by a large section of trade-unionists.

I have already mentioned the evidence furnished by the general election of 1895 of the political impotence of the New Unionism; and it must be added that the trade unions themselves are independent bodies, animated by very different spirits, and often acting in antagonism. The trades that fall within the provinces of different unions, and the demarcations of industry that arise under the transformations effected by new inventions have produced keen disputes between rival unions.

The tendency, however, to federation and organisation, both on the part of the labourers and on the part of their employers, is very manifest, and when labour disputes break out they are apt to assume much larger proportions than in the past. There are signs that these influences are likely to play a prominent part in questions of municipal government. The Paris Municipal Council, under the influence of its Socialist members, has more than once attempted to impose a nine hours day and a fixed minimum of wages upon the contractors who did its work; but the Council of State possesses in France a right of veto, and it has hitherto refused to sanction such measures. The same body has tried to prevent contractors from having any portion of the municipal work done by cheaper labour in the provinces, and then brought into Paris.[72] It has gone further, and has actually subsidised strikes from the public funds. The first proposal of this kind was made in 1884, on the occasion of the strike in the mines of Anzin. It was on this occasion rejected, but similar proposals were soon after accepted. A single municipal council subsidised from public money no less than twenty-two strikes. On some occasions, when the Paris Municipality desired to support the most dangerous of all strikes—those on the railways—the central Government annulled their act; on other occasions it yielded, adopting the compromise of giving the money to the families of the strikers when the strike was over.[73]

---

[72] Guyot, *La Tyrannie Socialiste*, pp. 114–15.
[73] Ibid. pp. 209–13.

The proceedings of the Paris Municipality have, in some respects, gone beyond any in England; but here too, as we have seen, it is the object of a considerable party to make the municipalities on the largest scale direct employers of labour. It is the desire of the trade unions that the municipal authorities should apply to them for their labourers, and should accept and enforce their rules about wages and hours, and constant political pressure is brought to bear upon Governments, with the object of bringing all State employment under trade-union rules, supplying from the rates and taxes any losses that may in consequence be incurred.

The attitude of the employers to the trade unions varies a good deal, according to the character of the latter. In the case of the larger, wealthier, and more conservative unions there is, I believe, little friction, and no real antagonism. In several trade unions there are rules expressly framed for the protection of employers against unjust demands, and employers have sometimes found appeals to the trade-union authorities the best means of settling disputes with their workmen.[74] In the case of the more aggressive unions a different spirit prevails, and employers find many modes of defence and retaliation. Sometimes they have taken the extreme step of refusing to employ members of hostile trade unions. More frequently they have made it an express condition of employment that there should be no restriction on non-unionist labour. They have guarded against sudden strikes by engaging their men for definite terms. When hostilities were manifestly arising, they have taken the first step, and anticipated a strike by a lock-out. Sometimes during a strike they have imported foreign labourers. Sometimes they have made themselves independent of native labour by setting up branch establishments in foreign lands, or by contracting for some portions of their work with foreign manufacturers. Sometimes, in trade disputes with their own men, they have refused to enter into communication with trade-union leaders. It is a feeling much

---

[74] See some examples of this in the *Memorandum of Rules of Association drawn up for the Labour Commission*, pp. xviii–xix.

like that which makes a landlord ready to receive deputations from his own tenantry about the rents or rules of his estate, but not from outside organisations; and it is worthy of notice that the Imperial Government has hitherto adopted this rule, and refused to permit trade unions to intervene in disputed questions between themselves and their labourers.[75]

The trade unions, on the other hand, do what is in their power to give their organisations an international character, so as to prevent the market from being flooded with foreign workmen. At home it is one of their great objects to affiliate different trades, and to induce them to support one another in their contests. In some recent instances they have succeeded in obliging vast bodies of workmen to strike, who alleged no grievance whatever against their employers, simply for the purpose of supporting the cause of workmen on strike in another trade or another district, and the paralysis of industry is thus spread over an area far larger than that of the original dispute. In these great strikes the interest of one class of labourer is alone considered, and it is the special object of the leaders to conduct the war in the manner which produces most inconvenience and injury to the country at large. It is the boast of one of the Socialist writers that, under 'the superb generalship of Mr. John Burns . . . the traffic of the world's greatest port was for over ten weeks completely paralysed;'[76] and attempts have been made, on both sides of the Atlantic, to dislocate the whole railroad communication, on which immense districts depend for all industrial life, in order to succeed in some local dispute. The calamities which the great coal strikes and the great shipping strikes have brought upon gigantic interests, and upon multitudes of men and women who were wholly unconnected with the matter of dispute, can scarcely be exaggerated. And it is upon the very

---

[75] See the indignant comments of Mr. S. Webb on the refusal of the Admiralty to recognise any person not in their employment as the representative of the workmen in trade disputes (*Digest of Evidence before the Labour Commission*, p. 20).

[76] Webb's *History of Trade Unionism*, p. 390.

magnitude of these calamities that the leaders of the strikes chiefly base their hopes of enforcing their demands.

A large proportion of English strikes are brief in their duration and very restricted in their area. They are a form of bargaining, wasteful indeed in their nature, but not permanently injurious to the national industries, and, in the judgment of some of the best authorities, they have not, on the whole, injured the workmen who were engaged in them.[77] A considerable proportion have succeeded, and a short suspension of wages, even in case of failure, is soon made up. But the great strikes can be only looked upon as national calamities. In many cases their immediate cost to the country has been at least as great as that of a small war, and it falls far more directly than the expenditure of a war on the labouring classes and their families. The distant and indirect consequences have probably been still more serious. Every great strike drives a portion of trade out of the country, and some of it never returns. The great industrial forces of the nation are permanently affected, and English industry, in its competition with that of other countries, sinks to a somewhat lower plane.

These great strikes are essentially of the nature of wars. They are governed by much the same motives as other wars, and are probably undertaken with neither more nor less wisdom. In some cases they are perhaps inevitable. More frequently they are due to false calculations of results, or to false estimates of conditions of trade; and pride and passion, and the personal ambition of individual agitators, enter largely into them. Sometimes it is a new trade union which wishes to force itself into notoriety and obtain the support of larger numbers. Sometimes it is an able and ambitious man who sees in a labour war the means of placing his foot upon the ladder that leads to municipal, or perhaps even parliamentary, success. The consequences of these great strikes are so

---

[77] See the evidence of Sir Robert Giffen (*Digest of Evidence before the Labour Commission*, pp. 42–43).

far-reaching that it is difficult to estimate them. In many cases they lead the workmen to utter and ruinous disaster, sweeping away not only the accumulated funds of the trade unions, but also the private savings of countless homes, and reducing hard-working men and innocent wives and children to the lowest depths of misery. Sometimes they are partially or wholly successful in their main object; but even then success often fails to compensate for the losses incurred by a long period of suspended work and by the restriction of employment that often follows. Sometimes the victory is more apparent than real, and the apportionment of gains and losses is not what at first sight might appear. There have been cases when so large an amount of coal had been extracted from the mine that prices sank to a point which required a considerable reduction of wages, and the reduction was resisted, and a strike ensued. The first result was a great rise in the price of coal, and the masters, having large quantities in store, gained enormously. The next was, that when this store was sold the men were taken back to work at the higher wages they demanded, which the enhanced price of coal abundantly justified. They congratulate themselves on their victory; but, in truth, it was the masters who had gained largely by the struggle, while the suffering fell partly on the public in the shape of increased prices, and partly on the workmen, who were deprived, perhaps for several weeks, of all wages. Nearly always after a great strike comes a time of restricted and uncertain employment, due to the fact that capital has been expatriated or rendered insecure, that capitalists find it necessary to retrench, that industries which were once wholly British have, in part at least, crossed the Channel or the ocean. Sometimes unanticipated changes of habit affect the issue. A great London cab strike is said to have accustomed multitudes to use omnibuses who had never done so before, and the habit, when once formed, persisted though the strike had terminated. Often, too, increased cost and scarcity of labour gives a great impulse to the invention of labour-saving machinery. The extraordinary development of this form of in-

vention in the United States is probably largely due to the
great cost of American labour. Always in these strikes the
community suffers severely, and generally in part permanently, and, if these labour wars succeed each other too rapidly, they must ruin the industrial pre-eminence of the nation,
and destroy or contract great centres of employment.

The federation of industries, enlarging the area of a strike,
is one great weapon which is employed by the working man;
but there is also a widespread desire to make use of the power
which democracy gives to the working classes to handicap
the employers in all disputes with their labourers. That the
increasing power of the working classes in the State should
be followed by an increased attention to working-class interests in both natural and desirable, and, as we have seen,
much that has been done has been very beneficial; but this
legislation may take forms which involve grave danger.

One of the most popular proposals, and one which can be
supported by the strongest arguments, is that measures
should be taken to prevent the immigration of foreign pauperism. This policy has been decidedly adopted by the United
States, which, of all countries, was most identified with the
opposite system, and in nearly all other great countries it is
in one form or another pursued. The change of opinion that
has taken place on the subject in the United States in our own
generation is exceedingly significant. Only a few years ago
Lowell, echoing the favourite boast of American statesmen,
spoke of his country as

> She that lifts up the manhood of the poor,
> She of the open soul and open door,
> With room about her hearth for all mankind.[78]

As late as 1868 the American Government, in a treaty with
the Emperor of China, asserted 'the inherent and inalienable
right of man to change his home and allegiance,' and unqual-

---

[78] 'Commemoration Ode.'

ified freedom of migration to the United States was frequently put forward as one of the most essential characteristics of the American polity. Since 1880 the stream has completely turned. The change began with the great outburst in California against Chinese labour. Exclusive Acts were carried by the California Legislature, but they were pronounced unconstitutional. But in a few years the Federal Government took up the question, and the United States have now been closed against Chinese immigration. By laws of 1885 and 1891 all persons who had been convicted of crimes other than political, all labourers brought over on contract, all idiots, lunatics, cripples, consumptives, persons with loathsome contagious diseases, girls and children or in a state of pregnancy, inmates of poorhouses, and also all paupers who seem likely to become a burden on the community, are excluded from American soil.

In the British colonies the old system of free or Government-assisted immigration has been abolished. Measures have been taken, both in Canada and in Australia, to diminish the influx of Chinese immigrants; and in the North American colonies at least a strong disposition has been shown to restrict the immigration of all pauper labour. By the Immigration Act of 1886, indeed, the Viceroy has already power to prohibit it. [79]

It does not appear to me that, either in America or in England, there is any valid argument of principle against such legislation. Every nation has a right to close its own door, and a country which is already overcrowded, where vast masses of native industry are unemployed, and where the State undertakes at national expense to support pauperism, can surely not be blamed if it refuses to admit torrents of foreign pauperism, which displace native industry, beat down the wages of native workmen, and appreciably lower the standard of life. The real question is one not of principle, but of expediency. In past periods of her history England has owed many of her most valuable trades, as well as some of the best elements in her national character, to Huguenot or Flemish immigrants.

---

[79] Dilke's *Problems of Greater Britain*, i. 120–22, 146.

Whether the evil of the present immigration greatly exceeds the good; whether it would be possible to discriminate between that which produces wealth and that which increases pauperism; whether attempts to restrict foreign immigration would not be followed by retaliatory measures, which would be peculiarly disastrous to a nation so migratory as the English; whether the principle of exclusion, if once admitted, could be restricted within reasonable limits, are questions which demand much careful and far-seeing statesmanship. It is extremely probable that, if the Home Rule policy ever effected a complete or even partial separation between the Governments of Great Britain and Ireland, a working-class agitation would arise in some parts of England to prevent the immigration of Irish labour. In France, where great immigrations of Belgian and Italian labour have had much the same effects as Irish labour in England, a strong movement in favour of the exclusion of foreign workmen has more than once appeared.[80]

It can, at least, hardly be doubted that, if the policy of importing cheap foreign labour in times of strike became common, there would be an irresistible pressure of working-class opinion in favour of laws forbidding it, much like the American and Australian laws against Chinese labour. Sometimes the Protectionist spirit has shown itself at home in still more decided forms. Among the proposals carried at the Trade Congress at Norwich in 1894 was one for making it 'a penal offence for an employer to bring to any locality extra labour when the existing supply was sufficient for the needs of the district.'[81]

In other ways it is possible for a legislature to do much to handicap the employer in any contest with the employed. It may do so by largely increasing taxation for the benefit of one class, and throwing the burden mainly upon another. It may do so by introducing into legislation trade-union rules about hours, and even about wages; by surrounding the employer

---

[80] See Guyot, *La Tyrannie Socialiste*, pp. 136–40.
[81] *Report of the Trade Union Congress*, p. 49.

with new restrictions, responsibilities, and limitations, and withdrawing the management of his work practically from this control. It is the ideal of some men to leave the whole cost and risks of a great factory in the hands of the owner, while the conduct of the business is placed mainly in the hands of the working men and of Government inspectors. In this direction much has been done, and much more may be done. But it can be done only subject to one inexorable condition—that all legislation which seriously diminishes profits, increases risks, or even unduly multiplies humiliating restrictions, will drive capital away, and ultimately contract the field of employment.

The form in which the spirit of Protection now shows itself most strongly in England is the limitation and regulation of labour, and it is the outcome of a spirit which is now passing widely over the whole civilised globe. No fact is more conspicuous in the nineteenth century than the strength of the reaction that has taken place against the Free Trade, or *laissez faire* principles which, within the memory of men still living, were almost completely dominant in the more advanced economical teaching of the world, and which seemed likely in a few years to control all the more civilised legislations. Whether we look to the despotic monarchies or to the democratic republics, whether we consider the crowded populations of Europe or the thinly scattered inhabitants of Australia or New Zealand, the same lesson may be learnt. Nearly everywhere the old Free Trade doctrine is a vanquished or a declining creed, and the chief disputes relate to the forms which Protection should take, to the degrees to which it may be wisely carried, to the advantage of establishing a preferential treatment in favour of different parts of the same empire.

In England, more than in any other great country, Free Trade holds its ground, and it still governs our commercial legislation. But England is very isolated, and, if I read aright average educated opinion, the doctrine has become something very different from the confident, enthusiastic evangel of Cobden. It has come to mean little more than a conviction that, if all nations agreed to adopt Free Trade, it would be a benefit to the world as a whole, though not to every part of it; that though protective duties are of great value in fostering the infancy of manufactures, they should not be continued when these manufactures have reached their maturity, or be granted when there is no probability that they may be one day discarded; that Free Trade is the manifest interest of a great commercial country which does not produce sufficient food for its subsistence, while its ships may be met on every sea, and its manufactures might almost supply the world; that cheap raw materials and cheap food are essential conditions of English manufacturing supremacy.

Even this last article is not generally held without qualification. Cheap food, it is beginning to be said, does not necessarily mean the very cheapest, and a system under which the greatest and most important of all national industries is almost hopelessly paralysed, under which land is fast falling out of cultivation, and the agricultural population flocking more and more to the congested towns, cannot be really good for the nation. It is more and more repeated that the great rush of prosperity that undoubtedly followed the repeal of the Corn Laws was largely due to the gigantic gold discoveries, which kept up prices while they stimulated enterprise; that the predictions of agricultural ruin made by the old Protectionists, which were once laughed to scorn, are fast becoming true; that, short of the absolute repeal of the corn duties, diminutions might have been made which would have greatly cheapened bread without ruining agriculture; and that if this policy was not adopted, it was because the preponderance of voting power had passed from the country to the towns. To those, indeed, who observe how large a proportion of the advantage of the extreme cheapness of articles of food goes simply to the middleman, and not to the consumer, it will appear very doubtful whether a low corn duty would have any perceptible effect on the price of bread.

What may be the final issue of this momentous controversy, on which the civilised world is so deeply divided, I shall not venture to forecast. If, a quarter of a century hence, this book should find its readers, they will probably be able to judge this, like many other questions that I have raised, with a juster judgment than contemporary critics. One thing, however, may be confidently said. It is, that the policy of regulating and limiting labour, which is now so popular; the policy of substituting in all industrial spheres administrative and legislative restriction for the free action of supply and demand; the policy of attempting to level fortunes, to change by law the natural growth and distribution of wealth, and to create a social type different from that which the unrestricted play of natural forces would have produced, belongs to the same order of ideas as the Protectionism of the past. It is clearly akin to the old policy of sumptuary laws, of embargoes, of trade regulations and monopolies, of feudal restrictions on property and industry, of strict commercial Protection. The policy that would exclude foreign labour from England, and submit all English labour to trade-union rules, leads logically to the exclusion of all goods that are made on the Continent by foreign labour and under foreign conditions. Free labour and free trade are closely connected. If, in England, those who oppose the first profess to be in favour of the second, this is only because most sections of the labouring classes believe cheap food to be altogether to their advantage, and because in the great division of industries in England they see no present prospect of obtaining protection for their own.

In the United States Protection is mainly defended on the ground that it keeps wages at an artificial height. In Australia and New Zealand we might naturally have supposed that a small working-class population, living amid the boundless possibilities of a new country, with every stimulus upon individual resources, would have chosen to be governed as little as possible, and would have allowed the whole subject of politics to sink into a secondary place. Though Australia contains few great fortunes, she is almost wholly free from great poverty, and wellbeing is so diffused that the average wealth of the colonists is said to be greater than that of any other nation in the world. The most prominent Australian statesman of our generation has stated that, at the end of 1892, the wealth of the Australian colonies 'amounted to 1,169,000,000*l.*, or 309*l.* per head of the total population.' 'The percentage of the accumulated private wealth,' he added, 'was higher than that of any other nation; the next in point of wealth was the United Kingdom; the third, France; the fourth, Holland; and the fifth, the United States, which were very much below that of the Australian colonies.'[82]

Yet there are few countries where State intervention is more exaggerated than in these prosperous colonies, and Victoria and New Zealand are probably the two countries in the world in which the theory of State socialism is most nearly realised. Compulsory eight-hour laws; steeply graduated taxation, especially designed to break up large landed properties; compulsory education, paid by the State; State railways; highly protective duties; an immense multiplication of government officials; a debt rising with astonishing rapidity for the purpose of expenditure in public works which in England would be left to individual enterprise—to all these things are the characteristics of these rising English democracies, where the working classes exercise the most complete ascendency. In Victoria, about 8 per cent. of the adult male population are said to be in Government employment.[83] The New Zealand land laws are especially remarkable for their stringent provisions intended to prevent all speculation in land, and confining its ownership to moderate properties and *bonâ fide* occupiers.[84] It is remarkable, too, that, in spite of the great influence the working class exercises over Australian and New Zealand legislation, hardly

---

[82] See a remarkable speech of Sir Henry Parkes (November 13, 1894), *New South Wales Parliamentary Debates*, 1894, p. 2204. Some interesting statistics about the average wealth in these colonies will be found in the *New Zealand Official Handbook for 1892*, pp. 86–8. Victoria seems to be the richest colony.
[83] Pearson's *National Life and Character*, p. 21.
[84] *The Land Laws of New Zealand, as enacted by the Land Act, 1892*, by Vincent Pyke (Wellington).

any country has witnessed labour conflicts in the form of strikes carried on with more persistence and violence, or on a larger scale.

In England the greatly increased organisation, both of labourers and of employers, is an inevitable fact, upon which all sound calculations of the industrial future must be based. The value of the trade unions in representing, sustaining, and extending working men's interests, both at home and abroad, can hardly be exaggerated, but there are great dangers that they may stimulate over-legislation and largely restrict individual liberty. If they reduce the quality and produce of English labour, by hampering and diminishing the work which each man is allowed to do; if they insist upon the worst workmen being paid as much as the best; if they oppose or retard the introduction of labour-saving machines which other countries have adopted; if they so diminish profits and increase risks that capital finds more profitable employment in other countries than in England—if they do these things, they will ultimately prove not a blessing, but a curse, to the working men of England.

The great hope of our industrial future is that the working classes will master these principles, and abstain from seeking proximate benefits at the cost of ultimate disaster. The long practice of public life; the evident desire of all Parliaments and Governments, for many years, to meet the legitimate demands of the working classes, and the wide extension of education, have raised up a large class of workmen who are fully aware of the true conditions of industrial success, and who have no desire to separate themselves by a class warfare from the bulk of their fellow-countrymen. It is observed that the older, wealthier, and more conservative trade unions are far less desirous of legislative interference than the new unions, and that they rely much more largely on their own unassisted action. It is also observed that these unions are by far the most permanent. The aggressive and belligerent type of trade union makes for a time a great noise in the industrial world, but such unions usually perish during periods of depression: not less than fifty of them are said to have been wrecked during the acute trade crisis of 1878 and 1879,[85] and since that period many others have shared the same fate; while the unions of the older school, and of more moderate policy, generally survive.

In such facts we have a good omen for the future. An advocate of the new unions has given a graphic description of the manner in which the organiser or leading official of an aggressive new union starts in his career full of belligerent ardour, but gradually changes his views as he becomes more prosperous, as his family grow up, as he begins to come into closer connection with the employers, and with the more well-to-do classes.[86] A very similar change is apt to pass over trade unions themselves when their funds accumulate, when their advantages as benefit societies become more apparent, when the responsibility of the management of large investments and the dread of financial disaster begin to weigh heavily on them. This is but an image of what takes place with individual men when the caution, the responsibility, the attachment to settled habits, and the increased knowledge of life which age brings in its train have mellowed the character, and toned down the crude enthusiasms, the undisciplined energies of youth. Conservatism has its deep roots in human nature, and there is a kind of tidal movement in human affairs which prevents the triumph of extremes. If times of depression and distress quicken the impulse towards violent experiments and revolutionary change, times of prosperity act in the opposite direction. If the clash of rival interests begins by generating fierce passions, it commonly ends by suggesting possibilities of compromise. If violent opinions and measures have for a time a free career, they infallibly end by arousing the timid and the apathetic, and producing reactions proportionally

---

[85] *Subjects of the Day* ('Socialism'), August 1890, p. 115.
[86] See the very interesting picture of trade-union life, drawn up by a skilled artisan, in Webb's *History of Trade Unionism*, pp. 431–58. This seems to me the best thing in the book.

strong. England has been saved from many dangers by her reactions, and the lassitude that follows a period of abnormal excitement has often given time for the formation of habits that will not wholly pass away. Whether a great social or industrial change is an evil or a benefit will often depend upon whether it is effected violently, suddenly, and prematurely, or by a gradual change of ideas, by a process of slow and almost insensible growth.

The best security of the industrial fabric is to be found in the wide division and diffusion of property, which softens the lines of class demarcation, and gives the great masses of the people a close and evident interest in the security of property, the maintenance of contracts, the credit and wellbeing of the State. In all the more civilised countries this process is steadily going on. Among the great countries of the Continent, France holds the first place in wealth, skill, industry, and thrift, and the peasant-proprietor system attracts to the land a far larger proportion of working men's savings than in England. Her first living economist computes her total annual savings at from 1½ to 2 milliards of francs, or from 60 to 80 millions sterling; and he mentions that in 1882 it appeared from official documents that the sum due to the depositors of the French savings banks was about 1,745 millions of francs, and that it had increased by 1 milliard 85 millions since 1875.[87] In England the accumulated capital of the working classes to to be mainly found in savings banks, insurance and co-operative working men's societies, trade unions, building societies, and a few other kindred societies, about which much accurate statistical information has been collected. Mr. Brabrook, the Chief Registrar of Friendly Societies, gave some valuable evidence on this subject before the Labour Commission, and he estimated the sum total of the accumulated capital of the working classes in England and Wales alone, in 1890, at the enormous sum of 218,374,046*l.*[88] Still more sig-

---

[87] Leroy-Beaulieu, *Le Collectivisme*, pp. 228, 237.
[88] *Digest of Evidence*, p. 35.

nificant is the evidence showing that, in the space of fifteen years before 1891, the invested capital of these classes in England and Wales had nearly doubled.[89]

Such facts clearly prove the fallacy of the sharp distinction that is commonly drawn between the capitalist and the working population, and each generation brings them more closely together by increasing vastly the realised and fructifying property of the wage-earning classes. This is the best of all guarantees against revolutionary projects. Public debts and landed property are the two forms of property which it is the special object of Socialists to plunder. If they succeeded, the savings bank of the poor man would sink in the same boat as the fortune of the millionaire; and most of the charitable funds, the provident and insurance funds, and the various forms of endowment which are the special property or for the special benefit of the poor, are either invested in Government funds or are a first charge upon land. The true owners of the soil are not merely those who hold its title-deeds. They are also the mortgagees and encumbrancers, who have a first claim on its revenues, and in this way the land of England belongs, to a degree that is seldom realised, to the very poor, and to provident and charitable institutions for their benefit. One of the most remarkable facts disclosed by the recent inquiries into the ground values of our great towns is, that ground rents have long been a favourite form of investment of persons of small means, as well as of benefit and insurance societies, charities, and trustees. It is only necessary to look through the reports of any great hospital, or charitable association, or working man's insurance company, to perceive how largely their incomes are derived from the very forms of property which the Socialist and the demagogue most bitterly assail.

That a wide diffusion of property can ever give complete and permanent security to a country which has no written

---

[89] See the statistical abstracts brought together by Mr. Mackay (*A Policy of Free Exchange*, p. 235).

Constitution protecting property or contract, and in which all power ultimately resides with a simple majority of the poorest and most uninstructed, I, at least, do not believe. With the growth of Socialism in all countries; with the manifest and rapid decline in the character of public men; with the increasing tendency of popular party politics to depend upon competing offers of class bribes; with the precedents of violation of contract and confiscation of property which Irish land legislation has established, it is certainly not surprising that a feeling of growing insecurity may be traced among the possessors of property. There are already plain signs—ominous for the industrial future of England—that they are beginning, in calculating risks and profits, to estimate as a serious item in the former category the possibility of plunder by their own Government, either in the shape of violation of existing contracts, of increasing restrictions on their industrial freedom, or of partial, inequitable, and confiscatory taxation. But, at the same time, every measure which by honest means tends to the diffusion of property and the multiplication of proprietors is of real value, and in this constantly increasing diffusion we possess the most powerful corrective of the Socialist tendencies of our time. The growth of the co-operative principle in industry and the multiplication of joint-stock companies accelerate the process. If it is true that, with the agglomeration of industries, great capital is more and more needed for successful industry, it is also true that a great capital is ceasing more and more to imply a great capitalist. It often consists mainly of the combination of a large number of moderate, or even very small, shareholders, and the chief industries of the world are thus coming rapidly to rest on a broad proprietary basis.

Co-operative industries in which the actual workers are at once the proprietors and the managers are, on the whole, steadily advancing, though their history has been a chequered, and in some respects rather a disappointing, one. A large proportion of the earlier co-operative enterprises failed through causes that may easily be understood. Great numbers of workmen prefer higher wages, with perfect freedom of locomotion and freedom from risk, to lower wages, compensated in times of prosperity, and after a long period of work, by a share of profits. Really skilled management is a rarer, a more difficult, and a more essential thing than a common workman is apt to imagine, and the large salaries by which alone it can be secured often seem inordinate to a workman's committee, which compares it with the wages of manual labour. The great fluctuations of industry; the many miscalculations and failures, balanced by occasional brilliant successes; the years of depression and declining profits that alternate with cycles of prosperity; the trying and precarious years at the beginning of an enterprise, when a reserve fund has not yet been accumulated, can only be successfully met by moral qualities of a kind that are not common in any class, and which the life of an ordinary workman is not much calculated to promote.

It is difficult to persuade workmen who are not too highly paid that it is necessary in a time of depression to reduce their wages in order to avert bankruptcy. It is perhaps still more difficult to persuade them, in times when large profits have been earned, that great portions of these profits should be put aside to meet the stress of bad years and commercial losses, to accumulate a reserve fund, to obtain new and improved machinery, to enlarge buildings, or to establish new branches, for which there seems no very pressing or immediate need, but which are at the same time essential to the ultimate success of their enterprises. Large industries also are among the many things in the world that cannot be carried on successfully without an amount of discipline and an exercise of authority that cannot easily be obtained in a system of republican equality. The spirit of command and the spirit of obedience must both be there, and there must be some power that can promptly and decisively enforce submission and expel inefficient or recalcitrant members. It must be added, too, that this form of co-operation is still in such an early and undeveloped stage that a few conspicuous disasters produce a disproportionate amount of discouragement.

On the whole, a broad distinction must be drawn between

co-operative distribution and co-operative production. The former, which depends for its profits on the suppression of the middleman, and on the great cheapness that may be attained by an enormous and rapid sale and very extensive choice, has proved of late years brilliantly successful. The purchasers have gained largely in the shape of diminished prices, and the shareholders, in a large proportion of these societies, in ample dividends. These societies are largely working-class institutions, though many of the most conspicuous are chiefly owned by, and profitable to, other classes. In 1891 there appear to have been 1,459 retail distributive co-operative societies in Great Britain, with 1,098,352 members, and profits of no less than 4,342,373*l*. had been realised on their sales during the year.[90]

There are also numerous examples, both in England and in other countries, of successful co-operative establishments for production. It is true, as I have said, that most of the earlier societies, and especially the State-aided institutions in France, speedily failed, but experience has done much to solve the difficulty. On both sides of the Channel the conditions under which such establishments can be successfully worked are now much better understood, and large numbers of industries have adopted the system, and are working it with respectable profits. Their success has not been conspicuously brilliant, nor has it been unchequered, but it has been, on the whole, real and lasting, and establishments of this kind are steadily, though not very rapidly, increasing. They do not appear to be greatly encouraged by trade unions, which generally refuse to invest any of their funds in them; the societies for co-operative distribution do not usually connect themselves with them;[91] and there seems little probability that they will so far displace individual capitalist production as to become the dominant form; but, at the same time, they have acquired a considerable importance within the last thirty-five

---

[90] Jones's *History of Co-operative Production*, i. 1.
[91] See Howell's *Conflicts of Labour*, pp. 460–61.

years. They are naturally viewed with much dislike by the Socialist demagogues who are trying to foment ill-feeling between the employer and the employed, for they do very much to reconcile these classes. They make the workers themselves capitalists, produce in them the feelings and instincts of capitalists, and place industry on a basis that gives no scope to class animosity. They have also a great indirect value in enabling working men to understand more thoroughly than they could possibly do by other means the true conditions and prospects of a trade, and the rate of wages which can be profitably paid. In all these ways they prevent labour wars, and tend to correct the fatal fallacy that capital and labour are essentially antagonistic.[92]

The establishment of such societies has been largely due to the Limited Liability Act making it possible to establish companies with moderate risk, and it has been much assisted by the growth of national education. The industrial uses of education are great and evident, though, as I have already pointed out, there are certain drawbacks, which practical men have now learned clearly to realise. They observe how the general effect of the spread of school education is to produce among the poor a disdain for mere manual labour and for the humbler forms of menial service, and they notice, with some concern, a greatly increased restlessness of character and a much stronger appetite for amusement and excitement. It shows itself in the increased love of gambling; in the growing preference for the hard work of the factory, with its free evenings, to the lighter work but greater restraints of domestic service; in the more fluctuating and nomadic character which domestic service has itself assumed. It enters, as we have seen, as an important element into the migration of the agricultural population to the great towns; and it is very apparent in the

---

[92] Mr. Howell has given a long catalogue of the more successful establishments of this sort (*Conflicts of Labour*, pp. 461–65). See, too, the excellent chapter of Lord Brassey (*Work and Wages*, pp. 247–60); Jones's *History of Co-operation;* Jevons's *Work and Wages*, pp. 144–46.

country districts, in an increasing disposition to choose casual and irregular work at comparatively high wages rather than regular and constant work at lower pay, and also in a greatly increased objection among agricultural labourers to isolation, which leads them to prefer to pay a high rent for a bad cottage in a village rather than a low rent for a good cottage on a farm. This desertion of the farms for the village has been justly considered one of the most significant facts in recent agricultural history.[93] On the other hand, education generally produces self-respect. It makes men quick to perceive and prompt to avail themselves of opportunities of improving their position, and thus tends to raise and to maintain the levels of industry. In all the higher branches, by developing intelligence, it increases power, and, where a work of difficult administration is required, it is almost indispensable. The prudence, foresight, self-control, and skill in management which are essential for successful co-operative work, are not likely to be found in an uneducated class.

The remarks which I have made about co-operation in production apply, with little change, to the various schemes of profit-sharing under which workmen receive, in addition to their wages, either a percentage on the whole profits of their work, or a proportion of such profits as are made in excess of a certain reserved limit. Schemes of this kind were much advocated by the Christian Socialists in England, and they have had some considerable success. They leave the management and risks in the hands of the employer, who seeks his profit in the increased stimulus given to industry, in the diminished need of supervision, in a closer tie of interest, binding the workman to his business, in the special attraction this form of industry presents to the more efficient workman. The bonus system is often so arranged as to come gradually into operation, to take the form of provisions for old age, and to depend largely on the length of time the workman continues in his employment.

---

[93] See the very interesting report of Mr. W. C. Little on the agricultural labourer before the Labour Commission (*Fifth and Final Report*).

The various systems of profit-sharing are only applicable to a limited number of industries. They work best in those which are at once profitable and steady, and in these they have widely adopted, and appear to have given a large measure of satisfaction. In trades where profits are precarious, violently fluctuating, and often, for long periods, suspended, they are rarely successful. In general, the trade unions dislike them. By establishing a close union between the employer and his workmen they withdraw the latter from trade-union influence; and strong objections are urged against the provisions which are intended to guard against strikes, against the minimum rate of profit which is often guaranteed to the employer before the workmen's profits accrue, against the tendency of the system to encourage increased work and unequal rewards, corresponding to diversities of industry and skill. The great strike against the South Metropolitan Gas Company in 1890 was a desperate but wholly unsuccessful attempt to break down this system. There is so much difficulty and complexity in its practical application that this form of industry is never likely to become universal; but wherever it has succeeded it tends, by establishing a kind of industrial partnership, to cure some of the worst evils of our time. There are said to be already seventy-seven profit-sharing firms in Great Britain and the Colonies, with over 16,000 persons employed in them.[94] In the United States, more than 10,000 workmen are said to be admitted to a share in the profits of the industries in which they are engaged.[95]

In France also the system has been largely and skilfully developed. In spite of all her political revolutions, the French laws permitting combinations of workmen are very recent. It was not until 1864 that some small amount of liberty was granted to working men's combinations and syndicates, and trade unions were only fully and formally authorised in 1884. It must be added, too, that though they have proved active and very belligerent bodies, they are not believed to comprise more

---

[94] *Digest of Evidence before the Labour Commission,* p. 33.
[95] *Forum,* March 1895, p. 57.

than 6 or 7 per cent. of the French working men.[96] On the other hand, the larger manufacturers, and still more the great industrial companies, have succeeded to a remarkable degree in uniting their interests with those of their workmen, and creating a strong and healthy sympathy between them. They have done so in many ways. They have built cheap cottages for their workmen in the immediate neighbourhood of their work, and where the workmen live at a distance they have organised a system known as the 'Economat,' for providing them with food at very cheap rates in their places of work. They have largely supported savings banks, pension funds, and sometimes gratuitous schools connected with their works. They have often introduced the system of adding a certain percentage of salaries after two or three years' service, and granting special bonuses to workmen engaged in works in which special exertions are required. They have given shares in the profits of their establishments mainly in the form of saving funds, increasing in proportion to the length of time the workman remains in his employment, and managed by a joint committee representing the employers and the workmen. They have also adopted the system of filling vacancies in their establishments by appointing chiefly the children or other relatives of their staffs. In the large shops a commission of from 2 to 3 per cent. is usually granted to the assistants who sell the goods.

In all these ways a strong co-operative feeling and interest is created, and industry receives a new impulse and a new stability. It is observed that this system, like so many other influences, works in the direction of large industries. The great company or the great manufacturer can do these things, but not the small employer. In the words of a valuable Government report, 'the owners of large private concerns, either by personal solicitude for the welfare of their men, or by a judicious distribution of annual gratuities, have generally

---

[96] *Report on the Relations between Capital and Labour in France* (Foreign Office, 1892), p. 6.

succeeded in retaining a staff of able and fairly contented workmen; but the small employers, on whom very often the worst, and consequently the most discontented, wage-earners filter down, have not been so successful. Often their circumstances prevent their doing more than just pay the current rate of wages, and their engrossing sympathy for their own wants and difficulties is a hindrance to their sympathising with the complaints of those they employ . . . and this in a measure accounts for the hatred existing towards the *petit bourgeois*.'

A natural consequence is that the best workmen prefer to work under a company or in a large firm, and, when the system I have described proves successful, they are usually completely alienated from trade-union politics. 'Workmen who join profit-sharing establishments,' it is said, 'desert the army of labour, and declare war on the syndicates.'[97]

In addition to profit-sharing, there are various other expedients for connecting the interests of employer and employed, and preventing ruinous trade quarrels. There is the sliding-scale system, according to which wages are advanced or diminished on a recognised scale, in proportion to the rise and fall of prices. It has prevailed largely in England during the last quarter of a century in the iron, steel, and coal industries, and, in a less degree, in the manufactures of lace and hosiery.[98] There is the system of piecework, which exists, though in very fluctuating proportions, in many industries, and which, beyond all others, establishes a fair proportion between wages and production, and furnishes strong incentives to industry and ambition. There is the system of paying work by the hour, giving the workmen large liberty of lengthening or shortening their day. Great efforts have also been made to substitute in

---

[97] *Report on the Relations between Capital and Labour in France* (Foreign Office, 1892), pp. 17–18. This very interesting report, which was drawn up by Sir Condie Stephen, gives an excellent account of labour relations in France. Compare Guyot, *La Tyrannie Socialiste*, pp. 232–34.
[98] See Howell's *Conflicts of Labour*, pp. 439, 448.

industrial conflicts arbitration for strikes. Conciliation boards and arbitration boards, on which both parties in the dispute are represented, and which consist of men in whose judicial qualities both parties have confidence, have attempted, with great success, to prevent and to terminate strikes. Sometimes these boards are permanent bodies. The North of England Board of Conciliation and Arbitration for the Manufactured Iron Trade, which was founded in 1869, has been the most successful, and the London Chamber of Commerce has shown itself very useful and active in the same direction. It is said that some three thousand disputes in the Northumberland coal trade have been settled by joint committees.[99]

The example has been chiefly set by France, where, as early as the reign of the Great Napoleon, conciliation boards were established, under the name of Conseils de Prud'hommes, for the purpose of settling disputes about the terms of labour compacts. Each of them is divided into a bureau of conciliation and a bureau of judgment, or, as we should say, of arbitration. They are instituted, at the initiative of the local chamber of commerce, by Government decree, and they consist of equal numbers of employers and workmen, with a president and vice-president, who were once appointed by the Government, but are now elected by the body itself. The success of these bodies has been very remarkable. From 30,000 to 45,000 cases are said to be annually brought before them, and in about 70 per cent. of these cases they succeed in reconciling the disputants.[100] In Belgium, Austria, and Germany, also, there are elaborate provisions for settling labour disputes.

In England an Act was passed in 1867 authorising the Secretary of State, under certain conditions, to grant a license for the formation of councils much like those in France, and,

---

[99] Howell's *Conflicts of Labour,* p. 439.
[100] Jevons's *State in relation to Labour,* p. 164; *Report on the Relations between Capital and Labour in France,* pp. 19–22; Samuelson, *Boards of Conciliation in Labour Disputes,* pp. 6–7.

while strictly limiting the subjects on which they might pronounce, it gave them powers of enforcing their awards; but this Act, as well as a later one which was carried in 1872, appears to have been a dead-letter, and conciliation and arbitration boards of a purely voluntary character have been found most acceptable both to employers and workmen. They have greatly multiplied, and boards of this kind, consisting of equal numbers of employers and workmen, have been established in a great variety of trades. Perhaps the most useful service rendered by the Government in this field is the collection of a large amount of accurate statistical information about the condition of work and wages in many countries.

In all these ways much has been done to mitigate class antagonism in industrial life. Much, too, is done by the Government to encourage thrift in the shape of savings banks and kindred institutions, which bridge over the chasm between the wage-earning and the wage-paying classes, extend to the working class the advantages of the national credit, and, by making their savings a portion of the National Debt, blend their interests very closely with the great property interests of the nation.

In France, and in several other continental countries, one great safeguard of property lies in the extensive subdivision of land, which raises up a bulwark against which Anarchist and Socialist passions dash in vain. In England this bulwark does not exist; for, although the legal owners have been shown to be a much larger body than had been frequently alleged, and although the real owners, who hold charges on the land, are very numerous, the ostensible ownership of the soil is in the hands of a comparatively small class, whose political power has greatly diminished. If the agricultural interest had been as powerful in England as in France, English legislation would probably have taken a somewhat different course during the last half-century; and, amid the ruinous depression through which English agriculture is fast withering away, the inadequacy of its political representation has become a great national evil. Extensions of the suffrage have not improved it. They have left the relative importance of town and country unchanged, and, by creating or deepening divisions between labourers and farmers, between Churchmen and Nonconformists, they have rather weakened than strengthened the interests of agriculture. Nothing, I think, can be clearer than that, in a democratic State, land should be in many hands. In this way only can it exercise its legitimate influence, and secure itself from injustice and extortion. It does not appear to me possible, in the existing conditions of English life, to defend with success the law of primogeniture in case of intestacy, and it is extremely desirable that all legal restrictions and obstacles that make the division of land and its sale in small quantities difficult and expensive, should be swept away.

It does not follow from this that the old laws favouring agglomerations of land should be looked on as acts of injustice or tyranny. They were intended to maintain in England a governing class who could be trusted to administer, for the most part gratuitously, county business, and at the same time to conduct the affairs of the nation with honesty and dignity. In spite of many shortcomings, this end was attained, and, under the government of her gentry, the English nation in its long and chequered past has achieved as large an amount of freedom, of greatness, of honest administration, and of internal prosperity, as any nation in modern history. Nor is it true that the interests of the poor have been largely or consciously sacrificed. Cases may, no doubt, be cited in English history in which class interest had an undue power in legislation, and things have been done in the past which cannot be justified if measured by nineteenth-century standards; but still, in every period of her history, England can well bear a comparison with the most favoured nations of the Continent. It would be difficult or impossible to find any country in Europe in which the general level of prosperity has been higher, the taxation more equitable, and the relations of classes more healthy.

The old order, however, has manifestly changed, and the

great agglomerations of property, which were once so closely connected with the prevailing political type, have become a source of political weakness and danger. The question how far it is likely that English soil will be more subdivided than at present is one of great difficulty and complexity. The system of compulsory equal division which, under the influence of the Code Napoléon, has spread so widely over Europe, has taken no root in either English or American public opinion. Traditional habits and ideas throughout the English-speaking world are strongly opposed to it, while the revolutionary party would probably dislike it, as strengthening the sentiment of hereditary property, and the rights of the family as against the claims of the community. If agriculture in England were prosperous, it does not seem to me possible that it would take the form of a peasant proprietary. The two forms in which such a tenure of land is most profitable are vineyards and market-gardening; but the first does not exist in England, and, in the face of foreign competition, the second can never play more than a very subsidiary part in English agriculture; while pasture, into which England is more and more turning, is not adapted for small farms.

The disappearance of the yeomanry, which is so often and in some respects so justly lamented, was not in any perceptible degree due to the laws of entail and primogeniture, and was probably only slightly accelerated by the enclosure of common land. It was mainly due to irresistible economical forces, which I have already traced, and which were closely connected with the growth of manufactures. When the small proprietor found that he could greatly increase his income by selling his farm and investing the proceeds in trade, or by selling his farm, renting it from the purchaser, and employing his capital in stocking it, one or other of these courses was certain to be followed. In our own day, if the ownership of land is not widely diffused among the farming classes, this is much more due to the absence of all wish on their part to buy than to any indisposition on the part of the landlord to sell. The political arguments in favour of a peasant proprietary are, indeed, even now far more powerful than either the social or the economic ones.

In Ireland, as is well known, great efforts are made to create such a proprietary; but the conditions of Ireland are unlike those of any other part of the civilised globe. It has been the deliberate policy of the Government to break down, by almost annual Acts, the obligation of contracts, and the existing ownership of land has been rendered so insecure, the political power attached to it has been so effectually destroyed, and the influences tending to anarchy and confiscation have been made so powerful, that most good judges have come to the conclusion that it is necessary to force into existence by strong legislative measures a new social type, which may perhaps possess some elements of stability and conservatism. In order to effect this object the national credit has been made use of in such a way that a tenant is enabled to purchase his farm without making the smallest sacrifice for that object, the whole sum being advanced by the Government, and advanced on such terms that the tenant is only obliged to pay for a limited number of years a sum from 20 to 30 per cent. less than his present rent. In other words, a man whose rent has been fixed by the Land Court at 100*l.* a year can purchase his farm by paying, instead of that sum, 70*l.* or 80*l.* a year for forty-nine years. The arrangement sounds more like burlesque than serious legislation; but the belief that political pressure can obtain still better terms for the tenant, and that further confiscatory legislation may still more depreciate the value of land to the owner who has inherited it, or purchased it in the open market, has taken such deep root in Ireland that the tenants have shown little alacrity to avail themselves of their new privilege.

What may be the ultimate issue of the attempt to govern a country in complete defiance of all received economical principles remains to be seen. The future must show whether a large peasant proprietary can be not only called into existence, but permanently maintained, under these conditions, and whether it will prove the loyal and conservative element that

English politicians believe. According to all past experience, peasant proprietors rarely succeed, except when they possess something more than an average measure of industrial qualities, and the Irish purchase laws give no preference to the energetic, the industrious, and the thrifty. On the contrary, it is very often the farmer who is on the verge of bankruptcy who is most eager to buy, in order to reduce his annual charge. The tendency of the new proprietors to mortgage, to sublet, and to subdivide, is already manifest, and some of the best judges of Irish affairs, who look beyond the present generation, are very despondent about the future. They believe that a peasant proprietary called into existence suddenly and artificially, with no discrimination in favour of the better class, in a country where industrial qualities are very low, and where the strongest wish of the farmer is either to divide his farm among his children, or to burden it with equal mortgages for their benefit,[101] must eventually lead to economic ruin, to fatal subdivision, to crushing charges on land. The new policy must also, they contend, almost wholly withdraw from the country life where it is peculiarly needed, the civilising and guiding influence of a resident gentry. Whether or not these apprehensions are exaggerated time only can show. Two predictions may, I think, with some confidence be made. The one is, that the transformation is likely to be most successful if it is gradually effected. The other is, that a great part of the influence once possessed by the landlord will, under the new conditions, pass to the money-lender.

We may perhaps derive more instructive facts bearing on the probable future of English land from the example of what is taking place in New England and some of the other parts of the United States. The competition of American wheat, which has ruined agriculture over a great part of England, is felt with still greater force in New England and New York,

---

[101] It may be observed that the farm of the peasant proprietor has been made by law personal property; so that if, as is very often the case, the owner makes no will, his sons have equal rights in the inheritance.

where the overwhelming influx of the products of the Western States has beaten down most prices to unremunerative levels. The first result has been a great removal of population from the country to the towns. The second has been a large diminution of the number of farms. In Massachusetts alone there were, in 1890, 1,461 abandoned farms. In the State of New York there were, in 1890, 16,108 fewer farms than in 1880. At the same time the steady tendency seems to be to larger farms, worked as much as possible by labour-saving machinery, and exhibiting a much greater variety of farming than in the past. Market-gardening and tree-planting seem to have rapidly increased, and much inferior land has gone out of cultivation. In Maine, which is called 'the Lumber State,' scarcely a third of the State is occupied by farms, and more than half of the farms are under wood. While the old farmers of New England, who were once the backbone of these States, are moving in great numbers to the towns, they are in some districts largely replaced by foreigners—chiefly French Canadians, who are accustomed to more economical habits and a lower standard of comfort.

Land in all these States has always been cultivated chiefly by its owners, but it is a remarkable fact that there appears to have been during the period of depression some movement in New England towards the English system of rented farms. In 1880, 91·8 per cent. of the farms were cultivated by their owners; in 1890, only 85 per cent.[102] In general all farming in the United States is conducted on a much larger scale than in the peasant-proprietor countries of Europe. In the words of the British Ambassador in the United States: 'With a very few isolated exceptions, there does not exist in the United States the class of peasant proprietors as understood in European countries. There are to be found in agricultural districts a few

---

[102] I have taken these facts from a very careful and interesting examination of American agriculture by M. E. Levasseur in a series of papers in the *Comptes Rendus* of the Académie des Sciences Morales et Politiques in 1895. These papers have, I believe, been republished in a book.

farmers whose farms are of only twenty acres or thereabouts, but the term "peasant proprietors" could not in any way be applied to them.[103]

A series of reports were presented to Parliament in 1891, drawn up by the different British diplomatists in the countries to which they were accredited, relating to the increase of diminution of the number of peasant proprietors, and of the debts with which they were burdened during the preceding twenty years, but the evidence accumulated is so imperfect and conflicting that it scarcely authorises us to draw any fixed conclusion. Thus it was shown that in that portion of the Austrian Empire where the peasant properties are large and seldom divided there is a far higher level of cultivation and a far smaller proportion of debt than in the part where the system of small farms and constant division prevails. In the German Empire, where the habit of letting farms is seldom practised except on princely estates, and where an overwhelming majority of the estates are managed by their owners, there is decisive evidence that the farmers who have suffered least by the long period of depreciation are those who are the owners of what are termed middle-sized farms, which range from about 18 to about 370 acres, and are probably, on an average, a little more than 60 acres.

In France the number of persons cultivating their own land is believed to have increased during the last twenty years by rather less than ½ per cent., but there has been a large diminution in the number of farm-servants. There has been a considerable movement of population, both from agricultural and productive industry, to commercial and transport occupations. The larger farms tend to increase, but the general average size of the plots of land cultivated is diminishing. Most of the peasant proprietors have very small holdings, but most of the land of France belongs to the proprietors of farms ranging from 23 to 115 acres. About 78 per cent. of the

---

[103] *Report of Sir Julian Pauncefote; Reports on the Position of Peasant Proprietors Abroad* (1891).

rural owners themselves till the land they own or occupy. The author of the report expresses his belief that, owing to 'the intensely frugal habits' of the French peasantry, their indebtedness has not increased, but rather diminished, during the last twenty years. This statement, however, seems to rest chiefly on conjecture, as there are no available statistics, and it is quite inconsistent with the experience of all other countries where the system of peasant proprietorship exists.

In the smaller countries the evidence of rapidly increasing debt is very great, and in some of the countries where peasant proprietorship is most extended the distress has been extremely acute. In Belgium almost the only peasant proprietors who were not poorer in 1890 than in 1880 were said to be found among the very smallest and poorest, who employ no hired labour, and cultivate their own land with their own children. In the Netherlands the only accurate statistics on the subject appear to be for the five years from 1883 to 1887 inclusive, and they are certainly abundantly significant. In that time the unredeemed mortgages of the peasant proprietors nearly doubled, having risen from 80,000*l.* to 158,000*l.*, and while the number of the very small farms not exceeding 2½ acres has increased, there has been a considerable diminution in the number of rent-paying farmers.

In some parts of Switzerland the number of peasant proprietors has greatly declined, but in the whole country it is believed to have considerably increased. This, however, is no real proof of the success of the system, for it is largely due to the much smaller number of peasant proprietors who now buy up neighbouring farms, and also to the marked tendency to break up the common lands. In Switzerland, as in nearly all other countries, there has been a rapid increase of the debt of the peasant proprietors during the last thirty years, and if it is not checked it will, in the opinion of the author of the report, seriously endanger their position. Much the same thing may be said about the Scandinavian countries, in which the system of peasant proprietors is popular, and works well, and is encouraged by several special laws. In Denmark, during the last forty years, the debt has increased from about 25 to more than 50 per cent. of the value of the landed properties.

These facts do not seem to me to point to any general movement in favour of peasant proprietors. At the same time, in England land will, no doubt, soon be held by a larger number of persons than at present. The laws that favoured its agglomeration have been repealed, and nearly all the social, political, and economical motives that led to it have either passed away or greatly diminished. If under the combined influence of agricultural depression and Radical finance the great historical properties come frequently into the market, it is probable that the new millionaires will often prefer to purchase a great place unincumbered by large tracts of farming-land, which now add little to the power or the social consequence of the purchaser.

Several important Acts have been passed within the last few years for the purpose of improving the condition of the agricultural labourers, and, if possible, checking their migration to the towns. Sanitary authorities and county councils have obtained large powers of closing or removing insanitary dwellings, acquiring sites, and building houses for the working classes. In London and several of the great provincial towns these powers have been largely exercised, and they have also, in some degree, been employed for the benefit of the agricultural labourer. Under an Act of 1887 allotments have been multiplied, and the Small Holdings Act of 1892 attempted to create a peasant proprietary on the lines of the Irish Purchase Act, by enabling the county councils to lend public money on certain conditions to small farmers for the purchase of their farms. Legislation of this kind is the first fruit of the extension of the suffrage to the agricultural labourer, and it bears much resemblance to the old Tudor legislation annexing four acres of land to every agricultural cottage. It is intended for the benefit of a poor, suffering, meritorious, and silent class, and in as far as it gives them healthier and happier lives it deserves all sympathy. Whether, however, in the face of existing economical tendencies, it is possible to create by law on any large scale a peasant proprietary, appears to me more than doubtful. There are manifest dangers in the disposition to place great compulsory powers of purchasing land in the hands of the new elective bodies, and to enable them to levy rates and accumulate debt for the benefit of a single class of their electors. But the elevation of the humbler levels of the agricultural population is a matter of the very highest national importance, and, when compulsory purchase is made on equitable terms, it does not appear to me in such a cause to exceed the legitimate powers of Government.

One of the most powerful of the earlier causes of the migration of labourers to the towns was the destruction by the factory system of the domestic industries which once flourished in the rural villages and in countless isolated farmhouses. Considerable efforts have been made in the present generation to bring back, on a small scale, some of these industries. Philanthropy has done something to stimulate the movement, and, both in France and England, manufacturers in the great towns have lately found it profitable to have portions of their work done by the cheaper labour of the country. It is a course which is bitterly resented by the town labourers and their representatives, and seems likely to become the cause of much labour dispute. It was one of the causes of the great lock-out in the boot trade in the spring of 1895; and I have already mentioned the attempt of the Municipality of Paris to prevent it. It is possible—though the suggestion can only be thrown out as one of distant and uncertain conjecture—that the progress of science may some day bring back to the country districts a larger portion of their old industries. If electricity becomes a cheap and easily managed motor force, it may make it possible to do many things in the cottage which can now only be done in the factory.

There is one form of agglomerated property which probably endangers the security of property in England much more than the great country estates. It is the vast town properties, which are in England in a very few hands, and which, being let at long leases, have risen enormously in value, owing to the general prosperity and efforts of the community. Few persons who have watched the Radical and Socialist tendencies of modern times can fail to perceive that it is this form of property which has proved most invidious, and which lends itself most readily to socialistic attacks. The immense increase of value, which is not due to any exertion on the part of the owner; the power which a selfish or unwise owner may exercise in obstructing the development of the community; the bad effects of the leasehold system, in producing buildings calculated to last little longer than the period of a lease, are keenly felt, and schemes for the special taxation of such properties, and for a compulsory transformation of leaseholds into freeholds, are acquiring much favour. It is greatly to be wished that the large town landlords would generally follow the example which has been set by a few members of their class, and make it their policy to convert, on equitable terms, their long leases into freeholds. Few things would do so much to strengthen property in England as the existence of a very large body of freehold owners in our great towns. The multiplication of small working-class ownerships, through the instrumentality of building societies, has in this, as in other ways, been one of the most healthy movements of our time.

The more intelligent Socialists are under no delusion about its effects. It is a characteristic fact that Engels, the chief disciple of Marx, was one of the bitterest opponents of the policy of making the working man the owner of his house, and, if he lives in the country, of a small garden. This Engels described as the 'bourgeois' solution of the labour question. He denounced it as the infamous device of the capitalist to buy labour cheap, as a cause of bondage for the working man, and a misfortune for his entire class.[104] In no quarter is the idea of a peasant proprietary more disliked than among the disciples of Mr. George.

---

[104] See on Engel's views the essay of M. Raffalovich on Working-class Housing in *A Plea for Liberty*, edited by Mr. Mackay, p. 219.

In considering the acuteness which labour troubles have assumed in modern days, a large place must be assigned to moral causes. The inequalities of fortune are undoubtedly felt much more keenly than in the past. The agglomeration of men in great towns, and the sharp division of those towns into the quarters of the rich and the quarters of the poor, bring into salient relief the too frequent contrasts between extravagant luxury and struggling misery. Education has strengthened among the poor the sense of the disparities of life, and by increasing self-respect and multiplying tastes and wants it raises the standard of what are deemed its necessaries. Wellbeing has greatly increased, but it has not increased as rapidly as desires. The breaking up, among large classes, of old religious beliefs has given an additional impulse to the restlessness of society; and when the hope of a future world no longer supplies a vivid and strongly realised consolation amidst the miseries of life, it is not surprising that the desire to obtain the best things of this world should attain a passionate force. And all this restlessness concurs with the unexampled opportunities for agitation which the conditions of modern life afford, with the growth of a great popular press which represents, echoes, re-echoes, and intensifies every discontent.

It concurs also with the new sense of power, the new vistas of untried possibilities, which triumphant democracy has opened to the poor. Nearly all the wide legislative movements I have enumerated are attempts to realise quickly and by compulsory action changes which, under the system of unrestricted freedom, had been steadily growing. Building societies and artisans' dwelling companies have anticipated legislative and municipal action in providing sanitary houses for the working classes, and they have succeeded in making their enterprises thoroughly remunerative. Pensions for old age and infirmity, and insurance against accidents, have long been leading features of unobtrusive provident societies, working without any compulsory powers, and resting upon a sound commerical basis. By voluntary co-operation and voluntary bargaining, unassisted by law, trade unions have succeeded in obtaining over large areas, and wherever it is economically profitable, nearly all those boons which legislators are now asked to enforce by law. But swifter and larger changes are demanded by the new democracy, and they are pursued often with effects which their authors had neither foreseen nor desired.

On the side of the wealthy, also, there is a much clearer realisation of the misery and injustices of life. Compassion in nearly all its forms has grown both wider and more sensitive. If the purely dogmatic elements in religion have waned, if the saintly type of character as moulded by the ideals of an ascetic and introspective faith has lost much of its old power, the philanthropic side of religion has certainly strengthened. Morality is looked upon much less as a series of restrictions and prohibitions than as a positive force impelling man to active duties, and chiefly measured by useful service to mankind. The unity of the race, the brotherhood of man, is more strongly felt, and there is a genuine and growing desire to open the spheres of opportunity and the great sources of human pleasure more largely to the poor.

Much in this direction has been done, chiefly by the great inventions of modern times and by the normal course of economical and moral growth, but largely also through the action of wise legislation and disinterested philanthropy. Education in nearly all its forms has been widely diffused. Picture galleries, museums, libraries, more sumptuous than any millionaire could collect, are the common property of the nation, and gratuitously open to all classes. Charitable institutions, enriched by the benefactions of many generations, and growing in full proportion to the growth of capital, bring the best medical and surgical appliances within the reach of the poor, and alleviate in countless forms their suffering and want. Noble parks and gardens are opened for their pleasure, and they have more leisure to enjoy them. The public domain, which is the common property of rich and poor, continually augments. Many artificial barriers have been broken down, and many paths to eminence and wealth thrown open to ability in every rank; and while the decline of pauperism and crime, the rise of wages, the prolongation of life, and the shortening of work hours, attest the substantial improvement in the condition of the poor, the range, variety, and cheapness of amusements have greatly increased.

The picture, it is true, is not unchequered. The land has become overcrowded. The strain of competition in many forms has grown more intense. The conditions of modern industry bring with them vast and frequent fluctuations, which increase the great evil of unemployed labour. Among the very poorest, misery is probably as acute as it has ever been. It is also true that many of the forms of pleasure which gave England the title of 'merrie England' have passed away or greatly diminished through changed conditions of life, through changes of tastes, manners, and beliefs. But for these last losses, at least, the printing press and the railway furnish ample compensation, and whoever will be at the pains to analyse the pleasures of rich and poor will probably be struck with the enormous proportion that may be directly or indirectly traced to their influence.

Envy is not a characteristic of the Anglo-Saxon democracies at either side of the Atlantic, and I do not believe that wealth honourably acquired and wisely, usefully, and generously employed, is ever likely to be really unpopular among them. Nor is it probable that they will ever to a large extent adopt the doctrine which is now so industriously propagated, that there is something immoral, and injurious to society, in living on an unearned income, or, in other words, on inhertied property. The number of men who are able to do so form, even in the richest countries, but a small fraction of the population, and many of the most useful and industrious lives may be found among them. To this class belonged William Wilberforce, and John Howard, and Lord Shaftesbury, and countless other philanthropists, whose services to mankind can hardly be overpraised. Great inherited properties usually carry with them large and useful administrative duties, and no class of

men in England have, on the whole, lived better lives, and
contributed more to the real wellbeing of the community, than
the less wealthy country gentlemen who, contenting themselves with the moderate incomes they inherited, lived upon
their estates, administering county business, and improving
in countless ways the condition of their tenants and of their
neighbours. It might have been better for these men, but it
would certainly not have been better for the community, if
they had thrown themselves more generally into the already
overcrowded paths of professional life, displaced poorer men
who were struggling for its prizes, or secured for themselves
a larger number of coveted Government appointments, paid
for out of the taxation of the nation.

The impulse of ambition may be sufficiently trusted to impel rich men of extraordinary abilities to the development of
their powers, and it is certainly no disadvantage to the world
if their circumstances and their aptitudes combine to lead
them to paths from which they never could have derived a
livelihood. It is possible that if Darwin had become a physician he might have earned a larger professional income than
his father. It is possible that if Sir Charles Lyell had applied
to the practice of the law his rare powers of collecting and
appreciating evidence he might have become a chancellor or
a judge. It was surely better that these great men should have
contented themselves with the 'unearned incomes' which
they had inherited, and should have devoted themselves to
pursuits which during the greater part of their lives were absolutely unremunerative. A man who has serious work to
perform in the world is in no degree to be blamed if he makes
it his object to minimise the cares of life by throwing his fortune, if it is in his power to do so, into forms that require little
thought, effort, or responsibility. English public life in most
of its branches has been largely filled by men who lived upon
inherited competences, took no means to increase them, and
gave their services gratuitously to their country.

It is quite right that a legislator, in adjusting taxation,
should take into account the fact that a realised property de-

scends undiminished from father to son, while a professional
income is a precarious thing, depending on the life and
strength of the man who earns it. It is, however, a false and
mischievous doctrine that the one form of property is less legitimate than the other. Society is a compact chiefly for securing to each man a peaceful possession of his property, and,
as long as a man fulfils his part in the social compact, his right
to what he has received from his father is as valid as his right
to what he has himself earned. In the one case as in the other,
no doubt the Supreme Legislature in England has the power
of confiscation. But moral right and constitutional power are
different things, and it is one of the worst consequences of the
English doctrine of the omnipotence of Parliament that it
tends to confuse them.

It is not the existence of inherited wealth, even on a very
large scale, that is likely to shake seriously the respect for
property: it is the many examples which the conditions of
modern society present of vast wealth acquired by shameful
means, employed for shameful purposes, and exercising an
altogether undue influence in society and in the State. When
triumphant robbery is found among the rich, subversive doctrines will grow among the poor. When democracy turns, as
it often does, into a corrupt plutocracy, both national decadence and social revolution are being prepared. No one who
peruses modern Socialist literature, no one who observes the
current of feeling among the masses in the great towns, can
fail to perceive their deep, growing, and not unreasonable
sense of the profound injustices of life. In the words of one
of the most popular of these writers, 'Jay Gould, the "finan-
cier," got more "pay" and held more wealth than Gladstone,
and Carlyle, and Darwin, and Koch, and Galileo, and Colum-
bus, and Cromwell, and Caxton, and Stephenson, and Washington, and Raphael, and Mozart, and Shakespeare, and
Socrates, and Jesus Christ ever got amongst them. So perfect
is the present system of pay!'[105]

---

[105] Blatchford's *Merrie England*, p. 139.

When in the immediate neighbourhood of the wretched slums of our great cities there are to be found societies where dignity is mainly measured by wealth, irrespective of the source from which it is derived and the purposes to which it is applied; when in the mad race of luxury and ostentation men are ever seeking for and inventing new and costly inutilities to gratify the freaks of fashion, and lavishing sums that might bring comfort to a hundred families on the pleasures of a single night, or on trinkets that are not really more respectable than the beads and feathers of the savage, it is not surprising that feelings should strengthen and opinions should grow that portend grave convulsions in the State. In these things law can do little, but opinion can do much. A sterner judgment of ill-gotten wealth and of luxurious, vicious, or merely idle lives, a higher standard of public duty, and something more of that 'plain living' which is the usual accompaniment of 'high thinking' are the best remedies that can be applied.

CHAPTER 10

Woman Questions

There is one other class of questions connected with the democratic movement in Europe which has during the last few decades risen rapidly in prominence, and which, though it has been incidentally touched upon in several of the preceding chapters, requires a somewhat fuller examination. I mean the changes which have taken place in the position and education of women, and the rapidly growing movement in favour of conferring on them some considerable share of political power.

There are few more curious facts in the history of opinion than the entire omission in the works of Rousseau and of the writers of his school of all mention of the political rights of women, although the first principle of their philosophy was that the exercise of political power was a natural and inalienable right. According to the 'Contrat Social' and the 'Emile,' no law could have any binding force unless it had been directly sanctioned by universal suffrage, and the sovereignty of the people was so sacred and inalienable that no contracts, no voluntary resignation, no consideration of expediency, could limit, or suspend, or annul it. Yet the very writers who preached this doctrine as a law of nature were content that one half of the adult population should be absolutely excluded by the other half from all political power, and should have no voice in the laws which regulate their property and, in a great degree, mould their destiny.

Rousseau wrote much, and sometimes with great acuteness, on the distinctions between men and women; but few writers of the eighteenth century asserted more strongly the essentially subordinate position of the latter. 'Women,' he said 'are specially made to please men.' 'All their education should be relative to men. To please them, to be useful to them, to make themselves loved and honoured by them, to bring them up when young, to take care of them when grown up, to counsel, to console them, to make their lives agreeable and pleasant—these, in all ages, have been the duties of women, and it is for these duties that they should be educated from infancy.' Even in their religious beliefs the subordination should be complete. Like Plutarch, Rousseau strongly maintains that a wife should know no religion except that of her husband, and that she should in her turn transmit it to her daughters. 'Even if this religion is false, the docility with which wife and daughter submit to the order of nature effaces in the sight of God the sin of error. Being incapable of judging for themselves, they ought to accept the decision of their fathers and their husbands like that of the Church.'[1] The only important exception to the prevailing tone among the writers of the Revolution was Condorcet, who, in an almost forgotten writing published in 1787, urged that it was impossible to establish the existence of rights of men anterior to social institutions without extending them to women, and that the same reasons by which it was contended that every man should have a voice in the government of his country ought to secure

---

[1] *Emile*, livre v. Compare Milton:

My author and disposer, what thou bidd'st,
Unargued I obey: so God ordains,
God is thy law, thou mine; to know no more
Is woman's happiest knowledge and her praise.

Paradise Lost, Book iv.

the same privileges for women, or 'at least for those who were widows or unmarried.'[2]

The tone of the political writers of the French Revolution is especially remarkable when we remember the vast place which Maria Theresa and Catherine of Russia occupied in the political history of their century; the pre-eminence attained by women in the social, intellectual, and even political life of France since the death of Louis XIV., and the very considerable place which women bore both among the agents and the victims of the Revolution. Few figures in that struggle are more striking than Madame Roland and Charlotte Corday. No writer of the age judged its events with a more eminent sagacity than Madame de Staël. No one concentrated against herself a greater measure of the revolutionary fury than Marie Antoinette, and she was only the most illustrious of the many women who perished on the guillotine. It is related that Napoleon, on one occasion, meeting the widow of Condorcet, who was herself an active Republican, said to her in peremptory tones, 'Madame, I do not like women to meddle in politics.' 'You are right, General,' she replied, 'but in a country where it is the custom to cut off the heads of women, it is natural that they should wish to know the reason why.'[3]

The few attempts, however, that were made during the struggle of the Revolution to claim political rights for women were sternly repressed. All female clubs, societies, and political assemblies were forbidden by the Convention. Women were excluded from the galleries of the hall where it sat; and Chaumette warned them that by entering into politics they abjured their sex and violated the law of nature.

In England, however, Mary Wollstonecraft published her 'Vindication of the Rights of Women,' which was intended as a protest against the doctrines of Rousseau, and which gave the first considerable impulse to a discussion on the subject.

---

[2] *Lettres d'un Bourgeois de New-Haven.* See, too, his essay, *Sur l'admission des femmes au droit de cité* (1790).

[3] Mme. de Staël, *Considérations sur la Révolution.*

It was not an able book, and grave faults and frailties that clouded the later life of the authoress did much to discredit it, but in its general tendency it is far from extravagant or revolutionary. Mary Wollstonecraft indulges in none of those attacks on marriage which have sometimes been connected with the movement. She speaks of it with reverence, as 'the foundation of almost every social virtue.' She dwells on the transcendent importance of chastity and morality, and on the essentially domestic character of the chief duties of women; and although she desires to assimilate in a great measure the tastes and studies of the two sexes, it is worthy of notice that she expresses a strong antipathy to women who are addicted to field sports. She complains, however, that in England women are taught to look to man alone for their maintenance, and to marriage as the sole end of life; to regard as unfeminine all serious studies that strengthen the understanding, and to cultivate as the chief female charm an exaggerated sensibility and dependence, and a proficiency in arts and qualities that have their empire only in the transient period of youth and passion.

Such a conception of female life was, she maintained, essentially false, and profoundly injurious to both sexes. If women are not educated to be the rational companions of men, they will inevitably impede their progress both in knowledge and virtue. It cannot be an indifferent thing that the education of man in his earliest and most susceptible years is committed to beings whose minds have been artificially cramped and stunted, and that the closest companion of his adult life should be wholly unfitted to sympathise with his more serious aims, studies, and occupations. Frivolity, vanity, dissimulation, superstition, and credulity are the natural fruits of the prevailing type of female education. In married life it throws a dark cloud over those long years when passion has subsided and when time has stolen away the charms that were so unduly prized. It gives the point to the sarcasm of a lively writer who asked 'what business women turned forty have to do in the world.'

But in the case of the many women who, with narrow means and contracted interests and enfeebled character, are obliged to fight the battle of life alone, the influence of such an education is still more disastrous. Our authoress quotes some curious passages from contemporary moralists showing how feebleness of body as well as of mind was regarded as peculiarly graceful in women; how they were exhorted to abstain from all energetic exercises; to conceal systematically all signs of high spirits or robust health, of serious interests or studies, or independent judgment, lest these things should mar their attraction in the eyes of men; how even female piety was inculcated, on the ground that 'a fine woman never strikes so deeply as when, composed into pious recollection and possessed with the noblest considerations, she assumes, without knowing it, superior dignity and new graces.'

Against all such teaching Mary Wollstonecraft indignantly revolts. She denies that virtues have a sex, and that those which are supremely precious in one half of the human race should be indifferent in the other; and she especially asks why cowardice, which is deemed shameful in a man, should be thought not only pardonable, but graceful, in a woman. She urges that, on the ground of natural rights, the claim of women to participate in the exercise of political power is irresistible, and that, on the ground of expediency, it is in a high degree important to the community that women should be inspired with a genuine public spirit. She maintains that it is grossly unjust that women, who are already heavily handicapped by Nature in the struggle for existence, should be excluded by law or custom from any honourable employment in which they might earn a livelihood. She considers the profession of a physician peculiarly fitting for them, and she contends that if restrictive laws were abolished women, by a natural process, would gravitate to such employments as were suitable to them. They have at least a right to an education as wide and liberal as that of men. She deplores, with great reason, the too sedentary lives which girls in her time were accustomed to lead, and urges that many of the faults and frailties of women are simply due to the custom of keeping them when young confined in close rooms, with no sufficient exercise, till their muscles are relaxed and their powers of digestion impaired.

These views would not now appear very startling, and it is difficult to realise the indignation they aroused. The political aspect of the case was only touched at rare intervals. Charles Fox referred to it in a speech which I have already had occasion to notice, and which was delivered in the May of 1797. He says that, 'with the exception of companies, in which the right of voting merely affects property,' it has never been suggested, 'in all the theories and projects of the most absurd speculation, that it would be advisable to extend the elective suffrage to the female sex;' and yet, he says, women have interests to be protected 'as dear and as important as our own,' and no one could deny 'that all the superior classes of the female sex of England must be more capable of exercising the elective suffrage with deliberation and propriety than the uninformed individuals of the lowest class of men to whom the advocates of universal suffrage would extend it.' What, he asks, is the explanation of this apparent anomaly? It is that the chief end of all healthy political systems is to obtain independent voters, and that by the law of nations, and perhaps of nature, the female sex is dependent on ours.

The subject was more than once touched upon by Bentham. He was struck by the anomaly and injustice of refusing females the small fraction of political power which is implied in a vote, while they have been suffered in nearly all countries to wield the supreme power of the State. At the same time he was of opinion that the prevailing prejudices on the subject were so strong that it was useless to discuss it.[4]

Bailey, the author of a very able treatise called 'The Rationale of Political Representation,' which appeared in 1835, was perhaps the first writer who seriously advocated the extension of the suffrage to women. The two great principles, he

---

[4] *Works,* iii. 463, 567; iv. 568; ix. 108–9.

maintained, on which the representative system should be founded are, that the end of government is the happiness of the community, comprehending alike male and female, as alike susceptible of pain and pleasure; and that 'power will be uniformly exercised for the good of the parties subject to it only when it is under their control, or the control of persons who have an identity of interests with themselves.' From these principles it follows that the exclusion of women could only be defended on one of two grounds. It might be said that their interests were so identical with those of men, that they were sufficiently protected by a masculine suffrage; or it might be said that they were so incompetent to exercise political power for their own good and for the good of the community that the disadvantages arising from any perfect want of identity of interests between the two sexes were more than compensated by the superior discernment which the male sex would bring to this task of government. The first of these arguments, it was answered, was refuted by all history, for nothing is more certain in the past than that the stronger half of the human race have almost universally used their power to oppress the weaker; that in the relations between men and women, as in all other relations, irresponsible power has been continually abused. Much has been done to improve the condition of women, but still 'the power of man over woman is constantly misemployed; and it may be doubted whether the relation of the sexes to each other will ever be placed on a just and proper footing until they have both their share of control over the enactments of the Legislature.' Much legislation, no doubt, applies to questions on which the interests of the sexes are identical, 'but in the actual relative position in which by nature the sexes stand, and must always remain, . . . separate interests cannot fail to grow up between them, and numerous laws must be directed to the regulation of their respective rights and duties. If the enactment of these laws concerning two parties who have distinct interests is solely under the control of one party, we know the consequence.'

Turning then to the argument from the alleged incompetence of women, Bailey acknowledged that in all existing societies the female sex may, on the whole, be inferior in intelligence to the men, but it is at least equally certain that the higher classes of females are in this respect superior to the lower classes of men. 'Women, for instance, possessing 500*l.* a year are generally superior in information to men of 50*l.* a year, although not perhaps equal to men of 500*l.* If this is a true statement, the obvious expedient is, not to exclude women, but to place their pecuniary qualification higher. Even the necessity of such a higher qualification may be doubted, inasmuch as, in that peculiar intelligence which is requisite for a judicious choice of persons to fill public offices, females are in some respects greater proficients than men of the same station. Female tact in the discrimination of at least certain qualities of character is universally admitted; and it can scarcely be questioned that such coadjutors would be highly useful in the selection of representatives. . . . Were a proper method of taking votes adopted, and such other appropriate measures employed to disencumber elections of what at present renders them scenes of rudeness and riot, the exercise of the elective franchise would be compatible with the most scrupulous refinement of feelings and habits.' If, Bailey says, the framers of the Reform Bill of 1832 had placed women on the same footing as men, they would have removed a grave anomaly and injustice, while they would have very slightly affected the composition of the constituencies. 'It would have been only widows or single women, keeping house, or possessing the requisite amount of property, that could have been entitled to vote, and it is difficult to conceive the shadow of a reason why they should be debarred from the privilege, except the tumultuous proceedings which are the unruly progeny of unskilful arrangements.'[5]

To this last argument there is one conclusive answer. It is, that at the time of the Reform Bill of 1832 no class of women

---

[5] *Rationale of Political Representation*, pp. 236–42.

demanded the franchise, and an overwhelming majority would have almost certainly disliked it. A long series of causes, however, have greatly altered the conditions of the problem.

One of the most profoundly important changes that have passed over England during the last century has been the destruction by a few great inventions of the old domestic industries which were once carried on in innumerable farmhouses, and the substitution for them of gigantic factories in which tens of thousands of women are daily employed. The effects of this great revolution may be traced in almost every field of English social and political life, and certainly nowhere more clearly than in the lives, the habits, and the interests of women. In some respects no one can doubt that the change has brought with it serious evils. From a moral point of view domestic industries were singularly useful. They left family life unimpaired, and they contributed powerfully to maintain the class of small farmers and yeomen, who form one of the most valuable elements in the community. Thousands of English and perhaps a still larger proportion of Ulster, farms would have been sold and amalgamated in large farms if the scanty earnings of agriculture pursued on a small scale had not been assisted by the industry of the weaver and the spinster. It is extremely desirable that men should not be wholly dependent on a single fluctuating industry—that there should be some subsidiary resource enabling them to tide over periods of depression and adversity. Domestic manufactures were in this respect peculiarly valuable, and they could be pursued when other industries were intermitted. They were the special occupation of the winter days, when the labours of agriculture were very slight.

The work of women, on the whole, probably fluctuates more violently than the work of men. As a rule, no doubt, the true work of a married woman of the labour classes is the care of her home and family, but the amount of labour this will involve varies immensely. It depends largely on the number of her children, on the age of her children, on the health of her children, on the degree in which they are employed in school or business outside the house, on the presence or absence of grown-up daughters to assist her in her task. A life which in one year may be crowded to the utmost, may in the next be most imperfectly filled. Under these circumstances the needle, the distaff, and the handloom became of great importance.

All this class of industry, however, has necessarily perished. It is impossible that the home-made article could compete in the market with the cheap and excellent products of machinery. Even in the sphere of artistic production machinery has so nearly rivalled the hand-made article that it has begun to dominate. It is only within the last few years that the mechanical imitations of lace have attained such perfection that the lace industry, which had so long flourished in innumer-cottages in the great towns of Belgium, has become almost unprofitable. The clothes of the family of the labouring man may still be often made at home, but even this has greatly diminished with the cheapening of the manufactured article and the diminished habit of domestic industry. Spheres of employment may have increased, but employments of a casual, intermittent, and secondary kind have probably diminished. In a rank somewhat higher than the labouring classes, indeed, the great fields of journalism and literature furnish such employments to many, and, without being pursued as a regular profession, they often turn a bare competence into an easy competence, and add some comforts and luxuries to lives which without them would be very dreary. But in general industry has become more concentrated and exclusive, and female labour has been largely transferred from the home to the factory.

It has been found necessary to apply to these vast organised industries an amount of legislative interference which would have been both impracticable and unnecessary at a time when weaving and spinning were chiefly accomplished at the fireside. Legislative regulation of industry has been in the past, and seems likely to be still more in the future, one of the most important duties of the statesman, and on this question the interest of women and men are by no means identical. Few questions are more difficult than the extent to which it is possible by legislative arrangements to protect women against the profoundly injurious physical effects of excessive labour, without practically excluding them from employments in which they might earn a livelihood, and fatally handicapping them in their competition with men. When two classes differing in physical strength, and differing also in the wages for which they are prepared to work, are in competition, separate interests must necessarily grow up, and when the regulations of labour are made exclusively by the representatives of one class, the other class are very likely to suffer. As we have already seen, in England and in most civilised countries the labour of women is now regulated by special laws, which are far more restrictive than those which are imposed upon men. They are excluded from night work, from underground work, from all factory work for several weeks after confinement, from agricultural gangs which consist partly of men. They are restricted in employments connected with dangerous machinery. Their hours of labour in vast departments of industry are specially limited by law, and they are placed in the same category as 'young persons' of the other sex who have not attained the age of maturity.

The arguments which have induced legislators to impose these special restrictions on female labour are very powerful. Whatever controversy there may be about the comparative capacities of the two sexes, there can at least be no doubt that women are physically weaker than men, and that the strain of excessive toil tells upon them more quickly and more fatally. They overwork themselves much more easily, and they are probably much more ready to do so. In some cases they appear to be more susceptible than men to the deleterious effects of unhealthy branches of manufacture. Thus lead poisoning is said to affect women both more easily and at an earlier age than men.[6] But, above all, the great fact of maternity clearly separates female from male labour. The fatal ef-

---

[6] See *Woman's Work*, by Bulley, Whitley, and Dilke (1894), pp. 133–37.

fects, both to the mother and to the child, of severe labour in the period immediately preceding and immediately following confinement, and of the withdrawal of the mother from the care of her child during the first weeks of its life, are now fully recognised.

But while there will probably be little difference of opinion, either among men or among women, about the necessity of much legislation of this kind, the question of more or less is one of extreme difficulty and delicacy, and it is one on which adult women may very justly urge that they ought to have a controlling voice. They complain that some parts of the factory legislation have driven them out of employments in which they once earned a livelihood; that they have artificially lowered wages which were already lower than those of men; that they fall with extreme severity on the large class of women who pursue trades which are in general slack and underpaid, but which become very lucrative under the high pressure of the brief fashionable season. They urge that every restriction which limits the efficiency of their work, by preventing them from working as long or as much as men, means their displacement by men in some branch of industry; that this process is going on at a time when, owing to many causes, women are much more frequently obliged than of old to work for their living; and that, under the keen competition of modern industry, ill-judging philanthropy or the jealousy of male competitors may very easily, through such laws, inflict on them irreparable injury.

One considerable body of reformers would drive women altogether out of the factories. Others would extend to adult women the Act which limits the hours of persons under eighteen years of age in shops, with the effect, as a large body of women believe, of replacing female by male workers in one of the fields on which the former most largely depend.[7] Scarcely a Parliament passes in which the area of factory legislation is not extended, and in which new special regulations are not

---

[7] Jevons, *The State in relation to Labour*, p. 87.

imposed on the work of women which tend to handicap them in competition with men. Thus, to take a very recent example, the Factory Act of 1895 brought laundries under the scope of legislation, introduced new limitations to the amount of over-time which women under special circumstances are allowed to work, placed restrictions on their home-work which will probably greatly diminish its amount, and much enlarge the power of the Home Secretary in excluding them from dangerous or insanitary employments.[8] And this legislation emanates from a Legislature in the election of which women have no voice, and it is largely due to the votes and the pressure or organisations of working men. Even the inspection of factories has, until very lately, been wholly in the hands of men. It was only in 1893 that, for the first time, two women were appointed factory inspectors.[9]

In the very remarkable preamble of the edict suppressing the *jurandes* and *maîtrises* in France which was drawn up by Turgot in 1776 there is a paragraph condemning the arbitrary restrictions on industries, that 'repel a sex which, through its weakness, has most wants and fewest resources, and which, by condemning them to an inevitable misery, gives its aid to seduction and debauch.' In the conditions of modern industry something of this kind, it is said, may very easily follow from the system of special factory legislation. It should never be forgotten that while in most things the interests of men and women are in harmony, in many of the great fields of modern industry they are the keenest rivals and competitors. If machinery has injured women by destroying the domestic industries, it has compensated them by a vast opening of other fields. It has dethroned physical strength, and, by the extreme subdivision and specialisation of industries which it

---

[8] A good summary of these provisions will be found in Miss Helen Blackburn's very useful *Handbook for Women engaged in Social and Political Work*. On the recent continental legislation on the subject, see Chauvin, *Professions accessibles aux Femmes*, pp. 208–10.

[9] *Women's Work* (Bulley, Whitley, and Dilke), p. 74. Mrs. Nassau Senior had been appointed poor-law inspector as early as 1873.

produces, it has even greatly diminished the value of skilled labour. Weak and inexperienced girls by the aid of a machine can and do perform tasks which would once have required strong and highly trained men; and in the great majority of cases they work for lower wages than men. There are exceptions, no doubt, the great cotton industry being the most conspicuous, but in most branches of industry their level of remuneration is distinctly lower. Even in shops, where such a difference seems least natural, the wages of female assistants are estimated at 33 per cent. lower than those of men.[10]

This difference of wages is due to several causes. It no doubt partly means that male work is usually in reality more efficient and less intermittent than that of women, and that women are more numerous than men, and more limited in the number of their employments. Something also is due to the old tradition of inferiority, which the changed habits of modern times have not wholly overthrown, and something more to the fact that female labourers are much less organised than men, and therefore less capable of making their bargains. These, however, are not the only elements of the problem. The standard of life always profoundly influences the rate of wages, and the cost and standard of living of an unmarried man is usually higher than that of an unmarried woman of the same class. A married working man is naturally the main support of his family, while the wages of a married woman are rather of the nature of a supplement, merely supplying the deficiency in the earnings of her husband.

These causes inevitably affect the comparative wages of the two sexes. But the fact that the general level of female wages is lower than that of men adds greatly to the severity of the competition, and makes it certain that a disposition will arise among male workers to banish female labour from the field, and, if they are unable to do this, at least to diminish its efficiency. The restrictions which factory legislation and trade-union rules impose on men are often a great grievance to

---

[10] Bulley, Whitley, and Dilke, pp. 51, 117.

some members of the class; but it is at least tolerably certain that they represent the real wishes of a majority of the workers. It is by no means so certain that a corresponding assertion may be truly made about the special restrictions and disabilities put upon women's work.

To say that working men, in advocating increased restrictions on the work of women, are not exclusively actuated by philanthropic motives, but partly also by trade jealousy, is only to attribute to them the ordinary feelings that influence all large bodies of competing men. Very few persons will seriously doubt that motives of this kind entered, in part at least, into the strong opposition shown by the medical profession to the admission of women; and in the so-called working classes they are not concealed. The trade unions which strenuously urge that women should be 'taken out of the mills' openly argue that by this means an overstocked market would be relieved and much of the overplus labour reduced.[11] The witnesses before the Labour Commission who desired that women's labour in the factories should be still further restricted, while they maintained that such restrictions would be beneficial to women, at the same time 'frankly admitted that their proposals were based mainly upon desire to get rid of the competition of female labour, which acted so prejudicially upon the men's wages and wellbeing.'[12]

I have no wish to overstate the case. Women are naturally more prone to advocate State regulations than men. It is by no means certain that, if they had a controlling voice in these matters, they would not desire rather more than less legislative restriction than at present; and only a small proportion of the women who would obtain votes would be connected with factory labour. Nor is the competition between male and female labour at present as acute as in many periods of the past. After many shiftings and vicissitudes the respective domains of men and women, in English industry at least, have

---

[11] Jevons, *The State in relation to Labour*, pp. 73–74.
[12] Spyer's *Labour Question*, p. 112.

become tolerably stationary. Of late years the proportion between the workers of the two sexes has varied but little, and the chief changes in female labour have been a considerable increase in the labour market of the number of middle-class girls, and a considerable diminution of the number of married women.[13] But the fact remains that Parliament is more and more interfering in the way of restrictions and regulations with the chief departments of industry, and that its legislation for women is widely different from its legislation for men. Separate and even antagonistic interests of a vital character have arisen, and the case for giving women some voice in legislation has greatly strengthened.

In addition, too, to such questions as the length of a day's work and the legislative regulation of the other conditions of female labour, many purely political questions affect women under the factory system far more than in other days. The market they supply is no longer chiefly a home market, and the enormous foreign and colonial trade, on which the factory system vitally depends, fluctuates with every change of policy. The question of Protection or Free Trade; questions of commercial treaties, of peace and war, of blockades, of the expansion or contraction of the Empire, of the relations of the mother country to her colonies, affect directly and immediately the means of subsistence of tens of thousands. In some branches of factory work, especially in the cotton manufacture, the majority of the workers are women, and more women than men are said to have been thrown out of employment in England by the great Civil War in America.

A change somewhat similar to that which was produced by the factory system is passing over the shopkeeping trade. The steady economical tendency is to substitute what the French call *la grande industrie* for *la petite industrie*. It is becoming more and more difficult for the small shop, with its scanty sale, to compete with colossal establishments depending for their

---

[13] See Miss Collet's report for the Board of Trade on the Statistics of Employment of Women and Girls (1894), pp. 71–74.

success upon rapid returns on a gigantic capital, upon vast sales at small profits. Prices which on a small, slow sale would fail to keep the shopkeeper from the workhouse prove abundantly remunerative when the sale is very large and very rapid, and thus the small shopkeeper is steadily extinguished by being undersold. One monster shop almost monopolises within a large district the supply of some great class of articles. If offers them at a low price and with an immense range of choice; it then proceeds to extend its business by bringing under the same roof the supply of many other wholly different industries; and the convenience of this combination gives it an increased advantage in the competition with the humbler providers of each. The growth of the joint-stock system, especially since the Limited Liability Act of 1862, gives new facilities for the creation of these vast establishments, while steam and the Parcels Post enable them to carry their competition into remote provincial towns and villages. Industry is thus steadily concentrating, and multitudes who in another stage of society would have been independent shopkeepers become salaried subordinates in a vast industrial regiment.

The change is inevitable, for it grows out of irresistible economical causes. It may be, and probably is, on the whole beneficial; but no one can deny that it has most serious drawbacks, and brings in its train a large amount of acute and unmerited suffering. Zola, in one of his truest and most powerful novels, has admirably depicted the desperate and unavailing struggle of the small shopkeeper against the overwhelming pressure of his colossal rival, and no careful observer can fail to notice how seriously this change has revolutionised the conditions of industry. The old paths have been to a great extent broken up. Numbers, after years of steady, honest, continuous labour, have been forced to seek new channels of employment; and the pressure has fallen with the greatest weight on the very class in whose lives and happiness habit and custom have the greatest place. In one important respect it has been especially disadvantageous to women, for it produces a tendency the exact opposite of that which grows out of the spread of machinery. Physical strength counts for much more in the monster shop than in the small shops it replaced. Women have been thus, to a considerable extent, expelled from what seems their peculiar province, and crowds of young men may be seen measuring ribbons or unfolding silks.

The change has greatly strengthened the case for removing as far as possible all artificial legislative restrictions which hamper women in seeking employments. It has altered greatly the number and proportion of women in the old industries, and much has been done, both by legislative enactments and by private efforts, to enlarge their circle. Post-offices, telegraphs, savings banks, and several minor posts in the Civil Service, in municipal bodies, and in railway administration, have been opened to them. They have multiplied greatly in authorship, in the newspaper press, in all the fields of art. The new and growing industry of typewriting, for which their flexible fingers are peculiarly adapted, is chiefly in their hands. A few have found means of livelihood on the platform or in the lecture-room, and a few others in inspectorships and in various somewhat exceptional administrative posts. Attempts have been made, though with no great success, in the Ritualist section of the Anglican Church to revive Sisterhoods on the model of those which in the Middle Ages sheltered and occupied the great majority of unmarried women. In the United States women have been very generally admitted to the profession of the law. There are a considerable number of female advocates, and by a law of 1879 women have been allowed to plead before the Supreme Court. Most European countries have refused to follow this example, though female advocates were for some time admitted in Russia, and though Sweden and Roumania have in this field shown themselves ready to follow the example of America.[14]

The special aptitude of women for the management of the

---

[14] The history of this movement will be found in Chauvin's *Professions accessibles aux Femmes*, pp. 233–39.

sick has been far more fully recognised. Nothing is better attested than that, in the power of quick and delicate observation of slight changes—which is at least one of the most essential qualities that are required for the successful treatment of disease—women are, on the whole, superior to men. As nurses they have always been pre-eminent; but in our generation, to the incalculable benefit of both sexes, the profession has been much augmented, and raised by skilful training to a much higher degree of competence. An Act of 1868 for the first time opened pharmacy to women, and after a long struggle they have at last obtained their footing as physicians. The United States had in this field preceded us, and female doctors appear to be both more numerous and more frequently placed in posts of influence than in England. In Great Britain, the University of Edinburgh led the way. In 1874 a special medical school was opened for women in London. In 1876 an Act known as the Russell Gurney Act authorised every recognised medical body to open its doors to women. In the following year they were for the first time allowed to follow clinical lectures in a London hospital. In 1878 a supplemental charter enabled the University of London to grant degrees to women in all its faculties, including medicine. Several other bodies have since followed the example, and up to the close of 1895, 264 women appear to have been placed on the British register as duly qualified medical practitioners.[15] It is not probable that female doctors will ever in general practice become very formidable rivals to men, but there are branches of the treatment of women in which their services are likely to be peculiarly acceptable. Exceptional talent in women, as in men, will no doubt be recognised; and very recently a new and vast field has been partly opened among the millions of Indian women who are precluded by their faith, even in times of extreme sickness and suffering, from any contact with a male physician. Should the establishment of female doctors prove successful in carrying the

---

[15] See Miss Blackburn's *Handbook for Women*, p. 42.

alleviations of science into this vast mass of uncared-for suffering, it would be scarcely possible to over-estimate the benefit it would have conferred upon humanity.

The Anglo-Saxon nations have not been alone in pursuing this path. The University of Zürich deserves a very high place as one of the chief centres of female medical education at an early stage of the movement; France, Switzerland, Belgium, and Italy have all their female doctors; and an Italian lady is now, or was very lately, professor of pathology in the University of Pisa. Russia was at one time eminently distinguished for its liberality towards women, and it admitted not only female doctors, but even female advocates. In the great wave of reaction and persecution, however, that has recently overflowed that country, these concessions have been lost. In 1876 women were excluded by an Imperial order from the profession of advocate, and a few years later they were excluded from all the higher studies in Russia, and no woman was allowed to practise medicine within the empire.[16]

The teaching profession had at the same time acquired a new importance, and there has been an immense increase in the number of women who are engaged in it, in the level of their competence, and in the salaries they can earn. Remarkable as have been the changes that have been effected in the education of boys, they have been less important than those which have taken place in female education during the closing years of the nineteenth century. Girls have fully shared with boys in the great impulse given to education by the Education Act of 1870; by the establishment of normal schools and art schools, and technical education; by the law for encouraging intermediate education in Ireland; by the improvement of voluntary schools that has resulted from the competition with School-board schools, and from the system of Government inspection and of payment by results. The excellent high schools and the ladies' colleges established in several parts of

---

[16] Chauvin, *Les Professions accessibles aux Femmes*, pp. 229–33, 236, 237, 260.

the kingdom are giving many thousands of girls of the upper and middle classes an education incomparably better than any which was attainable by their parents, and providing teachers for humbler institutions and for private families utterly unlike the half-trained governesses of the past.

The higher female education in England on a large scale has been, for the first time, systematically organised and seriously and intelligently pursued, and eight out of the ten universities of Great Britain, as well as the Royal University in Ireland, now throw open their examinations and degrees to women. Oxford and Cambridge, which in past ages were so largely endowed by women,[17] it is true, still withhold their degrees and their great prizes from them, but few persons believe that this will long be the case. In spite of a strenuous ecclesiastical opposition by such men as Burgon, Liddon, and Pusey, women have already been admitted within the circle of their teaching. The establishment of Hitchin, Girton, Newnham, and Somerville colleges; the opening to women of the great majority of university lectures, of the degree and honour examinations, and of the local examinations instituted by the universities throughout the country; the still more recent system of university extension, and the enormous development of popular scientific teaching in our great towns, have profoundly affected the knowledge, the acquirements, and the interests of women of the upper and middle classes. Few things in our generation are more remarkable than the facility and rapidity with which the movement for opening the universities to women has triumphed in Great Britain. The difficulties of discipline and the grave moral dangers that were so much feared have nowhere arisen, nor has it been found necessary to introduce any considerable change into university teaching.[18]

It is a movement which is by no means confined to England.

---

[17] See Miss Parkes's (Mme. Belloc's) *Essays on Woman's Work*, pp. 201–3.
[18] I am told that in mixed classes lectures become less catechetical than they used to be.

In the Scandinavian countries, in Italy, in Switzerland, in the United States, in the English colonies, universities have been thrown open to women, and strenuous efforts have been made to raise the general level of their education. Sophie Kovalewsky, whose recent autobiography has impressed and fascinated so many readers, was professor of mathematics at the University of Stockholm. French girls were entirely excluded from the educational reforms that were instituted by the Convention and under Napoleon I., and the great Corsican always maintained that female education should be of the most rudimentary description. But the laws of 1850 and 1867 established public schools for their primary education in every considerable commune in France, and the law of 1882 established compulsory education for girls. Under Napoleon III. excellent schools for their education in professions were established in Paris, and they were admitted to follow the courses of the College de France, and since the fall of the Empire they have been allowed to take university degrees in letters, science, and medicine.[19]

Germany, until a very recent period, was far behind most countries in the higher education of women, and in Prussia especially all movements for their introduction into the universities and for their recognition as physicians by the State were strenuously opposed. Out of 209 public schools for girls in Prussia, only a few years ago not more than 17 were under the control of lady principals,[20] and the opinion of the governing classes and of the universities was strongly hostile to all movements to assimilate either the higher education or the pursuits of the two sexes. The spirit of Prussian legislation was well shown by a law of 1850, which formally provided that women must never be admitted, either as members or as hearers, into any association which had for its object po-

[19] Chauvin, *Les Professions accessibles aux Femmes*, pp. 196, 202–6, 225; Ostrogorski, *La Femme au point de vue du droit public*, pp. 178–79.
[20] See an interesting paper on the 'Higher Education of Women in Germany' in the *Times*, December 27, 1893. See, too, the *Souvenirs de Sophie Kovalewsky*, pp. 220–21, 232–33.

litical discussion; and similar laws have existed in Austria and in several German States.[21] But in matters of female education Germany also has, during the last three years, made great concessions, and Hungary has entered resolutely on the same path.

It is with England, however, that we are now principally concerned, and in England, I think, the movement has exercised a much wider influence on female life than on the Continent. To me, at least, it seems to be almost wholly good. The married state is certainly not likely to be less pure or less happy because fewer women fly to it in despair as their only means of livelihood and occupation, or because men and women have learnt to sympathise more closely with each other in their graver thoughts and more serious interests. The profound and menacing chasm of opinion that in most continental countries divides educated men from most women, is in England largely mitigated, and a new spirit of enlightened tolerance is growing. The fears that were once expressed, that a highly educated woman would be apt to neglect her home duties, have certainly not been verified by experience, and it is not too much to say that for one woman who neglects those duties through this cause, there are hundreds who neglect them through frivolity or vice. The pedantry and the extravagances of taste and opinion which were once associated with the idea of a learned lady were not unnatural as long as such women found themselves isolated and unsupported, at war with the conventionalities of society, and exposed to a storm of ridicule and disapprobation. When their position ceased to be unusual and unrecognised, these eccentricities rapidly diminished.

Another and graver evil which was to be feared was that the strain of intellectual competition would prove too great for the more delicate organisations of women. But those who have chiefly directed the higher female education in England have been fully sensible of this very real danger, they have laboured

---

[21] Ostrogorski, pp. 172–73.

strenuously and successfully to prevent it, and they have been powerfully seconded by a great change of manners and taste which has insensibly passed over the nation. The beauty of perfect health and of high spirits has been steadily replacing as the ideal type, the beauty of a sickly delicacy and of weak and tremulous nerves which in the eighteenth century was so much admired, or at least extolled. A more healthy dress, a far larger amount of out-of-door exercise, a far larger share of active amusements, have accompanied the great intellectual progress, and I have heard that very acute observer, Professor Huxley, express a strong opinion that there has been, during the last half-century, a marked rise in the average physique of the women of the upper and middle classes in England. To the vast and increasing multitude of unmarried women, whether they be rich or poor, modern education has been a priceless blessing. However much it may fall short of an ideal standard, it at least sends them into the world far better equipped for the battle of life. It gives them more developed capacities, more serious and varied interests, and that discipline of character which habits of concentrated and continuous labour seldom fail to produce.

Connected with this subject, it is impossible for an attentive observer to fail to notice the great change which has taken place among the upper classes in England within a generation in the received conventionalities relating to the part which it is proper and allowable for a lady to perform in the world. The old Greek idea of the exclusively domestic life of a good woman, which still, in a great measure, prevails in Germany, has in England almost wholly passed away, and numbers of English ladies are as keenly and as actively engaged in public interests as average men. The change runs through all the fields of occupation, amusements, and habits. Some who are still living can remember when it was deemed unbecoming for a lady to walk unattended by a footman in the streets of London, or to drive alone in a hansom cab, or to travel, except under the gravest necessity, without a male companion. What would the generation of Hannah More and of Mrs. Trimmer have thought of an age in which ladies might be found throwing themselves into active outdoor games with all the zest of a schoolboy, mingling with male students at university lectures and examinations, appearing with perfect composure as lecturers and speakers on public platforms, organising and directing great political and social movements, climbing alps, joining keenly in field sports, travelling without any male escort over the civilised globe, studying freely and canvassing openly questions that lie at the very foundations of religion, science, and philosophy? Perhaps the only thing that would surprise them more would be the quiet, inoffensive, ladylike persons who do these things.

The causes and the consequences of this very evident change in manners would open out a wide field of inquiry, on which I can here barely touch. To some it seems to portend nothing less than a great moral revolution in the character of women. That some change is being produced can, I think, not be doubted; but its limits seem to me greatly exaggerated. Nature has established distinctions between men and women that can never be overpassed. In all ages the positions of wife and mother will be the chief positions to which women will aspire, and in all ages they will bring with them the same dominant interests and affections. It is in the finer shadings of character that change is perceptible, some lines of character growing fainter, while others deepen and strengthen. Women will probably remain in the future good and bad, selfish and unselfish, in much the same proportions as at present, but both their good and evil qualities will be somewhat differently mixed. In the modern type of woman we may expect to find more judgment, more self-control, more courage, more independence, a far wider range of sympathies and interests than in the past. She will become less credulous and superstitious, but she will also become a little colder and a little harder. Unselfishness will probably not diminish, but it will spring to a greater degree from recognised duty and acquired habit. The emotional, the impulsive, the romantic elements of character, with their dangers and their charms, will become less prominent. In the better class a strong sense of duty, dominated by an enlightened judgment, will be the guiding influence, and life will be brightened by a larger circle of unselfish interests and of worthy pleasures. In the worse class, blind, unreasoning passion will play a smaller part, but both religious and social restraints will be weaker; the appetite for excitement and novelty generated by an overcrowded life will increase, and worldliness will take at an early age a harder, a more sordid, and a more unlovely form. Few things are less beautiful than the worldliness of eighteen, maintaining amid all the whirl of dissipation and pleasure a steady eye to the main chance, estimating incomes and titles and prospects with all the calculating shrewdness of a sexagenarian lawyer.

It was inevitable that the great changes of education, circumstances, and manners that have taken place among women in the present century should have produced among them a stronger interest in political life. There have, indeed, been many periods when such an interest had before been felt. Addison has described vividly the fierce party spirit that divided female society in the closing years of Anne,[22] and at no later period in English history has the course of affairs been so largely modified by the influence of female favourites around the throne. In later days, such figures as Georgiana Duchess of Devonshire, or Mrs. Crewe, or Mrs. Macaulay, or Lady Jersey, or Lady Holland, or Miss Martineau, will at once occur to the reader; but the modern female interest in politics has taken a wider scope and somewhat different character, and questions of purely feminine interests have become more prominent.

At a time when the question of female education was rising rapidly into prominence, women could hardly fail to be struck with the fact that a large proportion of the free grammar schools, some of the best endowed educational establishments in England, had been founded in what are called less enlightened ages for teaching 'the children of freemen;' for

---

[22] *Spectator*, Nos. 57, 81; the *Freeholder*, Nos. 23, 26.

teaching 'all children' born in particular parishes; for granting 'maintenance, education, and training free of expense to poor children;' and that the benefits of these endowments have in the course of time come to be wholly or almost wholly monopolised by boys.[23] At a period when the State has undertaken so largely to subsidise education in all its grades, the claims of colleges and other institutions for female education to Government assistance naturally strengthened.

At a time, too, when a spirit of independence was growing among women, it was impossible that they should not resent the gross legislative injustices and inequalities to which by English law they were subject. Even in the present century it was a possible and by no means an infrequent thing for a vicious or tyrannical husband to debar the most innocent and virtuous mother from all access to her own children. He was at perfect liberty to place them, during their mother's lifetime, under the sole care and control of his mistress. It was not until 1839 that 'the Custody of Infants' Act was carried, which enabled the Chancellor or Master of the Rolls to secure to any mother who had not been guilty of adultery the care of her own children up to the age of seven, and free access to them at a later age.[24] An Act of 1873 extended this reform by enabling the courts, on special application, to grant a mother the custody of her children to the age of sixteen.[25] But with these exceptions, and subject to the right of the Court of Chancery in some extreme cases to interfere, legal power over the child was vested exclusively in the father. Even after his death the mother was not the natural guardian of her children. The

---

[23] For illustrations of this, see a remarkable essay of Mrs. Fawcett, in *Essays and Lectures on Social and Political Subjects*, by Henry Fawcett and M. G. Fawcett, pp. 195, 267. In France also it has been a matter of great complaint that when the property of the convents, which chiefly conducted the education of French girls, was confiscated, the State made no equivalent provision for their education (Giraud, *La Condition des Femmes*, p. 26).

[24] 2 & 3 Vict. c. 54. See, too, the instructive debate on this Bill in the Lords, July 30, 1838.

[25] 36 Vict. c. 12.

father might pass her by, and appoint another guardian, without assigning any reason and without consulting her. Even if he died without making any provision for the guardianship in his will, his nearest male relatives might claim it, to the exclusion of the mother. It was not until 1886 that the mother was recognised by the law of England as the natural guardian of her child after the death of her husband. The power of the father during his lifetime was untouched, and he may, if he pleased, appoint another guardian to act with his wife after his death, but the right of the widow was at least secured.[26]

In the matter of property the evils to be redressed were not less serious. Before 1857 a man who had abandoned his wife, and left her unaided to support his family, might at any time return to appropriate her earnings and to sell everything she had acquired, and he might again and again desert her, and again and again repeat the process of spoliation. A clause which was inserted in the Act of 1857, which established the Divorce Court, for the first time protected the earnings of a deserted wife, and an Act of 1886 secured her alimony from her husband.[27] In all cases, however, except desertion, the power of the husband over his wife's earnings was absolute. It is true that he was bound by law to support her, but only to secure her a bare maintenance; but it is also true that in numerous English homes a husband might be found living in idleness on the earnings of his wife, squandering them against her will, but with the full sanction of English law, in the public-house or the brothel. It was only after a long and strenuous opposition, after much ridicule, after many predictions that any innovation in this field would destroy the sacred institution of the family, that a law was passed in 1870 securing to women from the date of the passing of the Act the legal control of their own earnings.

It left, however, all other female property, with some insignificant exceptions, absolutely unprotected. By the common

---

[26] 49 & 50 Vict. c. 27.
[27] 49 & 50 Vict. c. 52.

law the wife possessed nothing of her own. She could not sue or be sued; she could make no contract without her husband's express consent. The personal property bequeathed to her by will after marriage, if it exceeded 200*l.*, was absolutely his; and although she had so far the right of property in her real estate that the husband could not dispose of it without her consent, he had during his lifetime complete control over the income derived from it.[28] It is true that the Court of Chancery had devised an expensive system of marriage settlements, by which, in the case of the upper classes, the common law was evaded and women were enabled to secure a real right in their property; but the great body of the middle and lower classes, including those who by industry or accident rose in the course of their married lives from poverty to affluence, remained under the provisions of the common law until the Married Women's Property Act of 1882 gave such women a full right to their own property, abolishing at the same time their privilege of obliging their husbands to pay their debts.[29] A few slight remaining grievances relating to contract and bequest were removed in 1893,[30] and in this field the rights of married women in England are now amply guaranteed.

It is remarkable that, in a country so little civilised as Russia, women's property had been from the earliest times perfectly secure, and remained unaffected by marriage. In the United States a series of State laws carried between 1848 and 1860 has nearly everywhere amply protected it. On the continent of Europe many different systems prevail. In some countries the position of women is even now little, if at all, better in matters of property than it was in England before 1857, though it is generally possible, by adopting a particular form of marriage contract, to improve it. It is, however, very evi-

---

[28] 33 & 34 Vict. c. 93. Some slight additional protection was given by an Act of 1874.

[29] 45 & 46 Vict. c. 75.

[30] 56 & 57 Vict. c. 63.

dent that the general tendency of legislation is towards the system of independence and equality which now exists in England and America. The system of treating all women, married and unmarried, as perpetual minors, who could only perform legal acts under the name of a male guardian, was only abolished in the Scandinavian countries in the third quarter of the present century, and the last vestiges of it in Switzerland only disappeared in 1881. Laws effectually protecting women's earnings were carried in Sweden in 1874, and in Denmark in 1880. In Norway a law of 1888 protected fully the property of married women. The Italian code on questions of married women's property and earnings marks a great advance on the French code, upon which it was chiefly based, and the new civil code in Germany shows with equal clearness the same tendency.[31] It is hardly doubtful that, before another generation is past, this great change in the conditions of married life will have become general throughout the civilised world.

In England, in the case of intestacy, there is still some inequality. If a man dies intestate, half his property goes to his wife, if he has no children, and the other half to his blood relations, but if the wife dies intestate the whole goes to her husband. A law of 1890, however, provides that in the former case, if the property does not exceed in value 500*l.*, it shall all go to the wife, and that if it does exceed that sum, she shall have 500*l.* in addition to her share of the remainder.[32] In the Divorce Court also the two sexes are not on the same footing; for while the husband can obtain a divorce by simply proving adultery, the wife is obliged, in addition to adultery, to prove cruelty, or desertion, or some other grave aggravation. A very valuable law was carried in 1878, and greatly enlarged and improved in 1895, granting judicial separation to poor women whose husbands had been guilty of aggravated assault, persistent cruelty, and wilful neglect to provide for the infant

---

[31] See Bridel, *Le Droit des Femmes et le Mariage* (1893), pp. 39–40, 85–98.
[32] 53 & 54 Vict. c. 29.

children, giving her the legal custody of her children under the age of sixteen, and compelling the husband to pay a weekly sum for their support.[33]

It is impossible to review these measures without perceiving that women have, till a very recent period, had grave reason to complain of English legislation. In essentially harmonious marriages, which form, it is to be hoped, the great majority, the inequalities I have described are probably unfelt; but it is the special province of the law to protect the weak against possible, though exceptional, abuses. In scarcely any other department of English law has the bias in favour of the rich been so strongly shown. Divorce, as we have already seen, was for a long time only possible for those who could afford the great expense of a private Act of Parliament; and the intervention of the Court of Chancery, by which the most serious wrongs inflicted upon women have been mitigated or redressed, lay beyond the means of the poor. Yet it is in poverty-stricken houses, where drunkenness and violence prevail, that these wrongs are most felt.

Something, no doubt, may be said to qualify the picture. I have spoken of the obligation of the husband to maintain his wife, and of his former obligation to pay her debts. As long as perfect liberty of bequest continues, it is hardly likely that the same amounts of money will be given to the girl as to the boy. The boy perpetuates the name and maintains the family of his parents, while it is the usual lot of the girl to bear another name, to pass into another family, to be supported by another man. The law of compulsory equal division of property after death, which prevails over a great part of Europe, has been of great and special advantage to women, as securing to them an equal inheritance with their brothers; but it is scarcely probable that any less drastic measure would effect this object. No one, however, can fail to see the peculiar hardship with which the great inequalities in the disposition of property by will that are general in England fall on that

---

[33] 58 & 59 Vict. c. 39. This Act came into force in the beginning of 1896.

large number of unmarried women who are by nature and education much less fitted than men to make their way in the world. Nor is it less certain that these inequalities are partly due to the influence of the law. The prevailing ideas of what is just and expedient on such matters are widely different in countries where the law encourages primogeniture and agglomeration of property, and in countries where the system of equal division prevails; and laws of intestacy, though in themselves not very frequently called into action, have a considerable indirect influence in determining the provisions of wills.

In the government of a family, strong arguments may be urged in favour of placing somewhere an ultimate and decisive authority, and it can hardly reside anywhere but in the head. This is the theory of English law, though it is not enforced as stringently as in ancient Rome or under French law. The most serious injustices to mothers of the law of guardianship have been corrected by the Act of 1886. But difficult questions still arise relating to the religious education of the children of mixed marriages. English law, like the law of nearly all European countries, gives the father the absolute power of determining the religious education of his children,[34] and that power is so complete that even a promise to his wife before or after marriage cannot affect it. This, it is contended, is the natural prerogative of the head of the family; and it may be added in its defence that women are much more likely than men to be governed by external and sacerdotal influences. The Austrian law on this subject, to which I have already referred, is perhaps more just than our own. At the time when the Concordat was in force it was necessary for all the children of mixed marriages to be educated as Catholics; but when this system was abolished the law did not establish, as in France and England, the absolute authority of the father. It was enacted in 1868, that in mixed marriages the sons should follow the religion of the fathers, and the girls

---

[34] On the continental laws on the subject, see Bridel, *Le Droit des Femmes et le Mariage*, pp. 149–50.

the religion of the mothers, unless the parents agreed on a different arrangement.[35] For a long period, as is well known, this was the general custom in England and Scotland in the case of marriages of Protestants with Catholics.

The question of the opening of professions to women is one of great difficulty, and the United States have in this respect gone somewhat further than Great Britain. Public opinion, and the provisions which in England confer on most professions a large measure of self-government, are probably in these fields more formidable obstacles than parliamentary action. In one case the law indirectly, and almost unintentionally, encourages female employment, for the head of a household pays taxes for his male servants, but not for his female ones. This tax was first imposed in 1777, during the war of the American independence; it was much increased during the great French war, when it was deemed a matter of public policy to discourage the useless employment of men, who might be enrolled in the army; and it has been continued in compliance with the prevailing habit of taxing especially those things which are in themselves luxuries, or which in general imply considerable wealth. It does not appear that a desire to encourage female industry had any part in it. The English law of breach of promise of marriage has been sometimes cited as an instance of the favour shown by legislation to women, as it is chiefly used by women against men. It has, undoubtedly, partially redressed some great wrongs, but hardly any law in the Statute Book has been productive of so much scandal and so much extortion, and its repeal would probably be, on the whole, a benefit to public morals.

The strong and growing interest, however, of women in political affairs, and the increased clearness with which the injustices I have enumerated were brought into relief, prepared the way for a movement in favour of female suffrage which has for many years been increasing. Its prominence has been more due to John Stuart Mill than to any other single

---

[35] *Revue de Droit International*, i. 385.

man. He brought it before the House of Commons as an amendment to the Reform Bill of 1867, and he advocated it powerfully in his treatise on the subjection of women, and incidentally in several other works. The case has been much strengthened by many subsequent measures, which have thrown open the doors of public life to women by giving them votes in a multitude of spheres which are very closely associated with politics. The Municipal Reform Act of 1869 gave them votes in all municipal elections. The Act of 1870 gave them votes for school boards. The Act of 1888 made them voters for the county councils. The Act of 1894, which transformed the whole system of local government and vastly extended the system of local representation, abolished in all its departments the qualification of sex.

A ratepaying woman is thus constantly voting at elections, and often at contested elections, conducted for the most part in much the same way as elections for members of Parliament. She votes for parish and district councils, for county councils, for school boards, and poor-law guardians. In nearly all these elections she may be a candidate as well as a voter. Large numbers of women have stood and large numbers have been chosen for such posts. Many of these elections are fought on purely political and party lines; and a vast proportion of the taxation of the country is now levied by bodies which women's votes contribute to elect, and of which women are frequently members. It is surely not too much to say that under such circumstances the *onus probandi* rests upon those who refuse to go one step further and admit them to elections for members of Parliament.

Of the reasons that have been alleged against it, several may be dismissed at once as manifestly absurd. It is said that the faculties of women are, on the whole, inferior to those of men; that there has never been a female Shakespeare, or female Handel, or female Raphael. It will hardly, however, be seriously contended that the exercise of such exalted powers is required for the average British voter, or that women have not, both in the past and in the present, shown themselves to be largely endowed with capacities that are very useful in political life.

The degree to which they have been admitted to take part in that life has varied greatly in different ages and countries. In ancient Greece and in ancient Rome they were jealously excluded, both by law and by public opinion, from all political functions. It is a curious fact, that among all the many insane follies of Heliogabalus, scarcely any act appears to have more scandalised his subjects than his conduct in enrolling his mother among the senators. When the emperor was assassinated, she shared his fate, measures were at once taken to prevent any repetition of such a scandal, and the emperor who had introduced it was devoted to the infernal gods.[36] It was not until the seat of the Empire had been transferred to Byzantium that supreme power was suffered to fall into a woman's hand.

But outside Greece and Rome the public part played in antiquity by women was very great. The names of Semiramis and Artemisia and Zenobia, of Deborah and Judith and Boadicea, will at once occur to the reader, as well as the picture which Tacitus has drawn of the German women. In more modern days women have in several civilised countries exercised the supreme power of the State, either as sovereigns or as regents, and they have often done so with brilliant success. Very few sovereigns in modern European history can be placed on a level with Isabella the Catholic, or Catherine of Russia, or Maria Theresa of Austria. Two of the longest reigns in English history have been those of queens, and no English reign has been more brilliantly triumphant than that of Elizabeth, or as blameless, prosperous, and constitutional as that under which we live. Even in France, which is the chief European country that has adopted the Salic Law, there have been no less than twenty-four female regencies; and it is a remarkable fact that it was not until the Constituent Assembly

---

[36] Lampridius, *Heliogabalus.*

at the opening of the Revolution that the regency was restricted by law to males.[37]

Who can question the administrative powers of the female founders of the great religious orders of the Dark Ages; of the abbesses of many vast and prosperous convents; of the many women who, in more modern times, have presided with eminent skill over great houses, created or managed great industrial undertakings, or wisely governed great charitable organisations? In the countries where charitable institutions have been best managed female influence has always been conspicuous. The many noble portrait groups in which Rembrandt and his followers have immortalised the lady regents of the great Dutch charities are sufficient to show the high estimation in which those ladies were held. In modern England the organising and administrative ability shown by women in poorhouses, hospitals, prisons, and schools, and in countless works of elaborate and far-reaching beneficence, will be disputed by no one who is acquainted with the social history of the century. How many fortunes wasted by negligence or extravagance have been restored by a long minority under female management! And where can we find in a large class a higher level of business habits and capacity than that which all competent observers have recognised in French women of the middle class? Who can doubt that the qualities shown by women in all these spheres are qualities that are eminently useful in public life? Such arguments, however, are superfluous, and seem almost absurd in an age when all idea of making the suffrage dependent on capacity or experience has been virtually abandoned; when it is given to tens of thousands of men drawn from the most ignorant and most dependent classes of the community; and when it is a main object of a considerable party in the State to increase the preponderance of such classes in the government of the Empire.

Another argument which appears to me to deserve very

---

[37] Ostrogorski, pp. 16–17.

little attention or respect is that derived from the inferiority of women to men in physical force, and from the fact that they are not expected to defend their country in the battle-field. Such an argument might have some force if it were proposed to enfranchise all women and all men; if it were probable that men and women voters would be divided into two distinct and hostile camps; or even if it were advanced in a country where universal military service was exacted. In England, military service is a purely voluntary thing, and only a small fraction of the population participate in it. No one would argue for the disfranchisement of infirm men, and of men who had passed sixty, because they were incapable of active service.

Even if a possible participation in warfare were required as a qualification for voters, this would be no argument against female suffrage. Women, like men, pay increased taxes at every declaration of war, and although they do not, like the German women described by Tacitus, or like the Irish women of the seventh century, accompany their husbands into the battle-field,[38] they have borne in all modern wars a distinct and most valuable part. Can it be said that an ordinary private soldier was more useful to the State during the Crimean war than Florence Nightingale and the band of nurses who accompanied her? Amid the manifold failures and abuses that marked the outbreak of the great civil war in America, the admirable organisation and the pre-eminent utility of 'the Sanitary Commission,' which was originally planned and worked by women, for the alleviation of the sufferings of the battle-field, were universally recognised; and the same may be said of the Red Cross movement of later years.

But, in truth, war and its concerns form but one of the numerous interests of national life, and there is no real reason why it should have any special connection with the right of voting. It has been said that votes represent force, as a bank-

---

[38] This habit in Ireland was forbidden by a law which was adopted in 697 at the instance of Adamnan (Joyce's *Hist. of Ireland*, p. 186).

note represents gold, and that it is a dangerous thing if preponderant voting power in the nation should be dissociated from preponderant physical force. The argument is a strange one in a country where the great majority of adult men have been for generations excluded from the franchise; and it has no real bearing on the question of female suffrage, for the women whose enfranchisement is asked would form only a small fraction in the electorate, and would certainly be dispersed, divided, and absorbed in existing parties.

It has also been gravely alleged that the whole character of the female sex would be revolutionised, or at least seriously impaired, if they were brought by the suffrage into public life. There is perhaps no subject in which exaggerations so enormous and so grotesque may be found in the writings of considerable men. Considered in itself, the process of voting is now merely that of marking once in five or six years a ballot-paper in a quiet room, and it may be easily accomplished in five minutes. And can it reasonably be said that the time or thought which an average male elector bestows on the formation of his political opinions is such as to interfere in any appreciable degree with the currents of his thoughts, with the tendencies of his character or life? Men write on this subject as if public life and interests formed the main occupation of an ordinary voter. It is said that domestic life should be the one sphere of women. Very many women—especially those to whom the vote would be conceded—have no domestic, or but few domestic, duties to attend to, and are compelled, if they are not wholly frivolous or wholly apathetic, to seek spheres of useful activity beyond their homes. Even a full domestic life is scarcely more absorbing to a woman than professional life to a man. Scarcely any woman is so engrossed in it that she cannot bestow on public affairs an amount of time and intelligence equal to that which is bestowed on it by thousands of masculine voters. Nothing can be more fantastic than to argue as if electors in England were a select body, mainly occupied with political studies and public interests.

It is possible, indeed, to contend that it is unbecoming for women to take any part or interest in political matters; and it is certainly not unreasonable to contend that it is very desirable, for their own sakes, that they should be kept altogether out of the arena. This, as I have said, was the opinion of ancient Greece; it is still the opinion of several continental nations. It has prevailed widely in Great Britain up to the present century, and it is by no means extinct. It is, however, surely too late to oppose such an argument to female suffrage in England. No single feature of our political history during the closing years of the nineteenth century is more conspicuous than the vast and ever-increasing part which women are playing in politics. Very few political organisations in the history of the world have attained in a few years to the dimensions of the Primrose League, and the example set by Conservative women is being ardently followed in the other political parties. Women now frequently appear on the platform, and scarcely an election occurs in which they are not active and successful canvassers. It is idle to contend with accomplished and irrevocable facts. The interest of women in politics, and the participation of women in politics, already exist. The concession of a vote is not needed to make them politicians, though it might make their politics more serious and less irresponsible. Can any one suppose that voting for members of Parliament is a more unfeminine thing than canvassing for them, more fatal to the beauty of the female character than voting for a county councillor, or a poor-law guardian, or a member of a school board?

The introduction of the ballot has also largely affected this question. It has almost taken away from elections their old turbulence, and has thus destroyed a powerful argument against female suffrage. It must, however, be added that this and some other influences have gone far to destroy the force of one argument on the other side. It used to be said, with truth, that the widows of farmers or of small householders were often removed from their homes, or were seriously impeded in their attempt to secure houses, on account of their political incapacity, the landlords and proprietors desiring the influence which the command of many votes could give them. This state of things grew out of a relation and dependency of classes which has now passed away; there are, I imagine, few cases in which it can occur.

Metaphysical arguments about supposed natural rights and about innate, universal, and unchangeable laws of nature, may, I think, on both sides be cast away. The inalienable right which, according to the school of Rousseau, every man possesses to a share of political power, and the irreversible law of nature which pronounces women to be the dependents of men, and unfit for any share in the ruling power, are equally baseless. It may, however, be truly said that where in political institutions great inequalities and anomalies are found, they may at least be expected to justify their existence by some proved utility. It is surely an anomaly that the purchase of a house or a piece of land should confer the right of voting if the purchaser is a male, but not if she is a female; that women who are landed proprietors or heads of great industrial undertakings should be surrounded by dependents and tenants who possess the right of voting through their favour, while the proprietor herself is denuded of all political power; that, in a land where the inseparable connection of taxation and representation has been preached as a cardinal principle of freedom, female taxpayers should have no voice in the disposal of imperial taxation; that women should vote for all the great public interests I have enumerated, but not for the highest public interest of all—a representative in the House of Commons. For such inequalities there are only two possible defences. One is, that women do not desire a vote. The other is, that if they possessed it they would employ it in a way which would be plainly injurious to the nation.

An argument against female suffrage which is often raised, and which has a considerable weight, is that the enfranchisement of women on a rating basis, by excluding married women, would exclude that section of them who are in general the most important. By the natural law of selection wives are, on the whole, the flower of their sex. They acquire an extent and kind of experience much greater than that of other women, and, if their time is more occupied, their judgment is usually much saner, more moderate, and more mature. No careful observer can fail to be struck with the tendency of the married life to repress the extravagances of judgment and feeling to which unmarried women are especially prone. If women were enfranchised on the same conditions as men, it is argued, the great majority of the most competent women, and a large proportion of the most serious female interests, would still remain excluded from representation, while under the lodger franchise the electorate in our great towns would be largely recruited by women of an 'unfortunate class.' It is not probable, indeed, that such voters would often care to go to the poll, and there is no reason to believe that they would exercise any distinctive or malignant influence in politics; yet their accession to political life would hardly be regarded, even by the most enthusiastic democrat, as an advantage.

This argument is a serious one, but its force has been considerably exaggerated. Married and unmarried women would not under the proposed measure be sharply or permanently divided. Great numbers of female voters would be constantly passing into the married state. Great numbers of married women would be constantly acquiring by widowhood the right of voting; and it is perfectly in accordance with the principle of basing the franchise on property that married women with independent property of their own should retain their votes in the married state. This would, indeed, be a natural consequence of the full recognition of married women's property by recent legislation. It is a principle which has been adopted in the Local Government Act of 1894, which for the first time permitted married women, provided that husband and wife are not both qualified in respect of the same property, to be placed with unmarried women and widows on the municipal and local register.

The contention that the proposed measure would cast a slur upon the marriage state, making it, in the words of Mr. Goldwin Smith, 'politically penal,' seems to me wholly futile. Does any one suppose that such a slur attaches to the military or naval services, or to those branches of the Civil Service which incapacitate men from voting? Married women would not lose their votes because they married, but because they ceased to be ratepayers; and it is hardly probable that any one woman who desired to marry would abstain from doing so for the sake of her vote. The establishment of female franchise on a property basis would probably have the great incidental advantage of imposing a real and powerful obstacle to the further degradation of the suffrage. Many who would advocate manhood suffrage would shrink from universal suffrage. It may, I think, be safely assumed that the British nation would not acquiesce in government by a Parliament in which female influence was preponderant, and women in Great Britain largely outnumber men. If, however, the suffrage of women were once admitted, it would not be easy to make a fresh anomaly by making male suffrage universal, and that of females dependent on a property qualification.

From one very formidable danger connected with female suffrage England is remarkably free. In France, Belgium, and Italy, and to a greater or lesser degree in all Catholic countries, there is a strong and evident divergence between the religious opinions of women and of men; and as in these countries ecclesiastical questions are in the very forefront of the battle, the result of female suffrage would be a sharp and dangerous political antagonism between the two sexes. It would increase in the most formidable degree reactionary and ecclesiastical influences. The secularisation of government, through the elimination of priestly influence from the fields of politics, has been one of the most marked tendencies in continental Europe, and every attempt to arrest it by the introduction into the electorate of a great body of priest-ridden electors would inevitably lead to grave political dangers. In England, however, and in most Protestant countries, religious questions occupy a far smaller place in politics; women are much less absolutely under ecclesiastical influence than in Catholic countries, and religious bodies are so divided that female suffrage could hardly affect to any dangerous extent the balance of religious politics.

Female suffrage in matters of education and in municipal elections has spread very widely through the whole English-speaking world; it has also been adopted by the Scandinavian countries, and several other countries allow women to vote, either directly or by proxy, in rural or communal elections. Their voice in the control of communal property is very ancient, and extends far into the Middle Ages. In the Austrian Empire this system is considerably developed, and it is remarkable that when Lombardy was annexed to Italy, many women lost a franchise which they had possessed in what was deemed the period of servitude.[39] Of purely political female suffrage, however, there are as yet but few examples. There are, indeed, some traces in the English history of the sixteenth and seventeenth century of members of Parliament returned by female electors, and the case has often been cited of Dorothy Packington, who, in the reign of Elizabeth, nominated two burgesses for the borough of Aylesbury in her quality of lady of the manor.[40] During the Middle Ages feudal tenures were often inherited by women, and those tenures carried with them no small share of political power. Bentham has noticed the curious fact that, at a time when women were excluded from every other kind of political influence, they voted equally with men in the election of the directors of that East India Company which governed despotically one of the most populous empires in the world.[41] In a few very modern constitutions women have some political rights. In Austria those who are large owners of property have the right of voting for members of some of the provincial Diets, though they can only exercise it by delegating it to male deputies.[42]

---

[39] Giraud, *La Condition des Femmes*, pp. 165–66.
[40] See Stubbs's *Const. Hist.* iii. 454; Ostrogorski, pp. 40–41.
[41] Bentham's *Works*, ix. 109.
[42] See Ostrogorski, pp. 72–77.

In Sweden they participate in some measure in the election of members of the Upper Chamber, as they vote for the municipal and rural bodies by which the members of that Chamber are returned.[43] In Italy widows and women separated from their husbands who pay the taxes which would give a male a vote, though they cannot vote themselves, have the right of designating that privilege to a near male representative.[44] In America direct female suffrage, since 1869, was granted in the sparsely populated State of Wyoming, in the Territory of Washington, and in Utah; but in the latter two cases it was speedily withdrawn. In the Isle of Man also it was conceded in 1881, but on a narrower scale than to men, for it applied only to possessors of real property. In 1892, however, it was extended to other ratepayers. In 1893 female suffrage on the same basis as male suffrage was granted in New Zealand, and in the following year a similar step was taken in South Australia.

In England the probable influence, either for good or evil, of a limited female suffrage based on a property qualification seems to me to be greatly exaggerated. It is not likely that it would be dominant and decisive in any field, and the tendencies it would strengthen would not be in the same direction. There can, I think, be little doubt that women are on the whole more conscientious than men—at least where the obligation of performing some definite duty is clearly set before them, and gives a serious character to their words and actions. At a time when there are many signs that the standard of morality in political life is declining, the infusion into the electorate of a large number of voters who act under some real sense of duty could scarcely fail to be beneficial. It would raise the standard of private morality required in public men, and increase the importance of character in public life. It would probably be a conservative influence, very hostile to revolutionary and predatory change. It would also probably

---

[43] Ibid. p. 78.
[44] Ibid. p. 84.

tend somewhat, though not in any overwhelming degree, to strengthen ecclesiastical influence, especially in questions relating to religious education. The wide personal experience which large numbers of women possess of the circumstances, wants, and temptations of the poor would give questions connected with the social condition of the masses of the people an increased prominence in legislation, and make it the interest of members of Parliament to give them an increased share of their attention.

At the same time it can hardly, I think, be doubted that female influence in politics would tend to accentuate some tendencies which are already dangerously powerful in English legislation. Women, and especially unmarried women, are on the whole more impulsive and emotional than men; more easily induced to gratify an undisciplined or misplaced compassion, to the neglect of the larger and more permanent interests of society; more apt to dwell upon the proximate than the more distant results; more subject to fanaticisms, which often acquire almost the intensity of monomania. We have had a melancholy example of this in the attitude assumed of late years by a large class of educated Englishwomen on the subject of vivisection. That a practice which may be and has been gravely abused is properly subject to legislative control will probably be very generally admitted. But it would be difficult to conceive an act of greater folly or wickedness than to prohibit absolutely the most efficient of all methods of tracing the origin, course, and filiation of disease, the only safe way of testing the efficacy of possible preventives and remedies which may either prove fatal or be of inestimable benefit to mankind. What tyrant could inflict a greater curse upon his kind than deliberately to shut it out from the best chance of preventing, alleviating, or curing masses of human suffering, the magnitude and poignancy of which it is impossible for any imagination adequately to conceive? What folly could be greater than to do this in a country where experiments on animals are so guarded and limited by law that they undoubtedly inflict far less suffering in the space of a year than field sports in the space of a day?

The spectacle of great numbers of most humane and excellent women taking up such a cause with a passion that would undoubtedly lead them, if they possessed political power, to subordinate to it all the great interests of party or national welfare, has probably done as much as any other single thing to shake the confidence of cool observers in the political capacities of women. It is true that they are not alone in their crusade, but it is only necessary to look down any annual list of subscriptions in such societies to perceive how enormously the female element preponderates. In the administration of justice; in measures relating to distress and poverty that may be mainly due to improvidence or vice; in all questions of peace and war, such a spirit would prove most dangerous. There have been ages in which insensibility to suffering was the prevailing vice of public opinion. In our own there is perhaps more to be feared from wild gusts of unreasoning, uncalculating, hysterical emotion. 'Les races,' as Buffon said, 'se féminisent.' A due sense of the proportion of things; an adequate subordination of impulse to reason; an habitual regard to the ultimate and distant consequences of political measures; a sound, sober, and unexaggerated judgment, are elements which already are lamentably wanting in political life, and female influence would certainly not tend to increase them.

Nor is it likely that it would be in the direction of liberty. With women, even more than men, there is a strong disposition to overrate the curative powers of legislation, to attempt to mould the lives of men in all their details by meddlesome or restraining laws; and an increase of female influence could hardly fail to increase that habit of excessive legislation which is one of the great evils of the time.

Different minds will form different estimates of the balance of good and evil in the tendencies which I have endeavoured faithfully to enumerate. It must, however, again be said that

English legislation has now fully adopted the principle of conferring the suffrage on almost the largest scale without any attempt to discriminate capacity or to estimate the manner in which it is likely to be exercised, and the distinctive evils to be feared from female influence in politics are, at least partly, due to the want of political experience, and would therefore probably be gradually mitigated. It may be added, too, that when it is argued that it is for the benefit of the nation that a new class of voters should be brought into the Constitution, this usually merely means that the special interests of that portion of the nation are likely to be more fully attended to and represented. Women form a great section of the community, and, as we have seen, they have many special interests. The opening to them of employments, professions, and endowments; the regulation of their labour; questions of women's property and succession; the punishment of crimes against women; female education; laws relating to marriage, guardianship, and divorce, may all be cited; and in the great drink question they are even more interested than men, for though they are the more sober sex, they are also, it is to be feared, the sex which suffers most from the consequences of intemperance. With such a catalogue of special interests it is impossible to say that they have not a claim to representation if they desire it.

They would probably find that, like other classes, they had greatly overestimated the value of a vote. The chief danger that befalls the interests of an unrepresented class is that those interests are simply forgotten, or at least postponed till more pressing claims are attended to. But, whatever may have been the case in the past, a review of the measures which have been carried of late years relating to women seems clearly to show that modern Parliaments are quite ready to deal with such questions. The great majority of the serious grievances under which women laboured in England have been redressed, and the practice of basing important legislation upon the reports of parliamentary commissions, before which representatives of all the interests concerned give full evidence, has secured them a certain representation. To a large number of women the concession of female suffrage would, I believe, still be extremely distasteful, as bringing with it duties and entanglements they would gladly avoid. But with the rapidly increasing prominence of women in English public life this feeling is manifestly declining; and if the demand for a parliamentary suffrage should prove growing and persistent, it is scarcely possible to doubt that it must ultimately triumph.

INDEX

BIOGRAPHICAL NOTE

William Edward Hartpole Lecky (1838–1903), Irish historian and essayist, was born near Dublin, educated at Kingstown, Armagh, and Cheltenham College and graduated B.A. in 1859 and M.A. in 1863 from Trinity College, Dublin. Although he had completed a course in divinity he abandoned his intention to become a clergyman in the Irish Protestant Church and turned his talents to history.

At age 23 he published his *Leaders of Public Opinion in Ireland* anonymously, receiving little notice. But he soon won rapid recognition with two learned surveys: *A History of the Rise and Influence of Rationalism in Europe* (1865) and *A History of European Morals from Augustus to Charlemagne* (1869).

Lecky's major work, in eight volumes, was *A History of England During the Eighteenth Century* (1878–1890) in which he aimed "to disengage from the great mass of facts those which relate to the permanent forces of the nation." A later, twelve-volume, edition of this work included five volumes titled *A History of Ireland in the Eighteenth Century* which drew praise from Lord Acton.

In 1895 Lecky entered Parliament and became a privy councillor. In 1902 he was nominated an original member of the new Order of Merit.

William Murchison is chief editorial writer for *The Dallas Morning News*. He holds an MA in history from Stanford University.

The Palatino typeface used in this volume is the work of Hermann Zapf, the noted European type designer and master calligrapher. Palatino is basically an "old style" letterform, yet strongly endowed with the Zapf distinction of exquisiteness. With concern not solely for the individual letter but also the working visual relationship in a page of text, Zapf's edged pen has given this type a brisk, natural motion.

Book Design by JMH Corporation, Indianapolis, Indiana
Typography by Weimer Typesetting Company, Inc., Indianapolis, Indiana
Printed and bound by Halliday Lithograph, Inc., West Hanover, Massachusetts